The Dream Weavers: Strategy-Focused Leadership in Technology-Driven Organizations

The Dream Weavers: Strategy-Focused Leadership in Technology-Driven Organizations

John J. Sosik
Penn State University, Great Valley

Don Jung
San Diego State University

Yair Berson
Polytechnic University

Shelley D. Dionne
Kimberley S. Jaussi
Binghamton University

INFORMATION AGE PUBLISHING

80 Mason Street
Greenwich, Connecticut 06830

Library of Congress Cataloging-in-Publication Data
The dream weavers : strategy-focused leadership in technology-driven
organizations / by John J. Sosik ... [et al.].
    p. cm.
 Includes bibliographical references and index.
 ISBN 1-59311-110-X (pbk.) – ISBN 1-59311-111-8 (hardcover)
 1. Leadership. 2. Strategic planning. 3. Industrial management. 4.
Technological innovations. I. Sosik, John J.
 HD57.7.D735 2004
 658.4'092–dc22

                                    2004001325

Printed in the United States of America

CONTENTS

**Part V
Realizing the Dream**

FOREWORD

I just returned from meeting with 20 senior executives of a large multinational firm brought together in Paris to discuss strategic planning for their respective subsidiaries. One of the consultants presented various models dealing with various inputs and outputs involved in strategizing. Despite all the differences in inputs and differences in outputs, at the center of all the models was leadership.

I am proud of the fact that the five far-sighted authors of this book are my former students and colleagues. They have made a significant contribution by extending the understanding and importance of full range leadership to its application to strategic planning. But rather than just writing what they thought about the issues, they modeled the process and completed a well-designed and well-executed investigation in 65 technology-dependent businesses, large, medium and small, of how 75 successful executives were observed leading strategic planning by their associates.

Strategy-focused leadership (SFL) is a process that uses technology to connect people, work processes, and opportunities in an organization to fully utilize available economic, social, and intellectual capital. Effective executive leadership envisions the strategy and creates the organization that links the available resources in the best way. Knowledge of such leadership is necessary in the dynamic contexts facing today's corporate executives and tomorrow's future leaders.

The Dream Weavers: Strategy-Focused Leadership in Technology-Driven
Organizations, pages vii–xiii
Copyright © 2004 by Information Age Publishing, Inc.
All rights of reproduction in any form reserved.
ISBN: 1-59311-110-X (paper), 1-59311-111-8 (cloth)

The book illustrates a novel qualitative *and* quantitative research approach to study how an executive first envisions a strategy and then integrates the available resources to carry out the strategy. Success is appraised in the stories about the executives and the accounts of their followers. The data for analysis come from videotaped interviews, surveys of direct reports, and content analysis of organizational documents. This multifaceted method deserves further exploration and utilization in future leadership research. At the same time, a multitude of practical lessons are generated for senior executives and promising leaders in organizations that depend on technology to achieve their missions. But the valuable lessons learned in this book are not limited to technology industries. For instance, traditional mining executives now need to envision new uses and customers for their products as well as better extraction, safety, and environmental protection processes.

I recommend this book heartily, for it provides a rich descriptive narrative of leadership processes at the upper echelon levels of technology-driven organizations, and has theoretical, empirical and practical merit. The lessons learned in this book will provide executives, leadership consultants/trainers, and graduate students with a solid understanding of SFL as it relates to practical applications and well researched models and methods of leadership.

Bernard M. Bass
Distinguished Professor Emeritus
Binghamton University
State University of New York

Bernard M. Bass, Ph.D., Distinguished Professor Emeritus of Organizational Behavior at Binghamton University in New York, is one of the foremost leadership scholars, having published a voluminous number of articles and books on leadership over his long and successful career. His professional background includes the publication of *Bass and Stogdill's Handbook of Leadership* (New York: Free Press, 1990), *Transformational Leadership: Industrial, Military and Educational Impact.* (Mahwah, NJ: Erlbaum), and *Leadership and Performance beyond Expectations* (New York: Free Press, 1985) and many other works. It is chiefly through the pioneering work and inspiration of Professor Bass that Professors Sosik, Jung, Berson, Dionne, and Jaussi were motivated to write this book.

PREFACE

This book is largely a product of strong and tightly woven professional and personal connections and bonds forged between the authors, colleagues and executives over time. Its origins can be traced back to June of 2001, when we reunited for the happy occasion of participating in Bernard Bass' Festschrift at SUNY-Binghamton. Inspired by this landmark event and our sentimental homecoming to the university where we earned our doctorate degrees, we were motivated by the belief that there is a need to better understand the kind of leadership behavior executives must display to spur performance excellence.

Yair Berson had already been pilot testing structured interviews with executives in high-tech organizations, which led us to an exciting discussion of writing a book on strategic leadership that would extend the work of our mentors, Bernard Bass and Bruce Avolio, to executive levels in high tech settings. Yair's enthusiasm toward the project was contagious and we were able to persuade Shelley Dionne, our long-time friend and colleague, and Kim Jaussi, a USC-trained researcher and former student of Jay Conger, who had just joined the SUNY-Binghamton "family," to become part of our project team as co-authors.

After returning from the Bass Festschrift, we continued to talk about the kind of study and the resources we'd need to provide a solid research framework for the book. After much discussion, we agreed to build upon

The Dream Weavers: Strategy-Focused Leadership in Technology-Driven
Organizations, pages ix–xiii
Copyright © 2004 by Information Age Publishing, Inc.
All rights of reproduction in any form reserved.
ISBN: 1-59311-110-X (paper), 1-59311-111-8 (cloth)

Yair's work by conducting videotaped interviews of executives from technology-driven organizations to identify common behaviors and traits that lead to organizational success. In addition to the interviews, we would survey the executives' followers to evaluate the leadership and organizational culture and examine successful executive leadership from multiple reference points. According to our plan, the book would summarize personal accounts of top executives' leadership styles tied to successful models of leadership to explain how to best develop effective leadership in technology-intensive settings.

Early in the project, we realized from our interviews of executives that today's businesses operate in turbulent, challenging and technologically complex environments. Technology systems that support business operations are pervasive strategic assets in the sense that they transfer one of the most important commodities in today's organization: information and knowledge. Employees, customers, partners, and suppliers also represent important strategic assets because they provide the ideas, innovations, and relationships that result in success. These people must understand how to best utilize technology systems to accelerate the dissemination of information and development of strategic knowledge and the creation of new products and services. To fully connect people, ideas and technology systems requires strategy-focused leadership (SFL). Thus, the primary aim of

FIGURE P.1
The Authors Re-Uniting in Binghamton, October 2003

this book is to describe how to put outstanding leadership into practice to achieve long-term strategic goals in technology-driven industries.

The fundamental principle guiding the book is that SFL is a *process* that leverages technology to make fundamentally sound connections between people, work processes and business opportunities to fully utilize the economic capital (increase in stock value), social capital (relationships with customers, partners, and suppliers), and intellectual capital (knowledge, skills and abilities of employees) of an organization. Executive leadership can envision the strategy (*dream*) and create (*weave*) the organization that has the very best connections to leverage each and every resource. Some executive leaders knowingly or unknowingly disconnect their people and in so doing, disconnect their organizations from being successful. Others work each and every day to make the connections that are critical to being agile and adaptive in today's rapidly changing markets.

From the latter group of executives, we distilled and report in this book important leadership lessons for achieving dramatically higher levels of individual, group and organizational performance. In essence, we found that displaying outstanding executive leadership doesn't necessarily require a commanding presence, genius level IQ, expertise, or even a strong command and control system. At the heart of outstanding executive leadership was an ability to envision a strategy for taking the raw inputs provided by their environments (e.g., people, technology, ideas, opportunities) and then weave them into an integrated pattern or system of social, technical and intellectual resources that ultimately produces dramatically higher levels of organizational success factors. To illustrate this process, we include dozens of stories and narratives from the executive leaders to offer you an in-depth look at what constitutes effective SFL in technology-driven organizations.

This book has several important and distinctive features. First, the sample of executive-level leaders is unique and should be of great interest and value to students of leadership and business professionals. MBA and other graduate students as well as business professionals from all types of organizations will be able to relate to the leaders in our sample, which cuts across technology-driven industries such as information technology (software, computers, microchips, telecommunications), services (media, retail, professional services), life sciences (biotechnology, health care), manufacturing (energy, defense, aerospace, construction, furniture), and finance (banking & securities, insurance). We interviewed 75 executive leaders (including many CEOs) from organizations in the U.S. and Israel. It is likely that readers will find someone or many in this book with whom they can identify.

Second, we describe in actionable ways what leaders do to be more successful in terms of SFL. Third, we measure and describe the type of culture that supports successful SFL. Finally, there are many MBA students and business leaders who are not yet in SFL situations, but certainly will be in the future. The narratives and learning points in this book should provide those individuals with the competitive edge by showing them how successful executives dream and then weave the complex tapestry of human and technical resources into effective strategic relationships with customers, employees, suppliers and business partners.

The book is organized around general themes derived from the results of interviewing executive leaders, surveying their followers, and analyzing archival data. The book is structured into five sections, including "Strategy-focused Leadership in Technology-Driven Environments" which presents foundation material in Chapters 1 and 2. The remaining eight chapters are grouped into four major sections: "Dreaming about Success," "Adapting the Right Pattern," "Weaving the Fabric of Success," and "Realizing the Dream." Each section contains two chapters and is sequenced according to eight processes essential for SFL. The research base for the book follows in the Appendix, which describes our methodology and the executives and organizations in our sample.

We are clearly indebted to the many people and organizations that helped us to realize our dream of completing this book. They include several of our graduate and undergraduate students who worked with us as part of our "virtual" research project team to help collect and analyze our data. In particular, we wish to acknowledge the assistance of Maria Peterson, Gary Generose, John Gronski, Dana Roos, Bill Young, Grant Galef, Steve Dunn, Mark Hellerman, Brian Viscusi, Wai-Ling Lam, Chen Cheng, Lisa Coutant, Michael Cranmer, Jacob Kretzing, Sean Hutchens, Michael Hall, numerous students from the High Technology Leadership executive classes (2000-2002) at Polytechnic University, the Yeda classes in Israel, Danielle Daks, and Lisa Sharaby. Their hard work and commitment to the project is greatly appreciated. We also thank all the executives and direct reports who participated in our study. We wish that we could acknowledge all of the executives in our study, but for reasons of confidentiality, we cannot. They have painted for us a much clearer picture of what a full range of leadership looks like in the upper echelons of high-tech organizations and how SFL can become the driving force of organizational success.

We thank Bruce Avolio, who gave us invaluable and insightful comments on the original interview protocol as well as initial and subsequent drafts of our proposal that significantly improved the book's organization and contents. Bruce has always challenged us to higher levels of personal and professional development, and for this we are grateful. A heartfelt "thank you" also goes out to Fran Yammarino for identifying *Information Age Publishing* as an appropriate outlet for our book. We also extend our sincere gratitude to Bernie Bass, who gladly agreed to write the foreword for us. His commitment and enthusiasm towards leadership research remains a constant guiding beacon for all researchers and practitioners after his 50-plus years of work. He will be a role model for all of us throughout our careers. From our professional relationships with Bruce, Fran and

Bernie over the years, we have found the true meaning of transformational leadership and experienced all the good that can come from it.

We have also benefited immeasurably from many individuals who have supported us all along our careers, especially while we were working on this book. Many thanks and much love go to our family members, who have made personal sacrifices while we have been associated with the SUNY-Binghamton "family:" Karen M. Sosik, Josephine and John G. Sosik, Ann Drost, Sin Choi, Austin and Celeste Jung, Miriam and Moshe Berson, Iris Goldberg, Peter and Luke Dionne, Jeff, Maia, and Peter Wright.

Several people played important roles in the preparation of this book. George Johnson, our editor, gave enthusiastic endorsement and editorial assistance throughout the project. Thoughtful comments from Boas Shamir, Phillip Laplante, John Mason and John I. McCool enabled us to make important improvements in the final manuscript. We also wish to recognize Mary P. Clark for designing our book's cover, and Rebecca Riley, Rick Gallagher, April Pumala and Corry Bullock for applying their conscientious and thorough administrative support to the assembly of the final manuscript. Their contributions have enabled us to weave together the ideas, stories and analyses and to realize our dream of sharing with others what we learned from this project. To all these people we say thank you.

John J. Sosik
Don Jung
Yair Berson
Shelley D. Dionne
Kimberly S. Jaussi
October 2003

PART I

STRATEGY-FOCUSED LEADERSHIP IN TECHNOLOGY-DRIVEN ENVIRONMENTS

Sandra Stevenson felt somewhat of a pang of sadness as she quietly left Bonita Technologies, the organization that she had co-founded ten years ago. The main reason for her departure was because she had become unhappy about the way Bonita's culture had changed dramatically once the German venture capitalists came in to raise $50 million to fund a variety of new product lines. Sandra longed for the days when Bonita was "like a family" and her associates were intrinsically motivated to work together to realize her dream of creating a successful biotech company pursuing a meaningful mission. But all that changed when the venture capitalists came in and her organization had to rapidly grow up. Suddenly her organization had a different feel and sophistication level. For Sandra, that meant it definitely was time for a change.

Since Sandra always loved creating and leading high technology enterprises, she planned to set up another biotech organization, Nova-Vignette Inc., along with three Bonita Technologies alumni. Their idea for the new organization was to build it around a fast-rising technology called *RNA interface*, a natural process in cells that researchers can harness to deactivate selected genes so that they can develop new drugs to treat diseases such as HIV, hepatitis C, cancer, or SARS. Inspired by her new mission in life, Sandra wondered how she would identify trends and business opportunities for her organization, what talent she would have to hire, what business relationships she would need to develop, and what technologies she would have to build upon and integrate into her organization. Sandra then realized that she was no different from any other executive leading a high tech organization. Bringing Sandra's idea into fruition would require her to master and demonstrate the fundamentals of strategy-focused leadership in the fast-paced, technology-driven, and fiercely competitive life sciences industry.

CHAPTER 1

STRATEGY-FOCUSED LEADERSHIP
Focusing on and Weaving the Dream

It takes a lot of courage to show your dreams to someone else.
—*Erma Bombeck*

Executive leaders of technology-driven organizations are responsible for connecting people, processes and technology to create performance excellence. Rapid advances in technology have provided executives with numerous novel business models and voluminous amounts of potentially relevant strategic information. Yet, as Nobel-prize winning economist Herbert Simon once noted, "a wealth of information creates a poverty of attention." This poses complicated challenges for executives who must display leadership that *focuses* their organizations' attention on strategies that add value for their stakeholders. In the pages that follow, we systematically introduce and explain the concepts, behaviors and tactics executives need to display

The Dream Weavers: Strategy-Focused Leadership in Technology-Driven
Organizations, pages 3–22
ISBN: 1-59311-110-X (paper), 1-59311-111-8 (cloth)

outstanding leadership for successfully navigating in intense and complex technology-dependent industries.

CHALLENGES FOR EXECUTIVE LEADERS

Ever since he was young, Michael Hagan dreamed of one day starting his own company. His dream became a reality in 1995 when Hagan co-founded VerticalNet to create online communities enabling companies to collaborate and conduct business with one another over the Internet. Since then he has been riding the turbulent and troubling seas of managing startup companies in a technology-based information economy. His rise to success at VerticalNet was fast and furious due to his highly effective strategic leadership skills. Hagan hired Mark Walsh, a charismatic and innovative individual, as CEO to launch VerticalNet's initial public offering (IPO) and to develop the initial business plan. As a result, VerticalNet had a successful IPO in February 1999 and by January 2000 its stock closed at $172 a share. Expectations were high and the future looked bright.

But by the end of 2001, VerticalNet took a nosedive. It experienced a dramatic reduction in new business opportunities and accumulated over $800 million in debt. Its stockholders and employees lost their confidence. The company laid-off a quarter of its employees, and was described by analysts as "not being *focused* on what they want to do." Walsh was ousted as CEO, and then the company gained and lost another high-profile CEO, Joe Galli (formerly of Amazon.com and Black and Decker). With almost all of its stock value disappearing, Hagen wondered if he could ever find a CEO with the strategic leadership required to keep VerticalNet from fading into the distant horizon. If so, what were the chances that this new CEO would be able to successfully implement it? What kind of leadership capability would be needed to support the strategic plan? Would the company's technology and employees support it? And how would it affect the company's customers, suppliers and shareholders?

The uncertainty posed by these questions prompted Hagen to assume the helm at VerticalNet, only to relinquish his leadership status as CEO and Chairman of VerticalNet in late 2001. In 2003, he re-emerged as CEO and Chairman of Nutri/System, Inc., a 32-year old diet and weight loss company. In his new role, Hagen faces a fresh set of leadership challenges including hiring the right people, developing a new marketing strategy, redesigning product offerings, and bolstering a strong brand name with technology.[1]

Unfortunately, this is not an isolated example of leadership challenges faced by executives in today's highly tumultuous and complex business environment. These challenges are especially apparent in the technology-dependent industries. These industries function in high velocity environments, characterized by immense turbulence, that pose critical challenges for leaders.[2] Given the rapid changes in technology development, product life cycles are significantly shorter and competitors can easily imitate products or services. Effective executives must translate these challenges to opportunities. Such leaders need to know how to recognize the unique resources they have and utilize these resources to achieve competitive advantage.

Many corporate boards and executives face strategic leadership challenges similar to those faced by Michael Hagen, especially after an initially successful stage of turning an innovative idea into a profitable product. More disconcerting is the mounting evidence that ineffective strategic leadership can destroy not only an organization's economic capital (accumulated stock value), but also its social (business relationships with customers, suppliers and partners), intellectual (knowledge, skills and abilities of employees), and reputational (intangible wealth related to goodwill and brand equity) capital.[3] Other organizations are finding it difficult to harness the power of advanced technology to assist executives to develop and implement new business strategies, despite the widely heralded promises of such technology and its documented success in some business settings.

In this book, we address these important issues by reporting the results of a comprehensive leadership research project based on structured interviews conducted in both the United States and Israel with 75 executive leaders, their followers, and the organizational cultures they have helped to create. Our executive leaders are CEOs, CIOs, CFOs, and other key executives of small, medium and large organizations that depend on advanced technology to support their mission to adapt to the rapid rate of economic, societal, and technological change required for performance excellence. These organizations represent a wide variety of industries and services, including telecommunications, computers, information technology, professional services, biotech and life sciences, manufacturing, finance, and others. You will recognize many of the organizations by name such as General Electric, Qualcomm, The Vanguard Group, and Barclays Global Investors. There are numerous other organizations in our sample with which you are probably familiar that we have used pseudonyms for because they requested anonymity.

Our aim in writing this book was to summarize practical lessons learned from executive leaders of technology-driven organizations on how to spur performance excellence. The lessons are presented using a variety of descriptive narratives provided by executives that are grounded in a robust research study which tests firmly established leadership models in these firms' upper echelons. Research has shown that these models allow top decision makers to transform the strategic assets of organizations (i.e., people, technology, information, operations) into successful corporations and that it is possible to use these models to train managers for institutionalizing change-oriented and innovative leadership and organizational development.[4] Readers interested in learning more about our sample, methodology and research models are referred to the Appendix. It is our hope that the lessons learned in this book will provide you with a solid foundation in strategy-focused leadership on which you can enhance your career and dramatically improve your organization's effectiveness—no matter what type of business you lead or manage in today's technology-based environment.

THE NATURE AND IMPORTANCE OF STRATEGY-FOCUSED LEADERSHIP

Imagine that you are the commander of an exploratory vessel on an expedition to Antarctica. What type of leadership role is expected of you? First and foremost is to define what your *mission* or basic purpose should be, including the focus of the work to be carried out, the reason the expedition exists, and the constituencies it is designed to serve. In other words, you are responsible for developing and articulating to your crew a compelling and motivating reason why you are undertaking your journey. You must also help determine your crews' objectives or goals that must be met along the way to attain your overall strategic goal. These include charting your course, employing the latest technology required for the expedition, supplying your ship with adequate food, tools, and supplies, training your crew, ensuring proper cooperation and communication among crewmembers, and motivating your crew through crises and safeguarding their welfare. You also need to adjust your strategic objectives based on changes in land, air, and sea conditions or unexpected emergencies, while commanding loyalty and commitment from your crew. In essence, you must engage in leadership that is *strategy-focused.*

Such were the leadership requirements for Sir Ernest Shackleton, the British polar explorer who with his 28 crewmembers in 1907 became trapped in the Antarctic ice 1,000 miles from civilization with zero contact from the outside world. While trapped, the men ate seals, shot their dogs and cats for food, played footer, and watched in depression and horror as the ice slowly crushed their ship the *Endurance* into a useless pile of wooden scrap. For 15 months, Shackleton and his crew faced and endured starvation, insanity, potential death and every other hardship possible, but his valiant and confident leadership inspired a fierce will to survive, and in the end all crewmembers returned home alive.[5]

But did Shackleton exercise good *strategy-focused leadership?* His voyage of endurance may also provide an example of poor strategy-focused leadership because his failure may have been entirely of his own making. For example, Shackleton and his journey were mainly driven by his ego rather than effective strategy and/or acceptable logic when it came to developing his mission as described in this newspaper classified ad:

> Men wanted for hazardous journey. Small wages, bitter cold, long months of complete darkness, constant danger. Safe return doubtful. Honor and recognition in case of success.

More importantly, his expedition was plagued by obsolete and inappropriate technology, inadequate planning and resources, poor preparation, failure to develop the skills for his crew necessary to reach their goal, and a mistaken belief that strength of character and determination were enough to overcome an under-funded, overambitious and ill-conceived mission.[6] How many of today's leaders similarly lead their organizations to new levels of heroic failure, instead of competent and consistent success? *In today's technology-driven business environment, executive leaders must possess the right set of tools and adequate resources to implement effective strategies and beat the competition.*

Just as Shackleton and his crew were subjected to daunting conditions, today's technology-driven organizations operate in unstable, challenging and complex business environments. And indeed, like Shackleton, some leaders of technology-driven organizations used their influence on followers to inspire and motivate them to deal with the risks by promising success and fame. For example, many leaders of "dot-com," or Internet companies, motivated their employees by offering them stock options and promising them quick financial success, rather than focus on achieving long-term strategic goals.[7]

When organizational environments are highly complicated and uncertain, competent strategy-focused leaders who motivate and guide processes yielding organizational success are needed and appreciated more than ever. These are the leaders whose strategy has both an internal and external focus. Their strategy considers employee selection and development, goal setting, communicating and rewarding, problem solving and resource utilization systems, while focusing on trends in the relevant industry and overall global business environment and potential strategic alliances. Such leaders gain more discretion from their awareness of these environmental conditions and from their excellent relationships or connections with their followers, business partners, customers, suppliers and technologies.[8]

But how does one acquire the skills associated with strategy-focused leadership? How should we measure this leadership process and the effectiveness of its outcomes? There is always meeting the revenue and profit numbers. There also is integrated communications with organizational stakeholders. Innovation and harnessing the power of new technology are also important. Another measure is a work environment or culture in which leadership is shared with organizational stakeholders. Continuous process and people improvement and expanded knowledge bases are also outcomes associated with such leadership.

In essence, strategy-focused leaders are at the "helm of the ship." They first "dream" or envision dramatically different and successful outcomes and then "weave" or form excellent relationships or connections within and between their organizations' *social systems,* comprised of customers, suppliers, partners and other constituents, and *technology systems,* comprised of equipment, machinery, tools, information, software, and know-how. They create, adapt and disseminate organizational strategy and build a learning-oriented and innovative organizational culture that is so essential in technology-driven settings. They also cultivate highly motivated employees within the organization to achieve these objectives, to ensure failsafe navigation through fair or stormy seas. Relationship building, employee development, and development of the firm's financial market value are essential for balanced success over the long-term business operation.[9] Therefore, we define strategy-focused leadership (SFL) as *a series of processes that determine the degree to which organizations are effective in making fundamentally sound connections between people, technology, work processes and business opportunities aimed at adding economic, social, and intellectual capital for shareholders, society and employees, respectively.* Employee and relationship development, technology adaptation/integration, and financial asset accumulation are the goals that strategy-focused leaders hope to attain through specific leadership processes.

STRATEGY-FOCUSED LEADERSHIP VERSUS STRATEGIC LEADERSHIP

Much of what we know about leadership in organizations up until 1980 was concerned with supervisors and middle managers. In recent years the attention of leadership scholars has shifted to executives who can exert a strong influence on the strategy and performance of organizations. We would like to clearly define and differentiate our concept of SFL from a more commonly used term, "strategic leadership." The phrase "strategic leadership" emerged from work on strategic management and consists of the following:

1. determining strategic direction;
2. exploring and maintaining core competencies;
3. developing human capital;
4. sustaining an effective organizational culture;
5. emphasizing ethical practices; and
6. establishing balanced organizational controls.[10]

Notice that these components of strategic leadership focus primarily on actual strategy formulation. While formulating strategy is a critical part of a strategic leader's job, it has been the focus of a great deal of research that looks at how leaders formulate strategy and whether or not they make sound strategic decisions.

Our work diverges from "strategic leadership" by not focusing on strategy formulation *per se*. Instead, we focus on *what effective leaders actually do* in order to produce a strategy-focused organization. We examine items 3 through 6 describing strategic leadership, and add several other critical aspects such as focusing on the core message and strategy; disseminating the strategy in the organization; developing and sensitizing employees to strategic issues; integrating the right people, technology and strategy; building ownership and trust; and reinforcing the core message and strategy by linking leadership and key performance indicators. By engaging in these processes, a strategy-focused leader will succeed in creating an organization capable of effectively implementing strategic plans and adapting to the turbulent organizational environment. Thus, our work on SFL, while overlapping with a subset of strategic leadership, examines in great detail a broader set of processes that create an organization capable of effectively implementing strategy to yield dramatic increases in intellectual, social and economic capital.

In order to understand how SFL processes impact an organization's intellectual, social, and economic resources, and how it contributes to create a successful organizational culture, it is instructive to review what we already know about strategic leadership, organizational culture, and performance. In other words, what does research tell us regarding the relationship between strategic leadership, organizational culture, and performance?

What We Know (and Don't Know) about Strategic Leadership

The answer to that question requires a comprehensive review of the emerging field of strategic leadership. Results of our review suggested the following key conclusions.

1. Organizations become a reflection of their top managers. The decisions made by senior executives, mostly top management teams and CEOs, have an impact on the bottom line of their organizations.[11] Organizations achieve strategic advantage by having access to unique resources. One such resource is the organization's leaders. Strategic leaders create a competitive advantage for their organizations by conveying a sense of organizational meaning or purpose,

which helps maintain or redefine institutional integrity and focus under conditions of uncertainty. Although we know that executives make a difference, we do not know *how* their interaction with their followers helps them implement their strategies and influence their organization's performance.[12]

2. We have evidence that the most senior executives of an organization are responsible for making strategic decisions. Indeed, early writers focused on the upper echelons of the organization. However, as we noted above, today's organizations operate in a complex environment that requires managers from all levels of the organizations to be actively involved in strategic decision making. Therefore, these managers need to possess the skills and influence necessary to make such decisions. Our unique sample that consists of interviews with executives and managers from a number of highly successful organizations in technology-driven industries confirm that while executives can provide an overall vision, managers of units within the organization provide the detailed strategic plan for their employees. Early research deemphasized the strategic role of mid-level management and has not examined the mechanisms by which strategic decisions are disseminated. Therefore, we intend to elaborate on these issues.

3. The leadership of top executives is a big missing piece in organizational research. Many studies explore the leadership style of supervisors or mid-level managers but neglect to focus on top executives' behavior.[13] Our book explores in detail the dynamics of top management teams at some of the world's biggest corporations. Unlike previous work, we combine descriptive information with detailed accounts by top managers and their direct reports.

Until recently, the strategic leadership field has relied upon the "upper echelon perspective."[14] Its primary focus was on top executives, their backgrounds and experiences, their relationship with their board of directors, and a variety of other factors that impact the strategic choices and ultimate direction of the organization. Studies of demographic and cognitive (related to thinking) characteristics of top executives and top management teams have shed light on our understanding of upper echelon issues.[15] While these upper echelon studies have produced important and valuable knowledge regarding strategic choices based on top management team demographics and composition, this focus is limited in its ability to view strategic leadership as it relates to the implementation and management of strategy at all levels throughout the organization.

To expand the knowledge base regarding the world of strategic leadership, we consider our notion of SFL as a process, and examine how it is transferred and implemented throughout the organization. Rather than taking a singular focus regarding the demographic and cognitive factors that influence senior executives' strategic plans, we examine the alignment of strategies and visions for successful implementation and creation/development of a strategy-focused organization. Our view is more consistent with contemporary views of strategy, which consider the day-to-day decisions of not only the leader, but everyone in the organization.[16] We are concerned with the leader's ability to influence and impact the decisions of every person within the organization in such a way that those decisions work toward maintaining immediate financial stability, while enhancing the long term viability of the organization.

All leaders devise strategies they feel will take their organization toward their vision, and thanks to the current field of strategic leadership research, we have a decent understanding of top management characteristics that lead to different strategic choices. What is much more complex and not well defined is *how a leader should align his or her organizational practices and processes to effectively implement the strategy selected* to maximize the organization's potential. In looking at these alignment practices and processes, we attempt to bridge the gap that exists in the strategic leadership literature between top executive characteristics, strategic choices, and successful organizational performance.

From our review of the existing academic literature on strategic leadership, it appears that we still know little about what specific leadership behaviors are used by executive leaders in their quest to motivate their individual employees, project teams, business units and overall organization to achieve performance excellence. Therefore, in this book, we provide answers to various issues on SFL with the following questions in mind.

1. *Do executive leaders generally view their leadership styles in a similar fashion as their direct reports?* To the extent that self-deception is a common source of executive career derailment as experienced by CEOs the likes of Gerry Dicamillo of Polaroid, Jill Barad of Mattel and Desi Desimone of 3M,[17] finding answers to this question is important to the viability of an executive's career.
2. *Does the common conclusion of most studies that leaders need to be very active hold at the executive levels?*
3. *Are passive forms of leadership used more frequently in the upper echelons of organizations?*
4. *How can leaders utilize their ability to create emotional bonds with their followers to promote organizational strategy and its implementation?*
5. *Can transaction-based forms of leadership also be effective if implemented correctly?*

It has also been unclear regarding the types of organizational cultures that are associated with leaders who engage in these behaviors. Therefore, we posed the following questions as well:

1. *What impact do these cultures have on how followers perceive their leaders to act?*
2. *Do these cultures correspond to the typical leadership styles of executives?*

Finally, also unknown are specifics on the types and content of vision and mission statements (which we refer to as "core messages") that these leaders create.

1. *Which core messages are more successful?*
2. *How are they crafted and communicated to organizational stakeholders?*
3. *How do they relate to the environment in which the organization operates?*
4. *How do they help followers derive important personal meaning out of their routine and mundane work processes?*

These are just a few of the questions that we will attempt to answer throughout this book.

A MODEL OF STRATEGY-FOCUSED LEADERSHIP

Scientific studies answer their research questions by framing them within a model of what is presently known about the phenomenon under investigation. These models are then expanded based on what is found in the investigation so that a better description and understanding of the processes associated with the phenomenon can be obtained. Because the study described in this book and its results are based on such a rigorous scientific investigation, the phenomenon of interest is SFL in technology-driven organizations. Therefore, we present our model of SFL as illustrated in Figure 1.1.

Our model describes the processes by which executives first envision strategy to take the raw inputs provided by their environments (e.g., people, technology, ideas, opportunities) and then weave them into a integrated patterns or systems of social, technical and intellectual resources. These patterns ultimately produce dramatically higher levels of financial performance, customer satisfaction, knowledge, communication, improvements in their people and processes and shared leadership. As shown in Figure 1.1, these processes involve dreaming about success (i.e., recognizing and initiating trends, focusing on the core message and strategy), adjusting the right pattern (i.e., selecting and developing people in line with the strategy, integrating the right people and technology), weaving the fabric of success (i.e., creating ownership and trust, "translating" organizational strategy to employees, supporting innovation and learning), and realizing the dream (i.e., reinforcing the core message and strategy, re-focusing the shape of future success).

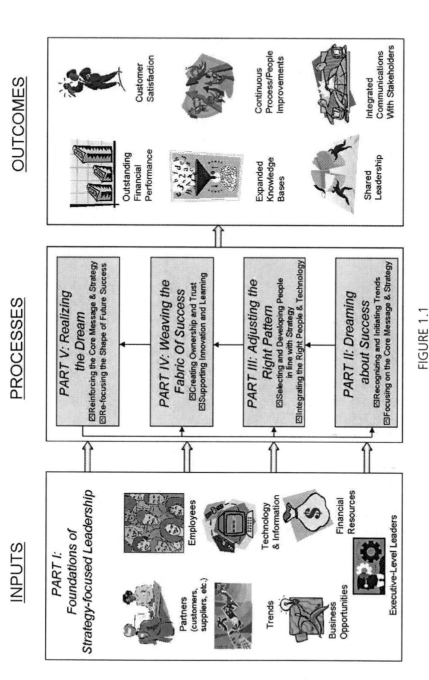

FIGURE 1.1
Dream Weaving Success with Strategy-Focused Leadership

Dreaming About Success

To dream about success, executives must recognize and initiate trends and focus on the core message and strategy. Trend recognition and initiation involves strategic networking and partnering and external monitoring. These processes are described in Chapter 3. Networking and partnering with customers, suppliers, industry partners and even competitors provides information regarding the wide range of events and trends that are likely to influence an executive's organization. This information is essential for realizing where the organization currently is and creating a vision of where it needs to go strategically in the future. Executives need to engage in environmental monitoring or scanning of key factors to assess the strengths, weaknesses, opportunities and threats that define their organizations' current and future positions. These factors include markets, economic conditions, demographics, technology, international politics, and socio-cultural trends.[18]

An example of this SFL process is radio station WARM in Scranton, Pennsylvania. In 1957, WARM was a little known broadcasting outlet owned by a future governor of Pennsylvania. It was powerful, 5000 watts at 590 on the AM radio dial, but no one paid much attention to its traditional mix of big band hits. Then, in early 1958, WARM was sold to the Susquehanna Broadcasting Company which sent Art Carlson to Scranton to turn sleepy WARM into what became known to hundreds of thousands of listeners as "The Mighty 590."

Carlson was a former New York advertising executive with a talent for recognizing trends and an ear for what great radio should sound like. In his first few weeks after arriving in town, he often lunched at a local diner and noticed that people tended to play certain popular rock and roll songs on the jukebox over and over. He also noticed that the people loved to discuss local news, sports and the weather. Carlson's ability to monitor the environment galvanized his vision and strategy for WARM: broadcast using echo chamber technology; use friendly and funny fast-talking disc jockeys who, when not on the air, are making connections with the listeners at live-promotional broadcasts and dances; play 40 popular rock and roll records; use a set of short vocal melodies called jingles; and present quality newscasts, sportscasts and weather forecasts.

Carlson's strategy worked practically overnight. Ratings multiplied within months and by the early 1960s, an unheard-of sixty percent of the radios in WARM's market (dubbed "WARMland" by the disc jockeys) were tuned to 590. WARM dominated its market until alternative broadcast technologies such as FM and the Internet overran AM radio by the year 2000. Thanks to Carlson's ability to recognize and initiate trends, his core message resonated throughout WARMland as an entire generation grew to know and love WARM.[19]

Focusing on the core message and strategy involves crafting and inspiring commitment to a vision and is described in Chapter 4. Crafting a compelling vision linked to a business strategy directs, guides, and motivates organizational members to work together for the good of the organization. Without guidance and motivation, employees lack direction and tend to pursue their own personal interests, sometimes at the expense of the organization's mission. Effective strategy-focused leaders know how to formulate a vision that will involve guidance regarding long term goals, but will also inspire other managers and employees to take an active role in initiating strategies for their units. A solid business strategy addresses what employees need to do in order to contribute and how an organization will attain its long-term goals through their collective efforts. An appealing and evocative *vision* inspires organizational members by conveying the ideal future of the organization, what it hopes to become in the eyes of its board, organizational members, and other stakeholders. The most successful visions are created jointly by leaders and their followers, exemplify ethical and pro-social values, and are *shared* with all organizational stakeholders. For example, Apple Computer's CEO Steven Jobs' vision of the role technology will play in schools of the future illustrates this process.

> Obviously, the computer has changed from a device of computation into a device for communication in the last few years. Now, its primary purpose is to be a tool and center for communication, whether it is distant communication over the Net or communication with other kids in your class by bringing in a video report made with iMovie. Our vision is that we have just begun. This is the tip of the iceberg of what we can do with these tools.[20]

Inspiring commitment to the vision and to challenging projects fosters the determination, willpower, and self-confidence required for effective employee and group performance. Commitment is an important motivational force that drives the extra effort needed to see projects through to their successful completion. Research indicates that commitment can be built through inspirational leadership that adds significant meaning to tasks, links employee's self-images to the successful completion of tasks, and shows how contributing toward the greater good may be morally uplifting.[21] Under such leadership, employees' routine tasks and mundane work processes become an important mission that they have to accomplish under any circumstances for the good of the organization. For example, Herb Kelleher, former CEO of Southwest Airlines, describes how commitment can be created:

> The important thing is to take the bricklayer and make him understand that he's building a home, not just laying bricks. So we take the building a home approach: This is what you're doing not only for yourself but for society: giving people who'd otherwise not be able to travel the opportunity to do so; making it possible for grandparents to see their grandchildren for the holi-

days, or for a working mom to take her son to see the World Series — for less than the cost of a ticket to the game. We constantly hold up examples of customer experiences and of employee efforts to make a difference.[22]

Adjusting the Right Pattern

To adjust the right pattern, executives must select and develop people in line with the strategy and integrate the right people and technology to support the strategic plan. Selecting and developing people in line with the strategy involves selecting the right followers and accelerating their development into leaders and is described in Chapter 5. Executives are beginning to recognize their employees as key strategic assets required to achieve organizational objectives stated in their strategic plans. Since employees provide the knowledge, skills and abilities (KSAs) required to attain these objectives, it is essential for strategy-focused leaders to systematically review their human resource requirements to ensure that the required human resources, with necessary KSAs, are available when and where they are needed.[23]

When these requirements are not met, strategy-focused leaders then must go through selection processes that match potential employees' personality and skills with the job requirements and organizational culture. A recent study co-sponsored by the American Society for Training and Development and Society for Human Resource Management was conducted to see how organizations use employee growth and career development initiatives to attract, retain and develop workers. The study identified Dow Chemical Company, Edward Jones, Great Plains, LensCrafters, Sears & Roebuck, Southwest Airlines, and South African Breweries as "exemplary practice" firms that have organizational infrastructures in place to support human resource efforts to attract and develop employees, and position or role competencies to provide employees with an understanding of the KSAs they need to acquire in order to advance. Because these organizations' cultures are unique and they commit significant resources (money, technology, development opportunities, people support) to employees, they focus strongly on communicating their strategy, mission, and vision to potential employees in order to find people who will be a good match.[24]

Even when requirements are met, strategy-focused leaders must continually nurture their employees to higher levels of KSAs through mentoring, delegation, and learning programs. For example, Proctor and Gamble CEO Alan G. Lafley has introduced a dramatic culture-shift by transforming the executive cafeteria on the top floor of its Cincinnati headquarters into a new training center that will develop the KSAs of P&G employees from around the world. According to Lafley, "I have made a lot of symbolic, very physical changes so people can understand we are in the business of leading change."[25]

Integrating the right people and technology involves team-building, team-leadership and aligning social and technology systems and is described in Chapter 6. Promoting collaboration within and between teams is essential in today's business environment given that nearly half of all U.S.-based organizations use teams as a basic building block for performing work.[26] Teams are used not only to harness the collective knowledge, skills and abilities of employees for solving complex problems, but also to form alliances with customers, suppliers and former competitors in joint-ventures. Given the highly complicated nature of today's job requirements due to advanced technologies, developing and maintaining high performing teams is one of the most strategically important responsibilities that strategy-focused leaders must carry out successfully. The importance of this function was noted by Joseph Deitch, CEO of Commonwealth Financial Network, a leading investment brokerage firm.

> Company success in this challenging economy turns on the abilities of the CEO and human resources professionals to attract great people, establish great goals, and build great teams. Establish lots of teams and leaders. This engenders passion and pride in project ownership, not to mention more productive brainstorming and effective consensus building.[27]

Properly fitting social and technology systems in organizations is a major strategic leadership challenge that has produced poor results so far. A recent study reported that 40 percent of all information technology (IT) development projects are cancelled before completion and that the primary factor accounting for their failure is a lack of SFL.[28] A separate study found an inverse relationship between the amount of money spent on IT projects and their success rates, with projects costing less than $750,000 achieving a lackluster 55 percent success rate, and projects costing between $5 and $10 million achieving a dismal 7 percent success rate.[29] More successful development, assimilation, and adoption of technology system into the firmly entrenched social systems of organizations, with their longstanding cultures, reward systems, trust issues, and reporting structures, will require leaders to pay close attention to the congruence between how the technologies are intended to be used by their designers and the traditional ways of conducting work embedded in the social system.

For example, the rapid development in IT is creating fundamental changes in the work processes in organizations. With advances in information and telecommunication technologies, more employers are offering flexible work arrangements for their employees such as telework. Flexible work schedules based on telework can increase employees' satisfaction and productivity as well as organizational performance. However, it is important to note that top management's awareness of potential benefits and problems that can result from telework has been shown to be a key factor for successful implementation of telework processes. In other words, top management's keen interest in embracing new technology is vital to organizational success under current business environment. That's because the extent that the development, implementation, and assimilation of technology into organizations is expected to increase as technology becomes a common medium for strategic leaders and their followers to interact in the future.[30]

Weaving the Fabric of Success

To weave the fabric of success, executives must create not only financial but also emotional/psychological ownership based on mutual trust and respect. They do it by sincerely conveying the goals as well as the challenges their organizations are facing. In effect, strategy-focused leaders "translate" their analysis of the business environment and their consequent strategic decisions to employees in the organization. This role of "leaders as buffers" becomes critical in technology dependent environments, where high uncertainty could harm employees' functioning. It is in these kinds of environments that emotional/psychological bonding is so critical.

They also must actively support organizational innovation and encourage self-learning processes. Creating ownership and trust involves gaining the commitment to the strategy and the trust of employees and is described in Chapter 7. Inspiring commitment among employees requires executive leaders to manage the impressions they make on others, to display a certain "stage presence," to project an image of confidence, power and trustworthiness, and to role model exemplary and ethical behavior that personifies organizational values.[31] As illustrated in the Shackleton expedition example, inspiring commitment by projecting a confident image is especially important during stressful times of hardship and uncertainty, when organizational members can lose faith in the mission and become de-motivated.

Inspiring commitment to organizational strategy by developing a workforce that is sensitive to market or other environmental changes is necessary for creating an empowered workforce. To empower means not only to give employees the authority to make decisions, but also to develop or bolster their confidence needed to identify what it takes to complete their work successfully. Confidence is based on one's knowledge of a task or subject area, one's ability to perform, and possessing the skills required by the requisite task. Such efforts are very difficult to sustain given the rapid changes in technology and employee skills required to keep up with such changes. These challenges are more devastating due to the economic, market and financial conditions that are dynamic and sometimes downright hostile. Our research indicates that gaining commitment to strategic goals requires that leaders challenge, mentor and coach employees, while displaying the highest levels of ethical standards in their behavior and decision-making. Leaders who use open communication channels and are effective listeners have followers who are more familiar with the organization's goals. Lee Kranefuss, CEO of Barclay's Global Investors Individual Investor business unit, recognizes the importance of communicating organizational strategy to empower employees:

> I spend a lot of time and I would argue the need to spend even more, talking about goals of the group and organization. I feel, in the absence of information, employees have the tendency to speculate and embellish on the pieces of information they do have. I want to ensure everyone is on the same page. We have spent so much time and effort building this high-functioning organization; we need to empower its most valuable component, the people.[32]

Supporting innovation and learning involves creating cultures that value change and adopt new ways of doing things and is described in Chapter 8. Facilitating organizational learning is a critical function that strategy-focused leaders have to play in today's highly complex and turbulent work environment, with its ever-changing competition, economic conditions, financial markets, technology advances, customer/client preferences, supplies of raw materials, services and labor, and governmental regulations. It is impossible for them to keep up with these conditions without leveraging the collective knowledge and skills of all members of the organization. To overcome this dilemma, many of today's most successful organizations, such as General Electric, Lockheed Martin, Vanguard, Qualcomm, and Unisys, are transforming themselves into *learning organizations* in which people at all levels, individually and collectively, are continually increasing their capacity to produce results they really care about. In these highly successful high-tech organizations, knowledge sharing and management are central to their innovative business operations and organizational culture. Leadership of such efforts requires the intellectual stimulation of all organizational members. Harriet L. Fader, CAE, president and CEO, Diabetes Association of Greater Cleveland notes that:

> A learning environment, in my opinion, is like a wonderful garden where people thrive because they have an opportunity to grow. By challenging your staff and expanding their skills, you create a more loyal staff and reduce turnover. In today's rapidly changing world, you need experienced staff members to be successful.[33]

Realizing the Dream

To realize the dream, executives must reinforce the core message and strategy and re-focus the shape of future successes. Re-enforcing the core message and strategy involves creating and sustaining strong *organizational cultures*, which reflect the shared behaviors, norms, and expectations of its members. This process is described in Chapter 9. For example, several organizations based in West Point, New York (e.g., www.PlatoonLeader.org and www.CompanyCommand.com) have used technology to facilitate organizational learning for the U.S. Army. The Army is changing its structure and culture to provide agile capabilities and adaptive processes powered by world class network-centric access to knowledge, systems and services. Their intent is to create a more enterprising, open, participative and collaborative culture adapted to the Army's more distributed and geographically dispersed theater of operations.[34]

Developing intellectual and social capital to support innovation and organizational change requires aligning the organization's overall goals for development with those of specific business units, groups and employees. The challenge for strategy-focused leaders is to align the often disparate personal, group, and unit agendas that have become incongruent or conflicting due to politics, self-centered motives and ethical lapses in judgment. Realigning employee's personal values according to organizational mission for higher levels of congruence has been linked to many positive outcomes that help the organization perform more effectively. In our experience, this usually consists of a solid goal-setting and reward system that encourages innovation and personal development. Richard King, CIO of Everfast, Incorporated, a privately held company in the niche home fabric and furniture retail market, highlights how goal alignment can be linked to building intellectual capital:

> The goals of our IT organization are formulated subordinate to the goals of the business. By doing this we have achieved a very good alignment with the corporate goals. Our goals are communicated periodically during regular meetings, they are also communicated in scope definition of projects and communicated as part of each employee's annual review. During the review process each employee is required to evaluate their performance and objectives relative to the goals of the company and the department.[35]

Re-focusing the shape of future successes involves assessing, opportunities, people, process and performance over time in relation to the organization's mission and strategy and is described in Chapter 10. A growing number of executives in organizations such as ABB, British Airways, British Telecom, Coca-Cola, Electrolux, Volvo and Xerox have recognized a need to mobilize and utilize their intellectual and human resources in addition to their tangible and financial assets. This recognition has given rise to the adoption of a more balanced approach to measuring the key success factors of organizational performance in relation to strategy. Traditionally, organizations measured their success primarily in terms of financial outcomes (e.g., stock price, net income, earnings per share, return on investment).

More recently, organizations have realized that financial success is a function of the development of human resources, the continuous improvement of organizational processes and relationships within and outside of the firm, and customer satisfaction. As a result, they are being held responsible by organizational stakeholders for maximizing the accumulated market value of the firm by concentrating on the SFL processes described above.[36] For example, Jack Welch, former CEO of General Electric, added over $321 billion dollars of market value to GE between 1981 and 1998 by focusing organizational strategy, relentlessly driving continuous improvement, and championing organizational development initiatives.[37] These examples illustrate that various functions that strategy-focused leaders perform are critical for achieving organizational success because they directly impact organizational effectiveness by identifying, designing and monitoring the key performance indicators that add to its economic value over time.

Assumptions of Our Model

The SFL model that we described above is based on several key assumptions. First, *SFL is a system* made of components that influence each other in a dynamic but predictable way. These include the executive leader, his or her followers, the organization and its culture, structure and operational processes, and the strategic situation. Particularly important is the *strategic situation*, which includes all the potential environmental and organizational stimuli that influence each of the SFL processes previously described.[38] Examples of environmental stimuli include degree of competitor hostility, unpredictability of competitor market activities, quality of supplier relationships, customer preferences, growth opportunities, rate and type of changes in technology, rate of innovation in industry products, amount of research and development in the industry, needed diversity in production and marketing methods to cater to different customers, and legal, cultural, political and economic constraints. Examples of organizational stimuli include followers' inclinations towards development along with their present KSAs, organizational culture, organizational structure (e.g., degree of formalization, centralization, professionalism, hierarchy), reward systems, employee orientation and socialization systems, work structures and preferences (e.g., individual versus team), and the leadership legacy left behind by previous executives. Aspects of the strategic situation are described in Chapter 2.

Second, *the core message or vision drives everything in the organization* in the sense that the SFL processes of recognizing and identifying trends and focusing on the core message and strategy propel the leadership processes that add economic value for the organization.[39] In other words, vision and its derivative organizational mission serve as the stimulus for developing SFL processes that ultimately lead to increased economic value for all organizational stakeholders. However, the vision needs to be adapted to the environmental and organizational stimuli so that it is meaningful, practical, compelling and consistent with environmental conditions.

Third, *no two SFL systems are alike* because no two organizations and their internal and external environments are alike. However, we will identify several strategies for developing the type of SFL that may be effective based on specific situations of the wide array of organizations in our study. The lessons derived from the wide range of organizations studied here and the technology they deploy to support their mission should be vital information for readers who are interested in harnessing the potential of SFL.

The tumultuous and unpredictable conditions of the business environment today, the challenges of succeeding in the Information Age, and the new organizational structures and business strategies that have emerged all demand that executive leaders take a hard look at the extent to which their SFL system contributes toward the development of economic, social and human capital. All the evidence points to the conclusion that developing sound SFL is the best way for executives to prosper today in the uncertain future. We now turn to setting the stage for SFL today and in the future by reviewing specific trends in the business environment, paying particular attention to how technology can enhance an organization's strategic situation.

CHAPTER 2

COMPETING IN A TECHNOLOGY-DRIVEN WORLD

Technology is a gift of God. After the gift of life, it is perhaps the greatest of God's gifts. It is the mother of civilizations, of arts and of sciences.
—Freeman Dyson

The technology-driven world is creating completely new ways to formulate strategies, facilitate work and business relationships, and create value for stakeholders. Such trends are creating a new context for executive leaders who must leverage technology to enable and empower their followers to successfully execute the organizational strategy. This chapter describes contextual characteristics of technology-driven industries and important trends in the business environment, paying particular attention to how technology enhances or neutralizes SFL in organizations. It also considers the unique challenges and opportunities for executives to attain long-term strategic goals in organizations.

The Dream Weavers: Strategy-Focused Leadership in Technology-Driven
Organizations, pages 23–42
Copyright © 2004 by Information Age Publishing, Inc.
All rights of reproduction in any form reserved.
ISBN: 1-59311-110-X (paper), 1-59311-111-8 (cloth)

TECHNOLOGY ENABLES STRATEGIC SUCCESS

Amy Turner-LaDow is no stranger to uncertainty and change. After successfully leading the ISO 9001 certification project at Anderson Consulting and supporting their clients' adoption and use of PeopleSoft software, she joined SCT, a suburban Philadelphia-based provider of advanced solutions and software for nearly 1,300 higher education clients worldwide. With 27 years of experience in the market, SCT provides solutions that turn data into information, and information into knowledge. This knowledge-based solution set, coupled with a professional and learning-oriented community of IT experts, sets the stage for results-based operational excellence. SCT and their core business have existed since the early 1970s, but their focus broadened as the technology and Internet boom began in the 1990's. However, beginning in the year 2000, SCT experienced several rounds of layoffs, restructuring and reorganization, resulting in the sale of two of their less profitable divisions.

Despite these challenges, Turner-LaDow points out that SCT has made it clear that its ultimate obligation is to its stockholders, and that it is focusing on its core competency of higher education in order to secure a viable future. As Vice President for support services for SCT's Global Manufacturing and Distribution Market unit, Turner-LaDow is responsible for client services leadership across all market units within SCT. She notes that one of the toughest challenges for SCT is to use the technology systems and knowledge they possess today to help the company expand in line with their corporate vision. Continually reinventing the company according to its vision, developing its employees, and maintaining its excellent reputation is a difficult task, but one she hopes SCT will accomplish through its people, technical infrastructure, and her role as a change catalyst.[1]

SCT is only one of many organizations today that depend on technology to sustain its business operations. Technology systems that support business operations are pervasive because information and knowledge are the most powerful resources in every business function in every industry. Technology also enables organizations around the world to implement global strategy in a timely manner and control their worldwide operations and subsidiaries more effectively. Most importantly, it allows organizations to evolve into truly global and transnational companies. Technology can accelerate the dissemination of information and development of strategic knowledge. According to futurist Alvin Toffler, leadership of tomorrow's organizations will require "continually seeking out new knowledge and applying it to teamwork and network interactions with others inside and outside of the firm."[2]

Strategy-focused leaders will need to guide their organization's knowledge management abilities to access, filter, and disseminate valuable information that can help generate new knowledge. They will need to hire multi-skilled experts who are capable of using technology to obtain relevant information and collaborate on complex and multidimensional tasks. As described in Chapter 1, successful implementation of IT-related systems (e.g., Internet-based accounting/financial systems and flexible work processes) requires continuous support and attention from top management. Strategy-focused leaders will also need to act as change catalysts that promote vision-relevant organizational development and facilitate the constant learning and sharing of experiences, insights and expertise supported by the organization's technology. Finally, strategy-focused leaders need to recognize the challenges involved in managing organizations that depend on technology. They must identify unique resources, especially individual skills, and develop them to provide strategic advantage for the organization. As a result, technology will drive internal changes and employee development.

James Morgan who has been CEO of Applied Materials for 25 years (the longest-serving CEO in Silicon Valley) demonstrates the benefit of a strategy-focused leader's proactive role in embracing new technologies. During his regime, Applied Materials' stock appreciated more than 5,600% and increased market share substantially. Many analysts have cited Morgan's forward thinking and bold strategies to develop and utilize advanced technologies for the firm's success in the highly competitive semiconductor industry. Applied Materials has already begun testing equipment for making their products targeted for the 2007 market and beyond.[3]

Strategy-Focused Leaders View Technology Systems as Potential Enablers of Organizational Effectiveness

Technology systems must be integrated into organizations so that they work in concert with the social systems in organizations. In other words, strategy-focused leaders must find ways to inspire their followers to view technology as a way that makes their work and interactions with other associates easier and more rewarding, and consistent with the organization's vision and culture, rather than as a threat to their authority, power, and control. Doing so may help to create social systems that embrace technology and the accessing, filtering and sharing of information as core values or norms that are central to the organization's mission. At the same time, strategy-focused leaders must also use technology to sustain a necessary sense of urgency and focus on the organization's strategy. What knowledge is available to help strategy-focused leaders attain this goal?

Knowledge of how to lead an organization that depends on technology is not always explicitly stated in best practices, corporate culture or policies, but is an essential element of success in virtually every organization—from small entrepreneurial start-ups to mature and established firms. The little research knowledge that is available is either too broadly or too abstractly described, based on anecdotal evidence that is not generalizable across organizational situations, or is targeted toward leaders of virtual teams, who interact with their physically dispersed members using information technology.[4] To build upon this limited knowledge base, we have launched the study described in this book to examine the real-life experiences, expertise, and insights of executives from organizations of various size and maturities in technology-driven industries. Our approach is consistent with the realization of many of today's most successful executives that the most practical way to derive knowledge is to tap the experiences, expertise, ideas, values and judgments that reside within individuals or are shared among groupings of people who work together interdependently.

Leadership must be increasingly shared throughout all organizational levels through empowerment, self-managed work teams, and participative decision-making processes when an organization needs to deal with ever-changing environment and facilitate innovation.[5] It is therefore important for every executive to develop a deep-enough understanding of the subject to know how to demonstrate SFL for his or her associates. As mentioned in Chapter 1, the strategic situation or context for SFL is very important to understand because it sets the stage, defines the playing conditions, and establishes the surroundings or environment. SFL does not exist in a vacuum; it operates in an interactive and ever-changing environment. Before we present our executives' ideas on SFL in subsequent chapters, it is instructive to examine what it means to be technology-driven *and* the trends in today's technology-driven work environments, so that you may obtain a clearer picture of your organization's strategic situation.

BEING TECHNOLOGY-DRIVEN

Organizations that are technology-driven share several characteristics summarized in Table 2.1. They face a rapidly changing, highly volatile environment with disruptive and destructive changes. Their environments are more dynamic (their technical, economic and social factors are ever-changing), diverse (they engage in different markets), risky, and buoyant (their markets and market emergence grow rapidly) than those for other organizations. They also are more technologically-sophisticated, endure stiffer competition, and undergo higher degrees of cyclical fluctuations in their business than other types of organizations.

TABLE 2.1
Major Characteristics of Technology-Driven Organizations

• Face a rapidly changing, highly volatile environment with disruptive and destructive forces.

• Have products and services often developed out of technologies that are only partially known or emerging.

• Introduce more offerings to the market due to shorter product lifecycles.

• Have extremely high levels of investment in R & D.

Technology-driven organizations have products and services often developed out of technologies that are only partially known or emerging. For example, Hyseq Inc. is a biotech company that is developing a new process for harnessing genetic variations to speed drug development. As more information and knowledge about alternative processes are obtained on a daily basis, more uncertainty about work flows, the product's features, and customers' demands are introduced into Hyseq Inc.'s work and decision-making processes. SFL is needed at Hyseq Inc. to place meaning on the uncertainty associated with such efforts and help employees deal with change.[6]

Technology-driven organizations also introduce more new offerings to the market than other types of organizations due to shorter product lifecycles. They also are forced to manage shorter product development cycles. As consumer demand grows for new products and services, one thing is inevitable: competition will force organizations to deliver products and services with more and more features—and to introduce those features in ever shorter time frames. For example, in the consumer electronics industry, innovative new products—with their promise to combine digital imaging, speech recognition, wireless communications, web access, e-commerce, and other online services—are being introduced at breakneck speeds. Transforming these challenges into opportunities for success requires strategy-focused leaders to motivate employees to effectively deal with pressures of rapidly transforming ideas into cooperative development efforts that yield successful products or services.

Fortunately, technology-driven organizations generally possess a large number of high-skilled technical workers. From a SFL standpoint, these workers are indispensable for providing the ideas, know-how, KSAs, and personal connections to deal with an uncertain environment. While these workers possess excellent formal academic or professional qualifications, they need to be selected on the basis of social criteria such as personality, motivation and inter-personal skills. By selecting staff with the right work orientations, strategy-focused leaders may have to rely less on formal systems of control and monitoring in order to extract high levels of performance from them.

Another characteristic of technology-driven organizations is their high level of investment in R&D. Some researchers[7] argue that it is at least 3% of their revenues, however, it is often much more. This feature allows for an emphasis on an R&D-driven strategy that banks on new products and services to proactively meet head-on the trends emerging from the environment. For example, Microsoft Chairman Bill Gates considers R&D spending to be important for supercharging his organization's performance. In 2002, he boosted R&D spending by about 20%, to $5.2 billion. Microsoft is designing a future version of Windows, code-named "Longhorn" and due later this decade. Gates says he spends about half his time at work with developers on the new program to help ensure the Microsoft's continued market dominance.[8]

Investment in R&D becomes more complicated in the high-tech environment where products are especially complex and product life cycles are extremely short. More than in other industries, in technology dependent industries competitors are often able to clone products while customers tend to be more sophisticated and discriminating.[9]

These are very harsh and extreme operating conditions facing executives of technology-driven organizations. One of the reasons we began this leadership research project was to discern who tends to do well in this environment and what they actually do to be behaviorally qualified to deal with the trends emerging in their environment and become a successful strategy-focused leader.

TRENDS IN TECHNOLOGY-DRIVEN WORK ENVIRONMENTS

Predicting the future is always risky. But in order to fully understand the potential strategic situation for executives in the forthcoming years, we need to put forth some predictions regarding the characteristics of leaders, followers and the work contexts as well as technology infrastructures in which they will be required to interact, on up to the point in time where we examine future work behavior. These trends are summarized in Table 2.2.

The Internet and its Expanding Role in Everyday Life

Taking an evolutionary view of technology seems essential given the rapid pace of technology innovation and change that has been associated with the Information Age. Perhaps the most significant technological trend has been the explosive growth of the Internet or World Wide Web as a major vehicle of business-to-business, business-to-consumer, and government services and procurement. As of 2003, the world distribution of users

TABLE 2.2
Major Trends in Technology-Driven Work Environment

- Dominance of the Internet and other information technology as basic means for work processes and functioning in everyday life.
- Integration of products, services, organizations, and technologies.
- Enhanced knowledge and elaborated expectations among shareholders and consumers.
- Increased need for continuous learning.
- Future-oriented culture that helps better embrace changes due to technological advancement.
- Flexible leadership and corporate governing structure.
- Empowered workforce through authority delegation.
- Strong emphasis on creativity and innovation as the most important source of competitive edge.
- Increased pressure toward globalization.

---

the Internet by native language was 238.5 million English language users, 238.1 million non-English European users, and 201.7 million Asian language users. The number of individual and business users is expected to grow exponentially.[10]

The Internet has fundamentally changed how strategy-focused leaders plan their "line of attack," design their organizations, collaborate with customers and suppliers, and interact with their employees. For example, the Internet has allowed former CEO Warren "Pete" Musser and his successors to shape Safeguard Scientifics, Inc. over time as a technology operating company that creates long term value for shareholders by focusing on technology related asset acquisitions. Safeguard acquires start-up technology firms, helps develop their business model, provides venture capital and managerial expertise, and then spins-off the start-up firm when it becomes more mature. Their strategy centers on "enabling the digital economy" and allows Safeguard to structure itself as a central hub with connections to partner companies that are nurtured and then spun-off over time. Safeguard has backed companies such as QVC, Internet Capital Group, US Interactive, and eMerge. The Internet has also enabled close working relationships across distance and time, not only with Safeguard's employees and partner firms who interact using virtual teams, but also with the customers of the partner firms.[11]

Information technology doesn't only help small, startup companies. It also helps large, global companies make their international operations more efficient and effective. For example, in KPMG, a global consulting company with more than 100,000 employees in more than 150 countries, knowledge management has become a major factor in their ability to compete and provide quality service to clients worldwide. The challenge of storing, retrieving, sharing and utilizing KPMG's valuable knowledge and other intangible assets was very exhausting due to the firm's extensive global reach until it developed and instituted a unique company intranet called "KWorld." This system is designed to streamline the process of knowledge management and help its employees to share information and collaborate on projects much more effectively. As one KPMG executive put it, "knowledge management is the enterprise integrator, the glue that holds everything else together."[12]

Beyond providing knowledge management support, the Internet is also fundamentally changing the way we function in life. Electronic devices, wireless communications, fiber optics, computation systems, satellites and global positioning systems are providing an infrastructure for information to be passed via the Internet. The successful integration of these systems was demonstrated under the brilliant leadership of U.S. Secretary of Defense Donald Rumsfeld and General Tommy Franks in the 2003 successful ouster of Saddam Hussein from power in Iraq. This was unlike any war in the past. This was a technology-driven war that involved a massive coordination and integration of many different technical and social systems. It was a case where the U.S. military leadership learned to leverage information and advanced technology to think big and win fast with its highly trained military forces.

That same strategy of learning to think big and produce quick and sustained victories is something that Andy Grove, the chairman and former CEO of Intel, considers essential for success in technology-driven industries. According to Grove, "The IT business will reignite its growth only if it can use these tools to actively reach beyond traditional *transactional* processing systems to *transform* other vital aspects of life." And this is already happening. Consider, for example, the following emerging technologies: Wi-Fi, voice over Internet protocol (VOIP), IBM's Websphere and on-demand computing, broadband to the home, e-commerce and e-marketing. Wi-Fi technology allows digital devices within a several-hundred-foot range to connect at broadband speeds to the Internet. This technology is used in 2.5 million homes in the U.S. and is popping up in organizations such as McDonalds, StarBucks and Kinkos as customers are now able to connect practically anywhere, anytime and with anyone.

And how they connect is being broadened by the convergence of data, voice, video and Wi-Fi over single Internet protocol infrastructures, which can save organizations large amounts of money on international communications costs. Besides merging media into single sources, organizations such as IBM and Salesforce.com are building software that links customers, suppliers and business partners and are selling it as a service so that organizations do not have to incur large lump-sum fixed costs. Instead they can purchase the software as a service on a more flexible "buy it when you need it" basis.

These services are increasingly coming into our homes. For example, it is expected that the number of broadband Internet or DSL telephone lines coming into U.S. households by the year 2005 will be 32 million, funda-mentally changing how people work, live, access health care and education services and do their shopping. Millions of people are logging onto online marketplaces or search engines, like eBay or Google to locate and pur-chase products, services or sources of information.[13] The availability of these resources is truly unprecedented and is making our work lives easier, more flexible, albeit faster and more stressful when it comes to the chal-lenges of keeping track of all the sources of information available.

Today's strategy-focused leaders often wrestle with the notion that infor-mation derived from the Internet is *uncontrollable* in the sense that the information may contradict their messages and reduce the commitment and motivation of employees. Information may be stolen by competitors or manipulated and distorted by malevolent individuals. However, some prog-nosticators argue that the Internet of the future will provide networked, intelligent environments that will give us more *control* over our intellectual property, but at the same time our actions will be more watched, tracked, controlled and compelled. These predictions are based on trends of intelli-gent appliances connecting us to our environments, knowledge becoming a medium of exchange, like money, and as essential as oxygen, and the bio-metrics (measurable physical and behavioral characteristics used to verify claimed identity) becoming more important for access and security.[14] These trends toward more controlled leader-follower or virtual team inter-actions via the Internet could contribute to a future work context that is inconsistent with intent of the designers of the Internet as an open forum for the sharing of information or organizational cultures that are based on trust, honesty and candidness while maximizing geographical flexibility. Indeed, perhaps the greatest irony is that *the future strategy-focused leader and his or her followers may find themselves more well-informed at the expense of being more controlled.*

Integration of Products, Services, Organizations and Technologies

In technology-driven industries, integration rules! When we use the term "integration," we mean the combination of various elements to form an innovative creation—whether it be a new product/service, partnership, or work process/tool. Today, we are seeing an amazing array of innovations that are the result of integration processes. In the life sciences industry, the blending of drugs and devices are producing major medical break-throughs for patients and profits for the developer organizations. For example, Medtronic Inc. is developing implantable drug pumps which are inserted into the abdomen to deliver a nerve-saving substance to the brain to treat Parkinson's disease. They are also perfecting an artificial pancreas that can monitor blood glucose levels and deliver the correct amount of insulin when needed, and have put steroid drugs into pacemakers to speed healing and reduce scarring for heart surgery patients.

Integration is not just limited to products. It's also evident in the tele-communication services industry and linkages between small startup and large corporate ventures. Comcast Corporation, a Philadelphia-based cable TV company, has developed broadband telephony services that partition telephone calls into bits of data and sends them over the Internet in packets. This integrated service has resulted in lower prices for consumers, more efficient processing of information and increased competition with organizations like Verizon and SBC Communications.

As electronic marketplaces continue to emerge, traditional bricks-and-mortar organizations are partnering with online marketers such as eBay to sell their products and services. eBay has successfully survived the burst of the Internet bubble and has partnered with Ford Motor Company, IBM, Sears Roebuck, and RitzCamera.com to further stimulate the growth of on-line marketing. Similarly, a growing number of large manufacturers are collaborating with or outsourcing work to startup organizations to best meet the needs of their customers. In its quest to satisfy its most prized customer (the Pentagon), Lockheed Martin has turned to Foam Matrix Inc., an Inglewood, California based producer of surfboards and sailboards, to collaborate on the manufacture of molded aircraft wings for precision targeted JASSM missiles. These missiles were used in the war to remove Saddam Hussein from power in Iraq. As a result of tragic events of September, 11, 2001 and the war on terrorism, many technology-driven organizations are bracing for disaster by forming business partnerships with companies that can provide backup power and datacenters, cybersecurity, extra telecommunications, and the tracking and securing of goods via global positioning systems.[15]

The continuing trends of product, service, technology and organizational integration require strategy-focused leaders to find ways to connect people, ideas and technologies to support collaboration, coordination, communication and innovation. The way business is performed has fundamentally changed from independent sources of brilliance, creativity, inspiration and hard work to interdependent and interconnected networks of people, teams, technologies and organizations. Strategy-focused leaders must identify who and what needs to be connected, and then make and support those connections in order to spur world-class innovation and further technological advances.

Elevated Expectations of Shareholders

The Internet has also made the tracking of financial and stock performance information much more accessible to current and potential shareholders. Because such information allows them to be more knowledgeable about company performance, these shareholders are becoming more demanding and are requiring strategy-focused leaders to add economic and market value to their investment so that they can achieve their earnings potential. They expect executives to provide leadership that increases the net worth of the stock they own.

But shareholders also expect executives of publicly traded companies to honestly and accurately report their firm's earnings according to generally accepted accounting principles, which is a not-so-common occurrence. In 2001 and 2002, the financial community and faith in corporate governance were shaken by the Enron and WorldCom scandals, which involved "entrepreneurial" executives who played the financial system for all they could get away with. Jeff Skilling, former CEO of Enron, and Bernie Ebbers, former CEO of WorldCom came under fire from the U.S. Congress for allegedly "cooking the books," destroying documents, and using fake accounting and structured deception to create a fantasy world, in which the value of their own share options was real enough, but many thousands of smaller people lost both savings and jobs. Societal confidence in the entire financial system has collapsed because of the unethical behavior of these executives. In response, Congress reacted by approving legislation to create new penalties, including long prison terms, for corporate fraud and document destruction, hold corporate executives legally accountable for the accuracy of financial statements, and require real-time disclosures on the Internet of important changes in a company's financial condition or operations.[16] The extent of CEO arrogance and greediness will hopefully never be the same.

In addition to calls for corporate accountability, organizational stakeholders are expecting executives and their corporations to be socially responsible. Organizations such as Co-Op America prepare and disseminate in-depth social profiles on organizations through the Internet. Stakeholders interested in the social responsibility ratings of a particular organization can access their website at http://www.responsibleshopper.org/.[17] A report on Hewlett Packard, for example, examines everything from executive compensation, unfair employment practices, superfund sites, and workplace reductions to forest-friendly initiatives. Social performance is summarized on the website in letter ratings as with Hewlett Packard, which got a "B" in workplace ratings, and a "B" in environmental ratings. With the public availability of such information, strategy-focused leaders need to think twice before they engage in any behavior that could potentially be seen as socially irresponsible.

Strategy-focused leaders also need to be concerned with the recent proliferation of social-betterment thinking on topics of such as globalization, creating ecologically sustainable economies, fostering spirituality and values in the workplace, community development and renewal, global governance and the fight against terrorism, antiracist strategies and solutions to eliminate the effects of discrimination, generational allowances of Social Security to fund surpluses into education programs, and labor unions countering growing corporate power with technology.[18] With greater attention given to executive unethical behavior and the need for social-betterment, there will be more emphasis on selecting strategy-focused leaders who can be fiscally, morally and socially aware and responsible to a variety of organizational stakeholders.

Prevalence of Leadership Training

Executives have come to realize that in a technology-driven world, the one fundamental source of competitive advantage is learning. As a result, an increasing number of executives are embracing the notion of "learning organizations," as organizations that possess a corporate culture that cherishes continuous improvement.[19] To create such cultures, organizations are investing in the development of their people by funding in-house training programs, corporate universities, university training of their employees, and leadership development firms. Organizations are committing more budget dollars to leadership training and development, including executive education and individualized executive coaching. U.S. companies spent an average $1,736 per employee on training in 2001 and an estimated $1,803 per employee in 2002, spending one-fourth of the total annually on executive and leadership development.[20]

The increased demand for leadership development has spurred several trends in the education industry. Leadership development consulting firms, such as the Center for Creative Leadership, Linkage, and PROVANT, are offering an increased variety of executive and general leadership training programs. A growing number of the world's most successful and innovative organizations, such as Johnson & Johnson, Royal Dutch Shell, Hewlett-Packard, The World Bank, and Arthur Anderson, also have developed and implemented their own leadership programs to grow leaders within their own organizations and to support corporate business initiatives of succession planning, corporate re-engineering, diversity, and employee development.

Leadership development is also prevalent in the advent of corporate universities, which provide an alternative to traditional university courses. Corporate universities leverage the experience of their senior managers who share their accumulated wisdom with students. For example, UNISYS CEO Larry Weinbach is a staunch believer in the power of corporate universities to develop the full potential of his workforce. Weinbach has championed the development and implementation of Unisys University, which offers classroom and online training on various levels of leadership knowledge. Employees enroll in courses to gain new skills, certifications and knowledge to advance their careers and the success of Unisys.[21]

We are also seeing a proliferation of universities delivering undergraduate and graduate programs in organizational leadership. A growing number of colleges and universities, including the University of South Florida, University of Nebraska, University of Oklahoma, and University of Richmond, have implemented programs creatively designed to accommodate the needs of traditional and non-traditional students. Compared to more traditional programs, these university leadership programs focus more on direct application of theory to practice, more hands-on learning, and the use of Internet-based learning and online communities for student support.[22]

If these current trends continue, we can expect to have strategy-focused leaders who have a broader array of leadership skills because of the plethora of education and training available. They will be more open to the continuous training and development of their associates, and used to sharing leadership information with their associates to solve the variety of leadership dilemmas that they face. They also will be comfortable using new technologies to locate information about their customers, competitors, employees and industry's trends and integrate this information into their organization's strategy. Finally, they are likely to be individuals who have a more proactive view on how to develop and maintain the knowledge, skills and abilities of their associates required for adding financial, intellectual and social value to their organizations.

A Sharper Focus on Culture

Cultural assessments are a means to understand the language, artifacts and symbols, patterns of behavior, publicly announced or "espoused values," and beliefs and underlying assumptions that define the way organizations operate. An increasing number of organizations are assessing their culture to initiate and better manage organizational changes as a way to deal with customers and environmental uncertainties. For example, at Sarasota Memorial Hospital, cultural assessment led to implementation strategies for a new integrated care delivery system that helped the hospital's leadership team overcome confounding factors of physician dislike of group work and aversion to standardization.

In the Swedish school system, administrators have successfully used cultural assessments to identify and remove stumbling blocks to total quality management and institutional core values of student focus, continuous improvement of learning and support processes and outcomes, administrative commitment, trust, and factual decision-making. At an organization where we have consulted, cultural assessment is being used to determine how to better integrate a new collaborative groupware technology into their "no-mistakes" culture, where making a mistake can be a "career-defining event." So far, the client is struggling with the adoption of the new technology because of its culture. According to one senior manager, the technology is being used so that "different units know who is doing what wrong, but more efficiently."[23]

These examples illustrate the need for strategy-focused leaders to realize that they help shape organizational culture by hiring and retaining associates who share their cultural beliefs, orientating and socializing associates in accordance with their cultural beliefs, and then acting as role models so that associates can practice and internalize their organizations' beliefs, values and assumptions. Because culture provides employees with the context in which social interactions take place, it can be either a springboard or stumbling block to an organization's effectiveness.

Based on current trends, one can easily imagine an organization attempting to implement a $6 million IT system such as PeopleSoft or Oracle systems. But suppose that the organization has a firmly entrenched hyper-competitive culture plagued with nasty office politics that have systemically infected all levels of the organization's hierarchy. Also suppose that middle-level managers show resistance to IT-based organizational changes due to their fear of losing control and/or power over their subordinates. Then the chances of successful implementation are slim to none. So we can expect strategy-focused leaders to ask more questions about how their organizational cultures can impede their planned strategies, and how these impediments can be overcome, or potentially changed into springboards with advanced technology.

The Advent of e-Leadership

The information technology revolution has influenced how new organizational systems now need to be restructured by leaders to adapt in the e-business context. Organic organizational structures, shaped by massive enterprise wide information systems, collaborative work flows, and geographically distant/temporally removed teams are required to achieve flexibility and openness in the current work environment. These configurations involve structural shifts from close adherence to a chain of command to little emphasis on the chain of command, from specialized tasks to continually adjusting job definitions, from vertical communication to lateral communication flows, from top-down decision-making to employee participation in decision-making, and from functional to divisional-type division of work.

Today's technically-adept workforce also expects to be able to work at home and at customer sites because of the convenience and flexibility offered by technology that supports any place, any time work arrangements. To this end, technologies such as Internet and Intranet conferencing, white-boards, document and database sharing, expertise locators, threaded discussion groups, instant messaging, chat rooms, handheld communication devices, groupware, and teleconferencing are being integrated into business strategies and operations at a dizzying rate. Such trends in technology and work-arrangements require *e-leadership* to mediate the social interactions of strategy-focused leaders and their constituents through advanced information technologies to motivate them towards a particular target goal or objective.[24]

Comprehensive enterprise-wide information systems have promoted collaborative sharing of information across organizational "stove pipes," causing shifts in power dynamics and networking. Widespread availability of information on company Intranets and the Internet provide followers with increased on-line networking opportunities via the technologies listed above, offering them alternative channels of information than provided within traditional management hierarchies.[25] These trends offer strategy-focused leaders an unprecedented opportunity to empower their followers to build more intelligent knowledge-based communities. Yet, the new technologies can also present strategy-focused leaders and their followers with the challenges of information overload, followers receiving messages that are discrepant with their leaders, and social isolation. These new work conditions will demand new organizational strategies, structures and techniques to help strategy-focused leaders respond effectively to new challenges and to create new opportunities. Strategy-focused leaders will also need to communicate their visions and expectations to build cultures where knowledge and information are essential assets required for collaboration, competitive advantage, and high quality relationships within and between associates, customers, business partners and suppliers.

Empowered Workforces

According to David Walker, Comptroller General of the General Accounting Office, "The key competitive difference in the 21st century will be people. It will not be process. It will not be technology. It will be people." To harness the full potential of human capital, strategy-focused leaders will need to conduct strategic analysis of present and future human resources requirements and workforce planning, obtain the needed employees, empower its employees to maintain a workforce with a mix of skills that match its needs, and motivate and reward employees to support strategic goals. Organizations such as the U.S. Coast Guard have been planning their workforce needs as far as 20 years out to avoid shortages that they encountered when they laid off 4,000 people in the mid-1990s. They have also used leadership development programs to empower their associates with increased KSAs, confidence and motivation in a hope of avoiding future leadership shortages.[26] In other words, the strategic focus for leadership development in the 21st century will be on empowering employees, rather than empowering managers.

The empowerment of employees, who now have increased leadership and decision-making roles, will be a common feature in tomorrow's organizations. Employees are already being called upon to generate ideas for new products, processes, and strategies. At Google, employee empowerment is being supported by the power of Intranet technology. Each of its 300 employees is provided with space on the company's intranet for listing ideas on topics that range from what might become new features on Google, new code or search algorithms, or a new way to improve the Google home page. On Fridays, the employees use the site to brainstorm their ideas. Promising ideas are quickly outlined on the intranet site and the individual who came up with the idea is put in charge of implementing it. Google faces intense competition from newcomers promising better and faster ways to search the Internet. As the competition becomes more intense, the leadership role is pushed down to employees who are closer to customers, processes and the technologies that support them.[27]

Trends of increasing employee empowerment present several opportunities for tomorrow's strategy-focused leaders. If the communication systems are robust and reliable, the amount and quality of information accessed and shared between strategy-focused leaders and their followers will surpass what was available to yesterday's most successful leaders. Strategy-focused leaders will be able to capitalize on locating and tapping into expertise, higher quality collaboration with followers, and enhanced ability to find the people capable of solving specific problems. They will have access to large bases of know-how about the decisions being made, the processes and policies within the organization, as well as information on customers, suppliers, competitors accumulated by the vast network of employees who serve as a distributed network of leaders. Of course, such benefits may only be derived if an organizational culture exists that is open, collaborative, committed, innovative and trusting of senior management. Given the amount of information their followers have, strategy-focused leaders now need to develop open and honest relationships with their followers, regarding the strategic goals and challenges that the organization faces. Effective strategy-focused leaders will need to express the right vulnerability that is necessary to form trusting relationships with their followers.

Emphasis on Creativity and Innovation

The rate of new technology development has far exceeded the rate of creative application of the technology to provide business solutions. Executives are therefore placing increased importance on the development of a creative workforce to provide a competitive intellectual capital advantage in today's technology-driven world. A poll conducted by Robert Half International, Inc. in 2001 revealed that the majority (89%) of the U.S. top executives polled said that their organizations are more proactively promoting creativity and innovation among their employees compared to five years ago.[28] This survey result is consistent with the attitudes of the CEOs of many of today's organizations that are fighting to eliminate the enemies of creativity and innovation: too much hierarchy and too many rules. According to John Brooks, President and CEO of Adherex Technologies Inc., a biotech company involved in finding treatments for cancer and other diseases, creativity and innovation is spurred by an open culture created by the organization's SFL:

> Innovation comes when people are free to use their imaginations and you've got to encourage that. You have to recognize the best ideas don't come from senior management all the time. We've come up with some bad ideas too, but that's what you want—people to feel free to bring up comments and talk freely about things.[29]

Many executives are also realizing that to thrive in today's competitive technology-driven world requires creativity and innovation being placed in the forefront of the minds of their employees. This view is held by Dave Colcleugh, chair, president and CEO of Dupont Canada Inc., which manufactures a variety of products from synthetics and polymers to automotive finishes. According to Colcleugh,

> Innovation is right at the very top of our vision statement. Many people have vision statements and put innovation in it but we take it very seriously. We think of ourselves as a science company. We try to brand ourselves as a science company and that is really the creation of knowledge. So clearly (innovation) is important to us.[30]

Spelling out creativity and innovation as *espoused* values is one thing. But investing in creativity and innovation is another. 3M Corporation has actually *enacted* these values by building its Innovation and Learning Center to create an environment that supports creativity and innovation. This center provides employees with creativity tools (e.g., videos, brainstorming technology) and a place where they rest, meditate and let the creative juices start flowing. It's a place where employees can listen to each other in a respectful, supportive, non-threatening environment, seek out the ideas of others, give ideas, and gain commitment and encouragement by being with others.[31]

Based on these trends, we can expect to have strategy-focused leaders who are more amenable to working to remove the stumbling blocks to creativity, whether they be in the organization, work processes, its employees, or its leadership. They will be comfortable nurturing creativity and innovation by building cultures that empower employees to not be afraid to make mistakes as long as they learn from them. They are likely to inspire employees to be creative and passionate about their work by making their work fun and meaningful. They will be used in employing advanced information technology (e.g., electronic brainstorming) to support the creative efforts of employees. They also will have a greater appreciation for the intellectual value of creativity and innovation based on its strategic importance as a form of competitive advantage, and be willing to put forth various incentives such as monetary rewards and company recognition to adequately compensate creative and innovative ideas and solutions from employees. Finally, they will allow individuals to craft their jobs so that they can choose the relationships with other employees and form new work procedures that lead to more creative products.[32]

Increasingly Complex Demands of Globalization

Growth in the international flows of trade, financial capital, technology, values, and ways of conducting business are all aspects of globalization and have important implications for strategy-focused leaders. Globalization has introduced new worldwide marketplaces, 24/7 operations, interorganizational and international business alliances, diversity in the labor force, production and service processes distributed across several countries, and what some call the "corporatization" or "westernization" of the world. As a result, there is a growing realization in executive circles that globalization offers an abundance of opportunities and rewards, while also promoting conformity and loss of diversity and the marginalization of the world's poorest countries that are less globalized.[33]

Globalization is not a new concept. Throughout history, advances in science and technology, ideas on government, society, culture, economics and religion have been passed across national boundaries, first from the East to the West, and today from the West to the East. These transfers of ideas and knowledge have benefited organizations, countries, and societies over long periods of time. They have introduced strategy-focused leaders to differences in cultural values that explain the distinctions in the way national cultures think about the meaning of life, what they value, and how they behave. Until the 1980's, executives at American car manufacturers ignored the traditional Japanese values of continuous process improvement, "just-in-time" inventory procedures, and long-term commitments to customers. Today, these concepts have now been institutionalized into the best practices of today's most successful organizations such as General Electric, Motorola, and Hewlett Packard. Indeed, globalization with its international trade of products, services, and ideas often carries with it a wealth of resources that strategy-focused leaders need to consider including business practices, training, leadership styles, regulation, and technology.[34]

Nevertheless, multinational corporations (MNC) need to continue to take into consideration cross-cultural differences, especially with regard to SFL practices. For example, a recent study conducted at a Fortune 50 MNC found that managers from Far Eastern cultures were rated higher on strategic planning as compared with their U.S. counterparts. One potential explanation for this finding is the future time orientation value that was found to characterize Far Eastern cultures. Executives at this MNC may now consider training procedures that will take into consideration such differences. Overall, we believe that global leadership in today's global business environment has become acronym for effective leadership among multinational companies around the world.

Advances in technology have increased the rate and pervasiveness of globalization and its effects on organizations. The Internet offers organizations an almost unlimited supply of marketplaces because in cyberspace the traditional assumptions and boundaries of space, distance and time no longer apply. Business transactions can occur with customers, suppliers, and employees anywhere and at anytime. For example, Vodafone utilizes a group of software engineers to work on developing new software, whose members are located in three different parts of the world—Boston, Hawaii and Bombay—to expedite their development processes based on advanced information technology. This web-based work process allows the company to work on developing new software literally around the clock, which cuts down the time and cost substantially.[35]

Globalization has also helped the acceleration of entire industries. Take for example the biotech industry, which in 2002 boasted 662 public and 3,600 private organizations across the globe. This industry has developed as world markets for genetic engineering of foods and animals, medicines, and biological weapons have expanded. Biotech activity in the U.S. has generated revenues of $25,319 million from 1,115 private and 342 public organizations employing 141,000 people. Europe has generated revenues of $7,533 million from 1,775 private and 104 public organizations employing 34,189 people. Asia has generated revenues of $1,001 million from 441 private and 91 public organizations employing 6,518 people.[36] However, the abundant number of biotech firms has resulted in over-competition in the biotech industry. In the mid-1990s there were about 350 biotech firms in the San Diego area, among which only 60 firms had any product on the market *and* only 30 firms were profitable in 2001. Continued successful leadership of these biotech firms will require thoughtful contemplation of the effects of globalization on organizational strategy.

The challenge for tomorrow's strategy-focused leaders is to take advantage of the opportunities of globalization, while avoiding its ill-effects. Detractors of globalization point to scenarios of greedy executives pressuring governments of Third-World nations to reduce their costly environmental rules and labor standards, resulting in environmental destruction and worker exploitation. Globalization has also been associated with population dispersion and displacement, marginalization of sectors of the population, social polarization, fragmenting institutions, increased corruption, crime, and problems for education, training, and the constructive use of human talent. These conditions favor the rise of authoritarian charismatic leaders, such as Idi Amin, Adolph Hitler and "Chainsaw Al" Dunlap, who leave a legacy of destruction and degradation. At the same time, globalization can be a means for spreading knowledge about the rest of the world, improving the skills of a diverse workforce, and generating international pressure to implement global standards for product and service quality, labor practices, and a clean environment.

Based on these trends, we expect that strategy-focused leaders will need to envision how to connect people, processes, and technology in and outside of their organizations in ways that add financial capital, but not at the expense of human and social capital. In the next chapter, we describe how strategy-focused leaders sort through the possibilities opened up by globalization and the other trends that describe the exciting and ever-changing strategic situation.

PART II

DREAMING ABOUT SUCCESS

After that first strategic planning meeting in her office, Sandra Stevenson experienced an intense sense of excitement, purpose, and optimism about her new organization, Nova-Vignette Inc. If even a fraction of RNA interface technology's promise could be realized by Nova-Vignette, many of the world's most dreadful diseases, such as cancer, could be treated by disabling genes that cause the diseases. At the same time, the technology could produce millions of dollars in new drug sales revenue for her organization. "What a meaningful and profitable venture this can turn out to be!" Sandra confided to her colleagues, as she walked down the corridor of their newly furnished office in the Vestal Corporate Park. Her dream of building a new company around a technology that promised to be the most important and exciting breakthrough in the life sciences industry in recent years was energizing and inspiring her with positive thoughts and emotions.

Sandra's enthusiasm was contagious as her colleagues couldn't help but feel a strong sense of confidence, commitment and camaraderie, based on the results of their initial SWOT analysis and scenario planning session, where they began to weave their dream of success with the realities of the marketplace and their industry. They all agreed that what they now needed was to develop their dream more fully and share it in a way that could be easily understood by their employees and the business community. It was now time for Sandra and her colleagues to enable their dream to take shape in a way that would guarantee the success of Nova-Vignette.

CHAPTER 3

WHERE DREAMS BEGIN
Recognizing and Initiating Trends

The first responsibility of a leader is to define reality.
—*Max DePree*

Leaders are often described as being responsible for interpreting events and defining reality for followers. As a result, they frame the way followers experience events so that followers can make sense out of their personal and strategic situation. These events emerge out of the business market or environment which serves as the context for executive leadership and is ripe with various organizational opportunities and threats. Executive leaders must be particularly astute in recognizing these opportunities and threats so that strategies can be created and adapted in a manner that is responsive to the market. Strategy-focused leaders use personal, professional and industry connections along with advanced information technology to spot and set important trends that influence their organizations' strategy. Simply put, this chapter suggests that organizational vision and

The Dream Weavers: Strategy-Focused Leadership in Technology-Driven
Organizations, pages 45–63
ISBN: 1-59311-110-X (paper), 1-59311-111-8 (cloth)

strategy stems from the executive's strategic networking/partnering and trend-watching/making processes.

FINDING THE SOURCE

Pause for a moment and think about who you would consider to be the most famous and successful corporate executives in history. What would you say they have in common? To answer this question, you could think of executive leaders who fit the "famous and successful" profile, such as Henry Ford, Sam Walton, Mary K. Ash, Andrea Jung, Meg Whitman, Jack Welch, Bill Gates, Steven Jobs, and Michael Dell. In our opinion, one important characteristic that they have in common is that all of these leaders were highly visionary. Simply put, they were *dreamers* who were able to make the connections required to realize their dream of success for their organization. They also had the ability to articulate their vision in plain language that everyone could understand and transform it into a reality that kept their followers motivated.

What was their secret of success for imagining and realizing their dreams? What was their "crystal ball" for searching for and then creating better futures for their organizations? In essence, they believed in a relational worldview that success requires working within societal and business systems where people, organizations and cultures are all interconnected and *interdependent*. They spent time trying to understand these connections rather than building their organizations in isolation. *By identifying these connections, they defined the context (reality) in which their followers and colleagues interact and work together towards accomplishing collective goals.* They were able to identify opportunities to produce stockholder wealth through knowledge and insights gained with their business connections. Their connections enabled them to spot and/or initiate business trends leading to their organizations' dramatic success. Their vivid dreams of success enabled them to craft an appealing and evocative vision of the future that grew out of their connections and comprehensive understanding of their strategic situation. Thus, they shared much in common with the strategy-focused leaders who we interviewed—our Dream Weavers.

We have found that the ability to dream is a required skill for executives of technology-driven organizations of all sizes—not just for the titans of business history. For example, Shannon K. Watson, CEO/President of GreyMatter, Inc., founded a small but successful IT services provider based in Wilmington, Delaware. Watson envisioned and created a dynamic work environment comprised of experienced and energetic IT consultants who have contributed to GreyMatter's success. According to Watson, it is important for executives to develop a broad network of business connections over the course of one's career, and bond with executives through professional groups and organizations, and with potential partners and customers through community services. Watson also emphasizes finding a market niche that can spur organizational success. For GreyMatter, this niche involves targeting Fortune 1000 companies who need solutions, not just staffing.[1]

But where do these dreams come from? How do strategy-focused leaders develop these dreams? Can any executive develop the ability to transform his/her dreams of organizational success into reality? Some research suggests that executive leaders vary in their ability to identify/initiate trends and make the right business connections required to realize their dreams. According to this stream of research, executives' social and cognitive capacity for such tasks is "hard-wired" into them at birth and sets limits on their success.[2] However, the executives we interviewed suggested that their ability to dream success for their organizations, while somewhat predisposed, also can be learned and developed. We now describe two important ways *any* executive can envision success for his or her organization: strategic networking/partnering and trend-watching/making.

STRATEGIC NETWORKING AND PARTNERING

As discussed in Chapter 2, globalization and technology are shaping the world into a more interdependent, smaller, faster, information and knowledge-based community. Globalization is requiring organizations to recognize where systems, products and services need to be made more similar, or where adaptations of product and services to local conditions are required. Technology is enabling work conditions to be automated, integrated and less defined by physical space and more by connection and contact, which results in a so-called "boundaryless organization." Technology is supporting work collaborations within and between many of today's most successful organizations. These collaborations are producing communities of interest and practice whose members find solutions to business challenges by exchanging information. Technology is also shortening product life cycles, timetables for designing training programs, and the restructuring of organizations. To gain the competitive advantage in this strategic situation requires the acquisition of information and knowledge. However, the world is far too complex for any one executive to leverage all the knowledge and skill bases required to successfully develop and orchestrate strategy and achieve dramatic success. To be successful requires executive leaders who can make the connections needed to acquire the ideas, develop insights for alternative versions of strategy, and implement and sustain the strategy.

The most successful executives we interviewed did not at first always have a brilliant strategy or dream percolating in the deep recesses of their

minds. But they did possess a broad and deep network of business connections that provided essential resources for the creation and ultimate realization of their dream. They nurtured their network of contacts to diversify
their ideas and plans and then used it to generate their own unique
dream—a dream that they truly believed in, internalized, and then got others to similarly internalize, connect to, and identify with.

Making such connections requires developing a *strategic* network of business partners who provide a base for ideas and future cooperative relationships. We emphasize the word *strategic* because business executives we
observed in the past might possess similar networks. However, they were
oftentimes comprised of constituents who had agendas that were incongruent with the organization's mission and objectives. By *strategic networks*
we mean relationships with key constituents (e.g., customers, board members, suppliers, experts, government officials, professionals) who understand and are committed to the organization's mission and objectives and
possess values that are consistent with the strategic interests of the organization.

As an example, consider the new approach that Chrysler took to build a
new car based on strategic networks. Chrysler has built all of its models
from scratch throughout its 75 years of corporate history. However,
Chrysler is now developing its new "Crossfire" sport car based on strategic
partnerships with Mercedes, Mitsubishi, and outsider suppliers in order to
reduce both development and production time. This new and innovative
approach will allow Chrysler to develop a new car in just 24 months of R &
D at a modest cost of $280 million.[3] Although there are several challenging
issues such as coordinating the engineering and manufacturing processes,
this example demonstrates many benefits that could be developed from
strategic networking and partnering.

Or consider the success of Greencastle Consulting. This six-year old IT
consulting organization that offers tactical and strategic IT services to organizations in the eastern U.S. Greencastle has enjoyed increased revenue
growth over the past six years. Its success comes from a clearly defined mission ("to implement client strategies and initiatives using process oriented
project management services that enable our clients to fulfill their definition of success") and core values (service, adaptability, loyalty, team player,
integrity, enthusiasm) that are frequently communicated by its senior leadership team to its key constituents. Celwyn Evans, Greencastle's founder,
told us that he builds relationships with potential partners by constantly
talking about the mission, objectives and values that define their organizational culture to all who will listen. In that way, he is able to identify who
are truly potential business partners and at the same time increase his
knowledge of opportunities and threats to the business.[4]

Strategic networking with customers is the first activity Lou Gerstner initiated when he left RJR Nabisco in 1992 to revitalize the then-ailing IBM as
its new CEO. Shortly after joining IBM, Gerstner boldly proclaimed that

"the last thing IBM needs now is a vision." Instead, he spent his initial days at the company visiting IBM's key customers to gauge what they needed and wanted. Gerstner also inquired about the customers' reactions to IBM's current products and services and what IBM could do to help them become successful. With this information, he was able to craft his vision of a radically transformed services-based IBM. In a few short years, IBM became one of the most profitable and innovative organizations of the late 1990s.[5]

Benefits of Strategic Networking/Partnering

We have found that strategic networking or partnering offers several benefits to executives who engage in this worthwhile activity. First, *network ing allows for a matching of mission, objectives and resources to attain objectives.* After failing in a prior "bricks-and-mortar" business venture, Jill Blashack refocused her mission on selling gourmet food, but through an alternative distribution model—multilevel marketing using Internet initiated home parties. She started her business called "Tastefully Simple" with $36,000, largely from a friend who later joined the company. Over time, she expanded her sales through networking at her parties. Each new party was another node in her network and growth expanded the company's sales to $78 million in 2002. Blashack's professional contacts provided the distribution model, an early investor, her sales force and her ultimate success. According to Blashack, *"Your network is everything."*[6]

Networking Also Provides Forums for Cooperation and Coordination of Diverse Activities

The development of product and services in technology-driven industries is complex, uncertain, and requires teamwork to meet the requirements of the highly demanding current market. As shown in the Iraq War which removed Saddam Hussein from power, the U.S. Army has transformed itself into a team-based and technology-driven organization. While doing so, it has reduced its armed forces by almost one-third and privatized many military tasks. As a result, the Army has increasingly become dependent on independent contractors. Tasks from mundane KP duty to complex communications services are now performed by private companies, such as KBR (a unit of Halliburton), Cubic, and DynCorp. We expect that success in leading and managing these relationships may depend on effective SFL initiatives outlined by the Army's top brass.[7]

As in the military, the executives in our sample who exhibited SFL recognized that partnering with organizations with congruent goals is one way to leverage the knowledge, skills and technology needed to meet market demand. For example, UCB Pharma's executive leadership team has fostered strong business relationships with co-marketing partners such as Pfizer, Inc. UCB licenses some of its drugs on markets where it has not yet established a presence, or in the form of in-licensed compounds, or out-licensed compounds, in Canada. In doing so, UCB exercises SFL that builds connections that add to the social and economic capital of the organization.[8] Another example, from our sample, is CEO of one of the largest U.S. telecom organizations. This CEO emphasized mergers and acquisitions as part of the company's vision. Moreover, he detailed the role of employees and managers in the success of these mergers. This example demonstrates how strategy-focused leaders leverage their extraordinary influence on their constituents to execute their networking strategies.

A third benefit that *networking provides is timely and rapid dissemination of new information, ideas and technology.* People like to discuss the latest news, rumors, and happenings in the organization and industry—its human nature. They also like to share and debate ideas and act as sounding boards for new business ideas and opportunities to make money. Many of the executives we interviewed stated that they often network among their own associates by engaging in "management-by-walking-around" (MBWA). Bob Still, an executive at Lancaster Radiology Associates, notes that MBWA lets senior management hunt for new ideas and interact with the creative thinkers "in the guts of the organization." At Lancaster Radiology Associates, executives are encouraged to be out of their offices working on building relationships, motivating, and keeping direct touch with the people who provide the pulse of the organization. "Oftentimes, the best ideas for our strategy," says Still, "come from our talented associates." In effect, these approaches reflect a strategy of encouraging organizational learning. Executives who disseminate information using networks within the organization provide a channel for learning both effective management practices and the strategy of the company.

Networking Also Provides Opportunities for Mentoring, Coaching and Leadership Development

The amount of collective professional knowledge and experience in conferences, professional organizations, workplaces, and community groups can be astounding. Dr. Terry Troxel, President and CEO of the American Institute for CPCU/IIA, uses professional meetings to discuss challenging organizational issues with senior members of the industry who have different management specialties and professional experiences. By discussing the ins and outs of a particular situation with his colleagues, Troxel gets ideas for adapting his strategy to future business trends in the insurance industry, and often, it proves successful for his organization. As a result of his efforts, Troxel's organization generated record levels of sales in 2002.

Similarly, an executive we interviewed from Qualcomm emphasized that he has tried to create and maintain an informal organizational culture and flexible work schedules for his engineering staff. These initiatives help his associates "feel safe to come up with and try out creative ideas." This inventive work environment coupled with a wide variety of group-based work processes helped the company develop and fine tune its highly acclaimed and successful wireless communication technology called Code Division Multiple Access (CDMA) and eventually made Qualcomm an icon for the information technology-based society we have today.

Another benefit of networking is that *it often yields marketplaces for financial resources, knowledge, skills and business partners.* One such marketplace is the Eastern Technology Council (ETC) which serves executive leaders of technology-driven organizations by providing valuable contacts, capital, and information with a broad variety of events, publications, and innovative services. Executives use the ETC to form vital money-making relationships. Many use the ETC to cut costs by taking advantage of ETC-negotiated discounts.[9]

Networking Also Provides Contacts Leading to New Business Opportunities

The successful executives we interviewed viewed themselves as primarily being responsible for searching out business opportunities and establishing the connections between people, resources, and technology required for transforming opportunities into realities. To find such opportunities, they spend a large portion of their time interacting with the people who help shape their organization's strategic situation. These people include their customers, suppliers, employees, and executives of other organizations. The ideas, skills, knowledge, and resources that flow among these people are regulated by the laws of supply and demand and the quality of the relationships between the people. The executives typically generated opportunities for success by recognizing the potential in others as collaborators to a dynamic collective knowledge and skill set based on relationships of loyalty and trust. In essence, they realized that their primary function was to find and connect opportunities, people, ideas, technology and other resources and make sure that all the pieces of the system fit and operate smoothly.

The critical role of the executive leader as connector and regulator of these relationships is highlighted by a top executive at a telecom company, who considered his SFL role to be

> a never-ending journey to align the company around the customer and the market, and the resources that are required to serve the customer and market. It's a very difficult issue to know that your organization is right since the market changes ever day. There's new competition and new products everyday, you always question whether or not you're facing the market in a way that makes sense. So, the primary goal is to focus on the alignment of the company with the focus of the business in the marketplace, to get the resources aligned properly.[10]

Finally, *networking can provide social support systems for challenging personal situations or issues facing executives and their associates.* SFL is much more than just providing a plan or structure to add economic value for shareholders. More importantly, SFL requires providing the "social lubricant" to address the emotional and personal needs of associates and their relationships with others who play an important role in shaping the organization's success. To illustrate, an executive we interviewed from a finance organization, who displayed a high level of SFL, used his senior leadership team as a strategic network to help his associates with work/family balance issues:

> . . . I spend most of my meeting time with my direct reports talking about personal issues. I try to be understanding and provide an opportunity to see if I can help. We have spent so much time and effort building this high-functioning leadership team; we need to keep its most valuable component, the people. I am very concerned about the amount of time people spend at work versus home/family time. Work balance is needed . . .

Another type of support system is comprised of members of the Financial Executives Networking group based in New York City. This group meets to provide assistance to executives looking for advice for overcoming personal challenges, such as job stress, divorce, career plateauing, or finding another job. The group represents an opportunity to find other people who understand the challenging experiences the executives are going through.[11]

To summarize, strategic networking provides strategy-focused leaders with a set of pathways for people, ideas and resources to come together. As such, networking can help you to collect information on trends, opportunities, and threats that must be considered for the development of organizational strategy and your professional career. Several benefits of strategic networking and partnering we have discussed are summarized in Table 3.1.

TABLE 3.1
Main Benefits of Strategic Networking/Partnering

- Allows for a matching of mission, objectives and resources to attain objectives.
- Provides forums for cooperation and coordination of diverse activities.
- Provides timely and rapid dissemination of new information, ideas, and technology.
- Provides opportunities for mentoring, coaching and leadership development.
- Provides contacts leading to new business opportunities.
- Provides social support systems for challenging personal situations or issues.

Building the Strategic Network

Now that we have established strategic networking as an essential and beneficial aspect of SFL, we need to describe how the executives who we interviewed developed and sustained their strategic networks of contacts. Given the variety of executives, organizations and industries represented in our sample (see the Appendix), we could not find one best way that all executives build their networks. However, we were able to distill several general guidelines for creating and developing a broad and deep strategic network of contacts. Follow these guidelines until your network grows to a manageable size and your knowledge and influence will increase.

- Develop *personal* contacts with executives inside and outside of your organization and industry. Conferences, professional organizations, corporate boards, college and university advisory committees and adjunct lecturing, and community/social/religious organizations are excellent venues to forge relationships with other executives outside of your organization. Mentoring junior executives, dining or golfing with colleagues, holding "all company" meetings or company picnics, and teaching leadership courses within your organization are excellent ways to connect with executives inside of your organization.
- Build reputational capital by role modeling high standards of ethical behavior and performance. *Reputational capital* is that portion of an organization's excess market value that can be attributed to the perception of the organization as a responsible domestic and global corporate citizen.[12] Enron's reputational capital was destroyed by the unethical behavior of its executive leaders that seeped into the organization to create a culture of corruption.[13] To avoid Enron's fate, many executives are considering the role of reputation in their strategies. Anthony Tebutt, President of UCB Pharma told us:

Whatever you want, we have the capability even though we're small, we have the talent, we have the know-how, the people that can pull it off. Our reputation and our name is growing. It takes time, it takes time to develop a name and a reputation but it is growing. We have a good reputation out there. The doctors who know us, who deal with us, they know we're not a front company and they enjoy working with us. And I think our heart is recognized . . . that we're professionals.[14]

Since relationships often depend on reputations, it makes sense that your organization's reputation should also receive the constant attention of its leadership.

- Create an organizational culture and identity that establish shared values and beliefs that allow employees to identify with the goals of the organization and increase your impact on both internal and external stakeholders.[15] Strong identities may become an organizational image, which executives can use to develop networks with other organizations.
- Demonstrate true personal interest in others and individualized consideration for *all* your constituents (e.g., employees, executive peers, customers, suppliers, partners). Both religiopsychiatric writings on personal development and scientific research on impression management suggest that the best way to connect with others is to ingratiate yourself to them by showing a true interest in them.[16] To be individually considerate of others means to recognize and appreciate the individual differences people possess, and to spend time coaching and mentoring constituents who can develop personally and professionally from your knowledge and expertise.[17]
- Use exemplification to not only provide followers with ideal practices but also to harness their effort and commitment to be part of your network. *Exemplification* means displaying morally, professionally, and performance worthy behavior designed to make your associates emulate you. For example, Sam Palmisano, CEO of IBM, is calling for his employees to return to IBM's basic core values—what he calls "the DNA of IBM." He not only talks about core values such as bold moves, diversity, and teamwork, he also has exemplified them by championing IBM's "e-business on demand" initiative, funding diversity programs and replacing a bulky strategic planning committee with streamlined executive teams.[18]
- Acquire conference attendance lists, professional association membership lists, direct mailing lists, and organization charts. These resources can be scrutinized to identify influential and knowledgeable individuals who can help you acquire and develop the employees, ideas, processes, technology and relationships that can help you achieve your organization's strategic goals.
- Use the Internet and Email to engage in computer-mediated professional networking. There are several ways to network via the Internet including

1. e-mail distribution lists (listservers) for executive or professional groups (any message that is sent to a listserver is automatically distributed to all email addresses on the list),
2. newsgroups providing open discussions covering diverse and specific interests, and
3. organization databases of members' interests aimed at fostering multi-professional networking and dissemination of information.[19]

- Develop a 10-second "core message" that describes your organization's distinctive mission and expertise and link it to your contacts' business problems and needs. The executives we interviewed indicated that since "time is money," it is important to inquire about others' business requirements *and* be able to quickly and effectively outline for others the essential purpose of your organization. Doing so "puts your company in their lives" by creating an image of your organization as a solution to their thorniest business problems and most pressing needs. We will describe the crafting and content of an effective core message in Chapter 4.
- Maintain an "electronic rolodex" of professional contacts on a Palm Pilot® or similar device. An electronic record of your contacts and their core competencies can serve as a handy reference guide for "go to" relationships. You can use this guide depending on the current status of your organization's strategic situation.

By using these techniques to build your strategic network of contacts, you will gain access to the resources required to build a successful technology-driven organization. Several of the executives we interviewed noted that doing so has helped them to expand their organization's knowledge base and strengthen their relationships with their key constituents.

THE ART OF TREND-WATCHING AND TREND-MAKING

Contemporary organizational theorists describe organizations as "living systems" that survive through continuous and successful interaction with their external environment. Oftentimes, organization's ability to adapt to changing environments becomes key to their survival and success. Over time, aspects of the environment change including customer preferences, technology offerings, and social trends. One company that has been quite successful in adapting to its environment is Corning. The pioneer in the materials development (e.g., glassware) is now the world's top maker of fiber-optic cable, which it invented more than 30 years ago. Corning, once known mainly for its kitchenware and lab products, gets most of its sales from the optical fiber and cable and photonic components made by its telecommunications unit.[20]

Equally successful in adaptation is Universal Instruments which first produced safety pins in 1919 and then transitioned to the tool and die business by the Great Depression. As the need for electronics grew following World War II, Universal entered the electronics assembly equipment manufacturing industry. Universal developed its niche in this market in the 1960s, and today its GSM® Platform has evolved into an industry standard.[21] In contrast, many technology-driven organizations, such as Lucent Technologies, Nortel Networks, Qwest, and Dynergy, have joined the ranks of the largest corporate failures in history because they have not been able to adapt to changes in their environments.

The degree of dynamic change in the environment influences the perceived uncertainty defining the strategic situation that strategy-focused leaders must face. The most successful strategy-focused leaders are sensitive to trends in environmental factors that can contribute to or detract from realizing their dream of success for their organization. These executives considered it important to "keep tabs on" the nature of society, economic stability, political stability, legal stability, the nature of the industry, the customer base, and the climate of the organization. Awareness of such trends allows executives to develop and revise strategy and structures that allow their organizations to adapt to, or even help shape, their environment.[22]

Organizations are not always required to passively wait to react or adapt to the changing environment. The executives of the more successful organizations we examined take a more *proactive* approach by actually changing the nature of their environments to help create the dream their founders envisioned. For example, consider the Vanguard Group, the world's largest pure no-load mutual fund company. Jack Bogle started Vanguard in 1975 because he felt that shareholders were not well served by the standard practice in the mutual fund industry, where funds are burdened by fund management companies seeking profits through their servicing of the funds. His dream, dubbed the "Vanguard Experiment," was that its shareholder would create their own management company to provide—at cost—the administrative services they needed. Today, Vanguard is considered by industry experts as a trend-setter and technology leader in employing e-business strategies and building solid relationships to meet the growing needs of investors.[23]

To be a technology leader, organizations must face particularly daunting environments marked by high levels of uncertainty, fierce competition, and rapid rates of change. Such environments demand SFL which *actively* perceives trends in the environment and plans for potential scenarios that may influence their organizations in the future. Fortunately, there are several common mechanisms that executives of technology-driven organizations can use to identify and help shape trends that will influence their future. The executives we interviewed highlighted two important techniques useful for influencing their environment and providing information for their strategies: environmental scanning and scenario planning.

Trend-Watching through Environmental Scanning

One such technique required for visualizing one's dream of organizational success is called *environmental scanning* (ES), also referred to as *external/internal monitoring* or *strategic intelligence gathering*. Psychologists sometimes describe being able to successfully survive and adapt to one's environment as intelligence. Using the "organization as a living system" metaphor, think of ES as a continuous process of intelligence—gathering information necessary for the survival of the organization, as breathing, perception and cognition are for the survival of a human being. ES functions serve to collect strategic information and competitive intelligence required to forecast alternative future scenarios needed for organizations to adapt to their environment.

The ES functions used by strategy-focused leaders typically follow the traditional Strengths Weaknesses Opportunities Threats (SWOT) model developed by Michael Porter.[24] This approach involves conducting an internal assessment of the organization's strengths and weaknesses. Many of the less strategically-focused leaders we observed in the past often argued that they assessed internal strengths and weaknesses primarily using financial and accounting measures such as ROI, ROA, revenue growth, inventory and accounts receivable turnover and net income after tax. However, the more strategically-focused leaders mentioned a more balanced approach using metrics of customer satisfaction, internal business processing, and employee development, along with the traditional financial and accounting measures. They also reported using operational and internal audits to identify areas for workflow improvements and for the streamlining/eliminating of processes that do not add value according to customer requirements. Based on results of our executive interviews, we suggest that *an internal assessment of performance be made on at least a quarterly basis using metrics that are linked to specific customer, internal process and human resource-related and financial objectives.*

In addition, an examination of the external events posing opportunities or threats to the organization should be conducted. Here the typical focal points of ES should include competition, technology, regulatory activity, customer preferences, pricing trends, and the economy. However, the executives we interviewed noted difficulty in identifying relevant information. The perceived difficulty stemmed from varying degrees of information reliability and validity, and the vast amount of information available. Sometimes, this difficulty resulted from very myopic and micro perspective in their business approach.

Despite these perceived difficulties, strategy-focused leaders have numerous resources that can be tapped into through ES to provide relevant, reliable and valid information. Scanning efforts should include searching as many of the following sources for information as possible. Many of the executives we interviewed established task forces or small teams responsible for identifying and surveying a wide variety of information sources. The following sources for obtaining strategic information need no prolonged and labored emphasis, for they are very basic and illustrate their own usefulness.

- Implementing and effectively utilizing "business intelligence" or "smart tool" software. The software works by crunching extensive quantities of data in search of trends, problems, or new business opportunities. Wachovia Bank has used *neural networks* to learn patterns of personal spending and to spot fraudulent use of credit-cards, resulting in a 70% reduction in credit-card fraud incidents. Wal-mart Stores, Inc. has used *expert systems* with "if-then" processing logic to mimic human expertise to accurately predict sales of almost every product at each of its 3,000 stores. A growing number of organizations, such as Ben & Jerry's, have implemented such software to track their products, monitor sales and complaints, and build customer loyalty. In fact, many of the top executives of organizations ranked among the *Business Week Fifty* top performing organizations identified neural network, expert system, and data mining software as key to their outstanding performance.[25]
- Reading newspapers and periodicals such as *The Wall Street Journal, The New York Times, Business Week, Fortune,* or *Fast Company*
- Selectively scanning business-relevant television and radio shows
- Getting data through market research studies, Gallup opinion surveys, and census reports
- Reviewing reports of "futurist" organizations that are in the business of analyzing trends. Examples of such organizations include Minnesota FutureWork (http://netco.tec.mn.us), On the Horizon (http://lucia.emeraldinsight.com), and Toffler Associates (http://www.toffler.com).
- Using data mining and text mining software to assist in performing competitive analysis using scenarios and simulations. For example, one text-mining approach scans over 100 geographically dispersed newspapers for a period of ten years in order to identify environmental changes and emerging trends.[26]
- Using Internet search engines, such as Google, MSN Search, or Yahoo!
- Logging onto online newsletters, listserves, newsgroups and blogs (personal Websites updated frequently)

- Using bibliographic type software tools adapted with online search features, such as Endnotes, Pro-cite and Reference Manager
- Reading journals and newsletters published by professional and trade organizations
- Perusing reports and databases prepared by information services such as Centris (http://centrisinfo.com), Knowledgestorm (http://www.knowledgestorm.com) or Reuters (http://www.reuters.com/).
- Having informal conversations with other executives and contacts on your strategic network
- Monitoring demographic data provided by industry of governmental agencies. For example, the U.S. Department of Labor (http://www.dol.gov) publishes a wide range of data on wages, health plan benefits, workers, and occupational outlooks that are helpful for recognizing the implications of workplace trends.
- Benchmarking to compare your organization's or industry's performance to another.

To summarize, a good ES system needs to reveal not only what changes have occurred in the past but also what is currently occurring or imminent. Remember that the purpose of ES is to use multiple sources of resources to corroborate or independently validate the information your ES efforts produce. Also, the primary goal of ES is to learn more about market trends including your competitors' products and activities and customer's needs and wants. All the information that you gather should be related back to your organization's original vision (the dream) and the objectives for attaining the dream outlined in your strategic plan.[27]

Trend-Making Through Scenario Planning

Once strategic intelligence information is collected through ES, the information needs to be used to envision better futures for the organization. The most successful executives we interviewed used a technique called *scenario planning* to think about several possible futures facing their organizations. Scenario planning provides several benefits to executives who use it to test their dreams of success for their organization against environmental possibilities. These benefits include

1. understanding of unconscious assumptions about the organization and market,
2. appreciating core competencies,
3. identification of opportunities in emerging markets,
4. contributions to contingency planning, and

5. quickening organizational response time in the face of actual crises and change.[28]

Scenario planning involves using the organization's best conceptual thinkers (e.g., senior executives and board members) to test the feasibility of alternative dreams of success against the fast and true certainties and unwieldy uncertainties of future environments. It focuses on understanding a few prototypical options that describe a range of possible futures. Scenarios are not plans. They are carefully crafted images and stories (dreams) that frame choices that may define the future. They serve to stimulate discussion about the organization's assumptions about the future and allow executives to envision possibilities about the future that are related to decisions that must be made today. They enable strategy-focused leaders to prepare for alternative futures by presenting possible details about what would be different from the present and learning from rehearsing reactions to these differences in the mind.[29] The multiple versions of the future not only help ensure the viability of the strategic plans and successful adaptation to their environment, but also for some it helps to create trends actually redefined the nature of their environments.

It is also important to remember that scenario planning is possible, meaningful, and beneficial only when strategy-focused leaders are willing to look at the situation with flexible and creative "out-of-the-box" attitudes. Oftentimes, we found that executives had before-the-fact or *a priori* assumptions and expectations (and even solutions!) before they developed and considered multiple scenarios. This approach tends to create a highly biased frame of reference based on their own experience and therefore doesn't allow them to enjoy full benefits of scenario planning. *The key to the scenario planning process is to look at the situation and issue with flexible and creative thinking.*

By demonstrating flexibility and creative thinking, Royal Dutch/Shell has successfully used scenario planning to deal with uncertainty and troublesome events including oil crises during the 1970s. Supplemented with computer simulations of multiple scenarios, scenario planners presented a series of stories to senior Shell executives. One scenario envisioned the emergence of OPEC and the rising price of oil as unstoppable driving forces that would dominate the global system for many years to come. (How right they were!) This forced Shell executives to re-examine the assumptions underlying their strategy and consider the implications of OPEC and supply and demand for oil. As a result, when OPEC announced its oil embargoes, Shell dealt with the oil crises better than its competitors and grew in size from eighth to second in its industry. Because of this initial success with scenario planning, Shell has used scenario planning for the last 30 years and currently produces three scenarios each year as part of its strategic planning process.[30]

Another way to understand scenario planning is by comparing it to traditional financial planning or budgeting spreadsheet models. Typically these models involve the elements of income statements (revenues, expenses) and balance sheets (assets, liabilities, owners' equity) which are linked together in a cause-and-effect manner over several period of time. These models present alternatives involving best-case, worst-case, and most-likely to occur scenarios. Under each scenario, the effects of many things that could happen, their likelihood of occurrence, and the effects on the financial position of the organization are highlighted.

As a strategic planning tool, scenario planning is a formalized and expanded form of the cause-and-effect processing logic used in financial planning of budgeting that is applied at the organizational level. However, instead of causal linear relationships between variables as in financial modeling, scenario planning creates alternate futures by organizing assumptions around categories of uncertainty:

1. clear trends,
2. unknowns that are knowable through research and
3. uncertainties that cannot be determined through research.

In other words, it requires weaving the unknown around the known.

Strategy-focused leaders use scenarios as powerful tools for increasing understanding and commitment to the organization's vision or dream of success. Scenarios present alternate forms of the dream with varying environmental conditions and outcomes. As such, scenarios force executives and their associates to realistically consider what it takes to be successful and how the competitive strategy depends on environmental conditions. The main purpose of scenario planning is not to predict the future, but rather to consider and develop a range of creative applications of the existing products, services, and situations so that a realistic and attainable dream of success can be visualized. The dream is eventually molded into a core message that is communicated over and over again to all organizational constituents. We describe this SFL process in Chapter 4 and revisit it again in Chapter 9.

How to Implement Scenario Planning

According to futurist-philosopher Peter Schwartz, creating scenarios is an eight-step process:

- Identify a focal issue or decision (e.g., Whether and how a hospital should merge with a competitor).

- Identify the key forces in the environment. This information is generally provided through the ES functions described above.
- Considering the key environmental forces, determine the driving forces that impact their organization.
- Rank the key factors and driving forces.
- Create and select the scenario logic. This involves relating clear driving forces with organizational, industry and global outcomes.
- Flesh out the scenarios.
- Derive implications for the organization.
- Select and monitor leading indicators and signposts for the key factors and driving forces.[31]

As an example, consider the application of scenario planning by a hospital CEO who we interviewed. This CEO, who is well known for his visionary and inspirational leadership, values scenario planning because it allows him and his senior management team, board members and physicians to search *together* for better futures for their organization—futures that his management team gets really excited about. He considers this approach to be superior to persuading his associates to accept and simply comply with *his* vision of a preferred ideal future.

The CEO and his associates used scenario planning to assess whether they should merge with a competitor during a period of hospital mergers and acquisitions in the late 1990s. As a result, the hospital decided not to merge and to remain an independent outpatient facility. The hospital radically changed its services and structure and today serves as a model for other health-care providers who offer state-of-the-art outpatient programs. The process enabled them to identify leading indicators and signposts that the market may be moving in a direction that would require merger or acquisition by another health-care organization in the future. With these indicators in place, the CEO knows more about his hospital's future and is more confident about inspiring his associates to go out to meet it.

The same kind of proactive envisioning of the future has recently occurred at IBM. In August 2002, CEO Sam Palmisano asked his strategy team comprised of executives from the supply chain, e-commerce, sales, R&D, communications and wireless business units to dream of a boldly different strategy that would put IBM back on top. His dream was to alter the very nature of how technology is delivered. Their team envisioned several scenarios allowing IBM to supply computing power as if it were water or electricity. From these alternative scenarios emerged one bold initiative and in late 2002, Palmisano unveiled the IBM's industry-driving concept of "e-business on demand."[32]

These examples illustrate the need for strategy-focused leaders to involve key stakeholders in the process of dreaming about alternative scenarios and how the organization can respond effectively and efficiently to meet the future head-on. To be strategy-focused means to support this approach for recognizing and initiating trends to create an appealing future for all organizational stakeholders. Strategy-focused leaders who paint an appealing picture of the future create meaning and purpose for organizational stakeholders, providing the important visual and emotional part of the core message that drives the SFL process. We turn our attention to the core message in the next chapter.

CHAPTER 4

FOCUSING ON THE CORE MESSAGE AND STRATEGY

He (or she) who has a "why" to live for can bear almost any "how."
—*Friedrich Nietzsche*

Exemplary or outstanding leaders are typically described by their followers as being inspirational and visionary. A leader's vision focuses followers on an appealing, idealized or evocative goal that they collectively share. The vision can motivate followers to high levels of performance targeted in the strategic plan. In addition to writing strategic plans, organizations typically create and publish the vision along with a mission statement that describes what they will do to reach the goal that is described in the vision statement. Oftentimes, however, these statements are too vague for followers to completely understand and find motivating. At the same time, followers often get bogged down trying to understand all the details in the strategic plan. Strategy-focused leaders favor using core messages, a simple yet informative communication about an idealized goal that the leader wants the organization to achieve in the future. This chapter describes how to articulate an inspiring and compelling core message and how the core message can be linked to organizational strategy.

The Dream Weavers: Strategy-Focused Leadership in Technology-Driven
Organizations, pages 65–86
Copyright © 2004 by Information Age Publishing, Inc.
All rights of reproduction in any form reserved.
ISBN: 1-59311-110-X (paper), 1-59311-111-8 (cloth)

THE CORE MESSAGE

Out of the many possible scenarios for the future eventually emerges one actual future. That future may or may not be planned for or even expected. It may turn out to resemble the "best case scenario," but most likely, it may turn out to be a very challenging scenario. In technology-driven industries, unexpected challenges and hardships are surfacing as never before to create uncertain futures. The uncertainty is due to a very rapid pace of operations, intense competition, high volatility, and disruptive and destructive changes in other environmental conditions. According to a senior executive in investment firm Morton Finance's IT services group, dealing with the challenges posed by uncertainty requires a long-term perspective that places importance and meaning on project work and organizational goals:

> In technology companies, things are more minute to minute, second to second. You just never know. The characteristic that you need to be successful in technology is that you need to have a much more longer-term perspective on the projects. You have to have an understanding of what's going on in terms of evolution and changes in technology, how they fit, why they are important . . . the biggest difference is the perspective, the time frame on projects, what the expectations are in the short-term and long-term. That can be daunting![1]

Over the course of history, for the individual, perhaps nowhere was the importance of maintaining a long-term perspective more so apparent than in the dehumanizing and uncertain environment of Auschwitz, the notorious Nazi concentration camp. Prisoners of Auschwitz endured every form of human degradation possible, including systematic and random murder, starvation, brutal cold, torture, physical and mental pain, slave labor, disease and selections for extermination in gas chambers. Millions of Jews, Slavs and Gypsies were killed and many committed suicide. The odds of surviving the horrendous conditions and all the selections for extermination were very poor. How many of us would give up when faced with such uncertainty and insurmountable odds?

One person who beat the odds was Dr. Viktor Frankl, a psychiatrist who endured and survived a three-year incarceration in Auschwitz and other Nazi concentration camps. He lived on to establish an approach to psychotherapy that proposes that man's deepest desire is to search for meaning and purpose. In studying his experiences with his fellow prisoners, Frankl concluded that prisoners who were more likely to survive were *those who had an appealing vision of the future.* For the prisoners, it might be to re-unite with a loved one, to help others in captivity, or to complete an unfinished work. For those who had a vision, or what Frankl called *purpose-in-life,* the days, weeks and years of stress became tolerable. This vision served as a source of motivation despite their inhuman and challenging living conditions and provided them with meaning for their existence and a will to survive.[2]

Frankl's experiences and existential approach emphasize how crucial a leader's vision is especially in challenging circumstances, so common in today's business environment. Many contemporary strategy-focused leaders create and provide a vision of an appealing future to inspire themselves and their followers to carry on despite challenging circumstances. Visions provide meaning for followers so that they can make sense out of the current circumstances and imagine how things can be better in the future. Several executives we interviewed crafted their visions into what we call the *core message,* a simple yet informative communication about an idealized goal that the leader wants the organization to achieve in the future. Leaders' visions are not simple slogans, the type one finds on company-issued key chains or business cards, but rather the overall approach the leader has for the future of the organization. Nor are these visions similar to a complex strategic plan for the organization. Rather, strategy-focused leaders craft visions that have a core strategic component but are conveyed in an inspiring way.[3] Crafting a strategic and appealing vision is a complex process and our interviews with SFL, described in this book, reflect these complexities.

The core message defines the work reality for followers and provides a powerful motivational force for followers who become committed to and identify with the goal being pursued. It provides hope and faith which humans find intrinsically satisfying. What makes strategy-focused leaders noteworthy is their ability to harness this powerful motivating tool to promote the strategic goals of the organization. Many followers could not and should not be aware of the detailed strategic plan of the organization. Those plans are aimed at Boards and top executives. However, the implementation of those plans, as well as the adaptation of an overall strategic plan to specific units within the organization, requires that mid-level managers and followers be aware of those strategic goals. Therefore, leaders must present the strategic goals to those audiences as well.

The challenge for strategy-focused leaders is how to present their strategies in a compelling way. How executive leaders formulate and communicate the core message to their followers often determines the effectiveness of their SFL.

ELEMENTS OF INSPIRATIONAL SFL AND THE CORE MESSAGE

What does it mean for a leader to inspire? Literally, the word "inspire" means to breathe into, to energize, to excite, to fill with life or "the Spirit," or to invigorate. Inspiration provides followers with the power to exert extra effort or go the extra mile required to successfully compete in today's technology-driven world. Today, simple performance to *meet* expectations is no longer sufficient for success. Instead, organizational success depends on *performing beyond expectations* by producing operational excellence, customer intimacy, quality of products and services, and development of human, intellectual, social and financial resources. Performing beyond expectations requires SFL that provides a very specific reason and meaning to followers as to why they should fully commit themselves and squeeze every possible minute of effort they could devote for their work.

A case in point is Norman Brinker who has founded several franchise restaurants including Chilis' Grills around the world. Brinker told one of the authors that he always tried to come up with at least a few reasons why his executives and employees should spend an extra 5 minutes before they go home everyday. Reasons included improving their career development, harnessing company success, and increasing shareholder value.[4] He figured that the extra 5 minutes and commitment he was getting from his 8,000 employees were adding up to 40,000-minutes of equivalent manpower everyday. That's like getting more than 80 highly committed employees for free!

In our sample, several organizations provided very specific reasons and inspiration to focus their members on working to exceed previous levels of critical success factors. Unicorn Incorporated, Pulte Homes and Everfast are examples of organizations providing operational excellence. ILR Global and Eastern Com represent organizations which have worked to improve customer intimacy over the course of their history. Qualcomm and International Chips are organizations seeking technological innovation to provide quality products and services. Union Bank of California, the Vanguard Group, and GE are examples of organizations that have emphasized the development of their resources.

Inspiring individuals, groups and organizations to perform beyond expectations requires executives to display inspirational leadership. Such guidance provides *meaning and challenge to followers' work, fosters teamwork, involves enthusiasm and optimism, and gets followers involved in talking about important core values and envisioning attractive future states.*[5]

The executive leaders in our sample displayed significantly higher levels of inspirational leadership than managers in a very large international sample assessing such behavior.[6] However, there was some variance in the frequency which the executives displayed inspirational leadership. Display of inspirational leadership was significantly higher among executives in manufacturing industries than in the information technology, finance, and services industries.[7] The majority of executives we interviewed used inspirational leadership fairly often, while some were more selective and limited their use of inspiration to crises. According to their direct reports, female executives displayed similar levels of inspirational leadership as male executives.

A top male executive at the media services organization Roote Information vividly described how he values using inspirational leadership at appropriate times:

> My firm belief is that to get people to deliver for your company, you have to get everyone believing . . . everyone believing that what the company does is important and what they do has an impact on how the company performs. You have to use a lot of inspirational leadership to show them those things because that's what makes the difference between a job and a mission. A job is no emotional commitment . . . but a mission, that is their life, the purpose of their life. When you get people on a mission, time doesn't matter, 9 to 5 doesn't exist. The level of commitment that you get from people is incredible, if you can tap into that.[8]

He went on to tell us that he strives to have employees who view their jobs as a meaningful mission, especially now that the demand for news is so high with the rise of terrorism and conflicts around the world.

Research indicates that when people view their work as meaningful and challenging, they become excited, highly satisfied and intrinsically motivated by the nature of the work itself. Like creative artists or sports figures who experience peak levels of performance, they perform the work for the sake of the work itself because they find it highly enjoyable.[9] According to Theresa Amabile, a noted researcher in the area of creativity, providing intrinsic motivation is a far better way to boost employees' creativity and organizational innovation than using carrots and sticks.[10] While financial incentives certainly are important motivators, wouldn't you rather be paid to perform a meaningful and important task than a mundane task?

Sometimes strategic leaders don't have a choice. For the Morton Finance executive we interviewed, one tactic for motivating followers working on mundane projects was to link the completion of the mundane work to more interesting and challenging projects:

> You can do great things by having great projects and throwing a lot of emotion and a lot of inspiration into them. And we've had success with that. For the mundane, you have to be realistic: the project stinks, it's ugly work, but you have to link the completion of the work to more interesting work and give them breaks so they don't burn out.

In either case, it is important for you as a strategy-focused leader to take the time to explain to your people

1. how their work contributes to your organization's overall mission,
2. why their work is important (regardless of whether it is exciting or mundane), and
3. that they are contributing to the overall success of the organization.

You cannot emphasize these motivational messages to your employees enough.

Inspirational leadership involves building team spirit. Fostering teamwork creates a sense of family and networks of task and social support that can help your people overcome the challenges they face. Consider, for example, Mighty Tech employees who work together to produce telecommunications systems. To work for Mighty Tech is to join an extended family, a community of individuals who support innovative technology and the relationships between the individuals that have made the organization successful. Mighty Tech goes to great lengths to make sure that their employees work together effectively. They do this by offering a variety of benefits and team-building events for their employees.

A similar case was found with John Yi, founder and CEO of San Diego-based KES, which specializes in providing software and other networking solution for government and corporate clients. Yi noted that "I tried to treat all of my employees as my friends and family members and emphasized collective success and benefits we will all enjoy when I try to motivate people around here."[11] As a result, KES was identified by the *San Diego Business Journal* as the fastest growing private company in the Greater San Diego Region. Their number one ranking was based on the percentage of KES' verified revenue growth from 1996 to 1998: KES grew a whopping 774 percent during that period!

Being enthusiastic and optimistic can help your people to gain a positive (and productive) attitude about the situations they face. A clear and positive vision of the future and strong purposes for organizations make for strong optimism. Research indicates that possessing a positive "can-do" attitude and belief system leads to high levels of performance.[12] As a strategy-focused leader, your enthusiasm also can be contagious and encourage groups of your people to share positive beliefs, thus creating a "can-do" culture. Karen Borda, founder and former COO of CB Technologies highlighted the importance of building a culture of collaboration for the successful emergence of her company past its start-up stage. According to Borda, "My enthusiasm often rubs off on my people, and vice versa. That's how we maintain the high level of energy needed for success in biotech."

Building strong cultures involves getting your people to share the company values and expectations for success. Talking about core values and envisioning attractive future states gets your people excited about being part of something that is bigger than themselves. The president of Mighty Tech identified personal ("honest, being direct, straightforward, making sure that the things you do you can be proud of") and business ("being dedicated, being entrepreneurial, having the spirit to get ahead, being goal-oriented") values that are important to Mighty Tech's mission "to be the complete provider of telecom service for the largest possible audience." He often refers to these values that are deeply held by the organization and society at large in his talks with his employees.[13] This is one way

TABLE 4.1
Ways to Use Inspirational SFL with Your Followers

- Make work meaningful and interesting. Show every follower how his or her work fits into the overall strategic plan.
- Talk about the importance of what your associates are doing.
- Foster teamwork and team spirit to support the strategic plan.
- Show enthusiasm and optimism regarding what needs to be accomplished.
- Talk to your followers about important company values and an attractive future.
- Get your followers to talk about ideas about possibilities for the future. Focus them on your organization's key success factors.
- Provide personal recognition to individual followers for their outstanding work and explain why their work is important
- Identify and articulate new challenges for the future of your organization.
- Raise the bar or performance expectations. Use stretch-goals.
- Publicize success stories of followers who exemplify core company values or who have performed beyond expectations.
- Work to become an exciting public speaker. Consider taking courses such as the Dale Carnegie course.

that Mighty Tech's president and other strategy-focused leaders attempt to motivate their associates. Several other forms of inspirational leadership are summarized in Table 4.1. Use these behaviors to motivate your followers to higher levels of motivation, commitment and performance.

How Inspirational Leadership Can Motivate Your Associates

Strategy-focused leaders understand how inspirational leadership raises their followers' level of motivation, commitment and performance. To illustrate, consider how the Roote Information executive, who manages his New York City-based company, perceived the connection between inspirational leadership and employees' commitment following the events of September 11, 2001.

Motivation and commitment is not a percentage of a person's time, not a percentage of a person's effort. It's a whole different level of relationship and it's very emotional. It's in here [points to his heart] and that's why you have to get in here as a leader and as a company because that commitment is whatever it takes. Consciously, I did not pay attention to my family the week of September 11th because I thought what I was doing here was more important at the time. I didn't go home for several days. My wife was very upset. My son knew that something was going on. But why did I do it? It wasn't because it was in my job description or because of the pay. It was because I thought what

I was doing was so important . . . If you really get this commitment, then you're getting so much out of people . . . it's different relationship, and once you tap into that, the company performs at a higher level.

The ideas expressed by this executive beautifully describe the essence of how people are motivated to higher levels of motivation and commitment. Typically, people are motivated to act in a certain way depending on

1.   how much value they put on the act and its outcome,
2.   how effective they perceive themselves to be in performing the act,
3.   their faith in themselves and others, and
4.   their level of commitment.

Research suggests that inspirational leadership builds each of these aspects of individual motivation. Inspirational leadership helps followers derive important personal meaning which motivates them to achieve more than they expected.[14]

The strategy-focused leaders we interviewed were able to get their followers to understand the importance of their work through open lines of communication. They placed great value on establishing and using communication networks within and between the business units they led. In addition to being good listeners and encouragers of inclusive dialogue, they used e-mail and other forms of advanced information technology to frequently communicate the core message to their followers. In their communications with their followers, they provided feedback about the internal and external events and how these events related to the core message and strategy of their organizations.

For example, the Roote Information executive truly believed that his presence at work immediately following the September 11th terrorist attacks was important. He placed significant value on his presence at work. By doing so, his action reflected Roote Information's core value of self-sacrifice. He made a moral statement that helping others is the right thing to do. His action helped to clarify for his staff the high standards that Roote Information expects from its employees. In addition, his action allowed him to express his identity as a person who believed in helping his organization to provide indispensable information tailored for professionals in the financial services, media and corporate markets during that terrible time.

In another example of his inspirational leadership while managing during and after the September 11th attacks, this Roote Information executive demonstrated how strategy-focused leaders utilize emotions to both motivate employees and convey a strategic goal of the organization. As part of their mission, Roote Information emphasizes neutrality in the way they report world news and avoids words like "terrorists" in their news reports.

Following the events of September 11, 2001, members of the editorial groups insisted on referring to the attacks as "terrorist attacks:"

> We had a problem with our people and their own values and the company and its values. I had to explain to them what is the mission of [Roote Information]. [Roote Information] is the eyes and ears of the world. This is the vision of the company. Personally, reading [Roote Information's] reports I felt these people were terrorists but we say "they" attacked the towers. So what I did to get people back on board was to show a picture, that one of our journalists took of the Chaplin carried by the firemen . . . killed in the towers, and told them that we got so much feedback from his family and others who were so moved by the picture. Our photographer has captured the essence of this men and his life's work. I was explaining to them that that's what [Roote Information] does, this is the mission of [Roote Information] and immediately it brought them perspective.[15]

This example illustrates how a strategy-focused leader can convey the mission of his or her organization, during challenging and chaotic times. The Roote Information executive was able to link the emotional event with the mission of the company. He utilized the historical picture of the FDNY (Fire Department of New York City) Chaplin carried by fellow firefighters, taken by a Roote Information photographer, to inspire employees about the importance of the company's strategic goals and their own role in promoting those goals. Like the Roote Information executive, other strategy-focused leaders are able to use emotional appeals to convey to followers what are the strategic goals of their organizations. Emotional and inspirational appeals serve to both motivate employees and communicate to them what is the essence of the organization.

By expressing to his employees that they were providing essential information during a crisis, the Roote Information executive enhanced his associates' self-esteem and self-worth. He also expressed high performance expectations of his associates and expressed confidence that they would be successful in contributing to Roote Information's important and worthy mission during the crisis. Self-esteem, self-worth, and self-efficacy are well-established motivational forces. They build confidence in oneself and one's associates and commitment to projects that are considered to be important to the strategic goals of the organization.

Being part of Roote Information's provision of timely, relevant and factual information to people around the world during the September 11th crisis represented an ethical dilemma for this executive. At that critical time, he had to make a difficult choice: whether to attend to the immediate needs of his family or attend to Roote Information's business. Attending to company needs at the expense of his family's needs was something that he thought was more important, so he made a personal sacrifice for the good of his organization. He wasn't motivated to do so based on his job description. Instead, he was motivated by his personal values regarding self-sacrifice, being part of a team, and performing a noble task. More importantly, he was motivated by his faith that what he was doing would help to clarify what the future held for the greatest amount of people.

Faith in a better future is a powerful motivational force and helps followers to view the essential aspects of inspirational leadership. Your followers are more likely to go the extra mile for you if you can instill faith in them, their abilities and the chances of creating a better future. Faith is closely related to commitment. People tend to become committed to projects or tasks in which they personally believe or are morally committed.[16] The Roote Information executive's strong faith in his participation in a noble task strengthened his commitment to his organization. Commitment allows for the continuance of a relationship, role, or course of action and the investment of efforts regardless of the balance of external costs and benefits.

As another example, Steven Jobs did not describe the creation of the Macintosh computer as a means to make money for Apple Computer in order to gain the commitment of his employees. Instead, he described the process as a "*mission from God.*" By linking specific actions to faith-based metaphors of the organization's mission, Jobs used inspirational leadership to motivate his followers through the creation of personal commitments. Of course, any leader's effectiveness at inspiring followers to new heights of success is a function of what he or she says (core message content) and how he or she says it (core message composition, style and delivery).

Core Message Content

The *content* is what the core message is about. Leaders who want to inspire their followers with their core message must effectively express

1.   the nature of the status quo and need for changing it,
2.   a future dream or vision and the values that support it,
3.   how the future dream or vision, when realized, will remove existing deficiencies and fulfill the hopes of followers, and
4.   the strategy for realizing the dream or vision.

These and other features of the content of core messages are summarized in Table 4.2.[17]

Several of these aspects of Verizon CEO Ivan Seidenberg's core message for the telecommunications industry are illustrated in a speech that he gave to the National Press Club:

... the bottom line of all this is that the current form of managed competition and economic regulation has run its course and is now more harmful to

TABLE 4.2
Content of Inspirational SFL Core Message

- Problem(s) with the status quo
- Focus on an appealing and/or evocative future (and the values that support it)
- How the dream/vision will remove the problems and fulfill follower's needs
- Strategy for realizing the dream/vision
- Time frame for the completion of goals
- Links the vision with rewards
- Highlights business and individual opportunities
- Links to tradition
- Cultural values
- Organizational stories and values (with justification)
- Collective history that links the past, present and future
- Emphasis on the collective, organization or team
- Building up of self- and collective-efficacy
- Leader's similarity to followers (to build followers' identification with the leader)
- Hope and faith
- Confidence in the vision

consumer welfare, investment, and market-based competition. It's time for a new approach to regulating the technologies that are at the heart of America's economic prosperity—one that allows the market to develop around what consumers really want.

Now, the basic elements of such a new system might be the following: Create a clear path—a clear path—for eliminating economic regulation at both the state and federal level on the entire communications industry, modeling it after the success of the wireless industry. For those of you who know this issue, reciprocal compensation, which is a big debate here in Washington right now, is a perfect example of why the current system needs a major overhaul. Focus public policies and regulation on those areas that are really meaningful to consumers. Some regulation is okay. Ensuring the availability of basic service, upholding service quality, and protecting consumer interests in the Internet Age, through open access policies. Enforcing privacy protections and meaningful enforcement."[18]

In his speech, Seidenberg used subtle humor and made references to popular icons in order to get the audience to connect or identify with him. After spelling out several reasons why governmental regulation has been a problem for the telecommunications industry, Seidenberg presented his vision of how government and the telecommunications industry should cooperate. He linked his vision to traditional American values. He then went on to present a compelling strategy for realizing his vision. Overall, Seidenberg's core message is rational *and* inspirational because it presents a strategy for obtaining a better future justified with logic and values that are emotionally appealing to the audience.

The top strategy-focused leaders we interviewed have core messages that highlight their companies' commitment to have cutting edge technological solutions. Their core messages focus on the strategic goals of the business, from exposing everyone to the Internet using new media opportunities to developing technology that offers innovative business solutions. The leaders we interviewed, who were rated by their followers as highly visionary, recognized the need to develop the skills of their workforce as well as to stimulate and motivate individuals to focus on customers' needs and identify with other key values of their organizations. In addition, those leaders emphasized a clear vision, communication to employees and, depending on the nature of the business, strong commitment to their customers as well.

Table 4.3 shows that both top and bottom rated leaders both focus on business goals. However, unlike the leaders who were seen by their followers as deemphasizing vision, strategy-focused leaders were able to present business goals in an inspiring way. They do it by focusing more on the individuals who actually execute the core message, and articulate collective rather than individual goals. Both the U.S. and Israeli strategy-focused leaders in our sample emphasized values and inspiration, while bottom rated leaders conveyed the goals of the company vaguely with less emotional appeal, as if they were presenting a mission rather than vision statement.

In constructing their core message, strategy-focused leaders typically talk about the values and traditions important to their organizations. At Magnum Credit Card, the executive we interviewed insisted that the organization's core values (*fairness, quality, customer satisfaction, respect for others, meaningful work, performance and strategy feedback, individual accountability, professional development, participative decision-making* and *teamwork*) be printed on the first page of the employment application form. Many executives included a historical perspective that links the organization's past, present and future to build a sense of consistency across time. Most of the executives focused on the importance of collective efforts for attaining long-term goals. All were hopeful and positive in their outlook.

The content of leaders' visions is also affected by the context of their leadership style and other issues, such as organizational size, and the leader tenure in the organization. Research has found that transformational leaders, who emphasize vision and inspiration, have vision that emphasize mostly optimism and the core values of the organization, but also strategic contents, such as specific mission and times to accomplish it. Moreover, leaders of smaller organizations tended to have more optimistic visions, and so were leaders with less tenure in the organization.[19] When crafting their visions, strategy-focused leaders must consider not only basic aspects of their organizations (such as size) but also how they are viewed by

TABLE 4.3

Examples of Core Messages from Executives
Rated on Vision by Direct Reports

Top Executives *(Rated High on Vision by Direct Reports)*	*Bottom Executives* *(Rated Low on Vision by Direct Reports)*
"I believe that organizations, regardless of their size, have to have a vision, and this is also connected to inspiration. A manager has to inspire the workers; the employees have to know what the organization's vision is and the values associated with it. Every employee should know the values, should have it even physically on his or her desk. I believe each manager should be very much involved in instilling inspiration."	"You have to see a vision of upward mobility. My goals for the future are to grow, not really large, but just enough constant growth to keep the business to be able to provide exceptional customer service. I would like to see my business maintain the integrity, credibility and character that I have worked very hard to instill. I certainly want to grow, but that's not the major thrust of my organizational goals."
"Our long term goal is to better understand our customers' business to make sure our services and our capabilities fit in with some of our customers work flow. You have to be adding value in a critical stage of a person's work and we do that for the financial and the media markets. Our vision is to be integrated with people's workflow and help them manage the flow of information and transactions."	"Our vision is that the organization provides professional education to people in risk management and insurance and set standards, technical standards for the business. And as I said before, ethical business standards are very much the overall rule type of approach to your customer and society."
"I think the important thing is to constantly be able to be in tuned with what are the best practices in terms of the process, technology of the solution. Not so much to want to be on the leading edge, but the cutting edge in the sense that you always set direction so your team will have enough time to prepare to gear up, to learn about the skill and create opportunities so they can in turn utilize those technologies as a kind of skill to get accomplished. So it is not necessarily one specific technology, one specific solution, one specific process. Moreover, always looking out into a year or two-year horizons, making sure the team has the skill sets to do and perform and provide those kinds of solutions for all."	"The main organizational goals of the company are to be number one. To make every business unit profitable and work for the customers. That's number one right now. Supporting that is we have to lower our loss and expense ratio which is a key metric in our in our business. We absolutely have to do that, which gets to the point that you have to grow and you have to plan at the same time in this business. Those two have to be balanced."

followers. Apparently, followers judge the content of their leaders' visions, also based on the organization's and the leader's demographic characteristics.

Core Message Composition

The *composition* refers to its structure, how it is framed through the use of rhetorical devices such as metaphors or alliteration. Several of the elements of inspirational composition are shown in Table 4.4.[20]

There are several techniques that strategy-focused leaders can use to maximize the inspirational effect of their core messages on followers and other constituents. All leaders need to align the interests, values and beliefs of their followers with their goals and ideology, so that followers will identify with and commit to the core message. In other words, leaders must align follower's personal and social experiences or frames of reference used to make sense and to guide actions that support the core message.

One method for framing the core message in the hearts and minds of followers involves the use of life images. Imagery can be used to arouse follower's sensory experience to produce a mental picture or sound that aligns with the leader's intentions or goals. Leaders who use *image-* and *emotion*-based words that evoke feelings, pictures, sounds, smells and other sensations are able to tap into followers' fundamental experiences of life—love, feeling, dreams, fears—and therefore align followers' values, beliefs and expectations with their own beliefs, goals, expectations and ideologies. For example, the word "imagine" evokes more emotion than "think," to "give a hand" is more appealing than to "help," and a "dream" seems more fascinating than an "idea." Practically everyone can relate to the imagery in Dr. Martin Luther King Jr.'s most famous speech:

> . . . I say to you today, my friends, that in spite of the difficulties and frustrations of the moment, I still have a dream. It is a dream deeply rooted in the American dream. I have a dream that one day this nation will rise up and live

TABLE 4.4
Composition/Structure of Inspirational
SFL Core Messages

- Image and emotion based words
- Metaphors and analogies
- War and/or sports-related terminology
- Identification of a common enemy
- Appropriate humor and self-deprecation
- Rhetorical devices (e.g., contrast, list, puzzle-solution)

out the true meaning of its creed: "We hold these truths to be self-evident: that all men are created equal . . ."[21]

Like King and all the great orators of history, whenever possible, you should use image- and emotion-based words to arouse the sensory images in your followers' minds and more fully engage them in what you have to say.

Another way to stimulate the senses of your followers is to use metaphors and analogies when you are communicating the core message to them. Consider how Russel Laraway, a former U.S. Marine, co-founder and present COO of ITG Pathfinders (an IT services provider), talks about the importance giving personal attention to employees.

> This is an absolutely critical element of leadership. The reason why is because—you know this is a Marine Corps metaphor—combat effectiveness. Your combat effectiveness or your ability to do your work well is very much affected by your personal life. Now in the Marine Corps, it is a very different animal. You could be on leave . . . home visiting your family . . . And one of your Marines from your platoon . . . could go down to Tijuana and get in a fight with a Mexican policeman, end up in Tijuana prison and when you get back, you have to answer with no excuses, why that Marine was down there in Tijuana. What was he doing and why he didn't know that he needed to stay out of trouble? That doesn't seem reasonable. But the Marine Corps has a really good reason for that that I think is important . . . It's this concept of combat effectiveness and how it is affected by the person's personal life . . . But you try on an individual basis to get to know your Marines in a very personal way, but not in a fraternizing way. In fact, you often know far more about them than they realize. But you need to know these things. You need to know why somebody might be messing up from day to day. And if you're aware that his kid is very sick and you can do something to help him through that . . . It helps the unit to become better. It helps the work environment.[22]

In this case, Laraway, like several of the executives we interviewed, used a military metaphor with a touch of humor to make his point more vivid and realistic for his audience. Sports metaphors, like war metaphors, can also be very effective because war, sports and business involve competition, being physically and mentally strong, and creating well-defined winners and losers. For example, many business people have participated in team sports during their lives. So they should be able to identify with terminology such as *hitting a home run* (accomplishing a goal), *holding the line* (defending against competitors), or *going to bat for him* (giving someone help). When followers can identify with such terminology, it is easier for them to understand and be motivated by the core message.

How a strategy-focused leader communicates what he/she says in the core message is also important. How the core message is presented and then heard by followers depends on the types of rhetorical devices used by the leader. *Rhetorical devices* are word phrases that are strategically positioned in a way that is designed to elicit an effect from a listener or reader. Professors Deanne Den Hartog and Robert Verburg of Vrije Universiteit Amsterdam identified the following rhetorical devices that can add inspiration to your core message: contrasts, lists, puzzle-solutions, position-taking and pursuits. We illustrate these with speech segments of executives and politicians.

- *Contrast:* Presenting two opposing choices (A, B) with one implied correct choice.
  EXAMPLE 1: A. *I challenge you to hope and to dream.* B. *Don't submerge your dreams.*
  EXAMPLE 2: A. *Ask not what your country can do for you.* B. *Ask what you can do for your country.*
- *List:* Cataloging the elements (1, 2, 3, . . . n) of an important concept.
  EXAMPLE 1: *1. Government of the people, 2. by the people, 3. for the people.*
  EXAMPLE 2: 1. *Blood,* 2. *toil,* 3. *tears, and* 4. *sweat.*
- *Puzzle-solution:* Presenting a headline (H) or question followed by a punchline (P).
  EXAMPLE 1: H. *Even in your wheelchairs, don't you give up. We cannot forget 50 years ago when our backs were against the wall, Roosevelt was in a wheel chair.* P. *I would rather have Roosevelt in a wheelchair than Reagan or Bush on a horse.*
  EXAMPLE 2: H. *As many of you know, we filed our application to provide long distance in Massachusetts on Friday, and hope to expand the footprint across all of our big states in the next several months.* P. *The trouble is, we cracked the human genome in less time than it took to open the long-distance market in a single state.*
- *Position-taking:* Listing various positions (P_n) on an issue before taking a position (PT).
  EXAMPLE 1: P_1. *Cutting our costs may increase our sales and boost our profits.* P_2. *But at the same time decrease our quality and customer relations . . . . PT. What a sorry way to keep our shareholders happy.*
  EXAMPLE 2: P_1. *We want global trade to lift hundreds of millions of people out of poverty . . . if it happens, it'll create a big market for everything American.* P_2. *But the gap between rich and poor nations could continue to widen and bring more misery, more environmental destruction, more health problems . . . PT. We have to continue to achieve America's destiny . . . and care about, know about, and understand what is going on beyond our borders, and what we're supposed to do about it.*
- *Pursuit:* Re-emphasizing the point (P) just made with another comment (PS).
  EXAMPLE 1: P. *Our annual global budget for everything from diminishing the nuclear threat to preventing conflict to advancing democracy to fighting AIDS is no more than what Americans spend each year on dietary supplements.* PS. *This is a big deal!*

EXAMPLE 2: P. *I feel incredibly lucky to be at exactly the right place in Silicon Valley . . . PS. at exactly the right time historically where this invention has, has taken form.*

All of these rhetorical techniques demonstrate that there is much more to structuring an inspiring and rational core message than spouting off prose from a mission statement. To get your people to become committed to a mission requires careful consideration of the best ways to appeal at both the rational and emotional level. While rational thinking can "sell" your core message to your staff, evoking strong and positive emotional responses can ignite their passion for their work, their commitment to the organization, and their willingness to go the extra mile for you.

Core Message Style

Style means the way that the leader communicates. Some of the executives we interviewed communicated in a friendly manner, while others appeared to be more forceful and dominant. Some were quite animated and dramatic in their interviews, thoroughly enjoying being in the spotlight and sharing their wisdom. Others were precise, guarded in their responses, and some even contentious and challenging as they considered their strategic role in the organization.

Some leadership scholars have found that leaders who are friendly, attentive, dominant, and relaxed in their communication with followers are seen as inspiring. When leaders are friendly and attentive, they signal that they are interested in others and are willing to forge business and personal relationships with others. According to the CEO of Eastern Com, who spends 1/3 of his time with employees, "My role is to provide information, guidance, direction, hope and support." Remember that a key attribute of SFL is the ability to forge connections with employees and other constituents in order to make things happen.

Being friendly and attentive is often difficult and not always realistic given the hectic schedules executives must keep. Despite these time management challenges, executives who communicate with dominant and relaxed styles signal self-confidence and control. These personal mastery traits are also traits associated with inspirational leaders. Employees often look to executive leaders for information and clarification on what external events mean to the organization and to them personally. Given the turbulent nature of technology-driven industries, employees' questioning of executive leaders is quite frequent. That is why the ability to communicate in a dominant and relaxed way is so important for leaders in the upper echelons of any technology-driven organization.

Core Message Delivery

While the content of the leader's core message is important, how the message is delivered may be even more important. Poor delivery can distract an audience or make the message unclear. Leaders differ regarding the way they actually deliver their speech, especially regarding their use of speech techniques related to sound (e.g., repetition, rhythm, balance) and nonverbal communication (e.g., facial expressions, body language, eye contact).[23]

The most inspiring business and political leaders of history were highly skilled at using these techniques to mesmerize audiences. Martin Luther King, Jr. and his protégé Jesse Jackson used repetition of key words or phrases (e.g., "I have a dream") and rhythm, strategic pauses and balance to enable recall of important core messages in their speech. Adolph Hitler was equally effective in capturing the attention of his audiences. A masterful orator, he started out speaking very slowly and softly, and then gradually progressed into a violent and thunderous verbal climax filled with much passion and emotion, but lacking of any significant logic. Sadly, practically the entire German nation, traditionally known for their rationality, fell victim to his flair for the dramatic and the destruction that it helped unleash on the world. Anyone who has viewed Leni Riefenstahl's propaganda film *Triumph of the Will* can plainly see how Germany fell under Hitler's evil spell.[24]

Non-verbal communication is also important for the successful communication of a core message. Leaders who deliver their message while making direct eye contact with their target are seen as trustworthy and credible. Maintaining a good posture goes a long way in creating images of self-confidence which are important for being viewed as inspiring and charismatic. Effective SFL requires a fair amount of "acting" or impression management on the part of the leader. *Impression management* involves behaviors one directs towards others to create and maintain a desired perception of oneself. Impression management is integral to the dramatic verbal and non-verbal forms of communication that inspirational leaders use to build personal images of being extraordinary and energizing to followers. Scott McNealy of Sun Microsystems, Michael Dell of Dell Computer, and Carly Fiorina of Hewlett Packard represent inspirational leaders who vary in terms of the images they present to the public, yet these leaders have produced a range of organizational outcomes.

A leader's display of emotions in articulating the core message for followers may depend on followers' perception of the consistency between the emotions displayed by the leader and the content of the leader's message. Strategy-focused leaders need to align the rhetoric of their core messages with nonverbal and expressive behavior which is seen as fluid, outwardly directed and animated. A study of the role of emotions and non-verbal behavior of politicians competing in the 1984 primary found that Walter Mondale's smile was perceived by voters as not being as emotionally expressive as Ronald Reagan's smile. Voters were more comforted and less angered with a happy/reassuring Reagan as compared with an angry/threatening Reagan. The study's results suggest that to been seen as credible, strategy-focused leaders need to pay careful attention not only to what they say and how they say it, but also to the how their facial expressions match the content of their core messages.[25]

THE CORE MESSAGE AND STRATEGIC PLANNING

Although inspiration and emotion can have strong impacts on technology workers, research has shown that after emotional and inspirational appeals, these workers are mostly influenced by rational and logical arguments. *That's why it is very important to remember that even the most creative employees (e.g., engineers and R & D professionals) in your organization not only need to understand organizational vision, but also receive some sort of structure that guides their creative work processes.*[26] The executives we interviewed emphasized the need to provide a compelling link between the core message and the strategic plan and to effectively communicate key aspects of the strategy to their people.

Most of the organizations in our study followed the typical strategic planning process[27] shown in Figure 4.1. First, they use SWOT analysis, their strategic networks of contacts, and other information sources to collect information and intelligence on the environmental conditions characterizing their strategic situation. This information is used to isolate important trends and develop alternate scenarios for the future. From these alternative futures, a vision of where the organization intended to be in the future and the purpose for the organization's existence are then developed. The vision serves as a means of communicating to employees the basic assumptions and core values, as well as the mission of the organization.

Vision statements and their derivative mission statements are developed through self-examination and the results of SWOT analysis. Vision statements are different from mission statements. A *vision statement* expresses the desired destination of the organization within a certain time-frame. A *mission statement* explains the main aim or purpose of the organization (e.g., who the organization intends to serve, what service consists of, how it is provided). Some organizations also develop a statement summarizing their core values, although values are often expressed in vision statements, where they have a stronger inspirational impact. Once these statements are developed, the objectives or goals of the organization are developed.

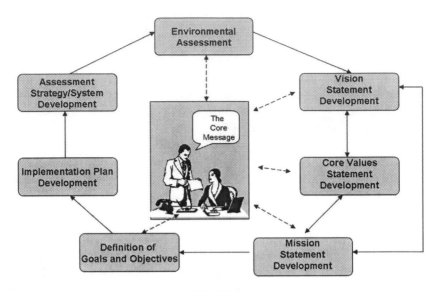

FIGURE 4.1
Typical Strategic Planning Process in Technology-Driven Organizations.

Objectives or goals describe what needs to be done to accomplish the organization's mission.

Note that at this point in the strategic planning process, strategy-focus leaders have all the necessary elements for the *content* of their core message:

1. the vision,
2. the mission,
3. the core values, and
4. the long-term and short-term goals.

They use these elements to create inspiring and compelling core messages and share them with all organization members over and over again to build strong cultures. In addition, by conveying their core message effectively, strategy-focused leaders may be able to kick-start a learning process that involves sharing information at multiple levels of the organization. Visions not only provide information, but also provide an example for employees on how important it is to share information for knowledge management.[28]

Ask Mighty Tech's president. He holds a series of department meetings every three months to communicate the core message to Mighty Tech managers and invited employees.

> I start [the meetings] off with a description of where [Mighty Tech] is as of that day. I describe all the things I want to do as a company, what changes I want to implement. And I consult with everyone in that room. Everybody has the option of speaking with, against, for . . . it's an open dialogue basically. So I go through all the points of where we are, what's going on in each specific area, what changes I want to implement based on our strategy.

We describe how strategy-focused leaders "translate" and share organizational strategy with their followers in Chapter 7.

When goals have been established, it is then possible to develop implementation strategies or action plans describing the details of how the goals will be attained. Finally, assessment strategies and systems are developed and implemented to provide performance evaluations of how successful the action plans actually were in attaining the goals communicated in the core message. Several of the executives we interviewed used the "balanced scorecard"[29] as a performance measurement system to keep employees informed of their progress toward attaining the key long-term goal spelled out in the core message. Russel Laraway of ITG Pathfinders uses the balanced scorecard to communicate performance expectations outlined in the core message:

> We have a framework for the scorecard now, and I am right in the middle of sending out the scorecards. The whole point is that everyone needs to see how the company is doing against it's stated goals . . . I will use the scorecard as a tool for telling them what they need to achieve . . . So, . . . it's not just hand out the scorecard and say see you later, figure it out. Yeah, it's probably obvious, but it needs to be very carefully dispensed, actually, to the subordinate leaders because there can be no misunderstanding of what's expected of them. So, use the scorecard as a tool to deliver those three things I talked about before. Deliver clear, concise guidance in the form of MBOs with a budget and say "go get it done."

Tracking the progress toward achieving organizational goals is critical. Without tangible performance indictors of key financial, customer, quality, and learning goals, the strategy-focused leader's core message remains a distant dream. To realize the dream requires collecting key indicators or measures of goals that are important for building customer intimacy and satisfaction, quality products or services, employee development and sound financial performance. Based on the feedback from such tracking systems, strategy-focused leaders make adjustments to their core message, their strategy and its execution. To be successful and competitive in technology-driven industries requires being adaptive. Information distilled from a well-designed performance measurement system that identifies the need for change can give your organization the edge.

Core Values Drive Business Results

George Harrison, the late Beatles' lead guitarist and songwriter, once sang "It's all up to what you value . . . " Perhaps he borrowed that phrase from research that confirms that an individual's behavior and action are often a function of his or her value system. Likewise, shared values produce strong cultures that guide the action of organizational members.[30]

One value-based organization that has adapted to the changes in its turbulent environment to achieve success is Scripps Mercy Hospital in San Diego, California. Scripps has been ranked among the top 50 hospitals in the U.S. for geriatrics. Its success is due, in part, to its strategic upgrading of its technology to meet market demands and sharing its core message and performance record on key success factors with its employees.

Core values are considered to be vital for guiding the behavior and actions of the Scripp's health systems' 10,000 employees and 2,600 affiliated physicians. A visit to Scripp's website (www.scrippshealth.org) reveals its emphasis on living its core values of *providing the highest quality of service, demonstrating complete respect for the rights of every individual, and caring for patients in a responsible and efficient manner.* Dr. David Shaw, Chief of Staff at Scripps Mercy Hospital, highlighted the importance of making associates understand the connection between core values and how they will help the organization to achieve it mission and realize its dream or vision of success. Shaw noted that Scripps values of quality, respect, accountability and efficiency produce pro-social behaviors that individuals recognize in his employees. This recognition allows patients, physicians, nurses, and other health care professionals, and community members to view Scripps as their choice for medical services and a national leader in the eyes of medical experts.[31]

It's that same centering of attention on the core message that allows strategy-focused leaders like Dr. Shaw to inspire their followers to performance beyond expectations. In technology-driven industries, where dreams can quickly turn to dust, realizing dreams of success requires careful attention to the creating the core message, effectively delivering it to the right followers, and connecting it to the strategy. However, realizing the dream requires the strategy to be implemented by people who are skilled, knowledgeable, and committed to the core message. In the next chapter, we describe how strategy-focused leaders go about selecting and developing people in line with the strategy.

PART III

ADJUSTING THE RIGHT PATTERN

Providing the leadership to guide Nova-Vignette was more challenging than Sandra Stevenson had ever imagined. Developing new drugs derived from RNA interface technology was likely to take more than a decade to get from lab to market. Sandra realized that "going the distance" would require a long-term commitment from people and technology working in sync with a strategy that could adapt to the ever-changing life sciences business environment. She would need to find, attract and retain high quality associates capable of adapting along with her strategic plan. They would have to possess a deep appreciation of technology and how it could be used to expand the business and increase its return on investment. To support Nova-Vignette's associates' efforts, she would also need to identify and develop cutting-edge and flexible technologies consistent with her organization's strategy.

Sandra's ideas about adjusting the patterns that she was weaving into her organization's dreams of success (her core message) were reinforced at an executive leadership seminar she subsequently attended. At this seminar, a panel of executives and leadership scholars concluded that the rapid pace of change facing high tech organizations requires executive leaders to constantly adapt their strategy to market conditions and trends. This would enable executives to make sense out of the complexities and challenges facing them and their associates, and then appropriately respond to those complexities and challenges. As a result of what she learned, Sandra went back to her office more determined than ever to figure out how she could best integrate the right people with the right technology using a more flexible organizational strategy.

CHAPTER 5

SELECTING AND DEVELOPING PEOPLE IN LINE WITH STRATEGY

The most magical and tangible and ultimately the most important
ingredient in the transformed landscape is people.
—*Carly Fiorina, CEO, Hewlett Packard*

Some executives tend to forget that their people have bottom line effects.
Employees interact with each other and with customers, suppliers and business partners and in the process form the relationships for conducting
business. The quality of business relationships enhances profitability
because it attracts customers to products and services, employees to career
opportunities, investors to securities, and suppliers to opportunities to
leverage successful supply chains. People represent the link pins in each of
these business relationships that hold together the complex networks for
conducting business in our global economic market system. This chapter
describes how strategy-focused leaders leverage the human resource function to select the right people who can support their core message and
strategy execution. It also describes how they rapidly develop their follow-

The Dream Weavers: Strategy-Focused Leadership in Technology-Driven
Organizations, pages 89–113

ers' competencies, so that SFL is shared throughout the organization to create strong cultures that achieve dramatically higher levels of performance.

POWER TO THE PEOPLE

While pursuing his graduate degree, one of the authors worked for a university-sponsored Small Business Development Center (SBDC). The SBDC was created as a resource to serve start-up and small business owners in the surrounding counties by providing assistance with business plans, seed and venture capital funding acquisition, marketing, human resources, legal and financial issues. While the SBDC provided a wonderful array of helpful resources for entrepreneurs and small business owners, many of the most exciting, brilliant and innovative strategic plans and core messages coming from its clients were unrealized. These were the dreams that turned to dust because *they were not effectively put into practice or executed by the right people.* The clichéd lessons that the author learned from his experiences at the SBDC were threefold: "talk is cheap," "actions speak louder than words," and "the people make the place."

Strategy-focused leaders recognize these clichés and realize that commitment to the core message and successful execution of the strategy *depends on their colleagues and followers.* It's the organization's people and their knowledge, skills and capabilities that can either make or break an organization's dream and distort its core message. For example, Bill Gates' success in developing innovative products and services at Microsoft is largely a function of his highly qualified, dedicated and loyal workforce. As at Microsoft, an organization's people comprise its *human capital* resource. Research indicates that organizations that invest in and utilize human capital resources to a greater extent are associated with higher levels of performance. Research also shows that organizations that have strong people values, such as 3M, General Electric, Wal-Mart and Disney, outperformed over a 50-year period those which were primarily interested in short-term financial returns.[1]

Human capital resources also allow organizations to create "network nodes" which enable them to maintain linkages with potential employees, business partners, customers, and other organizations. The network nodes can help execute the strategy and add value to the organization. Organizations such as ASEA Brown-Boveri, Microsoft, Southwest Airlines and British Petroleum have been particularly effective in utilizing their associates to create business opportunities and collaborative partnerships with other organizations. These relationships between individuals and organizations represent the *social capital* resources that strategy-focused leaders spend much of their time developing and facilitating.

Like executives in the organizations noted above, strategy-focused leaders of technology-driven organizations need to carefully match the knowledge, skills and capabilities required to accomplish goals outlined in their strategic plans with those people who can provide the right mix of human capital. They also need to make sure that the people in their mix of human capital possess personal values that are aligned with the values communicated in the core message. As described in Chapter 2, facilitating such alignment is quite difficult in highly turbulent and challenging technology-driven industries.

That's due in part to the way today's employees view their relationship with their employer. Rather than working in predictable business conditions, they work in constantly changing and uncertain conditions. Ever since high technologies became the central focus of business operations, more and more of employees' working relationships are becoming temporary and flexible, rather than permanent and standardized. Their skills and professionalism are valued more than their loyalty. Self-reliance and employment security have replaced paternalism and job security. Employees are now looking within and between professions for multiple careers and life-long learning opportunities, rather than linear career growth and one-time learning from traditional educational institutions. The introduction of new, integrated and advanced technologies has led to higher skill and intellectual requirements for the workforce. The demand for employees who are trained in more than one profession is also increasing. As a result, today's workforce is much better educated and qualified than ever.[2] At issue for executives is how to get and keep the best people capable of integrating their skills and knowledge of advanced technologies to support the organization's core message and strategy amidst the realities of today's workplaces.

We have found that such strategic situations and workplace realities demand that executives must do everything possible to recognize outstanding people in the interview process. Such people will not be selected only because they will make great followers, but because of their leadership potential.[3] The successful organizations we studied hire these people, fit them into the right jobs, and support them in all that they do, whether it's through rewards, training or recognition that helps them to grow. The unsuccessful organizations don't pay attention to person-job fit issues and don't work with people to improve their performance in their role. This requirement comes down to finding the right people, recognizing good people, and putting the right people in the right place. In other words, you must not only have the right people, but also have the right people in the right place.

Strategy-focused leaders also *rapidly develop their associates into individuals who are willing to share leadership responsibilities* across all levels of the organization. The ability of organizations to develop business associates more rapidly than their competitors appears to be a key sustainable competitive advantage in the life-sciences industry. Anthony Tebutt, President of UCB Pharma, highlights this requirement:

> And the point is that these business decisions are not the interests only of the company but the individuals themselves, because eventually an individual will suffer if they are not given a kind of direction they need to prove or perform. Eventually they'll find that the roles have passed them by and they're in a sad state. So that has been a major transition for a lot of the managers that we've inherited: teaching them how to be good business leaders, how to work with business plans and how to apply modern techniques to the pharmaceutical selling and marketing process.[4]

Throughout his interview, Tebutt emphasized the importance of developing people in line with the organization's mission, core values, goals and objectives in order to effectively compete in pharmaceutical markets. As Tebutt suggests, people represent an organization's most precious and unique resource—a resource that needs to be nurtured, developed and supported so that people, in turn, can support the execution of the organization's strategic plan. We believe that people's commitment toward long-term strategies and goals is what sustains an organization's competitive advantage in today's turbulent business environment.

Organizations such as the U.S. Army, SAS and Shell Oil have taken this approach for giving human resource management a strategic role, rather than a support role. The Army considers its HR function to be central to its strategy because it enables readiness and flexibility. Statistical software producer SAS, which boasts a 96 percent employee retention rate, has used its core value of "work/life balance" as a selection and retention tool. As a result, SAS has created a strong culture and a solid reputation, and been listed among *Fortune*'s list of best companies to work for. Also, Al Brendsel, director of Shell Oil's "talent pipeline" points out that at his company "HR is there to support business strategy."[5] It's about time that HR departments are beginning to receive the recognition and strategic importance that they deserve for their critical role in selecting and developing followers into leaders.

SELECTING THE RIGHT FOLLOWERS

Strategy-focused leaders view their followers as promising investments rather than burdensome expenses. One of the criticisms of CEOs of the "slash and burn" and downsizing era of the 1980s and 1990s was that they viewed employees as expenses or costly "cogs-in-the-wheel." The infamous former CEOs "Chainsaw" Al Dunlap of Sunbeam and F. Ross Johnson of RJR Nabisco relied on massive layoffs or merger-induced downsizing to boost their bottom lines. Sadly, the first place they cut monies from their budgets was personnel and training and development line items. This strategy for dealing with adverse environmental conditions sends a strong negative message to customers, their remaining employees, and the business community. Such strategies may have positive short-term effects on the bottom line, but often produce long-term declines in profits due to a lack of intellectual and social capital that ultimately feed financial capital over time.[6]

These antiquated short-term worldviews conflict with the more "people-centered" strategic perspectives held by many of the executives we interviewed. While providing suggestions for building successful careers in high tech industries, the Vice President for Strategy and Business Planning for an Israeli defense firm, exemplified the new attitude of today's strategy-focused leaders:

> You need to succeed in business with people and not fixate on their cost. That kind of success will lead companies to choose you because they'll notice that people around you go with you. Both results and cohesion matter together to them and to me.[7]

In other words, attaining dreams of long-term success requires SFL which searches for and values a cohesive network of people who possess the skills to fulfill roles that support the strategy.

Supporting a strategy that achieves success in technology-driven industries is easier said than done. Issues of environmental volatility and ambiguity, intense global competition, short product life cycles, and shortages in the labor supply have required executives to develop plans for eliminating or reducing inefficiencies and improve methods of production and service. High quality skilled workforces are needed to support the execution of such plans. However, chronic shortages of high quality workers have made recruitment and selection initiatives difficult. A recent study conducted by the Conference Board which surveyed 109 executives indicated that the number one challenge facing executives is hiring and retaining high quality employees. The study also reported that difficulties in finding high quality employees have been made worse by a need for general leadership competencies instead of technology skills and know-how that were so highly valued in the 1990s.[8]

These challenges were noted in our interview with Rich Sanders, Vice President for Operations at JNI Engineering:

> . . . high tech tends to have a lot more movement, transient. People are coming and going much more than [in] traditional [companies] where they tend to be more committed to the company. In high tech unfortunately, I think people have created the attitude that they are entitled to make a lot of money, a lot of stock options. And if you cannot provide growth and opportunity and wealth creation then [they say] "I am going to take my skills somewhere else." And so its becoming increasingly difficult to create constant

growth, constant creation of wealth for people who feel that they are entitled to it, and [they say] "if you don't provide it to me then I am leaving." So I think it's a challenge in high tech industries.[9]

Sanders went on to emphasize the challenge of finding individuals who can lead effectively because many of the individuals who rise up through his organization quickly are technology-savvy, but often lack leadership and interpersonal skills.

Despite these difficulties, high quality members of workforces must be identified and selected *one at a time* through effective personnel selection processes that identify people who possess the right knowledge, skills and abilities to perform in roles that support the strategy.[10] Workforce members also must possess values that are congruent with the core values of the organization. Fortunately, executives have a resource that can be quite effective in building a highly skilled, motivated and committed workforce.

Strategy as a Selection Guide

We have found that the strategic plan and core message can serve as a helpful selection guide for identifying and acquiring the right mix of human capital. When strategy-focused leaders engage in selection process they are concerned with recognizing external factors, such as the status of the market, but also emphasize the independence and choice of lower level managers to make selection decisions. Overall, they make sure that their selection procedures are integrated in the overall corporate strategy. By following the steps illustrated in Figure 5.1, strategy-focused leaders and their associates can use strategy as a selection guide. Typically, an organization's HR department scans its internal and external environments to identify recruits for positions that need to be filled. But according to David Dell of the Conference Board, everyone in the organization from CEO to the most junior associate should work together to find top-notch employees.[11] For example, the personal networks created by strategy-focused leaders and their associates can provide leads for promising recruits and help address the hiring and retention problems facing today's technology-driven organizations. Some executives used non-traditional sources of recruiting such as community fairs, industry conferences, microbrewery festivals, corporate sports leagues, home-and-garden shows, Internet websites, and asking current employees how to recruit others like them. These employees are often paid bonuses if the person they refer is hired.

Many of the executives we interviewed highlighted the central role of the strategic plan and the core message in their hiring practices. They noted the importance of integrating recruiting and retention goals into the annual strategic planning process. A case in point was found when one

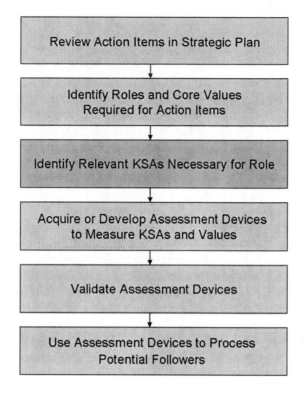

FIGURE 5.1
Steps in Selecting Followers in Line with the Strategy.

of the authors interviewed a senior vice president at Union Bank of California. He explained his company's very genuine and long-term strategic focus and commitment toward diversity and pointed out several potential benefits of promoting diversity for his company. He mentioned by integrating diversity initiatives into his strategic plan:

> One positive outcome of our long-term focus on promoting diversity rather than just a political slogan came in unexpectedly when we were looking for a new board member. We found a very capable and well-experienced female executive who was in high demand from other several banks that were much larger than we were. We couldn't compete against our competitors based on compensation packages. However, she decided to join us when she compared who were on the Boards in each company and realized that we have the most diversified Board including several female members.

The strategic plan outlines the financial, operational, customer-service, and employee development goals for the organization. The goals are accomplished through *action plans* which identify who, what, when, where and how objectives will be achieved. By reviewing the action plan steps, executives and their managers may better understand the knowledge, skills, abilities (KSAs), roles, and expertise required to successfully complete the action items or the tasks that support the strategy. This information can help them to profile the types of associates who can make valuable contributions to the organization. Those who fit the profile promise to be high-performing contributors to the organization because they are likely to possess the KSAs and values that are required to support the strategic plan.

Consider General Electric which has been quite successful in using its strategic plan as a starting point for finding high quality employees. GE develops detailed staffing plans that are integrated into its strategic plan. Selection criteria that are part of departmental plans link project task requirements to available human resources. GE also develops metrics for hiring and retaining quality employees and links them to performance plans, strategic objectives and compensation for departmental managers. Companies also adjust their recruiting policies based on market conditions and forecast. During the last decade, General Motors emphasized a retrenchment or cost reduction strategy and used job redesign rather than hiring new employees. Intel, on the other hand, addressed immense growth by aggressively recruiting new employees.[12] In these organizations, talent databases which track the current workforce KSAs, experience, and accomplishments are maintained as a source of promotions from within the organization. These practices have helped these organizations improve their ability to hire and retain the best employees, while reducing the cost of hiring, the time needed to fill positions, and the percentage of new hires who do not work out.[13]

These outstanding results may be difficult to achieve in organizations that do not possess GE or General Motor's size and economies of scale. Yet, many sources of HR assistance are available for organizations of all sizes. For example, the Society for Industrial and Organizational Psychology (SIOP), the largest professional organization for industrial and organizational psychologists in the U.S., offers a wide range of products and services that can assist strategy-focused leaders and their organizations to acquire or develop assessment devices to measure the KSAs and values of potential high-performing workers. Assessment devices and methods can be used to find individuals who are a "good fit" for the organization. These include surveys, tests and questionnaires assessing minimum qualification screens (training and evaluation ratings, biographical data), abilities testing (cognitive, general mental ability or "g," emotional, and job knowledge testing), personality and interest tests, structured interviews, and assessment centers (work samples, simulations, mini-training and evaluation).

According to a recent meta-analysis (a scientific study of the results of many studies), the best methods for predicting job performance are work sample tests, g tests, structured employment interviews, peer ratings and job knowledge tests. Often these resources have been tested for reliability and validity as part of their development; however, they need to be validated by HR staff or consultants in terms of their content, constructs (concepts purported to be measured), and criteria (outcomes they purport to predict) on a job-specific basis as expressed in SIOP's *Principles for the Validation and Use of Personnel Selection Procedures.* Only upon successful validation of the measures according to these principles should the assessment devices be used to select followers.[14]

Such selection procedures assist strategy-focused leaders to ensure that new personnel will experience "*follower-culture fit.*" This means that followers possess the technical skills and knowledge and the values that are required to be a long-term contributor to the organization and its core message. Value congruence between the follower and the organization and its culture has been shown to be a significant predictor of what attracts individuals to the organization, who is selected in personnel hiring decisions, and who decides or is forced to leave an organization. In addition, value congruence between the leader and follower has been found to be an important ingredient for jump-starting followers' performance.[15] As described in Chapter 3, the core message that the strategy-focused leaders develop and communicate to their followers is an important tool for developing and communicating the importance of follower-culture fit. Fit is important if strategy-focused leaders are to develop their followers into successful strategy-focused leaders who share a commitment to the core message.

Followers' Qualities and Talent to Search For

We asked executives in our sample about the qualities and talents that set successful managers apart from less successful managers in their industries. Given the high degree of ambiguity, intense competition, rapid work pace, and information overload faced by managers in technology-driven industries, we expected the executives to talk about the need for several cognitive (e.g., intelligence, complex problem-solving skills, knowledge), behavioral (e.g., participation, drive, collaboration) and personality (e.g., extraversion, persistence, integrity, responsibility, cooperativeness, optimism) qualities discussed in the leadership literature. To our surprise, the executives identified a wide variety of attributes (similar across industries) including values, behaviors and managerial skills, in addition to many of those we had expected. These attributes are summarized in Table 5.1 and can be used as starting points when you begin assessing the talent of potential hires in your technology-driven organization.

Several of the executives noted the importance of efficiency and strategic thinking attributes. Given the hectic work pace, rapid rate of change,

TABLE 5.1
Characteristics of Successful Managers/Followers of
Strategy-Focused Leaders

- Aware of leader expectations
- Positive toward core message
- Manages time effectively
- Communicates and networks effectively
- Broad/deep knowledge of technology (cutting edge and future trends)
- Problem solver
- Strategic thinker
- Team player (even from remote location)
- Experienced
- Emotionally intelligent and mature
- Optimistic
- Honest and trustworthy
- Shows respect for others
- Well-respected by others
- Mentors associates to improve their performance
- Entrepreneurial values (e.g., risk taking, self-motivated)
- Inspirational leader (embraces and promotes change)

and multiple job demands facing technology managers, time management issues came to the forefront. Things are much more minute to minute, second to second in technology-driven industries. Being a "trailblazer" (an individual with initiative, drive, and a sense of ownership) who utilizes his or her time efficiently appears to be necessary for success in technology industries. The most successful managers also embrace change because technology-driven organizations must adapt to many frequent changes in services, products and processes. These managers hire workers who like change and know how to manage change, not maintain the status quo. This entrepreneurial "take charge" mentality is not all that common in some of the more traditional IT organizations that CEO John Yi had worked for before founding the San Diego-based software company, KES. According to Yi,

> Because what I really hated in a large corporation was the "not my problem" syndrome: "I am doing this, after I do that, I'm going to throw it over the fence and its not my problem." And what that means is that a lot of times things fall through the cracks and you don't find out until it is too late. In entrepreneurial companies like KES, . . . people are looking at more of a bigger picture what needs to be done as a whole rather than just the pieces given to them.[16]

Many of the executives also valued team players who could contribute to *shared leadership* systems, where some strategic leadership functions, such as strategic thinking/ problem solving and forecasting technology trends, are distributed to mid-level managers. By shared leadership, we mean "the process of all members of the team collectively influencing each other toward accomplishing its goal."[17] Our finding is consistent with leadership scholar Robert House's comment that the "concentration of leadership in a single chain of command may be less optimal than shared leadership responsibility among two or more individuals in certain task environments."[18] Technology-driven industries appear to be one of those task environments. A notable example for this shared leadership system and team-based approach is Qualcomm where employees are highly encouraged to show initiative for their project and are given the authority to make decisions.

Technology is enabling managers to lead their associates from a distance and is changing where they can work, when they work, and how they communicate. Responding to the trends discussed in Chapter 2, many of the organizations employing the executives we interviewed have championed and implemented forms of the *virtual workplace,* in which managers and their associates work remotely from one another via technology systems. They use a variety of such systems including laptop computers with network links, e-mail, voice-mail, cell phones, pagers, instant messaging, group-decision support systems, video conferencing, and the Internet to collaborate and communicate with their associates across physical distance and time zones.[19]

The ability to effectively manage work relationships in virtual workplaces appears to be a criterion for success. As noted by Sandra Sherman, an Assistant President at Union Bank:

> An effective manager is somebody who can do it remotely. My boss, I feel, is a fantastic manager. He is a great leader and I feel very fortunate to work for him. He is there whenever you need him, be it through phone, if not in person. He will be here . . . He leaves you alone so you can do what you need to, but gives you just enough direction that you know what he is expecting. And can do it very effective remotely. He has staff all over the West Coast. I can't even count. So to me, this is where the industry is going and especially globally, being able to lead remotely and keep everything flowing.[20]

The effective communicating and sharing of information on technology trends and strategic issues among peers and associates in the managers' personal and professional networks also is important for success. In technology organizations, effective communication is "job one." Senior managers spend a great deal of their time in formal or informal, face-to-face or virtual meetings communicating with their associates or customers. These meetings require managers to use different types of leadership styles while communicating with others. Some require mentoring and coaching. Others need to be inspired or challenged. Some need participative leadership to hold them together as a team and get them to produce, project sales or provide service more effectively. Managing in technology-driven organizations requires managers to deal with a variety of different people and to be able to talk to them and lead them as unique individuals.

Terry Troxel, President and CEO of the American Institute for CPCU/ IIA considers effective managers to be first and foremost

> good communicators, both upward and downward . . . I would actually differentiate between my direct reports on that basis: who talks to me most, not necessarily most frequently, but most effectively perhaps, and who I feel I have the best understanding of what's going on in their area, so communication is extremely important in decision making. Obviously the ability to formulate what the issue is, and come up with a decision is very important, and continuity of work and the culture that we operate in is important as well.[21]

As Troxel suggests, effective upward, downward and lateral communication builds the vital information and social networks required for managerial success in technology-driven industries. We found a similar focus on communication and network building several other organizations, notably telecommunications innovator Qualcomm. At Qualcomm, effective managers know how to contribute and make the best use of human and information resources of the company. They take the initiative to tap into the company's information network and learn how to gain access to it. These successful managers are known as team players. They believe in the core message of the company and fit in with its culture. Managers can't be successful if they are at odds with the Qualcomm's culture. As a result, they become known for their loyalty. Most of the successful executives we interviewed have developed a support system among their colleagues and their superiors in their company through a series of informal or formal mentoring relationships.[22]

To navigate through these networks, managers also need the skills to integrate multiple sources of information into coherent solutions and to filter large amounts of information provided to them via their personal and computer networks. It appears that in technology-driven organizations, technical knowledge and expertise are valuable for career advancement and maintaining a professional image. According to JNI Engineering's Rich Sanders:

> Technology becomes a kind of overwhelming wave—a real source of power. It's really more powerful than everything else. So people who understand the technology, who are technologists, tend to rise up through the organization very quickly. These are the ones who tend to be CEOs or [are in] key management positions. In some cases, the management strategy is made on that knowledge of technology. Not necessarily on their leadership skills or their maturity or their skills. Those become secondary. Unfortunately, I think the high tech experience still wins.

Sander's sentiments were echoed in our interview with a top executive at Morton Finance:

> . . . to be successful in technology, you need to have much longer term perspective. You have to have an understanding of what is going on in terms of technology and evolutions and changes in technology. Ultimately it is very difficult for people to be on one side of the business to cross over to the other because their frame of reference is so much different.[23]

These executives' viewpoints are consistent with research conducted by one of the authors at a large multinational IT services corporation. In this particular organization, presenting oneself as a technical expert is a more effective strategy for managers than worrying too much about public impression management. Leaders are unlikely to be concerned about conformance to social norms in an environment in which social appropriateness is not often considered. For example, Bill Gates of Microsoft, Larry Ellison of Oracle, Steven Jobs of Apple Computer, and Scott McNealy of Sun Microsystems have been described as somewhat rebellious, maverick, and unconventional. Such proclivity for nonconformance is consistent with attributes of some strategy-focused leaders. Therefore, while strategy-focused leaders in IT industries may be very much aware of their personal expertise, ideas, and beliefs, they may be less concerned about their behavior and actions in social settings.[24]

While technology and management skills appear to be important, the "softer" interpersonal skills were also mentioned by the executives we interviewed. It is interesting to note that Daniel Goleman's research on *emotional intelligence* is consistent with our executives' views on the importance of interpersonal and leadership skills. Goleman reported that in a study of engineering managers at Bell Labs, the most successful managers were *not* those with the highest intelligence or IQ. The most successful were those engineers with the highest emotional intelligence or EQ. To be emotionally intelligent requires a mature, self-motivated and self-controlled response to events and people. Emotionally intelligent individuals possess a sense of hope and optimism. Hope involves faith that allows a person to set higher goals and to work diligently to achieve them. Optimism compliments hope in the sense that optimistic people "see the glass as half full" (rather than half empty) and realize that failures can be transformed into success with the right amount of determination, effort and faith.[25]

Several elements of EQ (emotionally awareness and maturity, optimism, people-oriented focus) were mentioned by executives as attributes of successful managers in their industries. Karen Borda, founder and former COO of the biotech firm CB Technologies, mentioned elements of EQ and leadership in her interview with us:

> Interpersonal skills are so important for success. At more senior levels I expect managers to be able to guide people through team issues, not dump them on HR, but rather play an active role. I expect them to coach others, to become more involved with goal setting and more proactive in helping us achieve our strategic goals. People want to be mentored. They want to be led—so we're looking for someone who can step up to the plate and do that for us. If you can sketch out what you want to be accomplished you can guide them into the role of a coach or mentor. It's also important that they be amongst the people . . . so they can inspire and challenge people to be problem solvers. This requires that they need to be self-confident—not to feel intimidated when someone from a lower level challenges them or asks 'why?' They really need the emotional maturity to get to the top and be respected by their colleagues.

Team-work, mentoring and emotional awareness skills appear to be integral to creating an organizational culture that has helped foster CB Technology's success in the biotech industry. The company has been around for ten years and has convinced several leading medical schools to use its software. CB Technologies has leveraged the good press from their initial successes to build solid relationships with much bigger pharmaceutical organizations.[26]

The importance of people skills also was echoed by Concord Inc.'s CEO:

> I think that good managers are extremely good in developing people, watching what is going on with people, and practicing diversity (which is a big goal of ours). And I think average managers do not do that as well. I think it is people skills.

While leading Concord Inc. into new products and markets based on cutting-edge technology innovation, this CEO emphasized that practicing diversity involves finding common ground among different people and distilling the common values that can bring different people together to achieve a real sense of community.[27]

The basis for SFL and managerial effectiveness in technology-driven organizations appears to be the fundamental moral values of honesty, trustworthiness and showing respect for others. These values can help strategy-focused leaders and their followers gain respect and admiration from others in return. Many of the executives we interviewed highlighted the importance of "strength of character." A common conclusion among these executives was that to "do the right thing" shows maturity and judgment and that people generally don't (and should not) get into customer relationships or leadership positions without strength of character.

According to Brian Duffy, President of General Electric's Auto Insurance division, unyielding integrity, honesty and respect for others build a strong foundation for leadership and customer relationships: " . . . integrity is the benchmark of everything, but basically it all starts at the customer . . . passion for the customer, do the right thing and do it with integrity."[28] As with GE's leadership, you should consider selecting followers on the basis of their strength of character. This quality, when possessed by members of your workforce, may serve as a collective asset base that just might help prevent Enron and Worldcom-type scandals from destroying your organization's reputation and its human, social and financial capital.

ACCELERATING THE DEVELOPMENT OF FOLLOWERS INTO LEADERS

In technology-driven industries, advantage goes to the first mover and victory goes to the quick. Those organizations that rapidly develop the knowledge, skills, and capabilities of their people are better poised for success. One way that strategy-focused leaders can develop their followers' full potential is to display what leadership researchers have called *individualized consideration* (IC) behaviors, which involve leveraging diversity and mentoring. An executive we interviewed who is CEO of a health care organization put it best, "*Our value system says we respect and develop everyone—individual by individual.*" IC behaviors are aimed at energizing followers to achieve their highest level of performance and capabilities.[29] Table 5.2 summarizes key IC behaviors that can be displayed by managers at all organizational levels, including executives.

The executive leaders in our sample displayed significantly higher levels of IC than managers in a very large international sample assessing such

TABLE 5.2
Aspects of Individualized Consideration Behavior

- Recognize that followers have different needs, abilities, and aspirations
- Treat each follower as an individual rather than just as a member of the group
- Spend time teaching, mentoring and coaching
- Be aware of followers' strengths and weaknesses
- Be flexible regarding followers' work/family balance
- Encourage and fund followers' education and training
- Help followers to develop their strengths (accentuate the positive)
- Delegate tasks that develop followers' strengths (don't "dump" on followers)
- Show empathy, care and concern for followers' professional and personal issues
- Counsel and coach followers who face challenging issues or tasks
- Build followers' self-esteem and confidence by validating and recognizing their motivation, work and performance
- Where and when appropriate, be a friend to followers without showing favoritism
- Protect inexperienced or naïve followers from nasty office politics

behavior.[30] However, there was some variance in the frequency which the executives displayed IC behaviors. Some spent little time displaying IC to their followers, while others viewed IC as an integral part of their SFL. This variation was based on the industry of the executive's organization. Display of IC was higher among executives in the life sciences industry than information technology and services industries.[31] Gender did not matter: female executives displayed similar levels of IC as male executives.

The lessons we learned from these executives concerning IC and follower development can be used in your organization to build your human and intellectual capital resources. When strategy-focused leaders display IC, they lay the foundation for successful mentoring relationships. Leadership scholar Bernard M. Bass suggested that leaders' reassurance helps followers be more ready, willing and able to cooperate in joint efforts.[32] Moreover, IC can be cultivated and nurtured not only with individual employees but also at the team and organizational levels.[33]

Organizations can create cultures that encourage coaching and development while providing consideration and recognition of individual needs. Paul Galvin, the CEO of Motorola, created a culture, where risk-taking is advocated and seen as the most secure approach. Employees are encouraged to be creative and develop new products. Without a doubt, you too can use IC behaviors to develop your own followers into future strategy-focused leaders and help ensure a lasting legacy of success for your organization. But what must you do to accomplish this? The answer is relative simple: pay attention to, initiate, and then reap the benefits from diversity and mentoring programs.

Leveraging Diversity

The next time you attend a business meeting, perhaps a corporate training or university course, or an industry conference, stop and look at the people around you. Chances are you will see a wide variety of people who differ from you and each other in more ways than the obvious. They may differ based on their gender, age, race, national origin, culture, values, attitudes, self-concept, religion, personality, life experiences, socio-economic background, family situation, physical and psychological (dis)abilities, sexual orientation, political views, profession, functional skills, among other individual differences. All of these differences provide each *individual* person you see with specific strengths and weaknesses that they bring with them to your meeting and to the workplace. As are the people at your meeting, organizations and today's market places are increasingly becoming more heterogeneous or diverse on the aforementioned characteristics. The challenge for strategy-focused leaders is to systematically harness the wide variety of strengths possessed by each individual follower to accomplish specific action items in the strategy, while systematically transforming individual followers' weaknesses into strengths.

Why should executives care about leveraging diversity? Continuing or emerging workforce trends suggest several reasons diversity can build strategic resources. A recent report published by the Society for Human Resource Management (SHRM) and *Fortune* magazine's surveying 361 HR executives indicates that diversity programs build social and financial capital for organizations by boosting employee morale, decreasing interpersonal conflicts among associates, and increasing productivity and creativity. Such programs also improve corporate cultures, build better customer relations, and facilitate the hiring of new employees. Given that qualified employees are increasingly becoming scarce, HR departments have to become more flexible in who they hire. Diversity programs seem to help in these areas.[34]

One way that the executives we interviewed leveraged diversity's constructive power was by recognizing that their associates have different needs, abilities, and aspirations, which can be added to form a collective basis of organizational innovation. In other words, they acknowledged their associates as unique individuals, not just members of a group. For example, several of the executives identified the need to differentiate between associates who are in technical versus managerial positions, and between associates who are working on projects at different stages of completion. Concerning the diversity among technical and managerial workers at SCT, Amy Turner-Ladow noted that:

> . . . the lifeblood [of IT companies] can be programmers or can be technological wizards, and so you really need to provide two distinct growth paths for your employees. You need to have the individual contributor that could be absolutely invaluable in the technology or in the functionality that they bring to the table. And then you have to have the management staff that's willing to adapt to manage or lead a different type of person. So I think that has been one of the challenges in the industry in general . . . that they're bridging the gap between who runs the show, is it the programmers that run the world? Or is it the managers that lead the world? And you really need to be able to assimilate both of those and make sure that they are valued, that the human assets really feel valued.

STC handles this issue by having a dual career path (technical employees vs. managerial employees) to cater to the career inclinations of each of the employees. They also foster a sense of camaraderie between these two groups by holding "all company meetings" and sporting events with teams comprised of players from each group of employees.[35]

Projects in technology-intensive organizations often span months or years and change as they progress over multiple stages of completion. During each stage, project team members often possess different emotions, expectations and levels of stress. It takes a special leader to recognize how these changing conditions affect followers as the projects progress. Such recognition is needed in order to tailor the type of IC behavior not only to the individual follower, but also to the follower within the unique project stage. This point is emphasized by a key executive at the Vanguard Group:

> There are people who are more skilled at leading a project that has a finite duration than people who are going to run a group. Because there's a certain sort of detail orientation that good project leadership really has, and strong use of resources that really bring your project to a tight close. Versus, someone who might be running that group for the long term, but using the technology project to enhance the way that group runs. I'm not really sure they're distinct from each other, but you can find one person with that strength over another person who doesn't have as much of that strength.

Vanguard also illustrates another way our executives talked about leveraging diversity— by treating each associate as an individual rather than just as a member of the group. Vanguard's website highlights their commitment to hiring a diverse workforce that reflects the surrounding community and society at large. The true essence of IC behavior is reflected in their executive management's affirmation that *even one person can make a difference.* They back up this platitude with tried and true HR programs tailored to the individual needs and aspirations of their associates. These programs include offering a variety of internal and external training opportunities through corporate and traditional universities, on-line job-postings, college planning and academic financial assistance/reimbursement, professional licensing and technology training, performance management reviews and career development programs, and life issues seminars on child development, aging and elder care, and health issues.[36]

Mentoring for Career Issues

A large number of Vanguard associates are "coaches" or mentors who train new associates during orientation programs, training processes, and in individualized "one-on-one" mentoring relationships over the course of their early careers. The relationships between the mentors and their protégés help build the social network within Vanguard and strengthen its organizational culture through the sharing of core values, norms and traditions. To motivate participation in this culture building activity, Vanguard's "coaches" are recognized and rewarded for contributions they make to the professional and personal development of the organization's future leaders. Like Vanguard, many other companies such as Bank of America and PricewaterhouseCoopers' use mentoring as a strategic practice to increase employee retention. In competitive labor markets, such as the high technology industry, increasing retention is a major HR goal. For example, in PricewaterhouseCoopers', mentoring has led to a large decrease of female employee turnover.[37] Similarly, in our study many companies employ mentoring programs to develop and retain their human capital resources.

Since ancient times, mentors have been recognized as socially capable and knowledgeable individuals who develop protégés by sharing their wisdom. The Greek philosopher Mentor provided wise tutelage to Telemachus while his father Odysseus was away on his adventures. Today, mentoring has been identified by many organizations as an effective means of leadership development. At CB Technologies and in her current entrepreneurial initiatives, Karen Borda views her time mentoring her direct reports as relationship building that will pay off with a bounty of future dividends:

> People want to be mentored, they want to be lead. I do touch base with people by checking with them and asking 'How are things going?' or 'Are you having any problems that I can help you with?' In many cases, people will seek me out. I always have an open door policy. I start off by building the relationship, so people will trust that I will be there when they need me. Once they realize that, they have no problem talking to me. I spend a lot of after hours developing my people through mentoring.

In its traditional form, *mentoring* is a form of social support in which individuals with more advanced experience and knowledge (mentors) are matched with a lesser experienced and knowledgeable individual (protégé) for the purpose of advancing the protégé's personal and professional development and career. Mentoring can also be provided through one's peers, professional networks or groups, and relationships with multiple mentors. Mentor-protégé relationships can be either informal or formal. Informal relationships develop naturally, as the mentor and protégé gravitate toward one another based on shared values, perceived or actual similarity, mutual respect or liking. Informal mentor-protégé relationships have worked for Warren Buffet and Bill Gates, Richard Nixon and Bob Dole, Scott McNealy and Jack Welch, Bobby Darin and Wayne Newton, and Maya Angelou and Oprah Winfrey. Formal relationships involve the organization matching the mentor and protégé, oftentimes supporting the relationship with training and resources. Vanguard's "one-on-one" program is an example of a successful formal mentoring program.[38]

Why should executive leaders care about mentoring? *Because mentoring builds human, intellectual, social and financial capital—the essential elements of SFL.* Mentoring has been found to produce a wealth of benefits for the protégé, the mentor, and the organization. For the protégé, mentoring can result in increased promotions and compensation, enhanced self-esteem at work, increased job satisfaction, career mobility, career aspirations, career advancement, career satisfaction, career commitment, decreased work alienation, and reduced job and role stress and burnout. For the mentor, mentoring relationships provide enhanced job performance and promotions, organizational recognition and reputation, feelings of competence and personal fulfillment, confidence in their own abilities, esteem among peers, greater internal satisfaction stemming from the job or career, and rejuvenation and generativity (the passing on of their beliefs and values to future generations). A successful mentoring process could increase employee productivity, effective socialization of young employees, enhanced organizational commitment among mentoring program participants, and reduced levels of costly employee turnover.[39] These benefits of successful mentoring process are mentioned by Terry Troxel at the AICPCU/IIA. According to Troxel

> Mentoring . . . isn't just in my office. I go out and see them (direct report protégés) and we get involved in particular projects . . . and it's always interesting. An example is when you're doing a personnel decision, when you're looking for a new hire. Talking to them about how you go about seeking those people, what qualifications are you looking at, how we are to approach the market . . . Obviously I draw on my experience and my own thoughts and I'm always interested in theirs . . . They've had some experiences too. So we do a collaborative "What you think of this?," "What you think of that?," "Should we be looking at *hotjobs.com*?," "Is it worth using the *Wall Street Journal* or *Philadelphia Inquirer*?," "Is it better networking through affinity groups that we have, or professional associations?" . . . "What are the characteristics we are really looking at for this position?" . . . So mentoring enters into all that, it's simply drawing on some of our collective experiences to make better decisions.

Troxel's inclusive style of interacting with his direct reports varies depending on the quality and history of their relationship. Most direct reports stop by his office three times a week. One direct report is in his office about 12 times a day because they have known each other for over ten years. For Troxel and his direct reports, the more frequently they interact, the more their organization learns and develops human and social capital through mentoring.

Mentors provide two broad functions to protégés as they work together to develop the protégé's knowledge, skills and capacities and advance the protégé's career: career development and psychosocial support. *Career development* functions provide vocational, job or task support to protégés and include sponsorship, exposure and visibility, coaching, protection, and providing challenging assignments. Sponsorship involves aggressively nominating the protégé for desirable lateral moves or promotions. Exposure and visibility efforts entail assigning responsibilities that allow the protégé to work with important organizational members who may recognize the protégé's potential for advancement. Coaching involves suggesting specific strategies for completing assignments and achieving recognition and career aspirations. Protection involves the shielding of the protégé from untimely or damaging contact from senior organizational members. Challenging assignments are used to stretch the knowledge, skills and abilities of the protégé and promote his or her personal and professional development.

While providing these career-related mentoring functions, several of the executives noted how they coach and challenge their associates by offering them the opportunities to complete action items linked to accomplishing goals in the strategic plan. Individual stretch goals linked to overall strategic goals are often used to provide vocational support to employees at Magnum Credit Card. We interviewed an executive responsible for HR information systems at Magnum. He is a true "people-person," who loves to mentor, motivate and involve his staff. He is recognized by his colleagues as a personable, and participative visionary leader who possesses the cognitive power necessary for planning and completing the many complex and critical tasks required of him.

He has developed what he calls the *down-payment approach* to building higher levels of protégés' knowledge, skills and competencies. Here's how it works. Imagine that you need funds to buy a new home. If you go to a bank and want to borrow $300,000, most likely you must have a 10-20 percent down-payment. You must show the loan officer that you have the ability to produce the 20 percent before he lends you the $300,000.

The executive uses the same approach for encouraging the personal growth of his protégés. When they are at stage number 1 in their development, he knows that they will progress to stage number 2 in let's say 12 months, but that is not necessarily their current job. What the executive does is to get them to work as hard as they can on their current job the smartest way they can, so that they can allocate enough time to learn the skill set of the next job. Most of his protégés take on this challenge (to work as fast and efficiently as they can) within their current job so they can allocate 10 to 20 percent of their time to learning the next level of skills.

The executive creates this opportunity for his protégés to experience new learning opportunities. Most protégés know that when he offers them new projects, it is considered an opportunity because that is where he is asking them for 20 percent down-payment. If they don't pay the down-payment they realize they will not get the "$100,000 loan." In other words, if they don't take on the opportunity, they realize they will never get to the next level. At the same time, if they take on the 20 percent down-payment, they recognize that the executive will always provide feedback to the skill set level they are at, so that by the time the executive is ready to promote, they have already paid their dues. He doesn't promote protégés according to their potential, he promotes them according to their actual performance. It may not be 100 percent of the performance of the next level skill set, but at least 20 percent while they are doing their current job. This unique mix of sponsorship, providing challenging assignments, and coaching has helped Magnum Credit Card to identify its next generation of strategy-focused leaders.[40]

Linking career development functions to strategic objectives is also important in General Electric's culture of continuous personal improvement. GE emphasizes to its employees that they should seek out people with experience from whom they can learn. Managers are identified as excellence resources for career development. Managers serving as mentors provide GE employees with vocational support and valuable insights on what knowledge, skills, abilities and personal connections are needed to achieve their full potential as contributors to GE. Brian Duffy explained his approach for providing his protégés with vocational support:

> I try to play coach and mentor. And there is a difference between the two. Mentor is the "behind-the-scenes guy" that is counseling somebody, helping them out through a problem or whatever. I want people to know they can come to me in a non-threatening situation, and I'm there to help them in any way I can. And then as a coach, my role is strategy and tactics, I'm trying to lead us through the under-writing cycle.

As a firm believer in the power of mentoring, Duffy sees his SFL role at GE as enhancing profitability, providing financial security solutions with outstanding customer service, and shaping his people into knowledgeable, continuously improving, and self-motivated leaders.[41] But career development is only one part of the mentoring equation. The psychosocial part of the mentoring equation deals with the protégé as a human being.

Psychosocial support functions prop up the protégé's human spirit and include counseling, friendship, acceptance and confirmation, and role modeling. Counseling addresses the protégé's personal concerns that may interfere with effective functioning in their job or within the organization. Friendship is a close social interaction where the mentor and protégé like and enjoying being together in formal or informal settings. Acceptance and confirmation provide support and encouragement to the protégé, demonstrate the value and worth the protégé as an individual, and affirm the protégé's self-concept. Role modeling involves the mentor displaying high work and ethical standards through exemplary personal achievements, attitudes, character, and behavior for protégé to emulate.[42] These functions allow mentors to help their protégés feel competent, confident and effective as they work toward achieving their organization's objectives. As noted by Shannon K. Watson, President and CEO of IT services provider GreyMatter, Inc., while mentoring others,

> you have to relate to the business side and the personal side. But they are two separate issues . . . first you have to be a good listener. A lot times, when a person has a concern, they just want you to listen. I often say, 'at the end of the day, you guys have to make a business decision. I heard what you have said and it makes a lot of sense. I understand why you are where you are at, but you also have to understand we have some goals here as the organization and the client have some goals we have to achieve. How can I help you to achieve

them? How can I help you put your personal concerns aside from that?'
That's probably the best way to start.[43]

In other words, providing solid psychosocial support involves good listening skills to attend to the emotional needs and subtext underlying the concerns of protégés. Psychosocial support boils down to being perceived as a friend who is there to help within the limitations set by general business acumen and the overarching strategic goals and the core message. Bill Reiser, president of Pulte Home's Delaware Valley Division makes it a point to form friendships with his followers whenever possible. He is particularly proud of his people's efforts to spur his division's growth from 200 homes in 1996 to 850 homes in 2002. According to Rieser, his direct reports are like "*comfortable old friends*" who can concentrate on the big picture of where the organization is going, and how they can best contribute to the vision on a daily basis.

> You know, my direct reports I view as friends. Certainly, if they come to me with a personal problem, you have to treat it in the environment that we are in the business—in a business environment. But certainly, I think outside of that I can be very helpful. You just have to make sure that a line is drawn. That's kind of an esoteric answer. I would do anything to help the people who work for me on a personal basis that's within the bounds that I can do as an employer.[44]

Lending a Helping Hand for Personal Issues

Any leader can coach and mentor followers regarding professional issues. But to truly display IC requires going the extra mile for your followers by helping with personal issues, if and when you are asked. Each of us comes to the work with personal issues that can affect our thinking, motivation, mood and interpersonal relations with co-workers and customers. We are all "in the middle of something." The spillover of personal problems into the one's work is a byproduct of the increasing challenges faced by today's employees who struggle to integrate and balance their work and personal lives. Workers are spending more and more time on the job, and have less time to tend to their family-related obligations. This causes stress, burnout and lowers productivity levels in the workplace. It's fast becoming a major corporate issue.

The traditional corporate view is that personal problems are supposed to stay at home. However, issues such as alcohol, drugs, divorce, or family breakups are increasingly creeping into the workplace and causing huge headaches for the traditional people who handle these issues—the HR department staff. But the personal issues of individual employees have cascading effects on all members of the organization. To say personal problems are personal and not part of doing business or what should matter to executives is senseless. Strategy-focused leaders need to talk about them and help find solutions for the problems.

Clearly, most senior executives do not have the time to address the personal needs of every employee. However, many of the executives we interviewed devoted a portion of their day to engage in "Good Samaritan" organizational citizenship behavior. Such was the case for a top executive at Eastern Com who told us:

> Probably 95 percent of the day is spent on business and 5 percent on [employees'] personal needs. The way you help the most [employees] is to ask if they want help. The first thing that I do is ask "Do you want to talk about it?" You really can't go in and tell an organization this big what to do. You have to let them know that their approach and your approach is one and the same. It is quite easier to fix things if the employees handle their problems on their own at first, and they then ask for [your] input later on. The other way you help is to remind them of [similar] situations that they had or you had. What you are doing then is pushing them in the right direction and helping them along the way.[45]

Being recognized by employees and community members as a role model with "all the right answers" was also something that the former CEO and President of ADS Business Solutions experienced. She has been profiled in the media as an incredible woman who grew up in the projects in the Bronx section of New York City, and went on to achieve greatness in the business world. In her case, she has been requested to help not only her associates, but also members of the general community:

> There are many, many people out there that believe that I am a loner that sits up in my home and very rarely beams out. The fact is there is [only] so much bandwidth that you can deal with [regarding employees'] issues and challenges. The more senior I have become as an executive, the less engaged I have become in dealing with personal problems, but you can't ever turn your back on issues . . . I have actually the general public writing to me asking me to help out with problems they have with their children, issues like that. I try to always make time for people and recognize, but I think the more seasoned I have become, the more effective I have become at coaching people to accept the responsibility to find solutions on their own. In other words, I have become more of a facilitator as opposed to the problem solver . . . So I think there is a way to achieve that balance where you area not cold or untuned to personal issues, but you realize you are on a mission to achieve larger end state. And you have to do that and balance the whole thing out.[46]

For these and other executives we interviewed, the general consensus was that because their followers are an integral strategic resource, they need to care about the personal problems of followers, but not too much! In other words, there needs to be an appropriate balance between caring, and caring to the detriment of time spent on purely business functions, such as planning, customer relations and day-to-day crisis management tasks. If the follower's personal issue was development-related, most executives felt more comfortable working to bring them from point A to point B. But if it concerned messy personal issues, such as trouble brewing at home that is affecting their work, or something of a medical nature, that's where the executives felt they were out of their comfort zones. Most of the latter cases are referred to and handled by their HR departments. In both cases, however, the issues were dealt with as quickly as possible in order to build strong relationships between the executives, the challenged employees, and the HR departments based on compassion, dignity and trust.

To summarize, this chapter has illustrated several ways you can develop your people and embrace them as a most vital element that drives a successful SFL system. To be an effective strategy-focused leader, always remember two things. First, in technology-driven industries, good followers are worth their weight in gold. Second (and most important), always maintain a good dose of nurturance, humility and compassion while relating with your followers. Never forget that we all enter and leave this world the same way.

CHAPTER 6

INTEGRATING THE RIGHT PEOPLE AND TECHNOLOGY

> Technology is destructive only in the hands of people who do not realize
> that they are one and the same process as the universe.
> —*Alan Watts*

Ironically, nowhere are people more important than in organizations
which rely on technology to accomplish their missions. Technology oftentimes constitutes one form of *structural capital* which represents the tools
and infrastructure that supports the human capital, including physical systems used to transmit intellectual capital.[1] Developments in science and
technology are continually creating more white collar and technical jobs,
changing the way we perform our jobs, altering social roles and norms for
a knowledge-based society where opportunity knocks for organizations willing to integrate human and structural capital. Various high technology-driven companies we studied ranging from IT firms, such as
Qualcomm, Eastern Com and ILR Global to investment firms, such as Barclays Global Investors and Vanguard, are using Internet-based systems to
link with key stakeholders to gain the advantage on their competitors. Life
sciences companies, such as UCB Pharma and Lancaster Radiology Associ-

The Dream Weavers: Strategy-Focused Leadership in Technology-Driven
Organizations, pages 115–139
Copyright © 2004 by Information Age Publishing, Inc.
All rights of reproduction in any form reserved.
ISBN: 1-59311-110-X (paper), 1-59311-111-8 (cloth)

ates, are exploring new ways to jump-start collaboration and communication among the users of their state-of-the-art products and services.

With the rapid pace of technological innovation and development in these and other industries comes increased demand for executive leaders who can provide their followers with the best tools to enable their organizations to achieve their strategic goals. In this chapter, we explain how SFL can satisfy this demand by driving collective actions to facilitate, synchronize, and integrate all of the various players and technology tools associated with an organization's critical initiatives as outlined in its core message. Integrating human and structural capital is a collective affair. An executive's ability to connect the right people and technology requires coordination and active cooperation by a large cast of motivated associates, all of whom must be committed to and intimately involved in supporting the core message and strategy.

VALUE-BASED BONDING OF STRATEGY, PEOPLE AND TECHNOLOGY

In the U.S. information technology (IT) consulting market, for instance, we saw firsthand how Greencastle Consulting built its reputation as a high quality "can do" enabler of their clients' project management and development needs. Working on projects that range from $3 million to $200 million in size, Greencastle has helped organizations such as SCT, PECO, Exelon Energy, General Electric, and Lockheed-Martin yield maximum value and return on their IT investments. Greencastle works to deliver IT projects within time, budget, and quality specs using associates with prior U.S. special forces military service.

Greencastle's founding partner and President Celwyn Evans has created a "special forces" military-modeled, strategy-focused, value-driven organization that is a prime example of our concept of an organization driven by SFL. Evans' role is to connect three vital components necessary for strategic success: his "go-to" people, his methods of coordination (cutting edge technology and management tools such as total quality management), and his customer's definition of success. The values identified in his core message are the glue that helps him make these connections. These values articulated by the founder cascade down the organizational levels and become a permanent part of the organization's culture.

Evan's SFL philosophy centers upon Greencastle's overarching mission to fulfill its customers' definition of success. The foundation for achieving this mission is a set of six core values: *service, adaptability, loyalty, teamwork, integrity,* and *enthusiasm.* These values provide guidance for specific attributes, skills, actions and standards that guide the behavior of Greencastle's associates. Evans communicates to his associates and key stakeholders the nature and importance of his SFL philosophy through Greencastle's "Mission Concept Model" shown in Figure 6.1. For example, associates are encouraged to be adaptive, respond to client's needs, be aware of trends in IT, and recognize leadership philosophies that can be applied in their daily operations. In addition, associates who demonstrate elements of emotional intelligence and shared leadership are recognized as successful high-performing associates and rewarded accordingly at Greencastle Consulting. These two leadership styles—building identification with the mission and rewarding positive behavioral performance—when used in combination, have been shown to be good predictors of simulated U.S. Army platoon unit performance during times of stress and uncertainty, conditions characterizing technology-driven industry work environments.[2]

A careful examination of Figure 6.1 suggests that Evans hires, trains and empowers a pedigree workforce with values that support Greencastle's organizational strategy. According to Evans, selecting and retaining his "go-to" people is a matter of value congruency or what we described as "follower-culture fit" in Chapter 5.

> You can categorize all workers in terms of "A" players, "B" players, "C" players. "A" players are categorized as the top 10% for a given job at a given salary. So, the folks that we bring on board at Greencastle, are "A" players . . . we have the top 10% . . . we're looking for folks who are really accomplishment-oriented, very goal-oriented, and who have demonstrated achievement, in their recent past assignments. In addition to that, we're looking for someone who has the same type of values, and we're a very values based organization, and so before we can [say], "Yes, you're an 'A' player, come join Greencastle," you have to be aligned with the values that we have as an organization.[3]

Because most of his followers have special forces military experience, they can understand what is required to work in a value-based organization. However, even the most talented followers require the very best tools and resources, or "methods of coordination," to support their efforts. Evans bolsters his associates' mission identification and effectiveness by providing them with periodic training and offering tools that support his holistic coordination methods including management aids (Kaizan, TQM, Malcolm Baldridge) and innovative technologies (artificial intelligence, network systems, bandwidth management, biometrics).

In essence, Evan's SFL is based upon three business principles that create, bolster and perpetuate success measured in terms of performance beyond expectations. First, success starts with a solid strategy, executed skillfully, that requires a *focus* on Greencastle's mission: attaining its customers' definition of success. Second, success is bolstered by building *integrated business processes supported by technologies* that deliver superior value to their customers. And third, success is perpetuated by building *quality* into

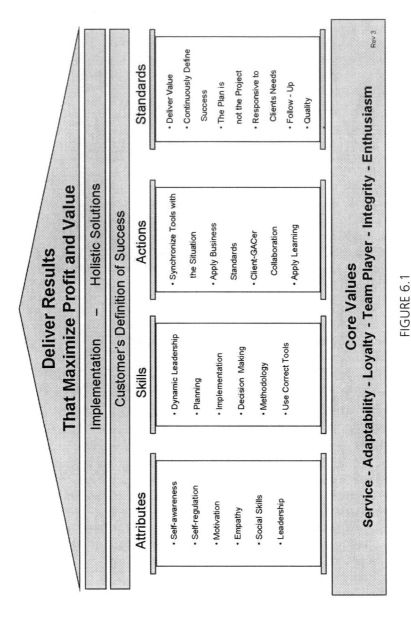

FIGURE 6.1

Green Castle Consulting's Mission Concept Model (Reprinted by permission).

the leadership and management process through a collaborative decision-making framework. Underscoring these principles is an emphasis on strategy support and evaluation at all levels of the organization, supporting the right people with the right technologies, and fostering synergies within and between employees, teams and organizational stakeholders. By connecting people, technology and his Mission Concept Model (core message), Celwyn Evans displays SFL and brings to life the old Welsh proverb, "He (or she) that must be a leader must be a bridge." Executive leaders like Evans weave dreams of organizational success and then make all the right connections to realize their dreams.

THE IMPORTANCE OF STRATEGIC FIT AT ALL LEVELS

A growing number of organizations are facing challenges in connecting their strategy, people, and technologies. With only 3 percent of the desktop computing market, Apple Computer has been forced to re-think how it will remain competitive. Apple is betting that music and movies are on the verge of establishing a profitable presence on the Internet. Apple has been aiming to grow its market share by positioning itself as a quality provider of the audio/visual computer media, such as movies and music files which can be downloaded from the Internet.

CEO Steven Job's strategy was to first create the electronic devices (iMac, iPod) to support the growing markets for computer movie and music editing and making. To do so, he leveraged the human capital of Apple's talented employees and provided them with technology support so that they could create innovative delivery systems for movies and music. His next step was to establish connections with providers of movies and music that customers could "rip, mix, and burn" onto Apple electronic devices. In April of 2003, Apple unveiled the iTunes Music Store, an Internet-based digital music service which sells songs playable on the iPod. One week after the store's debut, Apple's stock price was up 27%. Jobs also considered offering $6 billion to purchase Vivendi Universal Music Group, the world's largest music company. This bold move would provide Apple with more music products which could be directly downloaded onto their electronic devices for a fee. At the strategic level, Jobs is trying to align his vision of providing music with the technology and talent required to boost Apple's financial capital.[4]

Like Apple Computer, the U.S. Army is aligning people, technology and strategy. The Army's goal is to transform itself into a network-centric, knowledge based organization comprised of three basic integrated elements: change catalysts, intellectual capital, and infostructure. Change catalysts include transformational leadership, strategic cultural shifts, and innovation efforts that the Army's top brass have sanctioned in their strategic planning efforts. Clearly, the Army's upper echelons must communicate their core message and expectations to effectively lead these forces of change. For the Army, intellectual capital is the expertise, knowledge, insights and experience that reside in the military, civilians and the Army's industry partners. Infostructure represents the technical systems that support and connect all initiatives defined and driven by the change catalysts and intellectual capital.[5] The Army has been quite successful in its strategic integration efforts based on the awe-inspiring, creative and effective use of technology-based weapons and highly-skilled regular and special forces personnel in the Iraq War which removed Saddam Hussein from power and set the stage for *transforming* Iraq from a dictatorship to a democracy.

In contrast, consider the following unfortunate episode of failed organizational development through technology. An engineering firm that one of our colleagues consulted with was falling behind in keeping current with cutting-edge processes and tools. Most of the engineers were set in their ways and preferred to work individually rather than in the newly implemented system of work teams dictated by senior management. When they were forced to work together by the new team-based work approach, there was a lack of trust and collaboration. In addition, after the introduction of teams into the culture, personal agendas and big egos emerged and competition within and between teams and their members surfaced. In response, senior management decided that the answer to the problem was to install Intranet-based collaboration software designed to facilitate the generating and sharing of ideas and work.

A few months later, the organization made a significant financial investment in terms of technology and training to support this effort, and before long the system was up and running. But few used the system as it was intended to be used according to its designers and senior management. Instead of collaborating and brainstorming, the engineers spent a significant amount of their time trying to figure out how the system worked and how to make it crash, or puttering around researching it on the Internet. Even worse, instead of sharing their knowledge and making connections with other engineers and key stakeholders, they hoarded their knowledge and used any information passed onto them as fodder for political battles to add new levels of "toxicity" into their organization. Some even used it as a forum for basketball pools, jokes or rumor-mongering. Evidently, senior management failed to realize that the technology was not a good fit for the culture of the organization. At the operational level, the engineers were not personally ready to accept a technology that was inconsistent with their firmly entrenched culture.

These examples illustrate the importance of aligning an organization's core message and strategy, its people, and the technology that supports the way the people work together to accomplish strategic goals. The core message provides an understanding of the organization's purpose and broad goals, and the *strategic values* that guide behavior or actions that can attain organizational goals. In a sense, it's the organization's roadmap for success, but it is worthless without a carefully crafted integration of existing human and technical resources. Guided by their own personal values, people around the organization (e.g., employees, customers, suppliers, stockholders) provide the human, intellectual and social capital resources required to accomplish these goals through their behaviors, action and interactions. The relationships among people within and between the organization and its stakeholders are based on shared practices, norms, implied values, traditions, and legal and political constraints that all comprise an organization's *social system.*

The importance of articulating core messages based on organizational strategy and communicating them within the organization's social system to gain commitment from employees is well illustrated by Rick Sanders, Vice President for Operations at JNI Engineering:

> I drew something on the board up here that I want to go through. If you start with a compelling vision you communicate that to people. That floats down into a strategy. From a strategy you go into what the plan to achieve your strategy . . . Once you have that defined then you need to gain commitment from the group. Once you gain this and you set up metrics, its almost as if [you are] monitoring. People understand what they need to do. They understand their work in relation to total company goal. They understand the behaviors reinforced are team behaviors and as part of that they excel. They understand how they are being measured, the metrics and they are almost self motivated.[6]

The monitoring processes and metrics that Sanders spoke of are often automated through technology systems. Technology may provide the tools, methods, knowledge and processes that enable social systems to attain their strategic goals and realize their visions more efficiently and effectively. Technology systems are designed based on certain intentions for the use imagined by their developers, or what is called their *spirit.* Their structural features can be sophisticated, restrictive and comprehensive in terms of the way they shape the social interactions and attitudes of their users. These features and spirit describe an organization's *technology system* that creates structures for doing work and can promote certain work values and shared practices that affect decision processes and outcomes and create new social and technology systems that change over time.[7]

To illustrate, consider groupware systems, which are intended to promote collaboration and communication among users. However, these systems also may be used to strategically monitor work processes of a broad network of followers. Such systems may offer a technically efficient way to monitor behavior. But, they also may also produce dysfunctional social consequences such as restricting the cohesion of workgroups, fostering negative attitudes toward the technology among users, and promoting a "cover your behind" mindset of independence rather than interdepen-

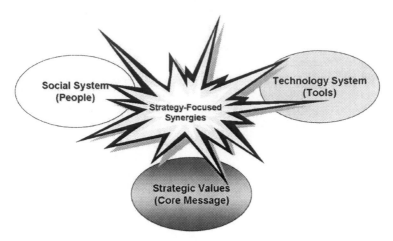

FIGURE 6.2
Strategic Fit Requires Aligning People, Tools, and Strategic Values.

dence among followers. The net results of technology being used for heavy-handed supervision can be social disturbance, suspicion, mistrust, and overall inefficiency of work processes and a shifting of values from interdependence to independence. Any inconsistencies in the values espoused by the core message, the people, and the technology can produce wasteful and costly outcomes for organizations. For example, it is estimated that about one third of all IT development projects are abandoned before completion. The resulting financial damage in the U.S. is about $100 billion annually. The reasons for failure center upon a lack of proper integration of the social and technology systems by the strategic leadership of the failing organizations.[8] These three elements (social systems, technology systems, and SFL) need to be aligned and synergized in order to reap the benefits of expanded knowledge bases, continuous process/people improvements and integrated communications with stakeholders. As shown in Figure 6.2, the integration of these elements becomes an essential task for strategy-focused leaders.

Strategic Fit

The degree to which an organization's strategic values are aligned with the personal values of followers and the values embedded in the technology as intended by their designers reflects the notion of *strategic fit*. At Greencastle Consulting, strategic fit means matching the appropriate "go-to" person with the best technologies whose features and spirit are consistent with values that support accomplishing Greencastle's mission of fulfilling their customers' definition of success. In this case, the corporate values of service and adaptability are required to fulfill the customer's definition of success. Service focuses Greencastle's associates on what the customer views as being a critical to their success. Adaptability allows associates to respond quickly and appropriately in rapidly changing situations with clients by generating creative solutions to complex problems and sharing leadership responsibilities.

Consider how these values are essential for understanding how Greencastle *intends* their associates to complete their projects, as described by Celwyn Evans:

> We always try to link people, processes, technology and strategy. We focus on the fulfilling the customer's definition of success by serving customers first and foremost and adapting to the situation as need be. We take our values very seriously. Another way of saying that is intent. So it's not just about the objective in terms of time, dollars, quality, and specifications. There's another component that is often missed and that is the leader's intent . . . To achieve an objective is a very easy thing. Because again you're working with the top 10% of people, you have the very best of technology and resources, so that's not a problem. Was the job accomplished according to the leader's intent? That's the key. A lot of the time, this is more important than just the objective. So, we've incorporated that into our methodologies, and again, getting back to how this started, the people at Greencastle.

At Greencastle, social and technology systems fit is measured at the strategic and tactical levels through surveys of client satisfaction with associates, systems performance ratings, and employee performance reviews. All of these ratings are tied to a multi-tiered balance scorecard system. Projects results are assessed and aggregated by project manager and then to the overall company level. At each level within the organization, from project experience to manager to company, Greencastle strives to fulfill customer requirements of success from a financial perspective, from a customer perspective, from an internal process perspective, and then from a learning and growth perspective. When the customer is satisfied with the consultant and the systems develop or implemented, Greencastle has delivered on the customer's intent and SFL has been successful in securing a good fit among strategic values, technology and social systems.

But are also many examples of situations where an executive's best intentions for a good strategic fit are not realized. Leadership scholar Bruce J. Avolio discussed the potential for strategic fit to go awry using an example that cuts across an organization's individual, group, and cultural levels. *Individual level* effects explain how individual followers are affected by the notion of strategic fit. *Group level* effects explain how work groups or teams are affected, whereas *cultural level* effects explain how an organization's culture or shared work practices, values and ways of thinking are affected.

Avolio noted that when an organization's social system has a deeply engrained culture of mistrust, individualism or a police-state mentality, the adoption of connective/collaborative technology, like Intranets and groupware, may elicit dysfunctional reactions from individuals. Users are likely to react to the introduction of new technology in ways that are inconsistent with the spirit of the technology, perhaps commenting *The technology is used to monitor our mistakes, not help us work together.* They are also likely to misappropriate or use the technology in a way that is not faithful to the intentions of the developers, perhaps rationalizing *I will release only my most essential data to my colleagues, but I'll be very selective in what information I share.*

Dysfunctional reactions from groups are also likely to emerge from the introduction of such technology into this organization's social system. For work groups comprised of individualistic members, the adoption of Intranets and groupware may be problematic, perhaps with members commenting *Our group has too many personal agendas for this system to work.* Here the collaborative spirit of the system is inconsistent with the individualistic values and norms of the work group. The individualistic norms and values carry over to how the group members are likely to use (or misuse) the system, prompting them to realize *When we brainstorm, our ideas are steel grey. The system has only allowed us to speed up the sharing of irrelevant or useless data.*

Avolio concluded his analysis of strategic fit by describing the cultural problems that can emerge as a result of poor strategic fit. When an Intranet or groupware system is introduced into a "dog-eat-dog," competitive, and politically nasty social system where mistakes are career-ending events, users are also likely to react in ways that are inconsistent with the spirit of the technology. For example, they may balk at using a group decision support system which features parallel and anonymous communication to promote expedited, frank, and open discourse, perhaps commenting *This is a no mistakes culture. I'm not talking about mistakes in ANY communication forum. Besides, everyone here is out to screw each other. All this system does is to accelerate the pace of screwing!* Users may also misappropriate the system by using it in an unfaithful way that is consistent with their culture, but inconsistent with the intention of senior management or the systems developers, perhaps commenting *Different units now know who is doing what wrong. Sounds more like People Grind to me.*[9]

Our point is this: Like all systems, organizations are comprised of social, technical and planning and monitoring (strategic) subsystems constructed from the connections within and between these subsystems and their external environment. Strategy-focused leaders, who are at the core of the system, are responsible for aligning the values that connect the social, technical and strategic subsystems. Poor alignment efforts can help explain why 70 to 80 percent of all technology systems fail when implemented. Therefore, strategy-focused leaders must learn how to create successful strategic alignments, and understand what type of leadership behavior works and doesn't work when it comes to fitting the right people with the right technology.

Success Versus Failure in Technology Adoption/Adaptation

Many of the executives we interviewed suggested that IT has become the foundation for nearly all of the strategic and tactical business operations in their organizations. The executives' sentiments toward IT are consistent with reports produced by the U.S. Department of Commerce indicating that by the year 2006, about half of the U.S. workforce will be employed by industries that are major producers or users of IT products or services.[10] Despite its pervasive presence in the workplace, IT has experienced an exceptionally high rate of project adoption/adaptation failures, with studies reporting failure rates ranging from 50 to 70 percent. Evidence from studies conducted both in the U.S. and in Malaysia indicates that a *lack of strategic leadership* is one of the leading reasons why these projects fail. In both cases, the lack of strategic leadership associated with IT project failure stemmed from executive or senior management that does not adequately champion the project, does not make decisions at critical junctures, loses interest in the project, and does not monitor the project consistently.[11]

To produce IT project success, executive-level support and facilitation of IT projects is critical. This generally involves high-level strategic project planning and goal setting, conflict resolution, prior setting and project sponsorship or championing. Executive-level support and facilitation provides the traditional leadership functions of initiation of structure and consideration of project team member needs. *Initiation of structure* is task-oriented leadership that involves the leader envisioning a project plan, organizing the work plan to accomplish the plan, and defining the way the work is to be performed. *Consideration* is relationship-oriented leadership that involves the leader showing concern, support and sponsorship for followers and their work. An extensive amount of research indicates that the higher the level of leader activity, where the leader is active rather than passive in initiating structure and being considerate, the higher the levels of individual and group effectiveness and satisfaction.[12] A leader's active involvement and provision of initiating structure has also been reported to have a positive relationship with creative and innovative performance among employees.[13]

This means that strategy-focused leaders need to be actively involved and enthusiastic in championing IT projects so that their enthusiasm rubs off on their followers working on the project. Enthusiasm can be quite contagious and has been shown to build high levels of commitment and identification with the project. When followers identify with the project, they link the values associated with the project (e.g., quality and service) to their personal and organizational values. They also become enthusiastic about what they are doing based on the consistency between the values. Enthusiasm often comes from inspirational leadership that shows followers that the work they are performing is important and grounded in the organization's values and core message. Inspiring followers fills with them with high levels of confidence, energy and enthusiasm required to successfully implement projects.

The role of inspirational leadership in spreading enthusiasm to followers is described by the CEO of one of Israel's largest cell phone service providers:

> I believe very highly in gut feelings. I believe that organizations, regardless of their size, have to have a vision and this [vision] is also connected to inspiration . . . A manager has to inspire the workers. The employees have to know what the organization's vision is. And beneath this vision, there should be a list of values. Every employee should know the list of values, should have the list of values, even physically on his [or her] desk. That's what happens in our organization. It has so for many years, we keep something like this on each employee's desk. It has the five values by which the company or in which the company believes. This is part of the vision and the inspiration for each one. I believe each manager should be very much involved in instilling inspiration and enthusiasm. A manager who does not put inspiration, enthusiasm and vision into his managerial baskets, so to speak, is a bad manager.[14]

Clearly, active participation and enthusiasm shared with followers via the core message can go a long way in fostering successful integration of IT projects into organizations. Enthusiasm and inspiration, as well as other aspects of transformational leadership, such as intellectual stimulation and individualized consideration, can increase the quality of climates in R&D project settings especially in manufacturing settings.[15] When leaders inspire, challenge, and develop their R&D teams, project members of the teams focus more on enhancing quality and are also more satisfied with their jobs. This is more critical in R&D where work is seen as more challenging and less based on routines as is the situation in process manufacturing.

Project failure can occur because some IT executives do a poor job communicating the goals of the project and how the project and its outcome fit in with the overall strategy and/or core message. These problems often stem from executives failing to attain general agreement on goals among senior management, IT staff and users. Or when they do communicate the goals, they are unclear or elusive; the goals change as the project proceeds.

The executives we interviewed varied in terms of how they communicated the strategic goals to their followers and explained how IT project goals relate their strategy. Some executives considered such communication as a top priority, while others favored sharing strategic goals to only top managers or Board members. For those who favored an egalitarian approach to strategic goal communication, goals are communicated at least on a quarterly or monthly basis in a variety of forums (e.g., "all company" meetings, business unit meetings, "brown-bag" lunches) to associates at all levels of the organization. At CB Technologies, employees are made aware of the strategic goals on a quarterly basis during "all company" meetings in which the CEO discusses strategy and the CFO talks about financial goals. Following the meetings, operational level managers translate these goals into what project teams or departments need to do. Monthly updates are provided via CB Technologies' Extranet system.

In contrast, the communication of strategic goals at one of International Chips' biggest units is more focused and direct. According to a senior VP of International Chips,

> The main goal is to be International Chips' top plant. It is also that this place's success is fulfilled and that it provides work for its employees. That's the general part. The more specific goals are judged in conferences of the managers . . . My part is to explain every time to the board, the managers, and to everyone this. People think that if you say it once, they got it but my experience is that the more general goals need to be constantly mentioned. We also have ways of getting input from the employees. We have every means, graphics, audible and whatsoever to distribute our current agenda.

The senior VP also told us that expressing strategic goals should be simple based on plain and simple language that can be understood by all employees. He argued that the purpose of the core message is to focus his people on being International Chips' top plant. Everyone in his organization understands this and has no problem keeping it in mind because he and his senior management team are *very proactive* in constantly finding new ways of sending that message via email, Intranets and other forms of advanced information technology. Their message is similar every time they communicate it, and as a result, employees are not confused about their core message and intent.[16]

Passive Leadership and Its Dangers

Over the course of your career, perhaps you or one of your bosses held the following attitude:

> Why mettle in the affairs of your employees? I don't care if they do or if they don't, it's their job and I'm paying them good money to do it. Besides, if and when they do something wrong, I'll let them know about it. I believe in empowerment and managing exceptions. Let them make their own deci-

sions, but if I see them doing something wrong, then I'll get involved. After all, if it's not broke, don't fix it.

At first glance, it may seem that this passive approach to leadership should be the norm for busy executives who do not have the time to take a more active approach to leadership. However, there are several problems with possessing this attitude toward leading others. First, SFL involves aligning the organizational values espoused in the core message with the personal values of followers at all levels of the organization. As we saw with the Greencastle Consulting and International Chips examples discussed above, strategy-focused leaders are proactive in facilitating this alignment. Second, empowerment is not the same as passive leadership. With passive leadership, the leader is not interested or actively involved in the followers' work. The leader avoids taking a stand on issues, doesn't emphasize results, refrains from intervening, and doesn't follow up regarding work progress. With empowerment, the leader builds the confidence of the follower by facilitating progress on self-initiated "small step" projects, delegating tasks that develop the follower's capabilities, and responding quickly to any requests for assistance. There is nothing passive in empowerment.

Third, an extensive amount of research has found that passive forms of leadership can have destructive effects on human and social capital, which oftentimes leads to less concentration on work, poor quality work, lowered net income, and low levels of productivity, group cohesiveness and satisfaction. Passive leadership strives to maintain the status quo through a leader's indifference, absence, and delays.[17] Leaders who rely on passive leadership tend to adhere to conservative strategy and present despair rather than hope to their followers at times of crisis. In a study conducted by one of the authors, three months before the demise of their unit, followers, unaware of the fate of their unit, described their leader as passive and desperate. They also rated their leader as one of the lowest in the entire organization on inspirational leadership. Therefore, today's turbulent business environment with its cut-throat competition requires strategy-focused leaders to be more proactive by identifying different needs from diverse customers and incorporating these into corporate strategy.

SFL aims to produce outstanding financial performance, customer satisfaction, expanded knowledge bases, continuous process/people improvements, shared leadership, and integrated communications with stakeholders. Outstanding financial performance requires proactive strategy and effectiveness from the perspectives the customer, the organization's processes, and employee development. Expanded knowledge bases and connections with stakeholders require a proactive assessment of the business environment, networking within the environment, and selection of employees and technology that can supply such expertise and connections. Clearly, the status quo will not do.

To avoid passive leadership, you must understand what passive leadership represents. Passive forms of leadership are comprised of two behavioral elements: *passive management-by-exception* (MBE-P) and *laissez-faire* (LF) leadership behaviors (see the Appendix for more details). MBE-P behavior involves waiting for things to go wrong before taking action. In other words, if it's not broke, the leader doesn't fix it. LF behavior involves leader delays, absence and indifference. With LF, we're really describing *non-leadership*: the leader simply could not care less.

The executive leaders in our sample displayed significantly lower levels of passive leadership in terms of LF than managers in a very large international sample assessing such behavior.[18] However, there was some variance in the frequency which the executives displayed MBE-P and LF behaviors. Some spent little time displaying MBE-P and LF to their followers, while others viewed MBE-P and LF as a form of empowerment and integrated it into their SFL. We also found that female executives, on average, displayed significantly lower levels of passive leadership than male executives.[19] Display of passive leadership was similar among executives across the industries in our sample. However, we found that the stage of the organization's life cycle (i.e., its age) was related to the frequency that the executives in our sample displayed passive leadership. In our sample, executives in emerging growth stage organizations were perceived by their direct reports as displaying significantly higher levels of passive leadership than executives of start-up and mature organizations.[20]

Among the executives of start-up organizations who were rated by their direct reports as displaying *low* levels of passive leadership was Rich Sanders of JNI Engineering. Sanders' self-assessment of his passive leadership was consistent with his followers' ratings:

> I'm not sure that I have a passive style at all. There are always priorities. Right? So I have to. There is too much to do and if there isn't, then you are overstaffed. So, with too many things to do, a successful manager will choose the things he lets fall through the cracks. And he makes sure he prioritizes his time on things that are important. So I am constantly prioritizing and spending my time on the most critical needs of the organization.

Sanders suggested that there is a natural tendency in followers that if they are not engaged or not being paid attention to, they tend not to be as diligent or as interested in performing their tasks. As a result, the followers' sense of urgency and their passion for their work will start to recede and they'll feel like their work is more of the "same old grind," instead of being intrinsically rewarding, satisfying, and important. For Sanders, there is a risk that if he focuses on certain parts of his organization, and not others (just letting them be), that his followers will feel like their work is not important, and their performance will decline. Clearly, some degree of monitoring with balanced scorecard metrics is necessary at JNI, but that process is grounded in inspirational leadership through Sander's commu-nication of his core message to his followers.[21]

In contrast, a few of the executives we interviewed were seen by their direct reports as displaying relatively high levels of passive leadership. For example, Richard King, CIO of Everfast Inc. (one of the more mature organizations in our sample), told us that he tends to use passive forms of leadership because his followers' professionalism, knowledge, and accountability often *substitute* for his passive leadership. According to King, he lets things settle naturally from time to time, but he makes a conscious decision to do so.

> A passive or non-active approach would be to make no decision. The main issue is accountability. When you expect accountability from people in your organization, you stress accountability and give them time and space to achieve this accountability. I always prefer not to take action when it inter-feres with the long term goal of personal accountability. Does this always work? No. Does it ever have a negative impact? Yes. But, I believe that the long range goal of accountability requires learning on the part of those strug-gling to be accountable. The consequences in the short term can easily be viewed as negative. However, the consequences viewed as learning are posi-tive. There is a paradox here. Generally, employees take on the responsibility and appreciate the time and space to learn to achieve accountability. When the task/job/project is completed, there is greater understanding and satis-faction. Over time, I think we all feel better and our performance is at a higher level.[22]

King's sentiments illustrate that when followers are accountable for their tasks, their knowledge and professionalism can substitute for con-stant active leadership, and as a result positive outcomes can occur.[23] For King, making a conscious decision to be passive allows his IT professionals to be empowered to learn new skills or technologies and to be accountable to him for showing how their learning can benefit the overall organization. In other words, passive leadership without accountability generally yields lackluster results, but selective passive leadership coupled with accountabil-ity on the part of the leader and followers may empower followers to learn for the greater good of the organization.

Another executive who we interviewed described the somewhat passive nature of his interventions in decision making in an example of a key meeting in his organization:

> There was a meeting regarding a line of products last week . . . I participated there as a guest. I was equal over there. I did not lead the discussion. I lis-tened. Usually I would walk out of a meeting and come back towards its end. The organization has to know how to run itself. The best organization is one that can run without its general manager, which means that the manager implemented all the tools put the things in place so everybody knows what to do. Anytime there's some sort of knot in the work it has to be untied.

For this executive leader, knowing when to sit back and let things settle naturally versus when to get involves is the key to being a bridge between people, technology, and the mission being pursued by his organization. Sometimes the bridge is there for support, and sometimes it is there reaching out over the gaps between human, social and structural resources to forge the strong bonds of alliances between people, teams and organizations.

MAKING THE RIGHT CONNECTIONS

Passive leadership may be appropriate in a select few organizations where followers' professional, knowledge, skills, or abilities can substitute for more active forms of leadership. But for most technology-driven organizations, the challenges of intense competition, rapidly changing environments, demands for constant technological innovation, and pressures to form networks with key stakeholders are no match for passive leadership. We believe that more active forms of leadership that inspire, develop, role model and challenge followers to achieve performance beyond expectations should create superior results. This set of leadership behaviors is referred to as *transformational leadership* and is described in detail in the Appendix.

As indicated by the results of our study, transformational leadership behavior is appropriate for executives in technology-driven organizations for several reasons. First, transformational leadership promotes change and adaptation. The executives who were rated by their direct reports as displaying high levels of transformational leadership told us they thrived in situations of radical change. To effectively promote SFL requires dealing with the stressful forces of change. A recent study conducted by one of the authors found that transformational leadership behaviors displayed by CEOs from 32 Taiwanese high-tech companies had a positive relationship with organizational innovation. When employees who perceived their CEO to be a transformational leader who displayed inspirational motivation and intellectual stimulation, their companies spent a higher percentage of money on R & D for new products development and eventually obtained a higher number of patents.[24]

Second, executives who display high levels of transformational leadership told us that they use their ability to influence followers to form effective networks with customers, suppliers and business partners. Such networks are vital for the gathering and dissemination of business intelligence and the development of long-term business relationships based on loyalty and trust.

Third, transformational leadership at the executive level often challenges internal organizational deficiencies. From the transformational perspective, bureaucracies that bog down innovation, collaboration and morale are organizational structures to be despised, destroyed and eliminated from the culture. In technology-driven organizations, bureaucracy is a beast of burden that transformational strategy-focused leaders are on a mission to slay. Finally, transformational strategy-focused leaders create conditions that allow followers to innovate. They build cultures that promote learning and innovation and support these efforts with the best tools and technologies whose spirit is consistent with the organization's culture. If the culture is not ready to embrace a technology whose spirit is consistent with the values of the core message, they introduce organizational change initiatives that foster the alignment of followers, technology and the core message.[25] To produce dramatically higher levels of performance, executives must display transformational SFL that connects the right people with the right technology in line with the right values as described in the core message.

Building Social and Structural Capital with Transformational SFL

The essence of SFL is making connections between people, processes, technology and the core values that underlie the organization's vision and strategy. The connections between the right people help to develop the organization's human and intellectual capital and shape the business relationships and social capital that are important for organizational success. For example, human and intellectual capital can be built by matching younger, more inexperienced followers who possess potential talent with more experienced followers who are committed to the organization's core values. Connections between people, processes and technologies create the structural capital that promotes innovation, collaboration and performance beyond expectations. As illustrated in Figure 6.3, making these connections is the job of the strategy-focused leader.

These ideas were vividly illustrated by the CEO of one of the biggest American telecommunications firms who told us that his executive leadership role was plain and simple:

> One of the roles . . . is you have to provide direction. You have to remove obstacles. You have to help change the system and provide resources. So I think there are some environmental things you have to do. But in the final analysis, people are accountable for their own actions. I have to make sure that we don't put people in a dysfunctional or "no-win" situation. I'm constantly working to make sure that people can win . . . It's all part of a never-ending journey to align the company, the people and the technology

Core Values: Inspire, Innovate, Challenge, Develop, Act Ethically

FIGURE 6.3
Building Structural Capital with Transformational Leadership

around the customer and the market and the resources that are required to serve the customer and the market.

He went on to say that the right people are the most important ingredient for success. People come into his organization through rigorous selection processes. They are then trained and paid well and stretched and challenged to perform to levels that they thought they were not capable of achieving. To sustain their high levels of performance, he gets them to really believe what they are doing is important through socialization and training programs and provides them with the technology tools they need to be successful. For this executive, SFL is all about facilitating success by plugging his people into situations where they can be successful.[26]

The socialization and training programs used by this executive are vital for development human, intellectual, social and structural capital. When his followers learn to master new knowledge, skills and abilities, they are developing their personal and professional capabilities. At the same time, their development is bolstering the human and intellectual capital of the organization. When his followers meet new associates and business contacts through professional or university training, or while working on projects, they are forming social capital. When his followers share that the core values and organizational standards and expectations through their acculturation and his leadership, they are building the structural capital that supports the organization's operations. When followers adopt and accept technology tools as useful means to support the core message, they are reinforcing the organization's structural capital. In guiding these efforts to build structural capital, strategy-focused leaders often must rely on advanced forms of information technology to harness the human, intellectual and social capital of geographically dispersed followers.

e-Leadership

One way to build structural capital is to leverage the power of *e-leadership*, the social process of influencing people through advanced information technology, such as the internet, videoconferencing, groupware, or e-mail.[27] Today, an increasing number of followers are separated from their leaders by physical distance, time zones and cultures. As a result, they are engaging in *telework* in which tasks are performed at a remote location either in real time or distributed over time. Teleworkers are required to perform multiple roles such as managing their personal and professional duties from their home. They are working on many projects that have discrete or continuous life cycles that need to be balanced with other obligations over time.

A recent study of e-leadership and telework at the Internal Revenue Service identified several benefits for strategy-focused leaders and their followers. For leaders, effective e-leadership of teleworkers resulted in increased productivity of teleworking followers, higher standards of the followers' work performance, and higher level of satisfaction with the process. For teleworking followers, effective e-leadership resulted in few interruptions and distractions, reduced stress, a sense of balanced work and professional lives, more focused time to plan and perform work, increased morale and reduced turnover.[28]

Despite these merits, when followers engage in telework, they also present e-leadership challenges for executives who are tasked with integrating technology into the organization to increase their followers' productivity and flexibility, technical efficiency, relations with customers, and to effective recruit and retain quality followers. As with any significant organizational change initiative, there are several operational and technical barriers that must be overcome to ensure the successful establishment of a foundation for e-leadership. From an operational standpoint, any follower's resistance to working at a distance via technology must be overcome.

Resistance can be overcome via education and communications that explain how the technology helps accomplish the core message and how it adds intellectual, structural and financial capital to the organization. Teleworking followers may feel that they are isolated from other followers. A sense of isolation can result in lower morale, lost creativity and lowered job satisfaction. Isolation can be overcome by periodic face-to-face meetings and active communication on the part of the executive via company-wide and personal emails. From a technical standpoint, technical support, equipment and security issues must be addressed. Communication and networking problems need to eliminated and backup plans for their eventual emergence need to be developed. In addition, the IT support group needs to understand that their role provides an essential foundation for the execution of the action plans associated with the organization's strategic goals.

The key to overcoming these challenges is to build a sense of trust between your senior leadership team and eliminate any sense of social isolation that may be experienced by followers by leveraging the technology's spirit and features. Trust is critical for managing any long distance work sit

TABLE 6.1
Suggestions for Effective E-Leadership

- Meet face-to-face as a group to set goals and clarify expectations before launching the action plans supporting the strategy. What happens early is critical!
- Use team names, visual images or logos that depict commonality, collaboration and team unity to create a common identity among remote followers.
- Utilize face-to-face and on-line training to reinforce shared leadership and self-management skills and provide remote followers with resources to be successful.
- Sponsor networking groups or chat rooms among remote followers working at a distance for information sharing and opportunities to bond.
- Train followers regarding the features and spirit of the technology. Show them how the organization can benefit from the technology and how the features and spirit of the technology are consistent with the organization's core values.
- Champion innovation and idea generation. To maximize the idea generation, use goal setting and rewards (transactional leadership). To maximize idea quality, supplement transactional leadership with intellectual stimulation and inspiration (transformational leadership).
- Don't introduce intellectual stimulation into the idea process too early. Questioning of assumptions and challenging of ideas can come across as critical carping. Instead, focus first on providing inspiration and goal setting that builds a foundation of trust.
- Build a sense of group identity and confidence among the remote followers by emphasizing the need to collaborate and the interdependencies among followers (transformational leadership).
- Develop personal and emotional connections by showing individualized consideration with each remote follower so that they stay motivated when distant (transformational leadership).
- Establish timeframes for responding to email and reward followers for quick responses. Role model timely responding to email. Be sure to stay in touch!

uation because followers working at remote locations are not only separated geographical, they may be separated psychologically on account of a
lack of similarity in cultures, experience, and values. They are also not subject to direct supervision, which is used to monitor followers in traditional
face-to-face work relationships. As a result, it may be difficult for strategy-focused leaders to trust remote followers, as it may be difficult for
remote followers to trust each other and their remote leaders. We discuss
how to build trust in Chapter 7.

Regarding the technology's spirit and features, our prior research has
found that features of network-based communication and decision support
systems (e.g., GDSS, email) such as parallel communication and anonymity
in brainstorming sessions of chat rooms, when coupled with transformational leadership, can elevate followers' confidence in their group and the
creativity of group products. Such features help submerge the individual
difference among followers and allow them to perceive a real sense of
esprit de corps or team spirit. Such confidence in their team can generate
high quality outcomes and creativity.

In such virtual settings, transactional leadership can also be effective in
leading efforts where quantity of ideas or production is more important
than quality. In these cases, it is important to set and clarify goals and
expectations for followers, evaluate their performance and provide feedback and coaching. Such leadership allows followers to do a better job with
time management, planning and organizing their work, and delivering
expected results in an accountable manner. These and other suggestions
for effective e-leadership, based on prior research,[29] are summarized in
Table 6.1.

STRATEGIC SYNERGIES
(WHEN SMART + SMART = BRILLIANT)

Over the course of history, some of the greatest advances in technology, science, art, music and business have resulted from synergistic collaborations
among talented people. It was Michelangelo and his 24 assistants who actually painted the ceiling of the Sistine Chapel. It was Bill Gates, Paul Allen
and Steven Jobs who were responsible for incubating the computer industry in which we witnessed Microsoft's phenomenal growth during the
1980's. Or consider, for example, the synergistic collaborations between
Alexander Graham Bell and Watson, Henry Miller and Anais Nin, Marie
and Pierre Curie, Pablo Picasso and Georges Braque, Steven Wozniak and
Steven Jobs, Aaron Copeland and Leonard Bernstein, Albert Einstein and
Marcel Grossmann, or John Lennon and Paul McCartney. In each of these
examples, talented and intelligent individuals joined forces to produce
synergies in which "the whole is greater than the sum of its parts." These

synergies emerge because the mind—rather than thriving on solitude—is clearly dependent upon the reflection, renewal and trust inherent in sustained human relationships.[30]

We believe that today's networked economy and advances in technology are enabling executives to promote *strategic synergies,* which connect people, organizations and strategies to produce much more efficient and effective organizational outcomes than ever before. Organizations such as Amazon.com and EBay are connecting with business partners in revenue-sharing programs in which the merchant partner (marketing and selling its products or services) pays a royalty or commission to the revenue-sharing partner who owns the Web site. By partnering with the Hill-Rom Company, the Coastal Cooperative of New Jersey, a start-up life sciences organization, is working to meet the needs of its member organizations with innovative beds, neonatal products, stretchers and other innovative solutions to their partner's business technology problems. Even school districts are harnessing the power of technology by integrating their funding raising initiatives with school-fundraising websites, such as Schoolpop.com and GreaterGood.com, which serve as on-line malls for selling the schools' fundraising products.[31]

There are many good reasons for strategy-focused leaders to form strategic synergies within and between organizations. Due to intense global competition and turbulence in technology-driven industries, speed to market is critical for success. Partnerships between organizations can greatly increase speed to market. Collaborations between organizations also can improve access to global markets. Market and technological complexity are constantly increasing. Collaboration allows organizations to pool their resources to acquire the total expertise needed to best serve the customer. For example, some companies that have traditionally been considered computer hardware manufacturers, such as IBM and Hewlett Packard, have transformed themselves into one stop technology solution providers which offer various technology services (e.g., deploying, supporting, and running technology-related services for clients).[32] Offering high-tech solutions allows their client organizations to focus their core strengths more effectively. In addition, given the large amounts of R&D spending in technology-driven organizations, partnerships can defray these R&D costs.[33]

An entire organizational development industry is emerging around the notion of strategic synergies. For example, *The Collaborators* is a Chapel Hill, North Carolina-based training and development organization founded on the principle that *in today's world people need to connect.* This personal connection, according to partners Vicki Field, Katie Donovan, Karen Monaco and Fay Kaft, creates meaning and the opportunity to exchange strategies, share information and harness the power of partnership. They believe that collaboration is the spark that engages people to develop professionally, personally and organizationally. They have shared common beliefs and values and use "teleclass" technology to deliver their training to a very distinguished list of corporate clients including IBM, LL Bean, Procter and Gamble, Corning, and Glaxo Smith Kline. They truly exemplify successful SFL in a small organization.[34]

Some of the research-based benefits of strategic synergies noted by *The Collaborators* and driven by SFL can also be effective in large organizations. Strategic synergies can open up creative interplay to generate new ideas by accessing knowledge, skills, experience and expertise of your associates. For example, Lancaster Radiology Associates (LRA) has embraced the *community of practice* concept as a tool to share ideas and best practices among its physicians and healthcare professionals. According to Bob Still, the senior leadership team at LRA has strategically designated specific Intranet pages for idea generation, evaluation and sharing. As a result, his associates have learned and developed through interaction, helped each other to solve complex medical problems for their patients, and have developed a stronger culture based on high quality standardized practices.

Strategic synergies can also help to take followers out of their comfort zone (the status quo) so they can identify buried opportunities through their fresh perspectives. Through his professional and personal connections, a top executive at Magnum Credit Card scans his business environment to find ideas to challenge his teams of followers to stay current regarding cutting edge trends and skills so that they can remain responsive to any forthcoming challenges.

> I think the important thing is to be constantly in tune with what are the best practices in terms of the process, and technology of the solution. Not so much wanting to be on the leading edge, but on the cutting edge in the sense that you always set direction so your team will have enough time to prepare, to gear up, to learn about the skills. [This is so] they can create opportunities . . . they can in turn utilize those technologies as a kind of skill set. So it is not necessarily one specific technology, one specific solution, one specific process. More importantly, it's always looking out in a year, two year horizons, making sure the team has the skill sets to do and perform and provide the kinds of solutions required.[35]

In other words, strategic synergies tap the power of diversity and harness the collective talent of followers. They use collective brain power and energy to enhance organizational innovation and identify important trends that will ultimately require adaptation and help re-shape the core message.

Achieving synergy also depends on harnessing followers to contribute and agree on the goals. Yet, leaders also need to link this agreement with sensitivity to markets and awareness of the need to change. According to the CEO of Vee Jay Communications:

> Things change, you think you're the only one, and suddenly there's a competitor that comes up with the announcement that came up with the same or

similar product and you have to provide an immediate answer. This is why you have to have good communication in the leading group. Good communication, then there can be a quick reaction to the things that happen. If everyone is on the same page or on the same plane, it is easy to react. If there is no agreement and no understanding, then every sporadic event could causes more rift . . . the trick is to set up your leading lines of marketing. You have to get them to agree on the method and should have agreement in understanding amongst them."[36]

Adapting to change was a common theme in many of the organizations we studied, including the Vanguard Group, where a Six Sigma quality initiative is integral to their organizational strategy. Remember that strategic synergies are built through the combination of imaginative thinking, trust-building and strategy-focused action. Imaginative thinking is essential for the continuous improvement of an organization's products, services, work processes and people development. Trust-building is a process of establishing respect and instilling faith into followers based on basic human virtues of integrity, honesty, and openness. Quality experts have always maintained that positive synergy between continuously improving work processes, people who trust each other, and a long-term strategy or vision can only be accomplished through team work or social *interdependence*, not independence.[37]

In summary, we have described how strategy-focused leaders achieve enhanced performance by strategically connecting their followers with key constituents and appropriate technologies. We have also pointed out several of the pitfalls of passive leadership at the executive level. Clearly, to fully integrate an organization's social and technical systems requires active and adaptive transformational forms of SFL. The challenge for strategy-focused leaders wishing to integrate social and technical systems is to achieve the "gel" that holds together these systems and makes the systems synergize in a way that their integration is greater than the sum of its parts. What we have described in this chapter and the little that scholars and executives know about e-leadership suggests that creating ownership and building trust may be two important elements of that gel. The bases for and methods of creating ownership and building trust are the topics of our next chapter.

PART IV

WEAVING THE FABRIC OF SUCCESS

As Sandra Stevenson's organization became more mature, she was faced with a set of problems that if not addressed would snowball out of control and run over her core message and vision of success. Her dream of building an organization around RNA interface technology, a highly skilled and knowledgeable workforce, and an adaptable strategy was suddenly resting upon an unstable pillow. Sandra was facing increasing levels of foreign and domestic competition and employee turnover due to the economics of the biotech industry. Among the employees who remained at Nova-Vignette were a contingent who were becoming distrustful of management, complacent, and generally set in their ways. This discontented group of employees was threatening to make Sandra's dream of organizational success turn to dust.

Weaving the fabric of success to strongly and securely support Sandra's dream would require her to find new ways to build and reinforce trust and ownership among her associates. She would also need to support and reward workplace values of innovation, creativity and learning in her organization. If Sandra would undertake such leadership initiatives, they could be directed at expanding organizational knowledge bases and developing continuous improvements in both her people and processes. Realizing the significance of the challenges facing her, Sandra scheduled a planning meeting with her senior management team to identify ways to instill and reinforce among her associates the values she articulated in her core message: customer focus, teamwork, loyalty, commitment, honesty, innovation, and continuous people/process improvement.

CHAPTER 7

CREATING OWNERSHIP AND TRUST

Every time Bush talks about trust, it makes chills run up and down my spine. The way he has trampled on the truth is a travesty of the American political system.

—*Bill Clinton*

Perhaps nothing is more essential to SFL than creating solid relationships with followers based on fairness and trust. Executives who display SFL get their followers to identify with them as trustworthy and exemplary role models and inspire them to excel in performance and show commitment to their companies. As a result, a sense of organizational ownership is created and shared among the followers, often leading to increased profitability. This chapter explores the peculiar rhythms of trust building and ownership creation: how to build a sense of employee ownership and mutual trust as a foundation for SFL; how base and deep levels of trust are established; how rewards are used to create a foundation for SFL; how character is developed for displaying exemplary leadership; how values can be used as empowerment tools; and how strategic goals are communicated to generate a sense of ownership among followers.

The Dream Weavers: Strategy-Focused Leadership in Technology-Driven
Organizations, pages 143–172
Copyright © 2004 by Information Age Publishing, Inc.
All rights of reproduction in any form reserved.
ISBN: 1-59311-110-X (paper), 1-59311-111-8 (cloth)

A MATTER OF TRUST

Trust is a topic that many people seem to mention when it comes to describing leadership. However, few are able to demonstrate trustworthiness or build sustained trust consistently over time on account of the imperfections that mark human nature. For instance, the trust of the American people was betrayed by Richard Nixon and Bill Clinton, when each of these former Presidents lied regarding their involvement in illegal or immoral activities. Tele-evangelists Jimmy Swaggart and Jim Bakker, along with former CEOs "Chainsaw" Al Dunlap, Michael Milken and Frank Quattrone betrayed the trust of their organizations' stakeholders when they displayed ethically questionable behaviors. At a broader level, the corporate scandals at Enron, WorldCom, Qwest, Adelphia Communications, and Morgan Stanley have eroded public confidence and trust in our financial and corporate institutions. Likewise, the sexual abuse cases involving Roman Catholic priests in the U.S. have called into question our fundamental assumptions about the integrity of the social fabric of the Church. As a result, the confidence, respect, and faith that people put in our Presidents, religious leaders, CEOs and time-honored institutions may never be the same.

These examples show that most people recognize trust as an essential element in forming high quality relationships, whether they are with friends or family members, or with employees, customers, suppliers and other key constituents in organizational settings. We propose that business relationships built on mutual trust form the foundation for SFL within and between organizations by providing the "gel" that bonds members of the relationship together. This bonding can create strategic synergies that yield dramatically higher levels of individual, group and organizational performance. According to the CEO of Vee Jay Communications, financial success at his organization is all about building trust:

> You have to create trust. That's it! On which plane that trust has to be built, that's a different story. Whether it's on a base level or whatever, your employees or workers have to trust you. Or if it's not correct, then they can argue with you, they can debate the issue with you. To know that you're open to opinions, that you can change your mind, they have to know that you're not some stubborn mule—you're open-minded. They have to know that if they tell you something that's confidential, it does not get leaked. I would say that it's not necessary being 'buddy buddy,' it's about creating trust. If you can't do that, then what's the use?[1]

The same is true at Pulte Homes, where constantly striving to build long-term relationships with customers based on loyalty and trust is their mantra for success. While building nearly 300,000 homes over the course of its history, Pulte Homes, a Fortune 500 company, has been honored as

"America's Best Builder," and was named the 2002 Builder of the Year by *Professional Builder Magazine.* In the spring of 2003, Pulte was ranked number 19 in the *Business Week Fifty*, a yearly positioning of the top companies in the Standard & Poor's 500. Pulte's honors are largely derivative of SFL which has yielded a 39 percent sales increase and 47 percent surge in profits and the acquisition of Del Webb, which builds homes for "empty-nesters" (people over 50 years of age) who represent the fastest growing segment of the housing market. According to Pulte executive Bill Rieser, trust enables Pulte to provide excellent customer service and technology-driven advanced construction processes:

> When you deal with selling a product such as a home, in our industry, we have to build trust. The customer has to trust us to do the job that they want us to do. And we have to trust each other that we are going to—as a team—be supportive of each other and our business. So honesty and trust go together. Integrity and conducting our business with a high level of morality are the things we want to do.[2]

Weaving the fabric of successful SFL and its outcomes requires moving beyond dreaming about a vision or core message. It involves initiating specific actions that build trust and followers' sense of ownership or commitment to the organization. It is not enough for strategy-focused leaders to "stare up the stairs," enraptured by a brilliant vision. They must also take the first step to empower their followers by instilling in them a sense of ownership and trust. *Ownership* represents a sense of pride in one's work, identification with the mission and core message, and commitment to the organization and the values for which the organization stands. *Trust* represents the willingness of an individual to be vulnerable to the actions of other individuals based on the expectation that the others will perform a particular action important to the trusting individual, regardless of the ability to monitor or control other individuals.[3]

Researchers describe three different types of trust that build different kinds of relationships between leaders and followers. *Deterrence-based trust* is based on fear of reprisal when the trust is violated and thus creates the most fragile and short-term relationship. *Knowledge-based trust* can be developed based on behavioral predictability that comes from past interaction. For example, you might develop a sense of trust when you have adequate information about your boss over time and reliably predict his or her future relevant acts. We refer to this type of trust as *base level trust.* Finally, there is trust that is based on a mutual understanding of each other's intentions and appreciation of the other's values, needs and desires called *identification-based trust.*[4] This form of trust represents the highest level of trust and is based on emotional bonds and connections.

We believe that strategy-focused leaders should strive to stay away from deterrence-based trust and move toward more active and desirable identification-based trust. Leaders can develop such levels of trust when they appear authentic to their followers, especially in crisis situations. One leader who develops identification-based trust despite tough situations, such as massive downsizing, is the CEO of Roote Information:

> I think you try to build up trust with your employees. You don't try to protect them from the truth. You try to be forthright and tell them. For instance, yesterday I said, you know, these 1,600 layoffs that we are making, it's over. What I don't want to tell you is that you can now relax and your jobs are all safe, right? We're still, you know, we just made an acquisition; we know that we're going to make some reductions based on that. We're still going through restructuring, we know some people will unfortunately lose their jobs for that. It's honesty and trusting them with information that creates a whole different level of relationship between employees and managers.[5]

Trust is especially important in technology intensive organizations, such as the ones we studied. These organizations operate in an extremely uncertain environment and employees need to rely on their trust in leaders as a source for stability. Leaders trust employees and team members by giving them the level of independence necessary to develop innovative products. Customers develop trust in companies based on the reliability of their products. We now turn our attention to the issue of building the base levels of trust that the CEO from Vee Jay Communications spoke about, and higher levels of identification-based trust noted by the CEO of Roote Information required to foster a sense of organizational ownership and commitment.

TRUST, STRATEGIC GOALS AND FEEDBACK

Trust is gained when a person is perceived as competent, open, concerned, and reliable. Stephen Covey described trust as a function of two characteristics: a person's competence and character. *Competence* has to do with a person's perceived abilities to perform a task. *Character* has to do with a person's perceived benevolence, openness to alternative perspectives, and integrity or reliability in being consistent in behavior and accountable for his or her responsibilities. Would you trust a kindly but naïve first year medical school student to perform open-heart surgery on you or your loved ones? Would you trust a Harvard Business School-trained investment banker formerly convicted of embezzlement with your children's college funds or financial planning? Probably not. In other words, trust is built upon consistent perceptions of ability, benevolence and integrity.[6]

A key challenge for strategy-focused leaders is building a base level of trust with followers and other constituents. One important reason for strategy-focused leaders to build trust is the ever-changing business environment we are facing today. In the hyper-turbulent strategic situations faced by technology-driven organizations, strategy-focused leaders are called upon to make sense out of the chaos surrounding them and to provide guidance on how to capitalize upon the hidden opportunities in the midst of the chaos. Followers, shareholders, customers, suppliers, and other constituents need to believe—they need to trust—that their organization is heading in the right direction, possesses the right people, processes and technologies to ride out the storm, and will eventually come out on top of the competition. This belief, which represents a base level of trust, emerges when followers perceive competence in their leader and their associates. We propose that base levels of trust can be built when strategy-focused leaders display what is known as contingent reward leadership.

Contingent Reward Leadership

Strategy-focused leaders must demonstrate competence when they work with their followers to set and achieve strategic goals and then reward their followers when the goals are met. According to Robert House, a prominent leadership scholar, followers perceive their leader as effective as long as he or she is instrumental in helping them accomplish their goals. House summarizes this relationship as follows:

> The motivational function of the leader consists of increasing *personal payoffs* to subordinates for work-goal attainment and making the path to these payoffs easier to travel by *clarifying* it, reducing roadblocks and pitfalls, and increasing the *opportunities for personal satisfaction* en route.[7]

Followers also develop a sense of trust in the leader because the leader develops a plan for taking on the challenges that face the organization, is accountable for the achievement of the goals, and follows through by recognizing and rewarding followers for their help in achieving the goals. Planning represents an active approach to dealing with strategic challenges and issues that may frighten followers. When followers perceive that a leader is actively setting goals, defining strategy to address their organizational concerns, and then rewarding them for positive outcomes, their concerns are likely to be allayed.

When faced with fears, mistrust or uncertainty, followers need to focus on what is most important. They need to understand that goals have been established to direct their attention to what is most important and motivate them to meet or exceed performance expectations. Goals affect behavior by

1. directing one's attention toward tasks necessary to attain desired outcomes,

2. encouraging task persistence,
3. mobilizing on-task effort and concentration,
4. facilitating development of strategies to enhance task performance and satisfaction, and
5. clarifying performance expectations by providing feedback standards against which performance can be measured.[8]

These effects on followers' behavior can build trust by initiating a structure for followers to follow, which suggests that they and their leader possesses competence in working toward performance outcomes.

To build this base level of trust, strategy-focused leaders must understand what contingent reward leadership represents. Contingent reward leadership is comprised of two behavioral elements: *goal setting* and *contingent rewarding* (see the Appendix for more details). Goal setting represent a wide variety of behaviors for accomplishing pre-specified objectives ranging from establishing targeted behaviors, actions and outcomes to providing periodic feedback on the progress toward the outcomes. Goal setting is most effective when a leader sets specific and difficult goals and provides feedback of results. In other words, goal setting spells out for followers what needs to be accomplished, how much effort is required to get the job done, what the outcome of the tasks and effort should be, and provides support and information on the advancement toward the goals. Contingent rewarding behavior involves exchanging reward and/or recognition for the accomplishment of goals. With contingent rewarding behavior, the leader provides support in exchange for the required effort and gives tangible (raises, bonuses, promotions) and intangible (praise and recognition) rewards to followers when they perform and meet agreed-upon objectives.

The executive leaders in our sample displayed significantly higher levels of contingent reward leadership than managers in a very large international sample assessing such behavior.[9] Female executives displayed similar levels of contingent reward leadership as male executives. Display of contingent reward leadership was similar among executives in all industries in our study.

Among the executives who were rated by their direct reports as frequently displaying goal-oriented contingent reward leadership was Bill Rieser of Pulte Homes. According to Reiser, goal setting is an important means of building base levels of trust and is a strategic tool for linking associates' efforts to key strategic outcomes outlined in balanced scorecards:

> We set certain objectives in customer satisfaction, financial performance, and employee performance and employee growth and then set objectives to achieve those goals down through the organization. Whatever my objectives are, they are the operating committee's objectives.

Rieser's frequent use of goals to align the expectations of Pulte's operating committee, his senior management team and his associates is common for executives who work for organizations recognized as outstanding performers. During the 1990s, perhaps no one has been recognized as contributing more to the successful building of financial, social and structural capital of his organization than Jack Welch, the former CEO of General Electric. In creating phenomenal amounts of capital for GE during his tenure, Welch developed a goal-setting system at GE that to this day helps to create success through development of human and intellectual capital. This system was described to us by Brian Duffy, President of GE's Auto Insurance division:

> GE has an operating cycle that is world-renown, that Jack Welch started. It starts right around this time each year [June], and it's called "Session One." In "Session One," my management team looks at an exterior five year forecast to try to figure out what's going on out there in the market. And we do a little dreaming and speculating regarding how our business is doing and then we do a SWOT analysis. We just really try to look at the threats and barriers and opportunities out there for business and try to reduce that to some numbers . . . as to what we think we can do against our competitors. Then come around September, we look at the short term aspect of the horizon, you know the rest of this year and next year, and really zero in on what the immediate term looks like regarding what do we need to do to make our forecast happen. What are the gaps we need to fill, both from a human resource perspective and from a capital perspective, money perspective, and from the organizational perspective?
>
> Then we get into an operating plan where we actually set budgets and targets and so forth. A lot of the goals for the organization emanate from setting the operating framework and that's somewhere around the beginning of the year. And then finally, right around the March or April time, we have what's called "Session C" and that's where we look at every employee of the company and rank employees from one to ten, and top 20, middle 70 and bottom 10 percent. We have to force rank them and for those in the top 20, we have to do everything we can to push them and make them excel and stay there. Those in the bottom 10 percent we have to work on the issues we've raised. It does not necessarily mean they are out of the company, we have to find that right niche for them, find the right motivation, maybe it's something we're not doing right. So we are constantly looking at that. That sets the table for the whole cycle to start again. Where do we want to position our employees in the next year? Relevant to what are they aligned with and what are the key deliverables or key success factors for the company.[10]

Several points made by Duffy are noteworthy attributes of the SFL process that we have discussed so far in this book. Duffy mentioned that he and his senior management team engage in SWOT and scenario planning exercises that we described in Chapter 3. These exercises provide strategy-focused leaders with expectations regarding what the most important industry and market trends will be. These expectations can be used for developing and ranking the most important and relevant strategic goals for the upcoming year. Duffy also alluded to short-term goal setting and the need to clarify expected outcomes and define specific action plans that describe the general means or methods for attaining the goals. Therefore, contingent reward leadership is all about clarifying for followers what needs to be done and ways to go about accomplishing these goals.

However, clarifying these goals also requires an active assessment of available resources GE currently has. This allows GE associates to identify any necessary resources they may need to acquire. As such, Duffy also described how he assesses the human resource base, identifying the "A" players, developing those associates who need developing, and finding the right job for people in the organization who may be mismatched in their current role. The process of identifying trends, prioritizing goals, and aligning people in the right roles or jobs that support the attainment of the strategic plan's key deliverables or success factors is the essence of SFL.

Once goals are established and communicated to followers, it is imperative that strategy-focused leaders provide timely feedback to followers regarding how well they are doing in pursuing their goals. Feedback allows followers to adapt their behavior, actions and level of effort as they work toward attaining their goals. The feedback should be provided in a timely manner so that followers have ample time to modify their behavior, actions or level of effort. Leaders who are able to provide specific and timely feedback, and thus create a sense of consistency for followers, are likely to build a base level of trust with their followers based on perceptions of benevolence. In other words, when you provide such feedback, you are likely to be perceived by your followers as being concerned with their successful attainment or achievement of goals. Consistent behavior that shows an interest in other builds trust over time.

Nowhere was this more evident than at CB Technologies, where founder and former COO Karen Borda worked for eight years to develop strong relationships with her associates. These relationships have paid off in the continued growth and development of CB Technologies. In describing the role of providing timely feedback to followers, Borda explains how being available for and supportive of your people is key to building base levels of trust:

> As the company grew, it became more difficult to do, but at least with my direct reports I take the time to set goals with them, and I do touch base with people. I ask "how are things going?" or "Are you having any problems?" In many cases, people will seek me out. I always have an open door policy. I start off by building the relationship [with my people] so people will trust that I will be there when they need me. Once they realize that, they have no problem talking to me. I spend a lot of after hours checking in with my people and helping them achieve what we expect them to achieve.[11]

Helping your followers achieve their goals is only half of the story when it comes to contingent reward leadership. The other aspect involves rewarding your people when they reach their goals or achieve expected levels of performance. It is well established that people repeat behaviors that are associated with positive consequences and avoid behaviors that are associated with negative consequences. Rewards linked to performance represent a type of positive consequence and allow employees to develop consistent expectations regarding their efforts, work processes, and outcomes. For many years, behavioral psychologists such as B.F. Skinner and others have argued that behavior is strengthened by positive consequences through instrumental and classical-conditioning processes.[12]

So it makes sense for strategy-focused leaders to provide consistent rewards that are in line with performance levels to reinforce followers' behaviors that contribute toward organizational goals. This sentiment is shared by IBM's CEO Sam Palmisano, who believes in the power of goal setting and contingent rewarding. When IBM shipped its storage devices ahead of schedule during the fourth quarter of 2001, Palmisano visited IBM's Poughkeepsie, New York facility and spent several hours walking the shop floor, buying the employees coffee, shaking their hands, and telling the employees that they were heroes who contributed to achieving an important goal.[13]

Palmisano used a combination of tangible and intangible rewards. Some of the more common tangible rewards that organizations provide to their employees include stock options, cash bonuses, merit pay increases, trips, company cars, paid insurance, gifts, refreshments, office parties, nice offices, and music piped into the office. Other more intangible forms of rewards can be just as appreciated by employees and include smiles, greetings, compliments, special jobs that develop important knowledge, skills and abilities, recognition, feedback on important or new tasks, asking advice or pats on the back. For the executives in our study who were leading technology-driven organizations, we found a wide variety of rewards being offered, which are listed in Table 7.1.

The most popular rewards used by these executives in our sample were monetary rewards, such as merit pay increases, bonuses, stock options and other financial incentives. The popularity of these rewards stems from society's placing of high economic value on the knowledge, skills and abilities of technology professionals, and the necessity of using future-oriented rewards, such as stock options, to foster ownership in small start-up firms. The use of monetary rewards, such as pay-for-performance, merit-based pay systems or stock options, is designed to build a sense of company ownership among followers. In most of the organizations that favored monetary rewards, the followers' behaviors were reinforced by tying the rewards to the successful accomplishment of the follower's individual- and team-level goals and then linking them to departmental or business-unit goals specified in a balance scorecard.

TABLE 7.1
Types of Contingent Rewards Offered by Strategy-Focused Leaders

- Merit pay increases
- Bonuses, gain-sharing distributions, and spot monetary compensation
- Incentive and stock option programs
- Promotions
- Awards (with plaques and checks)
- Monthly employee rewards (with gift certificates, cash or stock options)
- Public recognition via emails or company rallies
- Stretch assignments
- Education and leadership training programs
- Time off
- Flex-time (blending of personal and work time during the day)
- Chance to present ideas at a "Lessons Learned" meeting
- High visibility projects
- Personal notes of thanks
- Pizza (or other favorite food) parties
- Free on-site food services

For example, the Vice President of Technology at International Chips told us that his organization doesn't reward its associates based strictly on their effort. They measure success based on results. This attitude might sound tough and International Chips certainly doesn't ignore effort. However, after all, the bottom line in business is whether or not the organization reaches its strategic goals. In fiercely competitive technology-driven industries, the difference between success and failure is not based on the amount of work put in, it's all about meeting or exceeding performance goals established for building financial, human, intellectual and social capital.[14]

The same approach to rewarding and reinforcing expected performance is found at small start-up organizations such as PCC Ltd. and at large mature organizations like Roote Information. The CEO of PCC Ltd. told us that he is trying to develop a system to measure company performance, and at the same time the performance of the individual associates, the work groups, and the business units relative to what they've accomplished towards meeting performance expectations. In his opinion, it's important to examine work and reward performance at all organizational levels.[15] At Roote Information, linking specific and challenging goals to rewards across all organizational levels with a balance scorecard is a key driver of organizational excellence. According to Roote Information's CEO, this system, along with 360-degree feedback from subordinates, superiors, peers, team members, customers, or vendors, helps associates focus

on the behaviors they need to display to be rewarded for their performance.

> We keep a multi-level balanced score card, which we publish for every
> employee on the internal web [company Intranet]. It's very clear up front
> what our goals are, what our measures are, what's important to us, what's our
> expectations. We set them high so that it's not all that easy, you know, we do a
> green light for what we have achieved within a certain percent . . . yellow light
> or amber is for certain threshold we didn't target at all. We publish all of
> those and people are okay with this as a basis of that and there's one score
> card and the measures cascade. Then we do annual evaluation for everybody
> and employees are expected to get feedback. The boss is not just giving you
> his opinion or her opinion, they're giving you feedback and coaching based
> on the people that you work with, the people that you work for, the people
> that work for you, and so forth. And then there's always a third party discus-
> sion. So if I'm your boss, and I'm reviewing you, you're not going to get into
> an argument with me because I'm reinforcing. It's not just my opinion.[16]

One of the benefits of linking individual and group-level goals and
rewards to strategic goals is that the linkage shows followers how their
efforts fit into the overall corporate strategy. This can serve to push or
stretch the performance of followers to higher levels that exceed their
expectations. At GE's Auto Insurance Division, Brian Duffy encourages his
followers to take on challenging assignments that stretch their learning,
develop new knowledge, skills and abilities, and gain visibility. He considers these not as challenges, but as opportunities. Its all part of GE's corporate culture of building upon transactional contingent reward leadership
by taking people out of their comfort zone and using transformational
leadership behaviors to challenge them to achieve their full potential.
Duffy doesn't reward his followers just for the amount of effort they put in.
Instead, he sets expectations for taking on challenging assignments and
achieving stretch goals. When this occurs, he considers rewards to be justified:

> What I look for are associates who are willing to take on a tough assignment.
> I really look for that, because that's where you're really going to shine as a
> leader down the road. I think that those who just want to stay back in the
> background aren't challenging themselves. I look for aggressive folks and
> challenges, folks to take the tough assignments, seek out the impossible or
> what seems hard. And frankly if you're given an assignment or go out for an
> assignment and you don't have a knot in your stomach, its probably not hard
> enough. You're probably not pushing your self hard enough. And so I really
> look for those [associates] that stretch. We reward stretch. Those [associates]
> that are just doing something in their sleep will get by, but they aren't going
> to excel. GE has been founded on stretch performance. You only get stretch
> performance by reaching for something that looks unreachable.[17]

In addition to using stretch goals and rewards to attain high levels of performance, several of the executives we interviewed noted that it is vitally important that the rewards be distributed to the deserving followers *as soon as possible.* The proximity of the reward to the desired behavior helps followers to perceive a connection between the desired behavior and the reward. This idea, known as the "Law of Effect," was coined by Edward Lee Thorndike and states that of several behavioral responses made to the same situation, those which are *accompanied or closely followed by* satisfaction to the person will, other things being equal, be more firmly connected with the situation, so that when it recurs, the responses will be more likely to recur.[18] So, according to the Law of Effect, rewards accompanying or closely following desired behavior of meeting goals are likely to encourage followers to repeat their desired behaviors. One executive who uses this principle is Norm Thomas, the Director of Business Development at Qualcomm:

> I do use rewards as a tool to recognize people. The key is in most of these cases the reward and recognition must be right after, very rapid after good behavior or accomplishment. So distribute the reward the same day or the next day, or else it is really kind of limited in its effectiveness.[19]

Whereas the executives in our sample recognized the importance of distributing rewards in a timely manner, not all were sold on the importance of exclusively using monetary rewards in technology-driven organizations. For example, John Yi, KES Software's founder and CEO, told us that in the early days of his company, he immediately provided his deserving followers with bonuses, monetary compensation, or a combination of different financial compensation. But then he found out that these rewards had a negative effect on his followers' level of motivation and effort. That's because the rewards were perceived by his followers as more of an *entitlement*, rather than something they felt good about doing based on performance expectations. In other words, their motivation shifted away from being intrinsically related to the nature or importance of the task to something they were entitled to receive from management. If it was a very intrinsically motivating or interesting task they accomplished for the company, then Yi felt his followers valued what they did more than the actual monetary rewards. He now provides his deserving followers with a balance of monetary extrinsic rewards and non-monetary intrinsic rewards.

> It is a balancing act . . . I take a little more of a delayed approach. We have set bonus schedules here and annual reviews, cost of living adjustments, quotas, etc. Beginning every year on January 1, everyone gets the [cost of] living expense increase, in addition to their performance evaluation that is conducted at the end of our fiscal year. The bonus is also given out at the same time it's an annual event. And I try not to do monetary bonuses instantly or exclusively, so we also try to do gift certificates, things of that nature.[20]

Focusing exclusively on distributing monetary rewards, rather than balancing them with non-monetary rewards, can have detrimental effects on followers' creativity and innovation, which are essential forms of intellectual capital required for survival in technology-driven industries. A large amount of research has found that the expectation of reward can actually undermine intrinsic motivation and creativity of performance. The detrimental effects of extrinsic monetary reward appear to stem from a reduction of intrinsic interest in tasks. According to some researchers, tasks become less interesting when management only focuses on extrinsic rewards to boost employees' performance because they may perceive that they are performing the task not because they enjoy the task or want to perform the task, but because they will be rewarded by another person for performing it. As a result, they loose their sense of self-determination and self-control. In effect, they may perceive themselves as automatons controlled by "carrots and sticks," essentially being reduced to a professional version of "Pavlov's Dog in Pinstripes."[21]

This sentiment was shared by several of the executives we interviewed including Beth Bloom-Gardner, founder and President of the Bloom Institute, an executive coaching and development organization with many clients working in technology industries. Bloom-Gardner has conducted executive coaching and leadership development for over 1,500 executive and IT professional clients from organizations such as Citibank, Disney, Pennsylvania Power and Light, Borden, TRW Inc., Estee Lauder and JC Penney. She uses non-monetary contingent rewards in almost every opportunity she can find. Bloom-Gardner tries to be positive and provide positive feedback and recognition. She feels that providing recognition is critical because people need to feel good about what they are doing.

> What I find to be most affective is verbal affirmation. It's funny, because to see Corporate America trying to use monetary or different types of rewards, that seems to go against the norm. I think people just want to hear that they are doing a good job. I do. If someone says to me "I can't thank you enough, you have done an incredible job," that means more to me than money. Don't misunderstand me, we all want to be [financially] rewarded for what we do, but I think that [non-monetary rewarding] is critical.

Like the executives at GE, Bloom-Gardner provides challenging tasks, stretch assignments and opportunities that are aimed at developing her clients and associates. In the process of developing her associates, she provides support, stays in touch with them, and helps them with stubborn "roadblocks" to their professional career advancement. She has conversations with them to clarify what needs to be accomplished and follows up with them by providing frequent feedback.

> I think it is really important to challenge people and provide support, so we are not setting them up for failure. We want them to be successful. Some-

times I have found in the process of setting goals and challenge assignments, people become somewhat fearful about moving ahead. I think it is critical that you earn trust so that they feel support and are comfortable in that process.[22]

Building base levels of trust by providing non-monetary rewards to followers is also advocated and practiced by Rich Sanders, Vice President of Operations at JNI Engineering. At JNI, Sanders provides free Cokes, water, coffee, and Espresso machines on every floor of the office building. Every single JNI employee is entitled to these perks, which cost about $8,000 per month. Sanders also provides a free breakfast every Thursday morning. The breakfasts are social sessions where all employees come in and eat their breakfast together. Those kinds of rewards play an important part in supporting JNI's core value of teamwork. They also help create positive and trusting relationships among employees and help to build a positive and supportive work environment.

Sanders also rewards employees who attain their goals by renting a theater to view movies, such as the opening of the latest *Star Wars* movie. The employees take the afternoon off and they go to the theater to watch the movie. Or they take the day off to go to a local country fair and JNI provides the tickets. Or JNI brings in lunch for everybody. The only catch for employees who participate is that the event must meet two criteria or guidelines: it must involve *meeting as a group*, and it must involve *social interaction* and *relationship building*.[23] These events can build trust by identifying the commonalities among people, creating the ties that bind others together, and dispensing the social cohesion that sustains interpersonal relationships over time. What a wonderful way to reward people and build trust! For strategy-focused leaders, the gift appears to be in the giving.

TRUST, ETHICS AND EMPOWERMENT

Setting goals for your followers and distributing rewards to them for attaining goals is one way to build base levels of trust. In this case, the trust emerges when your followers recognize that you are accountable for their work focus, guide them toward their performance goals, and then follow through by rewarding them for their performance. This type of base level trust is generated by the implied "contract" or exchange relationship between the leader and the follower. In other words, there is an agreement, deal or transaction between you as the leader and your followers: if you provide direction and feedback and your followers meet your expectations for performance, then you will reward them. When both you and your followers consistently deliver on your side of the deal, trust is established.[24] Trust emerges because one party has demonstrated accountability and/or responsibility to the other party based on knowledge, skills and abilities that lead to competent task performance. Therefore, base levels of trust are grounded in the mind and body—accountability based on one's knowledge, skills and abilities.

But you may be asking yourself, *Why does trust have to be based on a contract?* or *How can deep levels of trust be built based on contractual deals, as if all relationships need to be legally instead of morally or emotionally binding?* The answer to these questions is that such exchange relationships are appropriate for establishing base levels of trust, but establishing long-term and deep levels of trust requires building upon a *moral or value-based* foundation that is shared by both the leader and followers. To establish deep levels of identification-based trust in leader-follower relationships, both parties need to identify with and be committed to shared moral values, character, standards and principles, which serve as guideposts for behavior. When these moral guidelines are ingrained in the self-concept of both the leader and the follower, the leader and follower are likely to share ideals, norms, and expectations of behavior. A deep emotional, value-based and moral connection emerges to enable the leader and the follower to bond together. As a result, they will implicitly understand or know what the other person will do. They can feel comfortable trusting the other person and will not have to solely depend on exchanging performance and rewards. In other words, deep levels of trust are grounded in a person's character—the will to do what is right according to your moral values.

Character can be defined as the stable and distinctive qualities built into an individual's life that determines his or her moral and/or professional response regardless of circumstances. Character is developed based on the relationships between personal attributes and behaviors that serve as its foundation as shown in Figure 7.1. That is, character is established by our habits. Our habits are developed by our behaviors and deeds. And our behaviors and deeds come from our thoughts and our will, motives and values. Bishop Fulton J. Sheen, the prominent theologian, philosopher and seminal televangelist, considered character to be in the will, not in the intellect. Sheen argued that "education trains only half a man, developing his intellect, but not his will; his mind, but not his character; it gives him knowledge of facts, but gives him no purpose or destiny."[25] In our opinion, it is the responsibility of the strategy-focused leader to fill in this void by providing followers with a sense of purpose and destiny.

A strong sense of purpose can be a strong motivating force for individuals. Sheen suggested that followers differ in terms of the amount of motivation or will they possess to perform either good or bad deeds. For example, some followers may possess 10 "units" of motivation, whereas others may possess 100 "units" of motivation. However, a follower with only 10 "units" of motivation can outperform a follower with 100 "units" of motivation, if he or she is guided by constructive or pro-social forms of leadership. Therefore, it is important for followers to seek and find positive role mod-

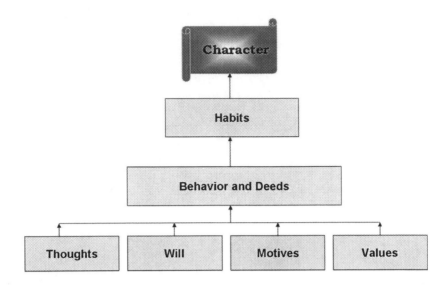

FIGURE 7.1
The Shaping of an Individual's Character.

els or pro-social leaders who can help shape followers' character. If Sheen's logic is valid, then it is important for strategy-focused leaders to exemplify or role model the core values that can strengthen the will and motivate and guide the behavior of followers and colleagues.

Demonstrating Exemplary Leadership through Idealized Influence

Today it is a moral imperative for executives to advocate exemplary leadership to build character in followers. Ethical fiascoes, such as those seen at Enron, show what leaders and followers are capable of when greed, arrogance and raw ambition are left unchecked. These vices need to be constantly checked against ethical guideposts, so that a myopic rush to fuel the economic success of an organization will not run amuck at the expense of character. Strategy-focused leaders concerned about their followers' character should take a personal and deep interest in their followers' most compelling virtues as well as their most noteworthy vices. In performance reviews or coaching sessions, they should focus their attention on the follower's predominant failing or vice, and by fighting against it, they can finally perfect the qualities contrary to the previous faults. In a sense, the follower's motivation or will is moved in the direction of perfection by transforming infirmities into strengths. This process is made tangible by training followers to look for the bad qualities or vices in themselves, whether they are pride, covetousness, lust, anger, envy, gluttony or sloth. It also involves training the followers to pay attention to and emulate the virtues and good or best qualities in others, especially in those of their leaders. Admirable virtues that strategy-focused leaders can advocate for their followers include prudence, justice, fortitude, temperance, faith, hope and charity.[26]

One way that the executives we interviewed were able to put Sheen's ideas into practice was to exemplify constructive forms of leadership by displaying idealized influence behavior for their followers and constituents. Exemplifying constructive forms of leadership requires that you, as a leader, engage in behavior that presents yourself as an appealing role model, so that your followers will want to emulate your behavior. For example, you may call for a return to basic virtues, ethical values or values espoused in the core message. But it is not enough for you to talk about these virtues and values. As an idealized leader, you need to consistently model the virtues and values—you must "walk the talk."[27]

Role modeling or exemplifying constructive pro-social leadership involves the leader displaying *idealized influence* behavior and followers attributing or reflecting idealized influence back to the leader.[28] Leaders who exercise idealized influence impress their imprint on their followers and in return their followers use this imprint to imitate the leaders. The leaders' beliefs, virtues, values, behaviors, goals, habits, and affections become part of the organization and tend to be reflected in their followers. It is as if all of these personal internal attributes of the leader shine on the followers. Because the glow of idealized influence is within the leader, it can be shined upon the followers so that they too can radiate the same values and behaviors as the leader. As a result, followers perceive the leader to displaying role model behaviors through exemplary personal achievements, character, and/or behavior. Several behaviors that strategy-focused leaders can display so that their followers can perceive them as idealized leaders are listed in Table 7.2.

An interesting aspect of idealized influence is that those who exercise it are often somewhat separated from the masses because their personal standards of ethical conduct and performance are significantly higher than those of the masses. It takes a special kind of leader to exercise idealized influence. Individuals with mediocre and weak characters succumb to the moods and fashions of the moment. They simply go along to get along. There are multitudes of these types of "leaders" (who behave more like managers—not leaders) in organizations. But the most innovative and idealized leaders are singular and unique—leaders like Sam Walton of Walmart, Lou Gerstner of IBM, Mary Kay Ash of Mary Kay Cosmetics, Herb Kelleher of Southwest Airlines, Don Clifton of the Gallup Organization, or Jeff Bezos of Amazon. It is as if each of these leaders "glow" or act as a

TABLE 7.2
Types of Leader Behaviors That Generate
Perceptions of Idealized Influence

- Demonstrate unusually high competence and achievement
- Celebrate followers' achievements
- Take personal risks that can benefit the organization
- Appeal to the hope and desires of followers
- Address crises head on
- Rise up and face the moral issues that affect the organization
- Demonstrate a high level of activity in organizational affairs
- Be willing to share the limelight
- Create a sense of joint mission and ownership
- Be positive and enthusiastic
- Set high moral and performance standards for all organizational stakeholders
- Show dedication to followers and the organization's core message

(Adapted from: Bass, B.M., & Avolio, B.J. (1990). Full range leadership development basic workshop manual. Binghamton, NY: Center for Leadership Studies, SUNY-Binghamton, p. 2.36).

bright beacon that guides certain followers in their behavior and energizes them to perform beyond expectations.

These famous leaders rely on trust and link it with ideology. In fact, the CEO of Eastern Com told us how important it is to him to maintain the trust level in the organization and to stand out as a moral guidepost for people both inside and outside the organization:

> There has to be healthy relationship between the people throughout the organization. Mutual trust, democracy, transparency in things where it's needed. Cheating and lying and destructive politics within the company are destructive, like in any company. Whatever you would want from your own society, from your own family, that's what you need here.[29]

It is important, however, to point out that the glow of idealized influence is also reflected back upon the leader depending upon the degree of value congruence, mutual liking and similarity with the leader. As most leadership scholars agree, "leadership is in the eye of the beholder."[30] What one person considers glowingly attractive or idealized may be considered to be repulsive by others. For example, in 1963, the 13-year-old Bill Clinton had a face to face meeting with his idol, President John F. Kennedy. To the young Clinton, Kennedy represented everything that he hoped to one day become. Clinton was enamored by Kennedy's inspiration, charm, wit and humor, his advocating of the values of self-sacrifice and personal courage, and his strong will to overcome physical disabilities to achieve a position of greatness. Clinton's admiration and identification with Kennedy was clearly evident as his face gleamed with joy while meeting with the President. In effect, Clinton was attributing or reflecting charisma back at Kennedy. However, other individuals present at the Clinton-Kennedy meeting may not have shared Clinton's perceptions, but may have looked to Richard Nixon as their ideal leader. The behaviors and attributions associated with idealized influence are evident in Figure 7.2 which shows this historic meeting of the two Presidents.

As in the Kennedy-Clinton "leader/follower" relationship, strategy-focused leaders need to be perceived by their followers as displaying idealized influence to build deep levels of trust with followers. In fact, the executive leaders in our sample displayed significantly higher levels of idealized influence leadership than managers in a very large international sample assessing such behavior.[31] Female executives displayed similar levels of idealized influence leadership as male executives. Display of idealized leadership was higher among executives in the manufacturing industry than in the information technology and services industries.[32]

Among the executives who were rated by their direct reports as frequently displaying idealized influence was the Vice President of Strategy and Business Planning for Ebor Tech Systems. This executive's idealized influence stems from a life history of overcoming the adversities of the Holocaust, meeting the challenges facing his country, making personal sacrifices for the good of his country, and espousing values that focus on peo-

FIGURE 7.2
The Attribution of Idealized Influence
(Used by permission of Arnie Sachs/ Consolidated News Photos).

ple. He was born in Poland, moved to Israel in 1950 and grew up in Haifa until he reached the age of mandatory military service. There he first worked as an Israeli Air Force communications specialist and then advanced up in responsibility to the rank of General, where he was the head of a division for three and a half years. Following his military service, he joined the International Security Board during the Barak administration and traveled overseas. Afterwards, he joined Ebor Tech Systems because he saw a place where he could apply his personal values to help other people become successful:

> For someone wishing to enter a strategic leadership position, let me suggest that you need to succeed in business with people and not on their cost. That kind of success will lead companies to choose you because they'll notice that people around you go with you.[33]

Another executive who was seen by her followers as exhibiting high levels of idealized influence is a former President and CEO of ADS Business Solutions. Like the Ebor Tech executive, she radiated idealized influence, which stemmed from her personal history of overcoming many barriers to reach high levels of professional success as a CEO. As a person of color who grew up in an inner city environment, she had many social and economic barriers facing her. However, her intelligence, spiritual values, tenacity, and non-conformist attitude enabled her to overcome these barriers and better herself by earning degrees from Harvard University and MIT's Sloan Management School. She rapidly climbed the corporate ladder at a large telecommunications firm and then joined ADS as their CEO in 2001. While achieving her phenomenal professional and personal successes, she has been able to touch the lives of many people in a way that defines the essence of SFL. According to this executive, her idealized influence has allowed her to demonstrate SFL over the course of her career:

> There are some people that have that ability to connect with individuals. I have been gifted in that way. And I say that very immodestly because I have people from 25 years ago that still write me long letters and send me little things telling me how I have touched their lives along the way. After everything that is said and done, that is the legacy that has the most profound meaning to me . . . that I have touched many, many lives along the way. Now, I hope that in the process in that journey I have brought profitability to those businesses that I have been a part of and improved the quality of service and improved the innovation of products and such, but the people legacy to me is the one that sustains me.[34]

This executive used idealized influence to develop and empower many followers and colleagues over her career. The impressions that she made on them were reflected back at her in the shared values that influenced their attitudes and behavior, and helped to shape their own success.

Values are Empowerment Tools

One way that leaders display idealized influence is by talking about the most important core values that are essential for achieving organizational success. For strategy-focused leaders, these values often are found in the core messages that they communicate to (and role model for) their followers over and over again. Values espoused and role modeled by strategy-focused leaders can serve as powerful mechanisms that guide and empower followers. This is important because followers need to develop a sense of independence in order to grow into their organizations' leadership positions.

Empowering followers boosts their level of confidence and independent decision-making capabilities. Values promote empowerment of followers because they serve as principles that can be applied by followers to make difficult decisions in new and complex situations without having to rely on the leader for guidance. If followers recognize that they are conducting themselves according to principled values, they are more likely to be confident in themselves and their decisions. For example, associates who work at Amazon.com are encouraged to make good value-added decisions without asking for permission. Associates compete for Amazon's "Just Do It" award bestowed on those who do something they think will help Amazon without getting their boss's permission. According to Jeff Bezos rewarding his people for valuing critical thinking that is independent and well thought through builds an empowered workforce.[35]

Several of the common values highlighted by the executives we interviewed who were rated by their direct reports as displaying very high levels of idealized influence are summarized in Table 7.3. According to these executives, the values listed below are important for achieving success in technology-driven industries.

Most of the executives we interviewed who displayed very high levels of idealized influence mentioned adding value for the customer and the organization as an essential organizational value that they espouse. If strategy-focused leaders and their followers are not creating value, whether it is in a one person "mom and pop" entrepreneurial start-up or in a mature 250,000-employee organization, they are not going to survive in the long-run due to the challenging aspects of the strategic situation discussed in Chapter 2. The challenge for strategy-focused leaders is to consistently considering how to create a linkage between the meaning of the work that the followers are performing and how their work is contributing to the overall financial success of the organization. It is very easy for executives of large mature organizations who have 250,000 employees to have a culture where their people don't understand how what they are doing is actually going to contribute to the overall success of the organization.

TABLE 7.3
Values Espoused by Idealized Strategy-focused Leaders

- Adding value for the customer and the organization (e.g., profit-making)
- Creativity/Innovativeness
- Teamwork
- Honesty
- Integrity (e.g., delivering on promises, being accountable)
- Ethical behavior
- Respect for individuals (e.g., fairness, decency, patience, tolerance)
- Focus on people (e.g., professional and personal development of associates)
- Pride and ownership of one's work
- Quality and continuous process improvement
- Entrepreneurship/Initiative
- Open communication with associates (e.g., constructive debate based on "what is said, not who said what")
- Spirituality
- Loyalty
- Trust
- Humor

To address this problem, strategy-focused leaders need to espouse value-enactment (putting core values into practice through exemplary behaviors) by articulating, role modeling and then rewarding very clear objectives set for the work that needs to be performed. Such an approach can foster employee ownership and commitment to achieving organizational goals. Several executives, including the former CEO of ADS Business Solutions, emphasized this point:

> The key is to get people fully engaged to understand how and what they are doing contributes to the bottom line and then to establish incentives associated with the quality of that that work. That has to do with understanding, for example, the whole structure of economics: how the surfaces of this enterprise basically are valued by a market place comprised of consumers, so ultimately our goal is to be able delight the consumer. So, how is what I am doing affecting that, even if I am several steps removed from interfacing with the consumer. How am I connected to bringing value to the enterprise?[36]

Besides promoting values of profit-making and building ownership, the executives who excelled at displaying idealized influence mentioned integrity, innovation, quality and showing respect for the individual as other important core values. While espousing these values, the executives try to put themselves in the position of the person who may be affected by their attitudes, values or behaviors, whether it is a follower, colleague, client, supplier or potential customer. For example, the CEO of Concord Inc. told us that certain key values are, as Thomas E. Ambler, Stephen Covey and other authors have argued, like a "moral compass" that always point people in the right direction.[37]

> When I first became a chairman the first time around in 1983, the people that worked with me, we had a group of six of us, five people reporting to me. One of the first things we did at the urging of some consultants, was to put down our values. A lot of them were fairly self-evident. One of them is integrity. Well, integrity has been around for 150 years [the age of the organization], it has not just been since 1983. But they [the values] had never been clearly articulated to the organization. It took us about two years to get them out, because we would put out a set, and then we asked for reactions and people would come back and say: "You are crazy," or "This ought to be there," and mention different values. But we finally got it finished. In about 1985, we put the values out and there is only one word that has changed since that time. . . . I do not think values should change, I think these are the rocks on which you hang your hand.

This CEO advocates the approach suggested by Jim Collins whose research suggests that *organizations that enact or live out their values enjoy greater success* than those that don't. Collins found out that highly successful organizations like Disney, Ford, Motorola, and Hewlett-Packard, had a core value-based ideology that guided them in times of upheaval and served as a constant bench mark, a rock-solid guidepost. Such values help to shape the foundations for all business relationships, all leader/follower interactions, all expectations between parties in business relationships, trust and ownership within organizations, and even the goals that focus organizations toward success.[38] This point is emphasized by the CEO of Concord Inc.:

> Our goals relate to our values. I believe that context is very important before you get in to content. Content is the strategies and the things like that. The context is how are you going to live? How are you going to do things? As I am fond of saying: our context is the values, our value system. [We have] seven big values that we really cherish. And as I keep pointing out to people: Values are sort of like buoys in the channel of commerce . . . strategies change, winds change, tides change. But if you have got those buoys that you always come back to, it does not matter what business you are in, you have got those basic values. And I think that if I have one goal it is that we continue to live our basic values.[39]

Another example of the importance of strong values and trusting relationships to delivering strategic goals comes from our interview with a top International Chips executive. At International Chips, where accuracy and keeping strict sterile conditions coexist with innovation and risk-taking, it is the role of SFL to allow maximum employee engagement. The mere belonging to the company is the indication that International Chips values trusting its people. As this key executive describes regarding the values he conveys:

First on the list is honesty, honesty without compromise. Everyone who comes to work here gets a very precious gift: we put trust in that person. I explain to them many times its importance. Second, perhaps, is giving everyone respect. Making sure we all look at each other without hidden agendas or raised eyebrows.[40]

Thus, according to these executives and several of their peers who we interviewed, certain core values listed in Table 7.3 play a big part in the way strategic goals are communicated and carried out through the organization.

STRATEGIC ROLE MODELING WEAVES
THE FABRIC OF FUTURE SUCCESS

International Chips' and Concord Inc.'s goals were largely a function of their organizational core ideology and values espoused and role modeled by their executives and managers. This is true for many organizations— both ethical and unethical. For example, Enron's organizational values of greed, arrogance and raw ambition fueled its relentless and duplicitous pursuit of organizational goals of maximizing stockholder value through a Byzantine system of off-balance sheet financing and a culture of secrecy. In Enron's case, these values were espoused and role modeled by Ken Lay and Jeff Skilling and led to the organization's eventual stunning collapse and demise. Lay and Skilling masterminded schemes that lined their pockets with millions at the expense of their employees and shareholders, and eventually fueled the energy company's tragic failure.[41] It is hard to believe that someone like Lay was characterized by many people as one of the most charismatic leaders of our time just a few years ago.

Unlike the executives at International Chips and Concord Inc., both Lay and Skilling represent everything that strategy-focused leaders who display idealized influence should *not* be! But what about strategy-focused leaders who exemplify idealized influence? How do they go about weaving the fabric of success by establishing and communicating goals throughout their organizations? We sought to answer these questions by reviewing the processes by which the executives who we interviewed (who were rated very highly on idealized influence) went about determining and communicating goals in their organizations.

Determining Strategic Goals

The various ways that strategy-focused leaders determine their strategic goals and the goals they pass down to their followers and colleagues through their organizations are summarized in Table 7.4. While perusing these methods of goal setting, you should realize that goals stem from the organization's strategic situation. They come from the requirements and demands of the environment that your organization operates in, from what your strengths and your weaknesses are, what you are good at, what you are not so good at, who your natural business partners are (or should be), what your personal and business experiences have been, and the history and traditions of your organization. They come from assessing what the most valuable strategies and markets are going to be in the next three or four years, understanding where those strategies will come from, and understanding your environment. When you engage in these goal setting activities, you will understand where your organization is at, where you need to go, and who amongst your people will be able to get you there.

Many of the executives who were rated very high on idealized influence also displayed high levels of goal setting behavior. They included executives from CB Technologies and Scripps Health. Karen Borda, former COO of CB Technologies, told us that the strategic goal setting process in her organization changed as the organization grew in size. Initially she and her co-founder/partner determined strategy alone. As the company grew, goal setting became more collaborative with the active participation of her entire senior management team. They focused their goal setting discussions on determining what they needed to do to be able to compete with their major competitor and what building blocks they needed to be successful. This changed however, after company got its funding. Their sphere of influence shrunk back and now only a key core group of senior management people set the strategy.

TABLE 7.4
Ways Strategy-Focused Leaders Determine their Goals

- Participative strategic planning and brainstorming sessions with the senior management team
- Surveying the types of needs of customers, clients and associates
- Strategic goals are translated into more specific and understandable departmental goals by CEO
- Linking of organizational values to market requirements
- Top-down vision, strategy, customer portfolio and MBO process
- Filtering down of operating committee and/or board of directors' objectives
- Vision, core message and SWOT analysis determines goals linked to balanced scorecard metrics
- Benchmarking or borrowing ideas from other successful organizations
- Independent accreditation or consulting feedback for adapting to the market
- Assessment of core competencies linked to market requirements
- Historical and traditional company goal setting procedures

A similar approach to goal setting is practiced at Scripps Health. Dr. David Shaw, Chief of Staff at Scripps Health, told us that he participates in strategic goal setting in an executive committee, which is 15 members representing the chiefs of all departments and major divisions. He meets with individual managers during monthly formal meetings, but also meets with some managers much more frequently to strategize, look at individual projects, and ask them for their feedback. He relies heavily on the past two Chiefs of Staff and engages in *a lot of brainstorming together.*[42]

Other executives took a more traditional approach to goal setting. For example, the Director of IT at Concord Inc. told us that they use a top-down vision strategy considering product portfolio and linking objective linear process to goal setting. To enable the strategic goal setting process within Concord, he strives to have very strong relationships with the top management of every business unit within the organization. Developing high quality relationships that foster frank and productive types of strategic discussions requires him to talk with the vice presidents of sales, manufacturing, and the general managers of all the division and to earn their trust by being accountable to them by delivering what is expected. "You've got to have rapport and good interactions. It's critical for this function and often time with some people it's not the case," says this executive.

Strong relationships are important for strategy-focused leaders to align all parts of the organization together to work toward achieving the strategic goals. Martin McElroy, CEO of Mercy Community Hospital, told us that he takes what he calls the "Oreo approach" to strategic goal setting processes:

> We have a pretty extensive strategic planning process. I am in the middle. I'm the white part of the Oreo. I have to take the goals of the organization and then translate them into goals for my different units and all the way down to make sure the people can focus on those goals. Our corporate goals are very broad. The business units need more focus.

McElroy recognizes that strategy-focused leaders need to know their people and be able to communicate with them. Some goals he and other executives set are financial in nature, others deal with quality, others deal with developing human resources. Strategy-focused leaders and their colleagues need to be able to reduce broad strategic goals designed for large organizational groups to more *specific* goals that are capable of being understood by members of specific departments. People with very different disciplines and knowledge need to understand what their role is in contributing toward organizational effectiveness. That's probably the harder part of the job of the strategy-focused leader's goal setting task.[43]

To summarize, most of the executives who were rated high on idealized influence and contingent reward described a very similar approach to goal setting. They establish goals on different organizational levels that are derived from their organization's vision, strategic planning process, customer portfolio and management-by-objectives (MBO) processes. And they distill these goals down into specific and clear key success factors describing multiple perspectives of business success. They establish financial goals, customer/client satisfaction goals, quality goals, and people goals. You might be wondering "Why are people goals listed last if they are so important?" That is because all other goals rests upon the people. Everything and every goal starts with people. These goals help to determine the business structure along with the SFL of the CEO and the Board of Directors. And from this they create the business model which followers are made well aware.

Communicating and Aligning Strategic Goals Across the Organization

It is not enough for strategy-focused leaders to effectively *determine* their organization's goals. They also must effectively *communicate* these goals to key organizational members so that everyone is "on the same page" and understands what is required of them to contribute toward achieving their organization's strategic goals. The strategy-focused leaders in our study who were idealized by their direct reports spend a lot of time making sure their followers know where their organization is at in terms of attaining their goals. They make sure that their followers have a good understanding of their markets and environment. As a result, followers understand that their leaders are trying to get them to achieve objectives that are honorable and achievable. Their leaders regularly communicate the objectives to their followers and colleagues and make sure everybody knows overall what the organization needs to accomplish during the year. In other words, strategy-focused leaders ensure that their followers and colleagues know exactly where they are and where they need to go. Some of the more prevalent ways these leaders communicated goals to their followers and colleagues are listed in Table 7.5.

Some executives we interviewed, like the CEO of Tele Spondence Inc., have established teams to make sure all the organizational goals are communicated and aligned within all the business units. It is very important that all associates at Tele Spondence know were they are trying to get to collectively, and what path will get them there. Besides, their CEO can't direct everything that is going on all by himself. Every manager needs to understand where the organization is heading, so that when they must face challenges, they can deal with them and take the right path for themselves—a path that is consistent with the organization's core message. But they always must know that they can expect their superiors and CEO to support them in the path they choose. This is accomplished by understand-

TABLE 7.5
Ways Strategy-Focused Leaders Communicate their Goals

- Informal "brown-bag" lunches and town meetings where executives present to followers and colleagues on a quarterly basis
- Formal performance review and next year MBO sessions
- Values statements disseminated to followers and colleagues
- Quarterly or monthly strategic and portfolio reviews with department managers
- Annual performance reviews
- "Real-time" commendations or requests for corrections
- Objectives communicated and assessed quarterly via multi-level balanced scorecards
- Strategic plans are shared with followers and associates
- Periodic progress reports on goal attainment reported in meetings
- Email and on-line bulletin boards
- Newsletters

ing what they are trying to achieve is consistent with what is described in the core message articulated by the strategy-focused leader.

At Tele Spondence Inc., the executives use a mix of innovative technology-assisted methods of getting the message out to followers and more traditional formal or informal "all-company" meetings. As their CEO told us:

> We communicate [our goals] through [online] bulletin boards, newsletters, individual e-mails. Since I been here, I have had around 2,000 e-mails from employees, and I have responded to every one . . . Sometimes it's not a very effective way of communicating strategy, I suppose, but I never tested this. But when I am sending an e-mail to somebody, they are at least telling their office [what I say to them]. Sometimes it's the most long term way to get the word out. So if people really see it directly, they will probably trust it more, that it was created honestly, that I was not afraid of making a mistake. I try to make sure there is no spin on it or positioning or any thing like that. Eventually everybody will know what I want. I also have meetings with employee groups. I have lunch meetings, meetings were I answer questions. I try to be as consistent as I can be in all those things, not necessarily saying the same things, but explaining to people why there are here, why they are going through so much pain, where we will get to some day as a result of all this, what are our values, why we will be a good company. I try to find every vehicle I can to do that right now.[44]

In other organizations where the executives were rated high on both idealized influence and contingent reward leadership, goals are communicated in a fairly formal and traditional MBO manner as shown in Figure 7.3. For example, at Magnum Credit Card, the Chief Technology Officer (CTO) of the Human Resources area drafts his business unit's goals at the

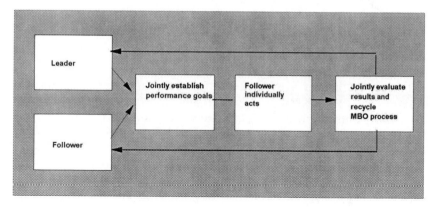

FIGURE 7.3
Formal Process for Setting and Communicating
Goals by Strategy-Focused Leaders.

beginning of the year as a document. He then sends it formally attached to an e-mail sent to his staff. The goals outlined in this document largely focus on three major objectives which he explained to us during his interview:

1. to improve efficiency,
2. to promote robust analytic skills for users, and
3. to support real-time point-of-service transactions.

In order for Custom to be successful financially, Custom must be profitable. In order for it to be profitable, it must be efficient. Just looking at human resource area, we must reduce the manual administrative aspect. Labor and technology will make us able to produce a large number of those transactions in a much more efficient way with less manpower . . . Second, also historically most HR organizations in big or small companies are not what I call analytically savvy. Most people only know how to input things or look at things from an individual record level . . . But they don't look at analysis [aggregated to the group level] in terms of trending. [For example, they don't ask] "What are the turnovers? What are the absentees? How are they all linked?" So again, during my tenure here we have provided a lot of this important technology, reports, and data bases. As HR managers, as generalists, we are required to provide some of these analyses. Information needed at the executive level is much more robust, and needs to be much more accurate and much more trending . . . Finally, I think most organizations with the advantage of technology, like the web, are driving towards the "self service train." [That means] the ability for their employees to be able to update accordingly and managers to be able to create transactions on-line and things of that nature. So those are pretty much my corporate objectives. To improve efficiency through robust analytic skills, the ability to run sale skills staff personality and even accordingly in expansion to the countries outside of the United States.

The CTO's email document to his staff clearly spelled out these expectations that outline his business unit's objectives. In his email, he asked his staff to develop their own objectives for the upcoming year. He then set up a time to review the objectives with his managers. Once they provide their draft copy to him, he reviews it and provides feedback and asks them to revise it accordingly. Then they both sign off and agree that these are the goals and objectives that need to be accomplished.

This process appears to be a very formal and traditional approach to the communication of strategic goals. But at the same time, Custom Credit Card's monthly strategy meetings set the stage for where high level organizational objectives turn into individual projects accomplished informally by Custom's employees on a day to day basis. As a result, the CTO knows that his staff understands the top three things that they need to do every day to support his business unit's overall goals. He makes sure to check in with them to see how they are coming along. If they need any help, he offers advice and support. Oftentimes he is delighted when this staff has a new system developed or when he is invited for a walk through of the prototype. During presentations such as these, he also provides feedback. He also provides feedback on systems designed to support customers in sessions where his staff do a "dry run" by offering suggestions for improvements.[45]

These examples illustrate how strategy-focused leaders effectively determine and communicate clear, timely and challenging goals to their followers and constituents. To be strategy-focused means to use goal setting and rewarding as a base for establishing base-level trust with followers, customers, clients, business partners and other constituents. Strategy-focused leaders who demonstrate idealized leadership solidify the foundation of trust with identification-based trust in relationships with their organizational stakeholders. Such efforts can support methods of learning and innovation that continuously invigorate the SFL process. In the next chapter, we turn our attention to the ways that strategy-focused leaders support learning and innovation within and between organizations.

CHAPTER 8

SUPPORTING LEARNING
AND INNOVATION

If you always think what you always thought,
you'll always get what you always got.
—*Gerald Haman*

Learning and innovation have become ubiquitous competitive tools in today's economy. Learning and innovation represent intellectual capital resources that are vital for technology-driven organizations that wish to be strategically focused. These organizations are relentless in their pursuit of continuous process improvement and adaptation to the forces of change in order to create or preserve a competitive advantage. To jump start these initiatives, strategy-focused leaders are championing innovation, building communities or practice, and deploying advanced information technology in their organizations and their connections with customers, suppliers and business partners. This chapter presents lessons learned from the executives regarding how to stimulate followers to be more creative and to think for themselves so that the entire organization can continuously learn, innovate and grow.

The Dream Weavers: Strategy-Focused Leadership in Technology-Driven
Organizations, pages 173–190
Copyright © 2004 by Information Age Publishing, Inc.
All rights of reproduction in any form reserved.
ISBN: 1-59311-110-X (paper), 1-59311-111-8 (cloth)

STRATEGICALLY BOLSTERING FOLLOWERS' BRAINPOWER

Anita Roddick founded The Body Shop, a global technology-driven retailer of more than 600 natural skin and hair care products. Roddick is one of many business leaders who recognize the growing responsibility of executives to be supporters of learning and innovation: "In the years ahead I see my leadership role as being an irritant, a gadfly—infusing creativity and creating an edge to everything The Body Shop does." Her perspective is in line with management guru, Peter Drucker, who has noted that innovation will be *the* core competency of the 21st century.[1]

Successful companies, like The Body Shop, rely on innovation and learning. Such companies initiate technological change, grow more rapidly, and utilize change for growth.[2] More than other companies, those companies that rely on technology cannot survive without innovative products and services. Such companies also compete in a global environment, unlimited by geography, which provides them with much more opportunities for innovation and boundaryless learning. In these companies, many of the leaders we interviewed noted that the creative people they employ are the source of innovation for their companies. In addition to inspiring the will of their people to succeed, these leaders hold themselves responsible for developing the intellect and knowledge acquired by their employees—collectively known as intellectual capital.

Strategy-focused leaders promote innovation and learning in their organizations. They strategically manage creativity and innovation using the transformational leadership component of intellectual stimulation to continually challenge and stretch their followers' "mental machinery" in line with their strategic objectives. Strategy-focused leaders also manage mistakes in the sense that they accept appropriate levels of miscues as long as learning is achieved along the way. In doing so, they avoid creating "no-mistakes" cultures which can snuff out innovation. They also provide followers with the infrastructure necessary for creativity. These conclusions are based on examples from the senior leaders we interviewed. Those leaders told us the methods they use to develop communities of practice and learning, and to build the cultures and organizational structures necessary for creativity. Finally, these executives harness technology to foster learning and innovation in their organizations, which is of critical importance for contemporary organizations.

Why Innovation and Learning Are Critical

Although organizational innovation is an important strategic issue in every industry, we believe that it becomes the most crucial issue in high-technology industries such as information technology (IT), consumer electronics and telecommunications. This is because these high-technology firms need to create and maintain a constant stream of innovation through new products and services in order to survive in very competitive markets. As discussed in Chapter 2, high-technology industries are characterized by thin profit margins, constantly changing technology and consumer preferences, and turbulent business conditions. As such, innovation is likely to be a key source of competitive advantage that generates new demands on their products and thus allows organizations to sustain successful long-term performance. According to Walter Bateman, Chairman and CEO of Harleysville Insurance, if you don't align innovation, learning, technology and business strategies, your company will die a slow death.[3]

Successful companies are those that rely on innovation and learning. Researchers have shown that firms initiating technological change tend to grow more rapidly and are more likely to survive the constant changes in their business environment. Companies that rely on innovation are more profitable and show more growth than companies that do not emphasize innovation.[4] Given the benefits of innovation, a growing number of organizations are emphasizing creativity and learning as paths for innovation. This is especially true when organizations depend on fast changing technologies, move to global markets, and employ individuals' personal power through various forms of empowerment or team-based work structures.[5] Such organizations operate in a fast-paced environment where new products or service concepts are introduced in decreasing rhythmic intervals.[6] In order to deal with such a hectic pace, managers need to develop innovative solutions. These solutions are also required when organizations deal with the increased competition associated with the global marketplace.

Organizations emphasize innovation not only in order to deal with their external environment but also to facilitate an internal environment that can attract an excellent workforce. Today's employees seek work in innovative corporations where they can express their personal power, voice their opinion, and be involved in decision-making. They are much more knowledgeable, self-motivated and highly educated than workers from previous generations. For workers in such organizations, innovation is manifested not only in the products or services they provide, but also in the way they administrate their operations, relying on innovative management techniques and create an internal environment of learning. Such organizations provide their workforces with the opportunity to develop and excel. Whereas the benefits of having a creative workforce are relatively obvious, many organizations face the challenge of leading creative people. Throughout this chapter, we present examples from the executives we interviewed and elaborate on their insights regarding how they manage their employees to achieve innovative results.

The Challenge of Leading Innovation and Learning

Creativity and innovation are not the same. While *creativity* refers to the generation of new ideas, *innovation* is the translation of these ideas into action.[7] This distinction is critical to understanding the role of leadership in fostering innovation. In fact, the relationships between leadership and innovation are not as obvious as one may think. Traditionally innovation was seen as an attribute of individuals. In this view, leaders are a hindrance to creativity and innovation.[8] Their influence on creative followers may be perceived as needless or irrelevant micro-management—a redundant and overbearing impediment to their creative efforts. For example, why would creative individuals need leadership at all? Given their excellent motivation and competence, such individuals may work well without leaders and even resent supervision.[9] Nevertheless, organizations recognize that having creative individuals does not necessary entail innovative performance. Innovation, unlike creativity, often requires concerted effort on behalf of a group of individuals.

The strategy-focused leaders we interviewed emphasized their role in promoting innovation in their organizations. Many of them recognized the challenge of managing creative people by giving the freedom necessary for innovation. For example, the CEO of C Communications, a major telecommunications company in Israel, briefly described his approach to innovative employees:

> I believe that a supervisor should not get too much into his employees' private affairs. The less you get into his bones, so to speak, the more creative, the more productive the employee is and the more initiative he shows.[10]

However, the challenge for executives is to also set the boundaries that help direct those creative individuals towards achieving innovation. The CEO of Concord Inc., a major information technology organization, notes:

> In an R&D organization, it is not as prescriptive, and so you know, establishing guidelines and boundaries are important, and then giving people freedom to operate within those boundaries is important. And the innovation of an organization really reflects as to how you set boundaries. If they are too narrow and too prescriptive you won't get a lot of freedom of thought and innovation. If they are too broad, you won't get the results you are looking for. So setting those kinds of boundaries is my responsibility and the responsibility of the leaders that I work with.[11]

Both CEOs recognized the unique aspects of managing creative individuals and the function of SFL not just to reinforce creativity per se, but rather to channel it towards innovation and organizational goals. This is a challenge for leaders because creative people often focus on the work and not on the organization. They develop their identity with the organization and its goals from their personal achievements doing their jobs.[12]

Strategy-focused leaders are those who are responsible for transforming individuals' creativity to unit or organizational innovation. They do it by broadening followers' identification in them as leaders to identification with the goals of the organization. Boas Shamir, a noted leadership scholar, suggested that leaders motivate their followers by increasing their identification with the goals of the organization.[13] In other words, they get their followers to see a connection between their personal values and self-image and the values of the organization and what it stands for, such as constant improvement and learning. In the process of transforming the creativity of their followers to innovation, these leaders also motivate them to excellent performance. This is exactly how strategy-focused leaders strategically link individual effort with innovation.

STRATEGICALLY LEADING CREATIVITY AND INNOVATION

Bringing about innovation is not a typical executive action for which one can provide prescriptions. Rules and procedures do not apply. However, in a special issue of *Harvard Business Review,*[14] leaders from extraordinarily innovative companies discuss how their companies repeatedly come up with great innovations. We believe that innovation is not something that only extraordinary companies can accomplish. Accordingly, we sought out to interview executives from both very innovative companies and companies that are not necessarily well known for innovation.

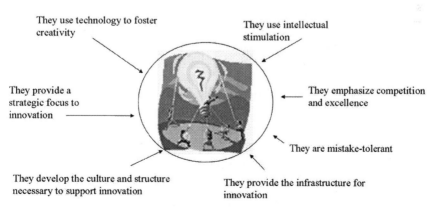

FIGURE 8.1
How Strategy-Focused Leaders Champion Innovation.

The executives who displayed SFL discussed several methods by which they support innovation. These methods are summarized in Figure 8.1. For example, they use intellectual stimulation with their followers and colleagues;[15] they highlight being tolerant of mistakes;[16] they provide the infrastructure for creative people to concentrate on developing their ideas;[17] they develop the culture and structure of the organization necessary to support learning and innovation; they are receptive to change; and finally, since the companies we examined were technology intensive, many leaders reported using technology to foster creativity and innovation. We discuss below each of these methods with examples from our strategy-focused leaders.

Achieving Learning and Creativity Through Intellectual Stimulation

Bernard M. Bass suggested that one of the main dimensions of effective (transformational) leadership is *intellectual stimulation*.[18] Intellectually stimulating leaders challenge old ways and habits of their followers, create a readiness for changing one's way of thinking, and display a willingness to think and develop new perspectives for current problems or work issues.

The executive leaders in our sample displayed significantly higher levels of intellectual stimulation (IS) than managers in a very large international sample assessing such behavior.[19] This variation was based in part on the industry of the executive's organization. Display of IS was higher among executives in the life sciences industry than in the services industry.[20] Gender did not matter: female executives displayed similar levels of IS as male executives.

Before strategy-focused leaders can intellectually stimulate followers to be creative and innovative, they must work hard to remove several types of stumbling blocks that can render their intellectual stimulation ineffective and useless. The major categories of stumbling blocks to intellectual stimulation are listed in Table 8.1.[21]

The organization may be a stumbling block to intellectual stimulation. At some organizations, like Sunbeam and RJR Nabisco during the reigns of

TABLE 8.1
Stumbling Blocks to Intellectual Stimulation

- The organization: its culture, structure, policies, etc.
- The organization's methods of solving problems
- The executive leader (himself or herself)
- The executive leader's followers
- The executive leader's superior or boss

"Chainsaw" Al Dunlap and F. Ross Johnson, being known as a creative thinker is risky and can end up as a form of career suicide. In other rigid organizations, most new ideas don't get implemented and those that do are not rewarded. What is not rewarded is often not repeated. Also, some organizations' standard assumptions for doing the work are procedural-ized and legalized and must be followed. Oftentimes, these organizations frown on and punish mistakes, so innovation and creativity are often avoided. What is your organization doing to put the brakes on your peo-ple's creativity and innovation?

Similarly, an organization's or team's methods of solving problems are often stumbling blocks to intellectual stimulation. In organizations like Enron, Worldcom, Adelphia Communications or Tyco, unethical, corrupt and/or faulty decision-making processes have led to disastrous results highlighted in the media. These organizations considered it a waste of time to return to and test their basic assumptions in their business transac-tions and decisions. Their cultures were so firmly entrenched that practi-cally everyone would start with the same basic assumptions. In these cultures, there was one right way to answer a problem—the way it had been done in the past according to company policy or shared norms or expecta-tions. Which of your organization's methods hold your people back from achieving their full potential to be innovative?

While it is easy to point to the organization and its methods as a scape-goat, it is often difficult for executives to point the finger at themselves when they are the ones who represent stumbling blocks to intellectual stimulation. Consider how *you* as the executive leader may contribute to the problem. Perhaps you feel uncomfortable questioning other people's assumptions. You might feel that you are simply not creative. Or you might possess the attitude that "if it ain't broke, don't fix it." In your mind, you might feel justified in continuing to use your old tried and true methods that have always worked for you. Isn't it time for you to recognize to your own beliefs, attitudes and behaviors that hinder your organization's cre-ative and innovative efforts?

Perhaps your followers are stumbling blocks to intellectual stimulation. They may rely on you to develop new ways to do their jobs. They may feel that brainstorming is a silly process reserved for "the creative types in Mar-keting." They also may avoid taking intellectual risks and therefore rarely come up with their own ideas. Or perhaps your people are politically-moti-vated "yes (wo)men" who think they they lack creativity and are afraid to show what they don't know. Such attitudes and perceptions are common in bureaucratic organizations or industries where compliance and regulation are the norm. What can you do to help your people escape this vicious cycle of negativity, cynicism and lackluster creative performance?

Most worrisome is the situation where your superior is a stumbling block to intellectual stimulation. Your boss may expect everyone to think like her. Or she may assume a "controlling interest" in stealing and embellishing new ideas from you and your staff. She also may be unreceptive to new ideas. She may even make fun of your ideas in public. Such behaviors may prompt you to make sure you do not act smarter than her or question her reasoning during meetings. Isn't it time that you took the initiative to help your boss change for the good of the organization and all of its stakeholders?

All of these stumbling blocks to intellectual stimulation should give you much to think about concerning the things that may be holding your organization back from achieving its full performance potential. They must be removed before you can begin to intellectually stimulate your followers. While there are no fast and easy prescriptions for removing these stumbling blocks, several ways to address are possible. Removing the organizational stumbling blocks requires a massive organizational change initiative, changes to the culture, or new executive leadership. However, the effects of these changes may take several years to be realized. Removing your own, your boss' and your followers' stumbling blocks requires a personal recognition that change is necessary and vital for career and organizational survival, commitment to change, and real learning and development in the areas of leadership and innovation. Fortunately, most colleges, universities and organizational development consulting firms offer courses and training on these topics. But in the end, the best and most effective solutions will come from *you* in the form of your deep and concentrated thinking and thoughtful discussions with your colleagues. What are you going to do to remove the stumbling blocks that are holding you back from championing learning and innovation in your company?

Once you have worked to remove these stumbling blocks, you can begin to display specific methods of intellectual stimulation. Most of these techniques are behaviors that you can display and are listed in Table 8.2.

Based on our research and work with our clients, we believe that *intellectual stimulation is highly related to innovation.* Indeed, research on leaders who promote innovation indicates that they explicitly require their followers to come up with innovative solutions, they define tasks in a broad enough manner that allows for followers' creativity, they don't present a problem in terms of its solution rather they provide the factual information that will help followers define the problem on their own. Finally, they work with a group of employees as opposed to dealing with separate individuals.[22] Specifically, leaders should allow a group discussion with members' sharing of relevant information. One of the executive leaders we interviewed described this as a process:

> If we encounter a technical problem within the company . . . you [the leader] gather the people, you sit down and discuss, trying to use everybody's ideas [in order] to cook up a solution . . . you come up with such innovative ideas in a process like this. Several years ago, I came across the process . . . leading to creative thinking and I utilize it in a methodical way. When there is any

TABLE 8.2
Methods of Intellectual Stimulation

- Question the assumptions underlying the problem at hand
- Look at the problem from different perspectives (e.g., the customer, venture capitalist) and time frames (e.g., long vs. short term)
- Redesign jobs, re-engineer work flows, and eliminate any processes that do not add value to your products or services
- Test new methods or ideas using demonstration projects
- Bring in outsiders add fresh perspectives to the problem at hand
- Turn problems inside out, assuming there are no restrictions of constraints
- Use metaphors to manipulate ideas
- Introduce humor and/or the absurd into problem solving sessions
- Identify and imagine alternate states of the problem
- Use brainstorming to generate large quantities of ideas
- Methodically evaluate ideas after brainstorming sessions
- Consider the context of the problem. Then enlarge it, or make it smaller to understand it nuisances.
- Learn and deploy Systematic Inventive Thinking or other creativity methods
- Establish a framework for solving problems to explain a flow of events and reduce the complexity and diversity of those events.

sort of a problem, I gather the people involved and I activate this process and this leads to quite innovative solutions.[23]

In addition to creating conditions for followers to share their ideas, intellectually stimulating leaders also use disagreements as a method of encouraging learning and innovation. Such leaders may counter employees' opinions and use disagreements to reframe followers' ways of thinking and help achieve integrative solutions. When leaders use these techniques, they create the conditions for followers to emulate them and form an environment that is open to criticism and consequently to change. Lee Kranefuss of Barclays Global Investors explains:

I wanted to create an environment where people felt safe to speak up and challenge me! I didn't want to be the only driver of discussion. I wanted people to think outside the norm and solve problems creatively. I wanted to create an environment where people could make decisions without being second-guessed.[24]

Such leaders also use their followers as a source of ideas that lead to innovation for their companies. Not only do these transformational leaders promote new ideas but in the process they also excite their followers by being enthusiastic about their ideas. The CEO of a large IT company describes how he uses intellectual stimulation to both identify creative solutions and motivate his employees:

> They [employees] can come to me with the most crazy ideas . . . if someone comes to me with an idea that makes me sort of jump . . . the more time I dedicate to examining this idea. And the more time I give it to see if it could be put into action. That's because I realize an idea that makes a person jump, an idea that brings a person to negate it initially means that it has something of an innovation in it. Something that has not been done before, something that is unknown. My people know it, they know they can come with anything. We then analyze it and see how it translates into action.[25]

The above are only a few examples from our analysis of the interviews we conducted with our strategy-focused leaders. These examples demonstrate that many of these executives associate intellectual stimulation with innovation. They do it by creating a work environment that encourages followers to stimulate rather than judge each others' ideas. Indeed, research has indicated that because innovation often depends on the input of multiple individuals, building the right working relationships among them becomes a key role of their leaders.[26] While intellectually stimulating leaders provide an open environment, there is often a much more radical approach to championing innovation and learning.

Inspiring Innovation by Being Tolerant of Mistakes

Thomas J. Watson, the founder of IBM, once said that "the fastest way to succeed is to double your failure rate."[27] Although this statement may sound extreme, it is clearly the gist of what our strategy-focused leaders, all of whom are senior leaders in today's high-tech oriented organizations, have indicated. The senior leaders we interviewed highlighted the benefits of creating an environment where failure is not associated with fear. Unlike lower level leaders, the executives we interviewed shape organizational policies and can fight the reasons why many individuals would avoid taking the risks to avoid punishment. Strategy-focused leaders recognize that in technology-intensive environments, risk-taking that breeds innovation. This recognition motivates them to work to change rules that inhibit employees' creativity.

In their book *The Failure-Tolerant Leader*, Farson and Keys suggested that another inhibitor of innovation is the judgmental use of feedback. Traditionally, leaders were taught to use feedback as much as possible. However, more recent research has indicated that in some cases feedback may actually hurt performance.[28] The use of feedback may signal to employees that they are being judged by their leaders. Rather than focus on judging employees' performance, leaders should take tangible interest in their work. Such leaders may facilitate their followers' willingness to take risks. In effect, many of the strategy-focused leaders we interviewed encourage risk-taking and even making mistakes. For example, a senior executive at General Electric noted:

> I look at all problems as opportunities . . . I try to look at the glass [as] half full as opposed to half empty . . . if there were no problems there would be no opportunities and no . . . inventions, nothing. So I encourage my employees to take risks. I let them make mistakes . . . as a leader I have the obligation to let people take that risk and allow people to fail. I don't want them [employees] to lose confidence, but I want them to have the pain of taking a risk, because if you don't take the risk, you don't get the reward. And if you just play defense the whole time, the best you can do is die. If you play offense you can win. I'm looking [to avoid] too quick feedback with them . . . sometimes there has to be a longer [period before giving] feedback . . . sometimes you get your best learning when you fail. And that's what we have to allow an environment that allows that freedom.[29]

However, letting employees make mistakes does not mean that leaders should not monitor the way employees perform. A key issue for leaders is how to balance the need to allow freedom and risk with their commitment to performance. Whereas most of the leaders we interviewed did not discourage mistakes that lead to learning, they were reluctant about making mistakes on *critical issues*. The two executive leaders below describe their philosophies regarding mistakes:

> I'm a lot more of a hands-off kind of person in that I think there's a ton of value in making mistakes and learning from them. I'd almost rather— depending on the scale—that they [employees] fumble or mess up a little bit so they can make mistakes and learn from them. When the stakes aren't that high, there's nothing to do but gain there.[30]

Similarly, the CEO of one of the largest financial information corporations noted: "Sometimes you have to let people make mistakes so that's how they learn. [It] depends on how critical the project is."[31]

There are benefits of being tolerant of mistakes.[32] Failure tolerant leaders help people overcome fear of failure by creating a culture where employees are encouraged to look beyond traditional views of failure or success. They show interest in the projects of their reports and make innovation part of the everyday, not an exceptional event. Whether an organization could harness innovation successfully or not depends on reducing the fear of making mistakes. In doing so, they encourage followers to make mistakes by admitting their own foul-ups or goofs. However, the success of innovation and learning depends not only on how leaders interact with their followers. From the interviews we conducted we learned that in order to facilitate innovation, senior leaders need to make sure that their work-force is free to innovate.

Emphasizing Competition and Excellence

Strategy-focused leaders recognize that internal competition leads to excellence, and excellence is a driver of innovation and learning. A num-ber of successful executives we interviewed also indicated that they tried to communicate a sense of urgency for changes and the need to be more competitive in order to beat their competition and survive. This is in line with the argument made by a number of researchers who have suggested that transformational leaders share their high expectations with followers to motivate them to go beyond their ordinary efforts and achieve perfor-mance beyond expectations. Karen Borda, who co-founded the bio-tech firm CB Technologies told us:

> I do this [achieve innovation] by setting up different teams and creating a lit-tle bit of competition. I assemble people from different levels and say 'you will make a presentation next week' to tell company what needs to be done—create! Review pressure sparks innovation."[33]

Some of our leaders also recognized their role as experts for followers. Followers can rely on them to support creative problem-solving by helping followers define and frame problems creatively. The framing of problems and methods to solve them often emerges from the core message and strat-egy. To work with new ideas or develop new products and services, follow-ers must understand that their work is meaningful and consistent with the core message. Followers need to be willing to explore new assumptions and be capable of changing their assumptions and methods of solving prob-lems in order to develop new and innovative ideas. In this way, strat-egy-focused leaders help followers to share the collective vision.

Providing the Infrastructure for Innovation

In order to support innovation leaders must provide multiple types of support, such as idea support and social support.[34] Idea support can come from both internal and external sources of training and development. Leaders may challenge employees to get them to come up with new ideas. One of the executive leaders we interviewed described this process of encouraging creative thoughts somewhat bluntly:

I sit with the managers, help them and request of them creativity, a different view on how we approach the market. For example, we tell the unit dealing with ads to remove the current idea from the Internet and create an interactive solution. The brainstorming that comes out of this is the possibility of an additional business.[35]

In addition to "requesting" creativity from their followers, sometimes leaders need to use outside sources, such as educational programs or seminars. However, idea support alone is not enough. In order to innovate, followers often need social support, especially peer support. The executive below describes how he provides the infrastructure to his followers for innovation and learning:

It [innovation] has something to do with the way they [employees] function in their role or their job. We provide educational programs where we actually train engineers or administrative staff to take the initiative to better themselves and learn new skills. We also send them to seminars and provide peer support.[36]

To summarize, we found that effective strategy-focused leaders often need to overcome organizational constraints in order to boost innovation in their organizations. They need to transform archaic policies that inhibit innovation to policies that are open enough to allow innovation.

Building Cultures and Structures that Support Innovation

Support for innovation, especially at higher organizational levels, involves protecting employees from potential organizational barriers to innovation. Effective strategy-focused leaders buffer creative individuals from demands that could harm their creativity. They provide technical support in terms of technology or other needs of creative work. Finally, at the stage of materialization of a project from an original idea, these leaders take care of the formalities necessary for successful implementation of the innovation.

In order to provide this support, leaders form organizational cultures that facilitate innovation. Many of the leaders we interviewed mentioned the types of cultures they created in their organizations. Creating such cultures involves using communities of practice or learning that spur innovation. *Communities of practice/learning* represent groups of individuals who are interested in a common professional topic and share their expertise on the topic among the members of their group. The members typically share a learning-goal orientation that is directed at expanding their collective knowledge base—and at the same time, their organization's intellectual capital.

When executives send out constant messages emphasizing communities of practice/learning and organizational innovation and display a favorable attitude toward changes through role modeling, it becomes part of their organizational culture and shared expectations that are conducive to creative behaviors and innovative work processes. We believe that innovative organizational cultures that supporting collective learning could serve as an important springboard for many innovative products and services. For example, an executive from a major publisher described how such a community operates:

> The creativity we have within our finance group is that we get to take that information and rearrange it in ways that make sense for our business. So in terms of challenging employees, within the finance department, the challenging part, that's motivating and makes the job more fun, is that we are not constrained by having to produce a document every month the same way. If we have another way to present this information that is more informative by all means let's look at it and see if it makes sense.[37]

As this executive indicated, a common trigger for creativity is challenge. For example, another executive from a major financial institution described how he creates such challenges:

> This challenge with new cooperation and new solutions is my central focus. I see in them the initial ideas and let them work it through . . . So, I'll sit them down every couple of weeks or on a monthly basis and say, "Do you have enough to do? Are you learning enough? Are you able to contribute? Do you have the opportunity to contribute what you want to contribute?" And typically when you are dealing in an environment where people are very highly motivated, they'll ask for more and you just give them more and watch it to make sure that they can handle what they have.[38]

Other leaders we interviewed discussed the sources of challenge for innovation. Some leaders suggested that challenge can come from emphasizing crisis, breaking norms, and figuring out original solutions to problems. For example, a highly esteemed Israeli executive leader discussed the role of crisis as a trigger of creativity, and what leaders need to do in order to channel crisis to achieve creative solutions:

> I think that struggle, crisis and pressure [lead to] creativity, and that [requires] a managerial attitude or atmosphere and [the leader to] instill dedication and loving or caring attitude towards the place of work.[39]

Finally, in order to institute innovation, such leaders build organizational structures that support a culture of creativity and innovation and help employees link their engagement in innovation with rewards or other support they can get from the organization. As described by the CEO of a major U.S. corporation:

So I think we have the mechanisms in place to where we can do it better than other companies. But it is never as good as you want it because you are continuously changing action and you are continuously making adjustments based upon what you have learned. So I think the feedback mechanisms are pretty good and we have the governing structure that allows us to change resources.[40]

Fostering Creativity and Innovation with Technology

Given the crucial role of technology in innovation, executive leaders need not only to have an excellent mastery of technology, but also to be able to use their followers for scouting activities, such as monitoring the development of new technologies. Effective leveraging of technology requires that leaders utilize their strategic networks to trace changes in technology. Such efforts are illustrated by Jon Boscia, CEO of the Lincoln Financial Group, a Philadelphia-based firm with $6.7 billion in assets. Boscia leverages his strategic network and followers' IT expertise to find new ways to promote creativity and innovation:

A CEO should lead the company in the efficient use of office suite products, PDA wireless usage, e-mail and intranet/Internet usage. To stay competitive, a CEO must study the ways competitors are using technology to expand their businesses. I have always had a deep appreciation for technology, and my working knowledge and usage has definitely increased since becoming CEO.[41]

Some of the ways that executives can stay current on technology's potential to enhance creativity and innovation are described by Martin D. Feinstein, President, CEO and Chairman of the Farmers Insurance Group, a Los Angeles-based firm which holds $12 billion in assets. According to Feinstein, executives have several ways they can understand the value of technology in supporting innovation:

I stay up on technology by participating in many of the meetings where technology issues are discussed. The CIO attends my staff meeting and is provided an opportunity to keep my entire staff up-to-date on key issues. I also encourage everyone to circulate interesting articles (about technology). Many IT articles are shared among the management team, looking at what the competition does, new ideas, or even old ideas applied differently. Recently, we have also experimented with transferring people out of technology into the business side, and vice versa. You can't force knowledge into someone or a group; people have to want to learn, and I believe a CEO's job is to create that atmosphere.[42]

Strategy-focused leaders are responsible for helping their followers make sense of technology and its potential to support a learning-oriented culture. Sense-making activities of leaders focus on linking technology use with achieving the goals of the organization and shaping cultures that value learning. Two of our executive leaders discuss below how they take advantage of technology to maximize innovation and learning. The first executive assessed his role as a champion of technology at GE: "Clearly, in this day and age, in 2002 and for the last twenty years or so, you can't be a leader if you are not leveraging the newest technology."[43]

The second executive specified how he uses a system of creative thinking to promote innovation:

> Let me explain to you how I built this nucleus of creative people that I work with at all times. There is a system called SIT. Did any of you ever hear something like this system? SIT stands for Systematic Inventive Thinking. This is a tool I work with at all times. This is something I discovered several years ago and the process that I use within the company . . . Very few companies took and implemented it as a work system. Our company uses it . . . for one thing [because] it is very technological and second, we believe that an innovative advantage will give greater value to a product.[44]

The SIT system originated in the former Soviet Union and has been refined in Israel through a very successful network of academic/industry partnerships. SIT blends academic knowledge from the marketing, strategy and technology fields with expertise in product and innovation management. Technology-driven organizations, such as Eastman Kodak, the British Broadcasting Corporation, Rubbermaid and Philips Consumer Electronics, have used SIT to creatively enhance their strategies in their quest to intellectual and structural capital.

While the executives we interviewed came from technology intensive companies, most of them mentioned technology as a strategic tool. In general, strategy-focused leaders facilitate innovation in a strategic way. They recognize that it is the strategy of the company that guides innovation and learning.

Providing a Strategic Focus

In the beginning of this chapter we differentiated between creativity and innovation. While creativity refers to the ability to invent, innovation means strategically inventing or channeling creative ideas and efforts into development of innovative products that serve to accomplish the goals of the organization.[45] Many of the leaders we interviewed clearly indicated that their purpose for innovation, as supported by technology, is to help followers to achieve strategic goals. Walter Bateman, Chairman and CEO of Harleysville Insurance, illustrates such efforts. Bateman uses an inclusive and participative approach in the process of identifying technology's role in supporting business strategies. Using a basketball analogy, he explains:

> Our IT guy is our point guard. He has the ball with the five-year strategic growth plan and heads the IT steering committee . . . [Through our collaboration, we are] making sure that Harleysville is not just growing for growth's sake, but making sure that there is a return on that growth. In order to deliver financially we need to know something about you compared to your environment and peers. That requires access to data.[46]

Bateman, like other strategy-focused leaders, works hard to align the IT steering and strategy committees so that they can set their collective sights on innovation. Since strategy-focused leaders structure activities that lead to innovation, they must be highly aware of organizational strategy, be selective when choosing the ideas that promote strategic objectives, and leverage technology to serve organizational goals. One common strategic objective of leaders is to maintain constant change within the organization to deal with external changes. This is how an executive of a giant multinational company described his strategic role:

> If I were to relate it to the challenges of the industry relative to other industries I would imagine that we need to be a lot more receptive to change. Not even receptive to change, we better be coming up with the ideas so that we can introduce new products that reduce prices and overall sales and still make money. We don't have the luxury of saying we just develop something great and now we can continue for [the next] 40 years. So we have to look for new and better ways to do things.[47]

RECAPPING SOME KEY IDEAS

We began this chapter by suggesting that innovation is absolutely critical for success in today's organizations. Innovation is the strategic tool managers probably use most to deal with the challenging business environment in order to provide value to internal and external customers. We also indicated that the relationship between innovation and leadership is not obvious. Some leaders may be seen as a hindrance to innovation, disturbing creative individuals in their pursuit of innovations. However, we also noted that while creative individuals may be smart, leaders are there to harness their skills to benefit the organization. In our interviews, we sought to identify what strategy-focused leaders do to promote innovation and we have described their activities in this chapter.

As summarized in Figure 8.1, the leaders we interviewed told us that they drive innovation by intellectually stimulating their followers and colleagues or by presenting goals as challenging objectives. Many of those leaders also indicated that they not only avoid punishing their employees, but even encourage them to make mistakes—just not the critical ones! Being tolerant of mistakes is what strategy-focused leaders do in order to facilitate risk taking and innovation. They recognize the strategic value of innovation by both using technology to induce innovation and stay competitive and by signaling to employees the links between innovative practices and the core message and strategy of the organization. Finally, strategy-focused leaders create competitive and challenging environments. They recognize that in order to support innovation they need to provide the infrastructure for innovation. They do it by building supportive systems, such as peer support and by creating organizational structures and cultures that favor innovation. We describe the role of organizational culture as the context for supporting SFL processes and achieving levels of success beyond organizational objectives in the next chapter.

PART V

REALIZING THE DREAM

Leaning back in her chair at the end of the day, Sandra Stevenson smiled with satisfaction as she gazed outside her office window at the beautiful autumn colors of the trees blanketing the mountains surrounding the Vestal Corporate Park. Just as Mother Nature rewarded spectators who had waited all year long to view Her vibrant display, Sandra's strategy-focused leadership was finally reaping what it had sowed. Her internal growth problems behind her, Sandra's Nova-Vignette organization was yielding bountiful profits, strong customer relationships, expanded knowledge bases, and associates who continually improved themselves and their work processes. She had built a true learning community of associates who shared responsibility for leading Nova-Vignette to new levels of success based on stretch goals, mutual trust, effective communication and commitment to the core message.

Sandra realized that all her efforts would be for fruitless if she had not taken the time to build a transformational culture that was shared and demonstrated by her associates. Equally important was her commitment to constantly revising, adapting and communicating her core message and strategy. This was important for recognizing the social, technological, economic and industry trends and for educating and informing her associates of what these trends meant for their organization. By weaving an integrated patchwork of talented people and cutting edge technology into a solid business strategy, Sandra had exceeded the expectations of her wildest dreams. She had woven the social and technological fabric that helped to realize her dream for Nova-Vignette, as it worked on its noble mission to help fight the world's deadliest diseases and improve the lives of people around the world. Content with her organization's progress, she packed up her briefcase, jumped into her BMW, and headed home to reconnect with her family.

CHAPTER 9

REINFORCING THE CORE MESSAGE AND STRATEGY

> Create and sustain a culture consistent with your strategic ideas.
> —*Stuart Wells*

Strategy-focused leaders realize that it is not enough to pontificate an inspiring core message and develop a brilliant strategic plan. The organizational values that underlie the core message and the skillful execution of the strategic plan must be socialized and reinforced to followers through a strong organizational culture. The values, norms and expectations underlying a strong culture can substitute for external management controls aimed at followers' compliance and create effective "internal controls" aimed at followers' identification seen in highly empowered workforces. This chapter describes how organizational cultures can raise the collective intelligence and performance capacities of technology-dependent organizations. We also summarize how the executives we interviewed created and developed their cultures that sustained and strengthened the values, norms and missions of their organizations.

The Dream Weavers: Strategy-Focused Leadership in Technology-Driven
Organizations, pages 193–213
Copyright © 2004 by Information Age Publishing, Inc.
All rights of reproduction in any form reserved.
ISBN: 1-59311-110-X (paper), 1-59311-111-8 (cloth)

THE PEOPLE CREATE THE PLACE

Top executives in today's technology-driven organizations reinforce their vision and personal values through various means. Successful leaders should be able to communicate not only strategy but also how the goals of the organization are relevant to the personal values and desires of the employees of their organization. To accomplish this objective, executives tend to have numerous interactions with their subordinates in various social and work-related settings. Subordinates find out what their executives emphasize and how they can help accomplish these goals. Direct interaction between executives and employees in an organization is an important part of instilling the core message and strategy they need to achieve the organizational mission and vision.

Imagine a multinational organization with subsidiaries in many different countries. Such an organization's structure is highly complex and its operation has to be coordinated through some type of normative means. Consequently, it is extremely difficult for executives in such organizations to exert their influence only through direct interaction. As the market place becomes globalized and organizations become more geographically dispersed, top executives at many large organizations are more likely to interact with their subordinates *indirectly* and they must find additional means to share core values and norms to infuse solidarity into their organization.

One highly effective solution to this problem could be provided through *organizational culture,* which describes the norms, values and work practices shared by leaders and followers of an organization. The interactive relationship between leaders and organizational culture and the need for leaders to effectively interact with their followers indirectly are succinctly summarized by leadership scholar Gary Yukl:

> Leaders directly influence subordinates by inspiring them to be more committed, building their self-confidence, and empowering them to take more initiative in carrying out the work. Direct leader influence on subordinates is a necessary part of transforming the organization, but it is not the only part. Another aspect of transformational leadership, at least for upper-level managers and administrators, is influence on organizational culture. By changing or strengthening the culture of an organization, a leader can indirectly influence the motivation and behavior of its members.[1]

Today, in virtually every technology-driven organization that is highly successful, there is a positive, unique and strong organizational culture. For example, 3M is known for its highly innovative organizational culture that was developed more than a hundred years ago. 3M's culture has motivated its employees to approach their work in the most creative ways they possibly could. Such emphasis on innovation provided an important guideline to employees that helped understand "the way things are done around here."[2] Subsequently, it has led to various innovative products and there have been numerous stories that symbolize how the innovation-oriented organizational culture at 3M has helped its employees to think "out of the box" and develop innovative and smart products. For example, the story about the 3M scientist who spilled chemicals on her tennis shoe—and came up with Scotchgard is well-known.[3] This example illustrates that a positive and strong culture makes an organization not only a desirable place to work, but also a more innovative and effective place to work.

Many people also credit the fun-loving organizational culture at Southwest Airlines as an important source for employee motivation and Southwest's remarkable business results. In an industry plagued by fare wars, recessions, oil crises, and other disasters, Southwest hasn't lost a penny since 1973 even during and after the terrorist attacks of September 11, 2001. From the company's top executive, Herb Kelleher, to mechanics to pilots, all employees are always happy to help their customers and show off how happy they are working for the company. This positive and fun organizational culture has received many kudos including consistently being listed among *Fortune* magazine's top 10 most admired companies.

Given these important issues related to organizational culture, it is beneficial for strategy-focused leaders to understand what culture is and how it functions. It is equally important for strategy-focused leaders to understand how they can influence the development of their culture and how they could utilize it as a strategic asset to transform their organization. Organizational culture is "a system of shared meaning held by members that distinguishes the organization from other organizations." [4] In other words, it defines who they are as a collective entity and represents core values that they try to accomplish. It includes the values and assumptions shared by members about what is right, what is good, and what is important. Organizational culture provides a social context in which employees interact and serves as "gel" that ties together various important constituencies in order to generate and mobilize collective efforts to accomplish organizational goals. Therefore, organizational culture has a tremendous influence on the attitudes and behaviors of employees.

How is Organizational Culture Developed?

In many cases, company founders and succeeding top executives develop and maintain organizational culture based on their personal values and philosophies. When they are creating an organization, they are imposing certain sets of personal values, expectations, and visions that become institutionalized. Leaders in organizations also engage various types of role-modeling and mentoring activities in order to pass along their core values to their subordinates. As a result, they develop what is called "organizational culture" which is reinforced and strengthened through employee selection, socialization, and other organizational systems such as performance evaluation and reward policies. Many employees learn more about their organizational culture upon their new employment through certain stories, rituals, and unique languages.

Although founders and successors are the primary source and influence of organizational culture, cultures are often developed and altered while the organization is interacting in certain types of environments, which imposes important constraints for the organization to survive. Unless they develop a flexible and adaptive culture such as those required in highly competitive and turbulent industries such as the information technology (IT) or professional education industries, they can't effectively compete against their competitors. For example, the American Institute for CPCU/IIA keeps its fingers firmly on the pulse of trends and developments in the insurance and professional certifications industries. Under Terrie Troxel's strategy-focused leadership, the AICPCU and IIA have adapted their culture and intellectual capital by revamping their curriculum and using new forms of IT to deliver exams and offer on-line courses.[5] Thus, the business environment is an important determinant to organizational culture.

We can also find two companies in the IT industry having two extremely different types of organizational culture reflecting their top executives' different personalities and values: Microsoft and SAS. Microsoft was founded by Bill Gates and Paul Allen in 1975 and has been an industry leader in providing innovative computer software products. Their mission is to enable people and businesses throughout the world to realize their full potential.[6] Employees at Microsoft have been working very hard to accomplish this goal. Toward this end, they have created an organizational culture that is very demanding and competitive. Many employees put in a rigorous 70-plus hours of work each week and are expected to excel in their area. The company rewards high performing employees with excellent financial compensations such as high salary, a generous stock purchase plan, and 401K plan. Without a doubt, this competitive organizational culture at Microsoft has challenged its employees to develop innovative products at a much faster rate than their counterparts do and makes Microsoft one of the most successful companies in the world.

In contrast, SAS is the world's largest privately held software company with more than 10,000 employees in over 100 offices in 50 countries. The company is in a similar industry with Microsoft and provides software solutions to about 90 percent of Fortune 500 companies with more than 40,000 customer sites. This equally successful software company, however, has developed a very different organizational culture from the one described above at Microsoft. SAS employees work in an environment that fosters integrating work and life and this has resulted in less than 5 percent of employee turnover rate, which saves the company $67 million each year. Although SAS employees are paid average salaries for their industry, they have been motivated by their corporate culture that values people. This fact is highlighted by their President and CEO, James Goodnight, who said, "Investment in people is essential to SAS Institute business success."[7] As a result, SAS has been named as one of the "100 Best Companies to Work for in America" by *Fortune* during all six years since the magazine has published the list. Therefore, it is important for strategy-focused leaders to recognize the various factors that contribute toward developing organizational culture in order to use it as a strategic asset.

FUNCTIONS OF ORGANIZATIONAL CULTURE

Organizational culture performs various functions that help create a more successful organization. First, organizational culture provides employees with some guidelines for their work processes and social interaction. In other words, organizational culture works as a sense-making device. This helps reduce anxiety, uncertainty, and confusion, which are always present in today's ever-changing high tech business environment. Organizational culture creates a sense of stability and psychological comfort for employees and allows top executives to control and coordinate various business activities. For example, the AICPCU/IIA's culture promotes and rewards continuous process improvement and change initiatives as a way of organizational life. According to Mary Ann Cook, Director of Curriculum at the AICPCU/IIA,

> Every day is about change—not just how to respond to change and manage it, but how to anticipate it and indeed be the driving force behind it. Here at the Institutes [AICPCU/IIA], we do the same thing. We're constantly evaluating our course content for relevance and timeliness. We feel very strongly that our compact with our students requires us to provide them with material that is current and that also alerts them to possible future changes in the social or regulatory or legislative arenas.[8]

Second, organizational culture can also provide a collective identity, which generates collective commitment among employees. Culture differentiates one organization from another. It conveys what kinds of values the organization stands for. Through these articulated values, employees generate commitment to go beyond their self-interests and work toward common goals. For the employees at the AICPCU/IIA, collective identity centers around the notion of professionalism, manifested through education, a commitment to ethics and experience in business.

Finally, culture serves as a control mechanism for an organization to maintain its solidarity. When a culture is created and strengthened through top management's active involvement and effort and through social interaction among employees, it attracts certain types of people who are able to fit right into the organization. For example, one of 3M's corporate values is to be "*a company that employees are proud to be a part of.*"[9] Employees who are attracted to such a culture tend to stay with 3M for a long period of time. This has resulted in a very low rate of turnover for 3M over the years. Although a strong organizational culture could become a liability that makes it hard to bring about changes and facilitate organizational diversity, it certainly can reinforce a top executive's core message and values and could raise the collective intelligence and performance capacities of the organization.

Given the many functions and benefits that culture provides to an organization, several of the strategy-focused leaders we interviewed devoted a lot of time to discussing how much they worked hard to develop and instill their organizational culture and values. Many of them expressed that top executives are the architects of corporate culture. For example, the founder of SNY Register Controls, which has provided retail control systems cash registers since 1966, emphasized the active role he played in establishing organizational values:

> We as a company believe strictly in integrity, honesty, and in fairness to employees and customers. We preach that all the time and if those things are done, then we never have to worry about who's walking behind you or who's opening the door. You just know you are doing the right thing. We preach that as the way of doing business.[10]

Lou Gerstner, the former CEO of IBM, also noted the very active role that he played in establishing a different type of culture in order to initiate changes and successfully turn around IBM in the 1990's:

> If the CEO isn't living and preaching the culture and isn't doing it consistently, then it just doesn't happen. This is a sine qua non—this is not a sufficient condition, but a necessary one.[11]

Like Gerstner, many of the executives we interviewed realized the importance of their leadership role in shaping a culture that focuses on adding to an organization's intellectual, human, social and financial capital.

CULTURE AS A STRATEGIC ASSET

Many organizations have used their corporate culture as a strategic asset to create more efficient and effective work environments. This is evident in numerous cases where the difference between successful and not-so-successful organizations could be found in the values and principles that underlie their internal organization.[12] These underlying values and beliefs are oftentimes translated into a set of management practices—how employees are rewarded, how decisions are made, and how resources are allocated. As a result, these systematized management practices based on a specific culture could ultimately affect organizational effectiveness. This is well-documented in the following passage describing IBM's founder Thomas J. Watson's ideas for creating culture and how they were used as a means to establish unique values that IBM represented:

> But the key to IBM's success was its finely tuned corporate culture, which prized excellence above all else. But it was a culture that reflected Watson's maniacal ego and encouraged almost blind obedience to his sometimes quirky convictions. Other business leaders encouraged corporate cultures that followed along strictly business lines, but with Watson, the emphasis was always on the personal. Other CEOs offered vague hints that employees should dress in a business-like manner. Nothing in the Watson dress code was left to change; every article of clothing fit Watson's image of the professional businessman. With its insistence on dark suits, dark ties, white shirts, starched collars, garters, and fedoras, Watson's dress code was supposed to make IBM employee always look presentable, but he also hoped to engender fierce company loyalty, which he believed was a vital ingredient in the IBM success formula.[13]

Perhaps the best example of organizational culture being used as a strategic asset could be found when an organization is undergoing a major restructuring process. A case in point is General Motors. GM's domestic market share had been sliding constantly from nearly 50 percent in the late 1950s to under 30 percent in 2000. The trouble was in part based on their rigid culture, "driven by financial considerations, allowed both foreign and domestic competitors to steal away customers with new products—like fuel-efficient compacts, minivans, SUVs, and eye-catching roadsters."[14] In essence, GM's culture was plagued with a risk averse, unimaginative, arrogant, and rigid bureaucracy.

When the CEO, Richard Wagoner hired Robert Lutz as Vice Chairman from Chrysler, Lutz's job was to change organizational culture at GM, which put the new thrust into the hands of younger people with less commitment to the status quo, and extended it later to other parts of the organization. Lutz's goal was to create a culture that was more in tune with the needs and wants of the customers and automobile market. He sought to create a culture that was more creative and innovative, with less concern with financial and engineering decisions and more concerned with marketing decision. He wanted to use the new organizational culture as a strategic asset to empower people and encourage engineers to think out of the box when it came to new car design. The huge success that Robert Lutz was able to accomplish in turning around the $180 billion company with over 350,000 employees allowed GM to regain a dominant position in the automobile market. GM shifted its focus from cost-cutting method to exciting new designs, which allowed GM to demonstrate its ability to respond to market demand and launched a record 21 new vehicles in 2002. The launches accounted for over $400 million in additional revenue and attributed to an increase in the GM's market share.[15]

Diversity as a Strategic Asset

One distinctive trend we face today in our business environment is cultural diversity. The trend toward diversity is fueled both internally and externally. Externally, organizations face their potential customers being increasingly diverse in terms of their gender, ethnicity, and age among other demographic characteristics. Shifting demographics are also creating a culturally diverse workforce that organization must employ given labor shortages and it in turn becomes an internal driving force toward more culturally diverse organizations.

Some executives look at cultural diversity as an opportunity to make their organization even more successful by creating an organizational culture that embraces diversity, while some executives look at cultural diversity as a threat or liability. The former is the case where executives use a diversity-embracing culture as a strategic asset. For example, senior executives at Union Bank of California value cultural diversity and are willing to go beyond ordinary efforts to make sure that cultural diversity does not just remain as a company slogan. Their proactive strategies have been reflected in various marketing programs calling themselves the "Bank of Lu Ping," "Bank of Anna," or "Bank of Rao" with facial pictures of different ethnic groups. These efforts create a very positive company image as an equal opportunity employer, which has helped the company attract and retain top-notch talent from various parts of the community and types of population they serve.

HOW STRATEGY-FOCUSED LEADERS
SHAPE ORGANIZATIONAL CULTURE

One important question that we tried to answer throughout our interviews with executives was how they shaped their organizational cultures. It was pretty obvious that different types of cultures emerged depending on the different developmental stages of the organization. Some executives from large and highly matured organizations such as ILR Global and Concord

Inc. focused on cultures that emphasized "how to maintain existing values and success," while executives from small and young organization such as KES and JNI focused on cultures that emphasized "how to communicate new values and change for growth."

The CEO of Concord Inc. articulated the importance of establishing core values and how to maintain them. It is quite instructive to re-visit his wisdom regarding the functions of values in creating and sustaining a strong culture.

> Values are sort of like buoys in the channel of commerce. I mean strategies change, winds change, tides change. But if you have got those buoys that you always come back to, it does not matter what business you are in, you have got those basic values. And I think that if I have one goal it is that we continue to live our basic values. One of the first things we did at the urging of some consultants, was to put down our values. . . One of the values we had was technology. We changed the word to innovation simply because innovation is broader than just technology. I mean you can be innovative in marketing and so on . . . . But that is the only word, and every other word is exactly the same. Starting with quality, ending with valuing the individuals. People ask me why is the individual last if it is so important? And I say because everything sits on the individual, I mean everything starts there. So we had this out in 1985, and it has been with us ever since.[16]

Compared to the company culture and values in a highly matured and established like Concord Inc., KES' espoused culture by the founder and CEO, John Yi, focuses more on growth:

> I would say take pride in what you do and do the best you can do. Always learn from your experience. I don't know if that qualifies as a value. And I can give you standard answers such as customer satisfaction and such like that. But I think it falls down to try to mix the goal of the business which is to grow. I firmly believe in growth. If the company doesn't grow there is only one other way it can go. So it is the combination of do everything you can to further the company and also fit in your personal satisfaction and values into it. And I think the company is really made up of all of those different qualities that the staff and the people bring.[17]

These examples illustrate that it is important to recognize that different types of culture are appropriate for different sizes of organizations at different stages of their development. While there is no proven formula that top executives could use to assess what type of culture is more appropriate for their organization at the current stage they are in, it is important to note that major changes are almost always necessary when an organization moves from one stage to another, say from the growth state to the maturity stage. It is also equally important to make sure that cultural changes are well accepted by followers.

Strategy-focused leaders should communicate with their followers why these changes are necessary and how the changes are going to affect them in the future. Ronald Kendrick, Executive Vice President of Union Bank of California, emphasized senior executives' important role of communicating with employees while they were going through a major merger process several years ago. The top management team including CEO of the company created an informal, open, and honest communication forum with employees and debriefed what's going on in the merger process. The weekly communication forum they created eliminated a considerable amount of uncertainty and anxiety from the employees and allowed them to focus more on their work than wasting their time speculating their uncertain future. Such effort from the top management eventually helped the company to complete the merger successfully and without losing many valuable employees.[18]

According to organizational development expert Edgar Schein, there are several mechanisms through which top executives influence organizational culture. First, leaders selectively pay attention to the things that are important to them. By communicating these priorities with their subordinates continuously, certain types of values and behaviors are reinforced and become part of organizational culture. For example, Alan Lafley, CEO at Procter & Gamble, focuses on establishing his company culture as one that values talent:

> It's Mother's Day, and Alan Lafley is meeting with the person he shares time with every Sunday evening—Richard L. Antoine, the company's head of human resources. Lafley doesn't invite the chief financial officer of the $43 billion business, nor does he ask the executive in charge of marketing at the world's largest consumer-products company. He doesn't invite friends over to watch The Sopranos, either. No, on most Sunday nights it's just Lafley, Antoine, and stacks of reports on the performance of the company's 200 most senior executives. This is the boss's signature gesture. It shows his determination to nurture talent and serve notice that little escapes his attention. If you worked for P & G, you would have to be both impressed and slightly intimidated by that kind of diligence.[19]

Second, top executives establish their unique culture by role modeling and mentoring. In other words, they reinforce the core message and strategy by showing followers how to fit into the organization through role modeling of their own actions. Mentoring and role modeling could potentially create and sustain a positive and high performing culture in an organization. Mentoring contributes to creating a very positive social context in which members of the organization could share core values and facilitate personal exchanges and engagement. When top executives consistently display through their own behavior what they preach, it promotes a more collaborative and collegial culture that strengthens organizational effectiveness.

Role modeling is well exemplified in the following way by Rick Sanders, Executive Vice President of Operation at JNI:

> Getting the best out of the best is very team oriented. Creating an environment in which people are not intimidated, afraid, where they feel they are needed, that they are appreciated, that their work has meaning. Once you create that environment and leading through example through the values that they see you demonstrating the team comes together. So honesty, openness, fairness, a hard work ethic. How do I motivate people to work hard? I get in at 6 [AM] and I leave here at 7 [PM]. I'm constantly working hard hours. I don't ask my employees to work those hours. In fact I don't monitor their work. All I ask for is that what they are achieving is achieved. They can do it how they choose to. They know that. So they want to be here. I don't have to ask them to be in here on the weekend if they have a job to get done.[20]

Finally, leaders influence culture by creating different types of criteria used as the basis for allocating rewards and other valuable resources. This signifies what is valued by the organization and helps employees establish accurate expectations.[21] For example, when a company values innovation, top executives can create HR policies that reward employees' innovative ideas and work processes. John Yi at KES echoed the importance of following up his employees' hard work with some rewards (both financial and emotional compensation) and demonstrated how he utilized this type of approach to create an innovation-oriented culture as follows:

> I think it's a combination of providing the financial compensation as well as providing maybe some kind of emotional support to your staff. And it's a combination and I'm still struggling. In fact one of the things that I take to my administrator director was she ran into my office with a couple of books and I forget the title but something like '50,000 Ways To Reward Your Employees'... and it could be something as simple as writing a note of thanks or sending an e-mail recognizing the accomplishment. One of the things that I try to also do is to replicate other companies' success. One thing that I tell my administrative staff is that I want to have food all the time, you know, cookies, chocolate candy, whatever. Small things like that.[22]

LEADERSHIP STYLES WITHIN ORGANIZATIONAL CULTURES

As part of our interview process, we also distributed three copies of a survey called the *Organizational Description Questionnaire* (ODQ) to the direct reports of the interviewed executives. This 28-item survey instrument measures different types of organizational cultures (see the Appendix for details).[23] Specifically, the ODQ generates cultural profiles of an organization based on how much it is transformational or transactional. Transactional elements in the culture's assumptions, processes and expectations are found in 14 items including the following statements.

- "You get what you deserve—no more, no less."
- "Everyone bargains with everyone else for resources."
- "Specific rules afford little opportunity for discretionary behavior."

In contrast, transformational elements of the organization's culture are summarized with 14 items including the following statements:

- "People go out of their way for the good of the institution."
- "Individual initiative is encouraged."
- "We believe in trusting each other to do the right thing."[24]

Respondents indicate whether each of the 28 statements are true, false, or "not sure." Therefore, when completed, the total transformational and transactional scores for each respondent could potentially range from –14 to +14. These scores are used to place organizations into cultural profile categories listed below.

The ODQ generates a cultural profile of an organization based on the transformational and transactional mean scores. There are nine cultural types that can be identified with the ODQ:

1. *Predominantly 4Is (Transformational)*
2. *Moderated 4Is (Transformational)*
3. *High-Contrast;*
4. *Loosely-Guided*
5. *Coasting;*
6. *Predominately Bureaucratic (Transactional)*
7. *Moderated Bureaucratic (Transactional)*
8. *Pedestrian* and
9. *Garbage Can.*

A detailed description on each of these ODQ cultural types can be found in Table A-2 in the Appendix.

At least three members from each organization in our sample rated their organization's culture using the ODQ. There was general within-organization agreement on the ODQ ratings and differences across the organizations. As such, we aggregated their ratings to produce one transformational and one transactional ODQ culture rating for each organization in our sample. We categorized the 65 organizations in our sample into one of the nine ODQ cultural types based on their transformational and transactional ODQ scores. Based on this procedure, our sample produced 2 *Predominantly 4Is* organizations, 40 *Moderated 4Is* organizations, 20 *Coasting* organizations; 1 *Predominately Bureaucratic* organization, 1 *Moderated Bureaucratic* organization, and 1 *Pedestrian* organization. No High-Contrast, Loosely-Guided or Garbage Can cultures were observed in our sample.

We then compared the mean (average) frequencies of leadership behaviors displayed by the top executives of these organizations available in our sample (as rated by their direct reports using the Multifactor Leadership Questionnaire –Form 5X) across the 6 ODQ cultural types or categories that emerged from our sample. Results of our analyses produced several interesting patterns summarized in Table 9.1 and Figure 9.1.

Regarding the executives' display of passive forms of leadership, executives in the organization with a *Moderated 4I* culture displayed less laissez-faire (LF) leadership than executives in organizations with *Coasting* and *Predominately Bureaucratic* cultures. Executives in the organization with a *Moderated 4I* culture also displayed less passive management-by-exception (MBE-P) leadership than executives in organizations with *Coasting* cultures.[25]

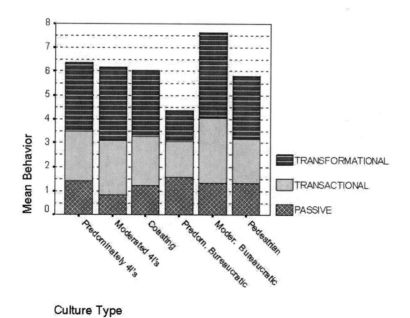

Culture Type

FIGURE 9.1
Mean Frequency of Display of Leadership Styles by Top Executives Across Organizational Culture Types.

TABLE 9.1
Means and Standard Deviations for Leadership Behaviors across Organizational Culture Types

Top Executive Leadership Behavior	Predominately 4Is		Moderated 4Is		Coasting		Predominately Bureaucratic		Moderated Bureaucratic		Pedestrian	
	M	SD	M	SD	M	SD	M	SD	M	SD	M	SD
Transformational												
II-B	2.83	.12	3.10	.43	2.72	.65	1.25	n/a	3.75	n/a	2.58	n/a
II-A	2.92	.47	3.24	.43	2.91	.63	.88	n/a	3.67	n/a	2.75	n/a
IM	3.21	.53	3.28	.43	3.03	.53	1.63	n/a	3.33	n/a	3.42	n/a
IS	2.83	.71	2.93	.39	2.52	.49	1.75	n/a	3.50	n/a	2.50	n/a
IC	2.54	.29	2.94	.52	2.57	.65	1.00	n/a	3.75	n/a	2.08	n/a
Transactional												
Contingent Reward	2.58	.35	2.96	.51	2.60	.54	1.25	n/a	3.42	n/a	1.92	n/a
MBE-A	1.63	.06	1.54	.55	1.52	.62	1.75	n/a	2.00	n/a	1.75	n/a
Passive												
MBE-P	1.80	.65	1.08	.55	1.47	.71	1.50	n/a	1.75	n/a	1.50	n/a
Laissez-Faire	1.00	.0	.57	.50	.97	.63	1.63	n/a	.92	n/a	1.17	n/a
Outcomes												
Effectiveness	2.64	.67	3.23	.41	2.98	.48	1.38	n/a	3.67	n/a	3.00	n/a
Satisfaction	2.72	.55	3.24	.37	2.98	.51	1.25	n/a	3.50	n/a	3.33	n/a
Extra Effort	2.74	.27	3.05	.51	2.77	.44	2.00	n/a	3.67	n/a	2.33	n/a
N (organizations)	2		40		20		1		1		1	

Notes: Sample (N= 65) represents top executive in organization within organizational culture type. II-B = Idealized Influence - Behavior; II-A = Idealized Influence - Attribute; IM = Inspirational Motivation; IS = Intellectual Stimulation; IC = Individualized Consideration; MBE-A = Management-by-exception (active) MBE-P = Management-by-exception (passive); n/a = not applicable.

Regarding the executives' display of transactional forms of leadership, executives did not differ on active management-by-exception leadership across the ODQ culture categories. However, executives in the organization with a *Predominately Bureaucratic* culture displayed less contingent reward (CR) leadership than executives in organizations with *Moderated Bureaucratic, Coasting, Predominately 4Is* and *Moderated 4Is* cultures. Executives in the organization with a *Pedestrian* culture displayed less CR leadership than executives in organizations with *Moderated Bureaucratic* and *Moderated 4Is* cultures. Executives in organizations with *Coasting* cultures displayed less CR leadership than executives in the organization with a *Moderated 4Is* culture.[26]

Regarding the executives' display of transformational forms of leadership, executives in the organization with a *Predominately Bureaucratic* culture displayed less inspirational motivation (IM) leadership than executives in organizations with *Moderated Bureaucratic, Coasting, Pedestrian, Predominately 4Is* and *Moderated 4Is* cultures. Executives in organizations with *Coasting* cultures displayed less IM leadership than executives in organizations with *Moderated 4Is* cultures.[27] Similar patterns were observed for idealized influence (behavior and attributes), intellectual stimulation and individualized consideration. Taken together, these results suggest that the leadership behavior of the top executives in technology-driven organizations does not necessarily correspond to the organizational cultures as perceived by their subordinates.

Several other interesting results were observed as depicted in Figures 9.2 through 9.6. First, among those companies whose culture was *Predominantly 4Is*, about 45 percent of the executives' leadership behavior was identified as transformational by their subordinates (Figure 9.2). In contrast, 33 percent of their behavior was identified as transactional and 22 percent was identified as passive. Interestingly, about 50 percent of the executives' behavior was identified as transformational the company whose cultural type was *Moderated 4Is*, while the percentage of the executives' behavior identified as passive went down to 13 percent (Figure 9.3). In addition, among those companies whose cultural type was *Coasting* (see Figure 9.4), which falls between the extremely transformational and transactional cultures, perceived leadership behavior among the interviewed executives was very similar to what we found among the *Predominantly 4Is* type. Therefore, perceived leadership behavior among *Predominantly/Moderately 4Is* and *Coasting* cultural types was mainly transformational (over 45 percent) followed by transactional and passive leadership.

However, in the *Predominantly Bureaucratic* cultural type we identified in our sample, only 30 percent of the executives' behavior was identified as transformational (Figure 9.5). A higher percentage of the executives' behavior (34 %) was identified as transactional. Interestingly, the highest percentage of the executives' behavior (about 36 %) among the *Predominantly Bureaucratic Culture* type was identified by their subordinates as *pas-*

Predominately 4I's Culture

Percentage of Total Perceived Leadership Behavior

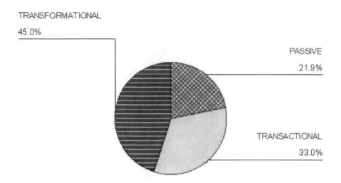

FIGURE 9.2
Mix of Leadership Styles Displayed by Top Executives in
Predominately 4Is Cultures.

Moderated 4I's Culture

Percentage of Total Perceived Leadership Behavior

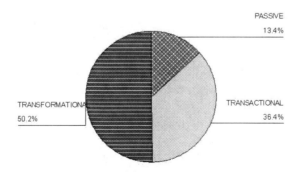

FIGURE 9.3
Mix of Leadership Styles Displayed by Top Executives in Moderated 4Is
Cultures.

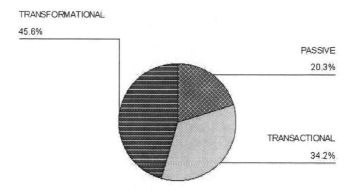

FIGURE 9.4
Mix of Leadership Styles Displayed by Top Executives in Coasting Cultures.

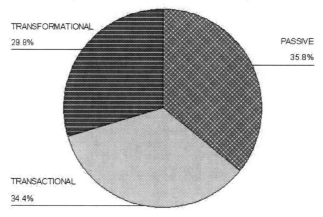

FIGURE 9.5
Mix of Leadership Styles Displayed by Top Executives in Predominately
Bureaucratic Cultures.

sive leadership. This relationship between highly bureaucratic cultures and fairly passive leadership was not unexpected because many of the executives were either being too passive in handling their managerial responsibilities due to their personality, or relied on a relatively passive style of leadership to handle their daily routines due to their very demanding work schedules.

This strong tendency toward using passive leadership might have been due to the nature of the work that employees perform in fast-paced high tech environments. The majority of the employees that these executives were leading and managing had advanced degrees and the necessary expertise and knowledge to make a decision based on their own judgment. As a result, many of the executives we interviewed tended to empower their subordinates and chose not to take action to intervene with their subordinates' work process. They preferred to let things settle naturally. In a sense, passive leadership style was the outcome due to the combination of some executives' personal tendencies, the highly demanding nature of high tech environments, and their knowledgeable employees, who might have perceived more active forms of leadership as unnecessary and redundant.

However, many executives noted that passive leadership could be used occasionally, but it would eventually lead to more problems than benefits in their fast-changing work environments. An example of when passive leadership style is chosen and how it eventually leads to negative consequences is illustrated in the following statements made by an executive we interviewed:

> So there is a risk that if you focus on certain parts of the department and not others and just let them be that they will feel like its not important what I am doing and the performance of those individuals goes down. So I think you have to monitor that and set the metrics up and continue to monitor. But that's difficult, to stay on top of things all the time. I think they tend to start thinking eventually that what they are doing is not important. That is a problem! It's a negative effect. We try to reinforce that my moving responsibility down the organization. We have managers that all have their metrics. We have group sessions where you are showing all your metrics. So try to engage and recognize everyone's contribution as much as you can.

Finally, another type of culture we identified among our sample was *Pedestrian,* which represents a somewhat mechanistic organizational culture. A *Pedestrian* culture is moderately transactional with little transformational nature. Change is typically unlikely and risk-taking is not encouraged in such an organization. The *Pedestrian* organization is relatively well structured with rules and procedures. However, executives in this type of culture tend to have real position power with little discretion. A typical *Pedestrian* organization is a not-for-profit organization with a number of volunteers whose commitment to the organization is generally low and leader's vision is not well articulated.[28] Therefore, we expected to find a significant percentage of the executives in the *Pedestrian* organizational cultures and their leadership behavior to be passive or transactional at best.

To our surprise, transformational leadership behavior was predominant (about 46%) among executives in *Pedestrian* organizations, followed by transactional (about 31%) and passive (23%) behavior (Figure 9.6). A plausible explanation for this unexpected finding is that some of the leaders we identified in the *Pedestrian* organization were newly appointed at the time of our interview and they were trying to initiate a lot of changes they needed to make in order to keep up with new Internet technologies, shifts in customer preferences, and turbulent market conditions. Furthermore, their organization was hit hard by the recent economy slowdown. In a sense, members of *Pedestrian* organizational cultures in our samples might have perceived a crisis situation which generated a lot of stress, anxiety, and uncertainty due to changes in the marketplace and their lack of adaptability. The leadership literature has identified some contextual and situational factors including perception of "crisis" that contribute to perceptions of transformational and charismatic leadership. When employees perceived that they were in the middle of "crisis" condition and observed their executives initiating some changes (such as reorganizing and restructuring their company to make it more efficient and effective) to offer attractive solutions and vision of the future, they may have been more likely to perceive their leaders as being transformational.[29]

Pedestrian Culture

Percentage of Total Perceived Leadership Behavior

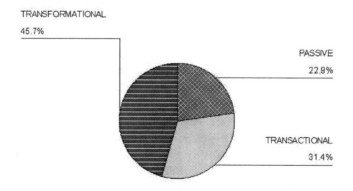

FIGURE 9.6
Mix of Leadership Styles Displayed by Top Executives in Pedestrian Cultures.

SOME POINTS WORTH REMEMBERING

In this chapter, we have described how leaders in organizations influence organizational culture and how it in turn influences organizational effectiveness. Throughout our interviews, it was obvious that the founders and top executives were cognizant of their role in creating and maintaining positive organizational cultures marked by empowerment, innovation, participation and diversity. Many of the executives indicated that they used their organizational culture as a means to communicate and reinforce their core messages and values. Since organizational survival depends on how well these values match up with the organization's mission and needs from their marketplace, the strategy-focused leaders we interviewed went beyond ordinary efforts to make sure that they had a unique, strong and positive organizational culture in place. Based on these findings, several conclusions can be drawn from this chapter.

First, leaders create and maintain organizational culture though various means. Sometimes, leaders constantly display certain behaviors to communicate what is important and desirable. Oftentimes, leaders build certain types of organizational systems such as performance evaluation and reward policies to reinforce their cultures. Second, some organizations used culture as a strategic asset. Members of the organization are more likely to embrace changes when they develop an organizational culture that emphasizes innovation and adaptation. We identified several organizations such as ILR Global and Union Bank of California where innovative organizational cultures made their restructuring process highly successful and profitable. Finally, we found that organizational culture and leadership interact with each other constantly. Leaders create and reinforce certain norms and behaviors within the culture, which in turn provides the leaders and followers with their work context in which they operate. In fact, we found a fairly consistent pattern of leadership styles across the cultural types. For example, when an organization had the *Predominantly 4Is* culture, the majority of executives we interviewed displayed transformational leadership behaviors. This could create a nice fit between executives' leadership style and organizational culture and past research has shown that such fit makes an organization more effective.[30]

In conclusion, today's high-tech organizations face highly turbulent technological and business environments. Customers' vastly increased access to information and suppliers has empowered them to demand ever-increasingly arrays of product features, higher quality, better service, and favorable price/cost ratios. These realities of the marketplace have put tremendous pressures on companies to increase their efficiency and effectiveness and, even more fundamentally, the innovation that they bring to product/process improvements and development. The new marketplace requires organizations to constantly transform themselves into more loosely-coupled, flexible and slim configurations. Toward this end, there is an added role and responsibility for strategy-focused leaders to create an organizational culture that is more adaptive and innovative. This new role of cultural change is often reflected in revisions to the core message as the organization changes over time. We examine this essential SFL process in our final chapter.

CHAPTER 10

RE-FOCUSING THE SHAPE OF FUTURE SUCCESS

The future is not a result of choices among alternative paths offered by the
present, but a place that is created—created first in the mind and will,
created next in activity. The future is not some place we are going to, but
one we are creating. The paths are not to be found, but made, and the
activity of making them, changes both the maker and the destination.

—*John Schaar*

As executives of technology-driven organizations diversify their products
and services and disperse their operations around the world, they are challenged as never before to continually re-focus their organizational strategies by fine-tuning the connections between people, technology and
strategy, to more fully develop their stock of social, financial, intellectual
and structural capital. This chapter summarizes how executives adjust their
strategies to make their organization more effective in the current business
and technological environment and to take charge of their future more
proactively. We pay particular attention to how they use connectivity concepts to align people, business partnerships, and value-added processes to

The Dream Weavers: Strategy-Focused Leadership in Technology-Driven
Organizations, pages 215–237
ISBN: 1-59311-110-X (paper), 1-59311-111-8 (cloth)

achieve strategic performance goals via performance measurement systems and the distribution of leadership within and between organizations in their strategic networks.

CREATING NEW OPPORTUNITIES THROUGH CONNECTIVITY

When former Delaware State Senator Bob Still first joined Lancaster Radiology Associates (LRA), the last thing that he could foresee himself as was a "creator of the future." But that's exactly what he has become in his role as LRA's COO. Today, Still finds himself continually building consensus among LRA's 27 physician owners, who are linked via a network of radiology practices, regarding the re-focusing of LRA's strategy and vision of maintaining excellence in clinical practice with its patients. This responsibility also involves moving the practice forward in a way that Lancaster General Hospital and other constituents deem necessary. Re-vitalizing the organization's culture and LRA's associates' professional views to be consistent with marketplace realities is what Still does best to keep LRA a highly successful and competitive organization. It is exactly this kind of inspirational leadership that strategy-focused leaders must display to help their organizations remain competitive and profitable in the face of changing markets and technologies.

Still's other major responsibility involves building and maintaining strong connections and lasting relationships based on loyalty and trust with LRA's business partners, employees and patients. This important role requires the sharing of information. Whether it's with patients, Lancaster General Hospital, or the LRA's management staff, Still is responsible for negotiating with them, motivating them according to LRA's business strategy, and establishing the information links between people, technology and strategy required for LRA's success.[1]

As organizations like LRA increasingly take advantage of technological connectivity within and between employees, customers, suppliers and business partners, the linkages that strategy-focused leaders are capable of making between people, technologies and ideas are expected to grow exponentially. These connections will allow for more opportunities for the outcomes of SFL depicted in Figure 1.1: outstanding financial performance, customer satisfaction, expanded knowledge bases, continuous improvements in people and processes, and shared leadership. As seen at LRA, integrated communications with organizational stakeholders allows organizations to thrive based on their strategic connections of people, technologies and ideas.

Economist John Mason elegantly describes this phenomenon of the power of *connectivity* that strategy-focused leaders use to produce beneficial outcomes:

Information generators thrive in an environment of networks because information is largely useless in isolation. Information becomes more valuable as more people have access to it. Metcalf's Law is usually given as the justification for this claim: the value of a network increases by the square of the number of members in the network. It seems that when more people share information, dialogue increases, more ideas are generated, productivity rises, and most of those involved seem to benefit. In networks, people treat each other as peers, and this gives individuals the opportunity to make their contributions as equals rather than as subordinates . . . This can create a tremendous *bottom-up* effect that seems to be a characteristic of very innovative communities.[2]

These types of aligned and integrated communities called *strategic networks* support the distribution of leadership functions within and between organizations and are created by strategy-focused leaders through the processes described in Chapters 3 through 9 of this book.

To illustrate, consider Samsung, Microsoft, Nokia, and Nextel. These are just some of increasing number of organizations that have added high levels of economic value for their shareholders based on the idea of connectivity. They have capitalized on a variety of complex business models such as "business-to-business," "business-to-consumer," and "business-to-all," which have fundamentally changed the way executives must develop and lead their organization's strategy and carefully synchronize their business activities. For example, executives at Samsung are rethinking the way they deliver products and services throughout the world using a "business-to-all" strategy. Microsoft has integrated the ideas of customers into its strategic planning by continuously collecting suggestions for system improvements and desired products and services. Customers are now partners in its SFL system.

Likewise, in 2002, Jorma Ollila, CEO of Nokia rolled out 30 new products (e.g., camera-phones) and licensed Nokia's software to other phonemakers to produce greater than expected profits estimated at $3.4 billion. Nextel Communications' CEO Timothy M. Donahue also yielded stellar profits by introducing DirectConnect, which provides walkie-talkie-like wireless connections. These examples show that SFL plays a central role in these initiatives in the sense that both CEOs first dreamed of a successful outcome, and then strategically created and aligned the connections between customers, product development and product delivery, which eventually added significant profits for their organizations.[3]

ALIGNING PEOPLE, PARTNERSHIPS, PROCESSES AND PERFORMANCE

One of the major themes that we have developed in this book is that executives must make the right connections between their people, business partners and opportunities, and value-added work processes and structures (which represent their organizations' strategic assets) to achieve outstanding performance. However, we believe that the alignment of these strategic assets should be seen as a moving target, constantly changing and shifting like sand bars that support the warm waters of Florida's Gulf Coast. Just as the sand bars shift with the rising and ebb tides, so too do the environmental elements of an organization's strategic situation. As a result, executives must constantly monitor the environment for changes and make the necessary adjustments and fine-tune the strategies and connections between an organization's strategic assets.

Given the never-ending shifts in an organization's strategic situation described in Chapter 2, the strategy-focused leaders we interviewed told us they worked very hard to be constantly vigilant of the characteristics of those moving targets. What some executives felt were relevant or desired performance targets or outcomes were deemed to be irrelevant by others. But most executives felt that the targets/outcomes need constant evaluation for relevance. This is because when you identify a performance target as relevant or irrelevant, good or bad, appropriate or inappropriate, you are basing your assessment on your past opinions, experiences, stereotypes and prejudices may be no longer valid or accurate. The problem is that your opinions, experiences and other viewpoints may be incorrect. They may have started out correct, but over time conditions of your strategic situation may have changed and your opinions and beliefs may not have been adjusted to reflect the realities of the new environment and its critical performance outcomes.

We were able to distill some common performance outcomes of SFL that were generally consistent among our interviews with the executives. Not only do the performance targets change depending on the characteristics of the strategic situation, but they also change depending on the age and size of the organization. In addition, some executives were more aware of their strategic situations and also more aware of their leadership behaviors that are generally associated with these performance outcomes. Such awareness can have a significant effect on the performance of the executive and his or her followers and organization, and is discussed below.

SFL Performance Outcomes

In Chapter 1, we identified six potential outcomes of SFL of technology-driven organizations:

1. outstanding financial performance,
2. customer satisfaction,
3. expanded knowledge bases,

4. integrated communications with stakeholders,
5. continuous process/people improvements, and
6. shared leadership.

These performance outcomes have a reciprocal relationship with SFL—they feed off of performance and each other and sustain each other over time.[4]

The primary performance outcome of SFL is *outstanding financial performance*—a healthy bottom line and cash flow that exceed the expectations of the Board and the shareholders. Let's face it: earnings and cash are the life blood of any organization. They are particularly important for technology-driven organizations which have extremely high levels of investment in R & D which require substantial cash outlays. Without healthy earnings and a positive cash flow sustained over time, there can be no core message, no development of human capital, no intellectual capital, or no structural capital. In other words, there can be no SFL. Without SFL, executives are not able to consistently deliver the financial results expected by shareholders and Wall Street analysts. In fact, one of the authors had an opportunity to attend the annual conference organized by American Society of Training and Development (ASTD) recently held in San Diego and found that the linkage between training and bottom-line performance was the most important issue resonated by many training and development managers.

Lee Kranefuss, CEO of Barclay Global Investors' Individual Investors business unit, highlighted the primacy and difficulty of consistently achieving outstanding financial results:

> It's the great scourge of the free market system, which is no matter how well you do, next quarter you got to do better. And no one lets you take a great performance and say, "Can I bank that one?" No, thank you very much, you've not set the level, it needs to happen again. It is a challenge. But, we've had a great run! Last year we pulled in almost $10 billion in total assets, which put us Number 3 against all equity mutual fund complexes in the country. So, we beat out most of the major names, coming out of nowhere, beat the names most people would have heard and seen and think of as the big fund families . . . Not withstanding the fact that you might be way ahead of where you should have in that point in time. So people will be looking at you saying, "Hey, we're still so far ahead of plan, this is wonderful, this is an unmitigated success," and what they notice are the changes taking place. They work off of the first derivative.[5]

Kranefuss suggests that it is important to realize that outstanding financial performance is largely a function of the people, processes, ideas, communication, and leadership that drive financial performance over time. Of particular importance to the executives we interviewed was customer satisfaction. We choose this term because it is a commonly understood and desired outcome of almost all progressive organizations. But the outstanding strategy-focused leaders we interviewed were able to achieve much more than mere customer satisfaction. They were able to create a consistent and strong sense of *excitement* for their customers.

The challenge of achieving more than mere customer satisfaction is that in our technology-driven world we are often trapped by the urgency of the moment—getting the work done not only effectively but also efficiently because we tend to focus primarily on the bottom line. But in the rush we lose something more important—the customer's concerns or interests. This is the mantra of Ted Garrison, our good friend and consulting colleague from Ormond Beach, Florida. Ted helps businesses in the construction industry to identify their customer's needs in order to add greater value for their customers. Perceived value is important because it often produces greater customer loyalty and increased profits.

One of Ted's favorite questions to ask his seminar attendees is: "What kind of customer do you want?" Usually some unsuspecting person falls into his trap and answers, "A satisfied customer." Ted laughs and responds, "You must be kidding—that is the last thing you want." After a pause where he gets some puzzled looks he adds, "The reason I say this is because 86 percent of satisfied customers will go to your competitor on the next job, so who wants a satisfied customer?" This occurs because "satisfied" means you did okay, but you certainly didn't "WOW" the customer, which is what's needed to create repeat business, customer loyalty and increased profits.[6]

This exciting "WOW" level of customer satisfaction is an outcome of SFL seen at organizations like ILR Global, a large computer and software service organization. At ILR Global, relationships with customers are managed by the sales staff or by consultants, and the customer services group manages the lists and press relations. There is a separate group that manages industrial relations, which is a discipline unto itself in most companies. That's true at ILR Global because they have a very specialized set of needs, but they want a solid return on their investment costs. ILR's Executive Director of Media Relations told us:

> To sell computers and software and services and WOW your customers, you need to know a lot about customers and about their industry. We have a lot of that knowledge. In fact, what's interesting is that Microsoft has just reorganized its sales staff largely by industry. That's something that we did in 1996. What drives the stock price are our customers. What makes our customers very happy are our great products and great services. So that's really what you have to focus on and that's not easy . . . we have very smart people out there, and we have a very big very complex company. So it's very hard work, but thank goodness the last few years we have been quite successful . . . The real strength of ILR is being able to put together everything for the customer— make it easy for them . . . the most important thing is taking the customer out and being more active with the customer. If we do that, I'm sure we're going to continue to do great![7]

The same is true at Eastern Com where its Vice President of Customer Service told us that WOWing the customer is so important that he has made it the vision for his organization. His core message is plain and simple: customer care. Specifically, *"Deliver it on time, make sure it doesn't break, and if it does fix it fast!"* His organization constantly strives for 100 percent reliability. He also works with operation teams to determine responsibilities, but since he works in customer service his goals are aimed at achieving complete reliability and satisfaction. According to this executive, his goals and the goals of operations and the supervisors in his organization need to be in alignment. If these goals are achieved, customers will continue to buy from Eastern Com.[8]

Other organizations, like ITG Pathfinders, are working very hard to achieve the "WOW" experience with customers. Russell Laraway, ITG's COO told us:

> A stated business goal [of ITG] is to improve—we have these ratings from our customers—our customer satisfaction ratings, which is going to be difficult to do, but we'll do it. We want to drastically improve our differentiation ratings from our clients. They saw us as very talented, very squared away, very good with technology, but they did not see us as differentiated, which is what prompted us a year and half ago to launch the brand platform, the brand architecture. That's a stated goal. All of these things kind of weave together. There are financial metrics, there are customer satisfaction metrics, everything, very measurable, of course, that ultimately add up to the big business goal, which is really wealth creation for the shareholders.[9]

Two additional outcomes of SFL are the *expanded knowledge bases* that result from the intellectually stimulating and connective leadership processes described in Chapter 8 and *integrated communications with stakeholders* described in Chapter 6. The strategic networks of employees, customers, suppliers and business partners can potentially generate continuing streams of ideas, innovations and opportunities. Supported by state-of-the-art technologies such as peer-to-peer, pervasive and mobile computing, strategy-focused leaders work to link nodes within their strategic networks so that communicating and processing will become truly ubiquitous. As more and more executives connect their people within and between organizations, integrated communications and processing will eventually pervade all industries and society. This has the potential to promote dramatically higher levels of organizational effectiveness.

Expanded knowledge bases are an outcome of Bob Still's SFL at LRA. Physicians at LRA are widely known as very highly skilled, highly trained, fellowship physicians. Still has built a community of practice which shares its expertise through traditional face-to-face meetings and an on-line web-based group decision support system that allows his associates to communicate, brainstorm, and access information outside of LRA's network.

At Concord, Inc. expanded knowledge bases are developed by getting all employees to be honest about their opinions and bringing them forward in a constructive way even if they do not agree with what the current strategy is. Simply put, Concord thirsts for its people's ideas and uses information sharing sessions, brainstorming, and employee focus groups to learn more about its industry. Management wants employees' views on how to do things differently because that makes for a much more healthy and innovative organization. According to Concord's CEO, "In quality terms, we need everybody's ideas, we just got to have them, or we will not succeed."[10]

Integrated communications with organizational stakeholders were evident at organizations like ILR Global through its individualized relationships with its customers, business partners and suppliers. These relationships are connected via a business grid environment so that computing can be done more efficiently and communication can be direct and effective. At Architectural Concepts, connectivity has also led to integrated communications with stakeholders. Bruce Weinstieger, a partner at the design firm, was particularly proud of this organizational outcome, which is important for sustaining a culture of total quality management:

> I think what our clients like about us is that they know they can get in touch with one of the partners at any time. The concept here is 'partners' and we make ourselves available to them. Yes, there are always staff members involved. They're on every project and we have to have staff here as well. But it is important to us to maintain that client contact for TQM.[11]

Continuous process/people improvements (CPPI) represent another outcome of SFL. The developmental processes of SFL described in Chapter 5 and the quality and innovation generating processes of SFL described in Chapter 8 are the drivers of CPPI. This outcome, a culture of quality that grows out of TQM processes, is critical for success in technology-driven industries given the rapid rate of change, importance of knowledge, skills, abilities and information as strategic assets, and the highly volatile environment with disruptive and destructive forces described in Chapter 2. To adapt to such a turbulent environment requires the CPPI of an organization's leadership and human resources, as the marketplace continuously demands different responses from the organization. CPPI entails

a. the never-ending reciprocal relationship between product/service improvement and customer satisfaction,
b. the constant enhancement of customer satisfaction by fostering a culture of trust, teamwork, high expectations and open communication with employees, customers and suppliers, and
c. a systems approach which utilizes objective data for analyzing/ enhancing processes to satisfy both internal and external customers.[12]

CPPI was evident at many of the organizations we studied, in particular, the manufacturing organizations where inspirational leadership was pervasive and quite effective in providing meaning for their CPPI cultures. For example, Bill Rieser of Pulte Homes exemplifies a strategy-focused leader who has provided meaning for his associates regarding the CPPI and quality culture at his organization. Rieser would like his customers to recognize the innate quality of his product—that their home is a Pulte home. And as a result, customers would have such a great satisfaction based on a great product, and Pulte would have a reputation in the market place that its brand would represent quality. According to Rieser,

> That would be the vision to create—to have people who believe—to recognize—our brand and quality are the same. It's interesting that what we do probably affects peoples' lives almost more than anything else. Educators obviously affect people's lives as they grow, but we affect how people live, and because of that, it is pretty exciting stuff.[13]

One of the most important outcomes of SFL is a culture of *shared leadership*. A culture of shared leadership is created by the developmental, intellectually stimulating, empowering and socialization processes of SFL described in Chapters 5, 8 and 9. *Shared leadership* means that the organization, as a whole, shares and participates fully in the leadership tasks of the organization. If empowered organizational members have the authority, self-efficacy and knowledge of the leadership tasks, they can accomplish much of the leadership formerly delegated to the middle or top managers. In a sense, the central focus of the leadership building process is shifting from "of" the team or organization to "by" the team or organization.[14] For example, organizational members can recruit and hire each other, actively motivate one another, provide feedback on performance, and direct the activities of the project teams. Shared leadership is one critical aspect of how strategy-focused leaders fully empower and develop their followers into tomorrow's leaders. Providing followers with the power and opportunity to make decisions based on the organization's collective skills makes sense when firms use strategic networks to take advantage of the unique knowledge, skills and abilities of people within and between organizations.[15] The shared leadership concept has emerged as an important topic in leadership research and practice since many organizations have adopted a more loosely-coupled structure and utilize virtual teams as a way to respond the fast-changing marketplace in today's economy.[16]

Shared leadership pervaded the cultures of many of the organizations we studied. However it was particularly evident at Greencastle Consulting Associates, which uses self-directed project management teams to monitor the strategic situation and execute the organization's strategy. In describing the shared leadership at Greencastle, Celwyn Evans told us:

I primarily work with the senior management consultants as part of my leadership team, and they don't need a whole lot of development, because they are very accomplished in coming to Greencastle. So, I'm more kind of ensuring they're aligning with how Greencastle operates. Are they utilizing the various enablers that we've put into play? So I see my role more as a mentor, or a coach, or a facilitator.[17]

It's the facilitation of an empowered and developed group of associates that enables strategy-focused leaders to reap the benefits of shared leadership as their organizations evolve over time.

SFL and Organizational Life Cycles

As human beings, we all go through various life stages—childhood, adolescence, young adulthood, middle age, and seniority. Each life stage has its own set of social, emotional, psychological and physical challenges. Moving from one stage into another is associated with potential crises. Organizations also go through various stages of development and transitions between these stages often can be problematic. Therefore, organizations should first realize different stages of their life cycles and identify unique requirements such as appropriate organizational structure, culture, work processes, and incentive systems in order to sustain continued success.

A recent announcement from Microsoft illustrates this point. After a decade of phenomenal success, the company has announced that it would start paying dividends and granting stock purchases instead of stock options to create more stable workforce and business structure. At Microsoft or any company, *each stage of the organizational life cycle calls for different leadership styles from executives and different performance outcomes required for success over time.* In fact, the age of organizations in our sample was *inversely* related to executives' display of laissez faire, MBE-P and MBE-A leadership, *and positively* related to direct reports' attributions of idealized influence to executives, and ratings of the performance outcomes of unit effectiveness, satisfaction with the executive, and extra effort.[18]

There are several classification systems of organizational life cycle stages. We choose to classify the organizations in our sample using I.M. Jawahar and Gary L. McLaughlin's concise and pragmatic classification scheme.[19] According to these authors, organizations go through four life stages:

1. start-up,
2. emerging growth,
3. maturity and
4. decline/transition.

In the *start-up* stage, organizations focus on developing and implementing a business plan, obtaining funding, and/or entering marketplaces. An idea for a new product or service arising through technological innovation emerges and begins to develop in the form of a new organization. Here the organization faces the well-known "liability of newness," where because it is working hard to become established, its most critical performance outcomes are funding, cash flow, and customer satisfaction. Creativity, innovation and inspirational leadership are required to establish the organization as a viable competitor in its market, which could use up the first 10 years of its life depending on economic conditions and leadership style. There were 20 organizations in our sample classified as start-ups, such as ITG Pathfinders, BB Net.com, JNI Engineering, Aye Tech.com, and CB Technologies.

What CB Technologies is today isn't what it started out to be. It began as a generalist consulting firm and provided information technology services to a variety of customers. Because of the concentrated number of pharmaceutical companies in the Philadelphia region, CB hired a significant amount of expertise which led them to develop a product. Now the company is strictly focusing on the product. The product electronically captures data of clinical trials and provides the services that go along with it. CB has been around for a decade and is now back to being a start-up company. Its goal is to go public. Being able to meet the financial goals of company and combine this with where they stand operationally will be required to get the sophistication they need for sustaining and gaining market share.[20]

In the *emerging growth* stage, the organization has achieved a sustained degree of success and is actively seeking and engaged in expansion opportunities. The organization has developed clear goals and objectives and a hierarchy of authority. Division of labor and formal systems have been established. The organization finds a market for its products or services based on technology it has developed or adopted. Clear direction and strategic goals reinforced with contingent rewards are needed to add structural capital to the organization. Here the most critical performance outcomes are CPPI, expanding knowledge bases, continued customer satisfaction, and outstanding financial performance. There were 12 organizations in our sample classified as emerging growth organizations, such as Diversified Data Services, Hartcourt, Magnum Credit Card, Rnet and Qualcomm.

Qualcomm has a tradition of classic research and development. That tradition worked against the company when they attempted to transition into full manufacturing. They overcame their transitional crisis and became profitable to the point where they could sell off the full manufacturing model and focus on their core competency: technological innovation. In fact, Qualcomm began as type of a think-thank. It hired lots of thinkers, classical thinkers and theatrical types, as opposed to applied scientists. Qualcomm continues to combat the very deeply entrenched attitudes in the world that are in favor of the main competing technologies. They perform many interesting experiments such as combining the two technologies so that they don't get bogged down in more matured technology.[21] It's those types of initiatives that Qualcomm tries to do to combat the lethargy that often leads an organization into the maturity stage.

In the emerging growth stage, the provision of clear direction and establishment of reward systems would seem to call for contingent reward and active forms of management-by-exception (MBE-A) leadership. However, we found that executives of emerging growth organizations in our sample displayed more passive (laissez faire and MBE-P) leadership than executives in mature organizations, and more laissez-faire leadership than executives of start-up organizations.[22] We expect that executives of these emerging growth organizations weren't "missing in action," like William Agee and John Sculley, the notoriously laissez-faire former CEOs of Morrison Knudson and Apple Computer. Instead, they may have been spending most of their time fighting fires and "letting things settle naturally" since organizations in the emerging growth stage typically find their environments neither threatening nor constraining.[23] In other words, they may have gotten themselves bogged down working "in" the business (of *technical details*) instead of "on" the business (of *strategy and leadership*), as noted by Steve Torres, CFO of Harcourt:

> Letting things settle naturally [passive leadership] can be effective with motivated employees and [giving them] the challenge of orienteering their way out of a tough spot. Orienteering is the use of a map and a compass. Some people like the freedom to come up with the full draft document with the full analysis. If you want a passive boss, I'm not the guy to work for. At the same time I'm not a micromanager. I am detailed oriented and I am a good follow-up person. And a good way to get me off your back is if you could give me specific answers as to when, where, how, who and what does the project really like? What are the big issues? And how are we approaching them?[24]

Yet in the emerging growth stage, it is important for strategy-focused leaders to learn to work "on" the business and not just work "in" the business. As executives, problems can occur when our technician nature that we nurtured during the start-up phase takes over. We think that focusing on technical detail is the essential part of the leadership of an organization, and that it is necessary to understand whatever the detailed problems are all about. Unfortunately, this is a shortsighted perspective, because strategically leading an organization is much more than focusing on solving narrow problems. Instead, it's about communicating with, developing and guiding followers along the long and winding road leading to the organization's long-term objectives. For Harcourt, that vision means being a leader in education, helping students and teachers pre-K through grade 12 by producing quality books that improve their lives.

In the *maturity* stage, the organization has grown relatively large, is well established in terms of markets and products, and its administrative structure is quite formalized and may evolve into a bureaucracy. The organization generally has been in existence for quite some time, typically more than 20 years. In this stage, executives often regard their organization as successful, respected industry leaders. Some organizations in this stage experience a slowed rate of growth, which may be a result of the overconfidence based on past successes. Other organizations may see such downturns in performance as opportunities to re-focus the core message and strategy and take advantage of their economies of scale to lead the organization into another period of rapid growth.

For mature organizations, the most critical performance outcomes are shared leadership, CPPI, and integrated communications to deal with stakeholders within the organization's established strategic network in a proactive manner. We found that executives of mature organizations displayed *less* of active management-by-exception (MBE-A) leadership than executives of start-up and emerging growth organizations.[25] For mature organizations, a mixture of transactional and transformational SFL may be most appropriate to maintain the existing internal systems and cultural norms that often substitute for MBE-A leadership, and to develop teamwork and shared leadership across the organization. There were 34 organizations in our sample classified as mature organizations, including Concord, Inc., ILR Global, International Chips, LRA, NC Utility, Morton Finance, Sheetz, The Vanguard Group, and Mercy Community Hospital.

The industry plays a major role in how effective a mature organization is in shaping its future. For example, the challenges today are obvious and significant for Mercy Community Hospital (MCH) and the health care industry overall: cost structures, physicians' malpractice insurance and other issues. Internal changes in the structure and culture of MCH also are challenging. The hospital's leadership is re-assessing its services throughout its system, searching for more conducive ways to be efficient and cut costs. MCH has several hospitals in its system which has led to a situation of over-capacity. They also have several hospitals that are closely related in functionality. That means that they may not be doing a good job probing the market. MCH also has to deal with many physicians who are in an uproar over malpractice. They are increasingly leaving Pennsylvania to practice in other states where the cost of malpractice insurance is not so prohibitive. Not to mention the changing nature of patients coming to hospitals, who are demanding at higher levels of service. As the industry itself is undergoing massive change, time will tell whether MCH has the kind of leadership associated with decline or the SFL required for transition.[26]

In the *decline/transition* stage, organizations become defensive about their products, services and even their existence. These organizations continue their maturity until they eventually decline out of existence, or retool themselves by streamlining and taking on small company thinking. In this stage, executives generally reassess the strategies currently used, and may re-focus their core message in an attempt to re-invent and re-vitalize the organization with transformational (specifically inspirational) SFL, before it is too late. No organizations in our sample were classified as being in decline or transition.

To summarize, to be a strategy-focused leader you must be aware of and pay careful attention to your organization's age, life cycle stage and its associated characteristics, so that you can match the appropriate leadership style to the organization's stage of development. Remember that transformational SFL is most appropriate in the early and late stages of an organization's life, whereas transactional SFL is most appropriate in the more stable emerging growth stage. Yet, a combination of transactional and transformational SFL may be most effective to ensure the continued success of more mature organizations.

Alignment Through Self-Awareness of Leadership Behavior and the Strategic Situation

In matters of leadership of technology-driven organizations, it's essential not to confuse dreams with reality. Intel's Chairman Andy Grove once wrote that executives most vulnerable to career derailment and organizational failures were those who lacked an awareness of how their leadership was being perceived by their followers, and how their business model failed to align with changing marketplace realities.[27] Consistent with Grove's viewpoint, *Fortune* magazine spotlighted five CEOs at the time—Jill Barad of Mattel, Gary Dicamillo of Polaroid, Desi Desimone of 3M, Jerry Sanders of AMD, and Paul Fireman of Reebok—and described them as lacking self-awareness of their leadership and living in denial of the adverse market realities facing their firms.[28] These examples illustrate the importance of an executive's self-awareness of his or her leadership behavior and how it affects an organization's people, strategy, stakeholders and critical performance outcomes.

The importance of self-awareness was noted by the Vice President and General Manager of Dial Rhodes, who studies karate, has a black belt and likens it to leadership perceptions:

> There's a lot of [karate] students who are at the lower belts. When you walk into that dojo, you don't even notice it. But if you think back to when you were a white belt, you were watching everything that those black belts did. [As a black belt or a leader] you always have to remind yourself that everybody's watching and looking at how you behave and the important decisions

you make. Leaders have the opportunity to change the culture and extend the organization, but instead of pushing back or addressing the [current] situation and saying they don't accept it, some just take it. Then the status quo becomes OK and the company stagnates.[29]

Self-awareness refers to a psychological state describing the existence of self-directed attention that considers what other people think about your role, impressions, or behavior. Most research has focused on self-awareness of the leadership styles of managers rather than executives. So we were interested in determining the extent to which the executives in our sample were self-aware, that is, generally viewed their leadership style in a similar fashion as their direct reports. Self-awareness of executive SFL would emphasize an executives' ability to pay attention to the verbal and non-verbal communication of others in response to his or her display of SFL behavior.

One way of assessing individuals' level of self-awareness is to examine their self-other rating agreement (how an individual sees himself/herself versus how others see him/her) and then categorize them as

a. *over-estimators*, those who produce self-ratings that are significantly higher than others' ratings of leadership behavior,
b. *under-estimators*, those who produce self-ratings that are significantly lower than others' ratings of leadership behavior, and
c. those *in-agreement*, who produce ratings similar to others' ratings of leadership behavior.

Each of these categories of individuals represents varying levels of self-awareness: those who are in-agreement are self-aware, whereas those who are over-estimators or under-estimators lack self-awareness.[30]

Research indicates that managers vary in the level of self-awareness of leadership behavior they display, and this variance is associated with different types of personality traits, impression management and influence tactics, and performance outcomes. The traits, behaviors and performance outcomes associated with managers who over-estimate, under-estimate, and are in-agreement regarding their transformational leadership are summarized in Table 10.1. In general, managers who are self-aware of their transformational leadership are associated with the most positive traits, display the most pro-social impression management and influence tactics, and are the best performers. While lacking in self-confidence, under-estimators are good communicators, build high levels of trust, are very good mentors, and are capable of good performance. In contrast, over-estimators tend to possess negative attitudes, display self-centered behavior, intimidate their co-workers, and are poor performers. Fortunately,

TABLE 10.1

Attributes of Leaders Who Are Aware or Unaware of their Transformational Behavior

	Self-Aware (In-agreement/good) Leaders	Under-Estimator Leaders	Over-Estimator Leaders
Personal Characteristics	• Emotionally intelligent • Healthy self-concept • Healthy level of public self-consciousness • Possess strong pro-social purpose-in-life • Positive attitude • Trusted • Most trusting • Committed to organization	• Lack self-confidence • May be too hard on themselves; believe in continuous personal improvement • Least publicly self-conscious • Lack strong purpose-in-life • Pleasant to be around • Most trusted • Somewhat trusting • Committed to organization	• Lack emotional intelligence • Hostile and belligerent toward others; easily angered by others • Publicly self-conscious • Possess self-centered purpose-in-life • Negative attitude • Least trusted • Untrusting/suspicious • Least committed to organization
Behaviors	• Adapt their behavior based on feedback • Exemplify positive behaviors • Effective rational persuaders • Very inspirational • Adept at exchange relationships • Good mentors • Make good job-related decisions	• Raise self-evaluations when feedback is given • Exemplify positive behaviors • Very effective rational persuaders • Inspirational • Adequate at exchange relationships • Most effective mentors • Make ineffective job-related decisions	• Ignore feedback from others • Intimidate followers • Poor rational persuaders • Lack inspiration • Poor at exchange relationships • Poor mentors • Make less effective job-related decisions
Performance Outcomes	• Very good; most innovative	• Mixed, but generally positive	• Poor, but can improve if they really want to

over-estimators are capable of improvement if and when they truly want to change.[31]

Understanding the profiles associated with under-estimators, over-estimators, and self-aware managers is important for exploring the level of self-awareness of the executives in our sample and predicting their degree of adaptability and alignment of their leadership behavior with their organization's people, processes, and performance outcomes. To gauge the level of self-awareness of SFL of the executives in our sample, we compared the executive's direct reports' ratings of inspirational motivation (IM) to the executive's self-ratings of IM discussed in our interviews. We focused on IM because this component of transformational leadership contains items assessing the core message developed and articulated by leaders, which is an essential component of the SFL of the executives in our sample.

Results of our analysis indicated that the executive leaders in our sample generally viewed their leadership styles in a similar fashion as their direct reports. Specifically, nearly half (47%) of the executives were self-aware. These executives, such as Bob Still of LRA, Bill Rieser of Pulte Homes, Norm Thomas of Qualcomm among others from Concord Inc., ILR Global, Eastern Com, Morton Finance and Roote Information, possessed accurate self-images of their inspirational leadership. Such awareness is necessary for selecting appropriate information from the environment to modify behavior and correctly react to feedback from others within and outside of the organization. The ability to scan the environment for feedback and be adaptive may be necessary for successful SFL.

One third (33%) of the executives under-estimated the impact that inspirational leadership had on their followers and organizations. While the executives in the under-estimator sub-sample lacked self-awareness, research summarized in Table 10.1 suggests that they may have what it takes to build a culture of shared leadership since under-estimators are typically very good at building trust and developing followers into leaders. However, twenty percent of the executives over-estimated their inspirational leadership. The over-estimators were generally associated with organizations that have recently struggled with their financial performance. With proper training on leadership and self-awareness and a willingness to be more active in displaying transformational leadership behavior, we are confident that these executives can develop the skills to build healthier organizational cultures and improve their organization's effectiveness.

NURTURING THE GARDEN OF
SHARED LEADERSHIP WITH SFL

People today are very much health conscious and want to take the lead in proactively finding the way to longevity and quality of life. In this regard, scientists are finding that the road to longevity and quality of life may cross over the *life bridge*, where nutrition is more than the sum of its separate parts, and through the process of culturing, a *synergy* of health promoting compounds is created. In other words, plants get their nutrients from the soil, and animals and humans depend on plants for their sustenance. If the soil is filled only with chemical isolates (it's dead), critical nutrients remain locked in place and are unavailable to our plants. What is needed is "living" soil, filling a complex organic garden with an array or network of beneficial interconnected chemical allies that make the nutrients in the soil a living sustenance for plants.[32]

And so it is with SFL, which is all about *growing* people! The executives who displayed SFL were able to cultivate rich gardens of their own, where the garden is really a culture of shared leadership in their organizations. Growing a culture of shared leadership is *unlike* growing a conventional garden (organization) where we dump chemical fertilizers (extrinsic individualistic rewards) on the plants (followers) and dictate to the plants how they are to grow. Traditional top-down approaches to leadership are like holding pots for what we tell followers they need to grow or produce in isolation.

Whether in gardens or organizations, "it's not nice to fool Mother Nature," using unnatural formulae to grow plants, people or performance outcomes. As in all natural phenomena, the garden of shared leadership is governed by scientific laws and does not prosper with isolated elements of the leadership system—leader, followers, core message, strategic plan, rewards, environment and organizational stakeholders. Instead, SFL systems prosper based on the rich connections and synergies between the elements in the leadership system, who become allies that share a positive core message that binds them together based on common values. Shared leadership is a "garden" where we replenish the followers' motivation and commitment with new relationships, opportunities, ideas, knowledge, skills, and abilities. This is the way we "work the soil," the learning environment, allowing it to become teeming with cognitive, social, emotional, and moral nourishment on the terms of the natural laws that govern leadership systems. As a result, followers and their associates and teams exert extra effort and become alive with much cooperative activity, information flows, innovation, learning and development. How well are you cultivating your garden?

Creating a Successful Future Together

We must realize that SFL is not something that happens *to* us; it happens *with* us. Conventional strategic leadership wisdom would suggest that the upper echelons, working within the organizational hierarchy and extrinsic reward systems, dictates leadership messages down to the followers regarding what the organization needs to do to achieve its goals. However, SFL's ultimate outcome is to grow its people and expand its strategic network—its life blood of information, ideas and talent—in healthy and positive organizational cultures of shared leadership. Realizing this outcome means recognizing that we must practice SFL by connecting and working together with customers, associates and other organizational constituents, so that all the elements of the SFL system will work *with* us. Relying on the connections of these elements as they interact with the guiding vision of the core message is the true genius of SFL and its shared leadership outcome.

This collective approach to creating an organization's future was evident at many of the organizations we studied that possessed the *Predominantly or Moderately 4 I's* cultures described in Table A.2 and discussed in Chapter 9. In fact, there were 42 organizations (64% of our sample) with these types of culture including ADS Business Solutions, Barclay's Global Investors, Concord, Inc., General Electric, Greencastle Associates Consulting, Greymatter, Inc., ILR Global, International Chips, and Eastern Com. In these organizations, it seems that everyone is likely to be constantly talking about purposes, vision, values and fulfillment, without fixating on the need for formal agreements and controls.

In these cultures, the executive leaders do not just inspire their followers, but the followers also to inspire the executives and therefore create a true form of shared leadership style in their respective organization. Everyone is helping everyone else in the company. Moreover, everyone is accountable for the task he or she performs regardless his or her organizational position. It's really a two-way shared approach to leadership with frequent meetings where they talk a lot about the business. It involves constant contact and constant communication. When everyone in the organization is thinking about and discussing the important elements of the organization's core message, a collective future is being shaped—a future everyone finds meaningful and exciting.

SFL for Today and Tomorrow

No executive in any industry that depends on technology can ignore the threats and opportunities that the future will bring. And no tech executive can develop strategic objectives without a sound understanding of how the future may play out and affect his or her organization. As Abraham Lincoln once said: "*The best thing about the future is that it only comes one day at a time.*" These are reassuring words for executives of technology-driven organizations, whose futures often come much too fast and have dizzying effects on almost everyone in their industry. As we described in Chapter 2, the future will bring many challenges, trials and tribulations to executives. However, our extensive interviews with executives in technology-dependent industries, who were successful and otherwise, yields some valuable lessons for those of you who aspire to master the processes of SFL. The lessons that we have learned from these leaders are summarized in Table 10.2 using the mnemonic C I LEAD and provide helpful guidelines for facing the future with courage and confidence, one day at a time.

Here are our observations regarding these key lessons on SFL:

- *Every strategy-focused leader needs to adhere to the Marine's motto "Semper Fidelis."* One of the best ways for you to be "always prepared" is to be aware of trends in the ever-changing business environment with an eye out for potential threats, and opportunities to partner with customers, suppliers and talented industry members. Being internally and externally vigilant and hungry for knowledge of the industry and the world is essential for strategy-focused leaders to be adept at making the right connections and spotting patterns in the market. Being prepared also involves being self-aware of your leadership style and how it affects your organization. Participating in upward and 360-degree feedback assessments typical of many leadership develop-

TABLE 10.2
C I LEAD: Key Lessons for Tomorrow's Strategy-focused Leaders

Connect	• Build personal and professional networks built on trust and reputation
	• Connect the right people and technology
Inspire	• Emphasize ideals and meaning of the organization's values and work with an appealing core message
	• Have passion for your work and your people
Look	• Constantly scan the business environment for trends and potential connections with customers, partners, employees, etc.
	• Be self-aware of your leadership style and how it affects the organization
Execute	• Follow through on strategy-implementation (make sure things get done)
	• Display active forms of leadership that energize your people
	• Create and measure high performance outcomes and cultures
Adapt	• Challenge, adapt and reorganize frequently
	• Constantly create, experiment, innovate and share what is learned among associates
Develop	• Hire people smarter than you, develop and connect (with) them
	• Build a shared leadership and learning culture that engenders trust, communication, and accountability to internal and external customers

ment and executive coaching programs can help you to become more self-aware of your leadership style.

- *Put people first, strategy second.* Given the nature of the information economy that supports the operations of contemporary organizations, the knowledge, skills and abilities of your people are your organization's most important strategic and reputational assets. It was both ironic and interesting that we have found through the interviews we conducted for this book that people (the human assets—*not* the technology assets) emerged as *the* most important source of competitive advantage in a number of high-tech organizations. The process of spotting smart people (who comprise the human asset base) through professional and personal networks, recruiting them, trusting them, and then pruning and nurturing them in jobs of increasing complexity and interdependence is the rock upon which the best strategies are supported. Such a people-orientation is best accomplished when executives are passionate about their people and organization's work. This passion is often contagious and keeps the fire burning in your followers. As Albert Schweitzer once said, "In everyone's life, at some time, our inner fire goes out. It is then burst into flame by an encounter with another human being. We should all be thankful for those people who rekindle the inner spirit." What connections can you make to re-ignite your associates' inner fire?
- *Don't forget to cultivate your garden.* Your SFL can provide a rich array of nutrients that can nourish your associates' ability to yield bountiful financial and intellectual harvests. Your ability to connect your people with other human, technical and strategic resources will become increasingly important in tomorrow's business environment that will demand even greater degrees of flexibility, innovation and connectivity than today. As a result, your people will demand more and more information and connectivity, especially in innovative environments that yearn for learning, excitement, and challenges. Fostering shared leadership based on trust, communication, information flow, and accountability to internal and external customers can help you to sustain a culture that values learning and build an organization that can adapt to the competitive environment.
- *When it comes to SFL, get things started NOW and be sure to focus.* Alan Lakein, the Harvard Business School graduate who invented the concept of "time management" in 1968, taught his students to constantly ask themselves: *What is the best use of my time RIGHT NOW?* Vince Lombardi, the legendary football coach of the Green Bay Packers, always allowed for planned and unplanned activities, never procrastinated, and focused on what was essential for success. If you take such a proactive approach to SFL by strategically connecting people, processes, technologies, ideas to key performance targets, you have little to fear from the challenges that the hyper-turbulent information-based

economy throws at you. By the same token, if you lose out by reacting to every fickle shift in the economy and isolating the elements of your SFL system, don't expect the SFL processes to provide you with any results.

- *Don't expect SFL outcomes without executing your strategy and measuring its critical performance targets over time.* Dreams can go only so far; be sure to follow through and execute the strategy you espouse in the core message. This is critical given the results of a *Fortune* magazine study indicating that 70 percent of the CEOs who failed in their jobs suffered from bad execution of their corporate strategy. They simply were not able to get things done, fell victim to decision gridlock, and didn't deliver on their commitments.[33] To gauge the progress being made toward attaining your mission, you need to track critical performance measures from the financial, customer, internal process, and learning and development perspectives using balanced scorecards. You will then be well prepared to create cultures that spur high performance linked to your mission and core message.

SOME FINAL THOUGHTS

Now we come to the end of our discussion of SFL, which is really just the *beginning for you.* It's an exciting time when you can start weaving the dream for the future of your own organization, hopefully making it a better place for your followers, associates, customers and constituents—all the many people who are touched every day by your leadership. No matter whether you are a corporate executive thinking about your next major organizational restructuring or acquisition, an entry level manager grasping fundamental management principles, or an MBA student thinking about setting up the next generation of Oracle or Cisco, your leadership can have important and profound effects on the lives and future of many people. We hope that you will share our enthusiasm about leadership that we have gained over the years through our research, teaching and consulting together as friends and colleagues. We feel that leadership is the most awesome and powerful human force in the universe. And that's something we truly believe!

Just think of all the great achievements in philosophy, medicine, science, literature, art, politics, social work, education, spirituality and religion that have emerged over the course of history from the power of an individual leader working in communion with empowered and committed followers. What a wonderful difference leaders like Rosa Parks, Andrew Carnegie, Pope John Paul II, Viktor Frankl, Mahatma Gandhi, Herb Kelleher, Nelson Mandela, Mary Kay Ash, Eleanor Roosevelt, Albert Schweitzer, Lech Walesa and Norman Vincent Peale have made in our world!

And in the business world, consider the legacy, innovations, personal and organizational development, and market and economic value added by great CEO leaders like Bill Allen of Boeing, Sam Walton of Wal-Mart, George Merck of Merck & Co., Darwin Smith of Kimberly-Clark, James Burke of Johnson & Johnson, David Maxwell of Fannie Mae, William McKnight of 3M, Katharine Graham of *The Washington Post*, David Packard of Hewlett-Packard and Charles Coffin of GE. These CEOs were selected by *Fortune* magazine as the "10 greatest CEOs of all time." They had one thing in common: *they possessed a deep sense of connectedness to the organizations they ran, the employees they inspired, and the customers they served.*[34] This sense of connectedness is the essence of SFL.

Like these leaders, if *you* exercise SFL authentically and consistently over time, success will be waiting around the corner for you and your followers. It just takes a dream, an ability to connect the right people, technology and strategy, strong convictions that what you are doing is right and meaningful, and the collective motivation and commitment of people willing to make the dream a reality. To highlight this point, we leave you with one final "executive" quote from a true strategy-focused leader and founder of a global social work organization, who over the course of her life made all the right connections and as a result has made our world a better place:

> People are often unreasonable, illogical, and self-centered; forgive them anyway. If you are kind, people may accuse you of selfish, ulterior motives; be kind anyway. If you are successful, you will win some false friends and some true enemies; succeed anyway. If you are honest and frank, people may cheat you; be honest anyway. What you spend years building, someone could destroy overnight; build anyway. If you find serenity and happiness, they may be jealous; be happy anyway. The good you do today, people will often forget tomorrow; do good anyway. Give the world the best you have and it may never be enough; give the world the best you have anyway. You see, in the final analysis, it is between you and God.[35]

We hope that these inspiring words of Mother Teresa, coupled with what you have learned about SFL, will challenge you to answer one final question: *Are you strong enough to show your dream to someone else?* The world is waiting for your answer.

APPENDIX

RESEARCH BASE

Many progressive-minded executives and academicians are advocating collaborative approaches to understanding the leadership phenomenon. These approaches include using larger samples of study participants than anecdotal case studies, joint interpretation of research results by the researchers and study participants, and emphasizing practical lessons for the study participants' organizational development initiatives.[1] We adopted this progressive approach that integrates practices employed by our interviewed executives with a well-developed and widely validated scientific framework while doing the research for this book. In this appendix, we describe the research methodology used to collect and analyze the data used to derive the lessons learned from the executive leaders who participated in our study. We also provide an overview of the executives and their organizations so that readers can identify with the executives in our sample and better understand the lessons discussed in the previous chapters.

HOW THE EXECUTIVES' LESSONS WERE DERIVED

The process for deriving the lessons on SFL was empirically based, involving data collected from both primary (interviews and surveys) and second-

The Dream Weavers: Strategy-Focused Leadership in Technology-Driven
Organizations, pages 239–275
Copyright © 2004 by Information Age Publishing, Inc.
All rights of reproduction in any form reserved.
ISBN: 1-59311-110-X (paper), 1-59311-111-8 (cloth)

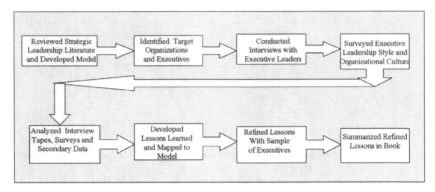

FIGURE A.1
Overview of Research Process for Deriving the Lessons
Learned from the Executives.

ary (organizational records and literature) research methods. Figure A.1 provides an overview of our research process.

Review of Strategic Leadership Literature and Model Development

We performed a comprehensive review of the existing literature on strategic leadership in order to determine what is already known *and* what is not known about strategic leadership. We reviewed major books published on strategic leadership over the past 20 years as well as over 100 articles on the subject obtained from various research databases in leadership research. Based on our review of this extensive literature, we identified what is known (and unknown) about strategic leadership that executives should know and described them in Chapter 1. Our literature review also afforded us with eight SFL processes that we used, in part, to develop the model shown in Figure 1.1.

Identification of Target Organizations and Executives

To help the broadest array of executive leaders possible, we targeted executive-level leaders (e.g., CEOs, CIOs, CTOs, CFOs, COOs, Presidents, Vice Presidents, Directors of Business Units) from a variety of technology-dependent industries. Our study participants were senior- or executive- level managers who are actively involved in the long-term goal-setting in their organizations, responsible for identifying industry trends, creating strategies, organizational structures and cultures for their organizations, and adding economic and market value for their shareholders. We included organizations from industries that were on the cutting-edge regarding the development and/or adoption of advanced technologies, and as a contrast, included some organizations from industries that relied on technology to a lesser extent. Thus, we targeted the following industries: information technology (software, computers, microchips, telecommunications), services (media, retail, professional services), life sciences (biotechnology, health care), manufacturing (energy, defense, aerospace, construction, furniture), and finance (banking & securities, insurance).

Our study was approved by the Institutional Research Review Committees of our respective universities. These committees are responsible for ensuring that the rights and privileges of study participants as human subjects are protected, and that the study is conducted in an ethical manner while providing benefits for its participants and society. After our study was approved by these committees, we selected 100 executives from the industries noted above, who would be representative of key executives in today's technology-driven industries. These leaders, like other leaders today, either deal with the challenges of the current economy or must demonstrate how they can make their companies even more successful.

Interviewing of Executive Leaders

For the 75 executives who agreed to participate in our study, we scheduled and conducted structured interviews with them. Structured interviews involve asking fixed questions with precise wording and sequence that provide consistency for all participants in a study. In our study, the interviews assessed each organization and its environment and strategy, the nature of managerial work in the organization, and leadership behaviors of the executives. Our structured interview questions were developed, validated and previously used by one of the authors. The interview questions are shown in Table A.1.

Using these questions, we worked with small teams of graduate students to conduct 1-hour videotaped structured interviews of the executives. The graduate student teams received comprehensive training on human subjects' protocol and how to conduct structured interviews prior to their par-

TABLE A.1
Structured Interview Questions

Company

Please describe

1. The company and its environment - market, products, competition, customers, strategic goals, developmental stage, future plans
2. Unique characteristics (challenges and opportunities) of the company

Managers

Tell us about the:

1. Leadership style, managerial tools, what characterizes successful versus less successful managers in the company, main challenges and opportunities
2. Unique characteristics of managers in high-tech versus other companies; between start-up/dot.com versus established high-tech companies
3. The main differences between employees in managerial versus non-managerial positions in high-tech companies
4. The main differences between characteristics or challenges of high-tech managers in various managerial levels (team leader, head of department, CEO)
5. Different qualities needed from high-tech managers in various project stages

Leadership:

Leadership Construct		Questions
Inspirational leadership (idealized influence and inspirational motivation)	1.	How often do you use inspiration of leadership to motivate your employees? (Probes: Give an example; Interviewer can give an example of an inspiring behavior)
	2.	What do you do to motivate your employees to work harder?
	3.	What values do you encourage? (Probe: interviewer can give an example of a value)
	4.	What is your vision for the unit you manage? (Probe: if the reply is none, ask for mission or long term goals).
Intellectual stimulation	5.	How often do you challenge the way your employees' think?
	6.	How do you help your employees solve problems they encounter? (Probe: Problems with a project, with peers, with a client, with you?)
Individualized consideration	7.	How often do you spend time attending to your employees' personal needs?
	8.	How do you, as a manager, help them when they have a challenge at work?
	9.	How do you approach dealing with their personal problems?
Contingent reward	10.	How often do you reward your employees just for the amount of effort they put in? Give an example.
	11.	How do you set goals for your employees? How do you reinforce their performance on these goals?
Management by exception	12.	How often do you need to use warnings in order to ensure that tasks are completed appropriately and on time?
	13.	Describe a recent situation, in which you had used warnings, how did your employees react? (Probe: - Every manager has to use warnings sometimes...
Passive leadership	14.	How often do you prefer not to take action and let things settle 'naturally'? (Probe: can this policy be effective sometimes? When did it have a negative impact on your followers? On you? On the work produced?
	15.	How do your employees react when you are less actively involved in their work?
	16.	Describe a situation where you chose to be passive.
Strategy	17.	What are the main organizational goals of the company and your activity? What are the goals of your unit? How do you determine these goals? How are they related to your supervisors' goals? How aware are your employees of these goals? How do you communicate these goals to them?

ticipation in the project. The authors personally conducted several of the interviews. A brief overview of each executive interviewed and his/her organization is presented below.

The focal point of the structured interview were questions, validated in earlier research,[2] to assess the executive's self-reported leadership style or behavior, described in terms of Bernard Bass and Bruce Avolio's Full Range of Leadership (FRL) model, which is the foundation of extensive training of individuals from industry, education, military, religious, and non-profit sectors. This model represents a refinement of Bass's seminal work on transformational leadership and describes specific leadership behaviors across a very diverse range.[3] The FRL model proposes that every leader displays some amount of laissez-faire, transactional, and transformational leadership behaviors; effective leaders, however, display more transformational and transactional contingent reward behaviors and fewer laissez-faire behaviors.

The most passive behavior is *laissez-faire*, characterized by delays of action, absence, and indifference. Three forms of transactional leadership are included in the FRL model: passive management-by-exception (MBE-P), active management-by-exception (MBE-A), and contingent reward. *MBE-P* leadership involves setting standards but waiting for deviations to occur before correcting the problem, waiting for problems to arise, reacting to mistakes, and intervening reluctantly. *MBE-A* leadership involves actively searching for errors, paying selective attention to deviations, and rectifying problems as detected. *Contingent reward* leadership involves setting goals, clarifying desired outcomes, exchanging rewards and recognition for accomplishments, suggesting or consulting, monitoring, providing feedback, and giving followers praise when it is deserved.

Transformational leadership goes beyond transactional leadership in that followers are motivated to do more than what is required. There are four behaviors (called the 4I's of transformational leadership) and one attribute associated with transformational leaders: *individualized consideration*—giving personal attention to followers to promote their development and achievement; *intellectual stimulation*—enabling followers to question assumptions, to try new things, and to think of old problems in new ways; *inspirational motivation*—communicating high performance expectations through the projection of a powerful, confident, dynamic presence; and *idealized influence*—displaying role model behaviors for followers through exemplary personal achievements, character, and/or behavior. Idealized influence also may be attributed to the leader by followers. A significant amount of research indicates that transformational leadership produces more positive influences on individual, group, and organizational performance than do other leader behaviors such as contingent reward, MBE-A, MBE-P, and laissez-faire.[4]

Surveying of Executives' Leadership Style and Their Organization's Culture

To substantiate the self-reports of the executives' leadership behavior, we administered the Multifactor Leadership Questionnaire (MLQ-Form 5X) to three subordinates of each executive to provide an independent quantitative assessment of the executive's leadership behavior. The MLQ was developed by Bass and Avolio to measure the FRL behaviors described above and has been shown to possess sound psychometric properties. In other words, the MLQ is a reliable and valid measure of the leadership behaviors it purports to measure.[5]

To assess the organizational culture in which the SFL system is embedded, we administered the Organizational Description Questionnaire (ODQ) to three different subordinates/associates of each executive. The ODQ was designed by Bass and Avolio as a tool to help managers clarify the link between leadership style and the characteristics/quality of their organizational culture. This instrument also has sound psychometric properties.[6] Based on data provided by respondents, the ODQ classifies an organization into one of nine cultural types based on transactional and transformational cultural scores: Predominantly Four I's, Moderated Four I's, High-Contrast, Loosely Guided, Coasting, Moderated Bureaucratic or Internally Competitive, Garbage Can, Pedestrian, and Predominantly Bureaucratic or Internally Competitive. A description of these cultural types and their meaning is presented in Table A.2.

We also collected organizational artifacts (e.g., company publications, annual reports, public relations literature), so we could assess how leadership values, vision and shared practices are reflected and communicated within and outside of the organizations. To summarize, we used multiple methods of data collection to describe how executives of technology-driven organizations provide leadership necessary to meeting their business challenges.

Analysis of Interview Tapes, Surveys and Secondary Data

Each interview videotape was transcribed by our research assistants into a text file. Videotapes from interviews with executives from Israel were first translated from Hebrew to English. The text files were input into *NVivo*, a qualitative data analysis program, and a coding scheme was created as themes emerged from the interview. Using this qualitative approach provides a rich description of the dynamics of SFL, allowing for common themes to emerge across different leaders. Also, we created the coding scheme as it emerged rather than forcing the data into an *a priori* or prede-

TABLE A.2
ODQ Culture Descriptions

Organizational Culture Name(s)	Description and Number in Sample	Related Probabilities
PREDOMINATELY and MODERATED FOUR I's	These cultures are characterized by the Four I's of transformational leadership. The more negative the transactional score, the more the culture of the organizational is purely transformational. At this extreme, everyone is likely to be constantly talking about purposes, vision, values, fulfillment, without emphasizing the need for formal agreements and controls. The lack of transactional specifications may make it difficult to be certain about what people will do. Trust is internalized rather than dependent on formal agreements and contracts. As the transactional score becomes less negative, or even slightly positive, the culture will place more value on agreements, exchanges and rewards for performance. The increase in transactional score leads to a greater balance in the organization's culture. (N = 2 Predominately and N = 40 Moderated 4 I's)	Expressiveness is likely to be high as in most families. The organization's structure is likely to be loose, decentralized and flat. The organization is flexible, adaptive, dynamic, informal, bottom-up, with emphasis on the potential of its individual employees and the organization to grow and improve. Creativity is likely to be high in this environment, with particular emphasis on questioning the methods to improve performance. If transactional scores are extremely negative, newcomers and outsiders may have a problem knowing what to expect.
HIGH-CONTRAST	This "high-contrast" culture tends to be characterized by the Four I's of transformational leadership coupled with a similar high level of transactional leadership. (N = 0)	The high transactional score is likely to moderate some aspects of the transformational culture. You're likely to see a great deal of both management and leadership activity, with conflict over the best ways to proceed. There is likely to be chafing and battling against the rules and the old ways of doing things, but much of the conflict is likely to be constructive. Maintaining a balance between the two will require trust in the individual and organization. This will be particularly true where trade-offs must be made between short-term gain and individual rewards for the long-term benefit of the organization.

LOOSELY-GUIDED	In this organization members tend to be independent of each other except when temporarily connected by informal leadership. Formal agreements are at a minimum in this culture. **(N = 0)**	This organization is highly unstructured. Whatever gets done occurs on the basis of informal leadership efforts. Predictability is low, but there is some degree of flexibility.
COASTING	For both of the transactional and transformational culture scores, respondents indicated that half of the items were characteristic of their culture while almost another half were not. Or, they had many questions about the items and responded by selecting "?". The culture in this organization is neither extremely transformational nor extremely transactional and falls in the middle of the range. External controls, for example, are balanced by self-controls. **(N = 20)**	Managerial and leadership activity tends to be moderate in amount, and the organization is likely to coast along but not as well as it might with the resources and opportunities it possesses. Little change is expected as the organization putters along. This pattern may represent an organization that is simply maintaining its current position.
PREDOMI-NATELY and MODERATED BUREAUCRATIC or INTERNALLY COMPETITIVE	These cultures are highly transactional in orientation and lacking in much transformational leadership. Respondents did not feel that many of the transformational items were characteristic of their organizational culture, while most of the transactional items were characteristic. The higher the transformational score becomes, the more the internally competitive aspects of the organization are moderated by concern for the individual, concern for new ideas and a longer-term perspective. **(N = 1 Predominately and N = 1 Moderated Bureaucratic)**	Self-interest is more important than the interest of the group. Employees watch out for their own interests. Short-term goals prevail. There is much attention to controls, directions and standard operating procedures. The organization tends to be an internal marketplace where much is negotiated according to the "rules of the game." The organization's structure is likely to be stable, centralized, tight and tall with a clear top-down chain of command. Employees have little discretion and are watched, driven and controlled. The organization tends to be rigid and mechanistic.

(continued)

TABLE A.2
Continued

Organizational Culture Name(s)	Description and **Number in Sample**	Related Probabilities
GARBAGE CAN	This organization tends to lack leadership and managerial transactional activities. Individuals in this organization are unable to offer a clear description of their culture. Consensus is likely to be absent. (**N = 0**)	Everybody "does their own thing." The organization is a garbage can of fruitless activities. There is very little cooperation. Agendas depend on who shows up at meetings, and individuals carry problems around with them waiting for an arena in which to participate and to air their grievances. The organization is anarchic without either clear purposes, visions and values or clear rules and regulations.
PEDESTRIAN	Little gets done within this organization that is not a consequence of formal arrangements. Little changes. Risk-taking is avoided. There is a general sense of structure and procedure which can take on different forms depending on the transactional items that were identified as true. (**N = 1**)	The organization is moderately mechanistic. Leaders have and practice little discretion. Work is routine. There is little commitment to the organization or to other members. If respondents selected "true" to items largely representing management-by-exception, the structure can highlight what is right. If the items to which they responded "true" were more oriented toward contingent reward, then the structure would highlight the exchange of effort and good performance for rewards.

Notes: Adapted from Avolio, B.J., & Bass, B.M. (1990). *Manual for advanced workshop: Full range leadership development.* Binghamton, NY: Center for Leadership Studies, State University of New York at Binghamton, pp. 13.16–13.18. Reprinted by permission. The ODQ produces two overall scores—the Transactional Culture Score (TA) and the Transformational Culture Score (TF). The maximum score on either scale is 14 and the minimum is -14. Based on these two scores, the organizations in our sample were placed into the ODQ Culture Name categories.

termined set of codes. This type of inductive research insures that we obtained a picture of what is actually occurring through executives' eyes instead of finding things we hoped to find.[7] Once the interviews were coded, correlations between themes were examined to detect relationships between the executive leader's vision, her/his leadership as perceived by followers, and her/his self-perception of the FRL behaviors he or she displays.

To provide a quantitative and independent perspective of the organizations' SFL systems, the MLQ and ODQ survey data (provided by subordinates of the executive leaders) were entered into data files for SPSS (a statistical analysis program), aggregated by executive leader/ organization, and then the leadership, outcome (unit effectiveness and followers' extra effort and satisfaction) and cultural scales were computed. Feedback reports of the aggregated results were provided to the executives so that they could understand and develop their leadership styles and cultures, perceive relationships between them, and interpret and apply the results of our research.

The secondary data, consisting of the organizational artifacts such as information published by the organization on its website or documents from the organization that were available for us, were used to validate our interview and survey based findings. For example, we compared executives' speeches that were published on a website of one of the companies with the content of the interviews done with the same executives. Such comparisons yield more consistent and valid conclusions regarding the leader's style.[8]

Derivation of Lessons Learned and Mapping Onto Model

Once the data was coded and analyzed, we identified several themes that were common across the organizations sampled in the research project. These themes corresponded to important elements of SFL. The themes were then mapped onto our model of SFL shown in Figure 1.1 based on the conceptual similarities and/or relationships with the leadership processes derived from our preliminary review of the strategic leadership literature.

Refining of Lessons Learned with Executives

The lessons learned were then summarized and presented to a random sub-sample of 10 of the executives interviewed. We provided the summaries to the executives so that we could provide additional feedback to the host organizations for their organizational and leadership development initiatives. By sharing of this information, we also were able to bring together members of our research team and some of our study's participants to jointly reflect, interpret and refine the information. Research has shown that this approach allows for opportunities to bring new information to light, better understanding of leadership concepts, and the accumulation of a richer and broader spectrum of information deemed relevant and useful by other executives. We used the comments provided by the sub-sample of executives to refine the lessons learned from our preliminary data analysis.

THE ORGANIZATIONS AND EXECUTIVES IN OUR SAMPLE

Our sample consisted of 75 executives from 65 different organizations cutting across a broad range of industries using various degrees of technology to support their operations. We now provide a brief description of each organization and executive. Pseudonyms are used for those organizations and executives that requested anonymity. The companies are listed in Table A.3 and described below alphabetically within industry sub-group within five major industry groups (finance, info tech, life sciences, manufacturing, and services).

Finance: Banking and Securities

Barclays Global Investors
This 30-year old organization pioneered a revolution that transformed the investment industry with the introduction of the first index investing strategy in 1971 and the first quantitative active investing strategy in 1978. Barclays is a 2,100-employee U.K.-based financial services giant that started out as part of Wells Fargo, the San Francisco bank. A carefully crafted reorganization in 2000 created an IT structure that is aligned with the organization's mission. Barclays is currently delivering enterprise solutions such as Windows, Collabnet, and the Common Platform. In 2001, Barclays managed $769 billion in investors' money and generated revenues of $11.4 billion. We interviewed Lee Kranefuss, CEO of Barclays Global Investors Individual Investor Business, who was educated at Cornell University and the Wharton School of the University of Pennsylvania. Prior to joining Barclays in 1997, Kranefuss worked with the Boston Consulting Group, gaining experience with retail, institutional/financial, and technology clients.[9]

TABLE A.3
Organization Sample Description

Organization within Industry Sub-group	Number of Employees	Organization's Age in Years	2001 Sales [Fund Assets]
Finance: Banking and Securities			
Barclays Global Investors	2,100	30	$11,360,000,000
CompGraphics	n/a	n/a	n/a
I Trust Bank	n/a	68	$159,000,000
Magnum Credit Card	28,000	11	$3,205,102,000
Morton Finance	57,700	70	$424,000,000,000
Union Bank of California	9,300	50	$24,000,000,000
Vanguard Group	10,500	27	[$540,000,000,000]
Finance: Insurance			
AICPCU/IIA	200	60	$23,852,483
General Electric	300,000	124	$125,900,000,000
Info Tech: Computers			
Comptech	1,600	22	$301,904,000
ILR Global	319,876	79	$81,186,000,000
International Chips	80,000	30	$26,500,000,000
JNI Engineering	220	10	$75,000,000
Info Tech: Consumer Electronics			
Oswold Services	13,000	62	$4,000,000,000
SNY Register Controls	40	37	n/a
Info Tech: Software			
Adocuments	10,000	21	$1,533,910,000
ADS Business Solutions	800	10	n/a
CB Technologies	200	8	$6,000,000
ITV, Inc.	410	15	n/a
Kane Tech	7,000	31	$187,200,000
KES Software	120	10	$15,000,000
Mega Software Israel	n/a	4	n/a
RDN Cognition	200	7	n/a
SCT	2,100	35	$345,000,000
Info Tech: Telecommunications			
Aye Tech.com	30	3	n/a
BB Net.com	90	5	n/a

(continued)

TABLE A.3
Continued

Organization within Industry Sub-group	Number of Employees	Organization's Age in Years	2001 Sales [Fund Assets]
Info Tech: Telecommunications (continued)			
C Communications	3,500	9	n/a
Concord, Inc.	24,000	150	$6,270,000,000
Dian Technologies	200	6	n/a
Eastern Com	241,000	4	$67,000,000,000
Mighty Tech	600	32	n/a
NAGMEA Tech	15	21	$1,000,000,000
PCC Ltd.	3,000	4	$735,800,000
Qualcomm	6,500	17	$2,700,000,000
Tele Spondence Inc.	41,000	19	n/a
Vee Jay Communications	150	9	$36,200,000
Life Sciences: Healthcare			
Lancaster Radiology Associates	30	30	$20,000,000
Mercy Community Hospital	2,000	100	$8,000,000
Scripps Health	1,500	110	n/a
Unified Hospital of New York	5,200	167	n/a
Unitary Medicine Associates	690	12	$115,000,000
Life Sciences: Pharmaceuticals/Biotech			
UCB Pharma	8,819	74	$1,149,444,984
Solid State Plasma	n/a	6	n/a
Manufacturing: Construction			
Architectural Concepts, Inc.	25	28	n/a
Pulte Homes	9,400	51	$5,300,000,000
Manufacturing: Defense & Aerospace			
Ebor Tech Systems	5,000	25	$765,000,000

(continued)

TABLE A.3
Continued

Organization within Industry Sub-group	Number of Employees	Organization's Age in Years	2001 Sales [Fund Assets]
Manufacturing: Energy			
Dial-Rhodes	7,500	163	$1,300,000,000
IS R&D Inc.	31	9	n/a
NC Utility	2,800	150	n/a
Manufacturing: Furniture			
Everfast, Inc.	1,700	66	n/a
Manufacturing: Metals & Machinery			
BA Reading	1,200	81	$750,000,000
Unicorn Incorporated	1,150	84	n./a
Services: Media			
Harcourt	1,000	12	$10,000,000
Roote Information	18,140	151	$5,600,000,000
Scoope Tech Services	140	21	$1,640,000,000
Services: Professional			
Bloom Institute	3	10	n/a
DGM Information Systems	n/a	34	n/a
Diversified Data Services	250	16	$15,000,000
Greencastle Associates Consulting, LLC	14	6	$1,800,000
Greymatter, Inc.	14	6	$2,042,333
ITG Pathfinders	35	4	$3,100,000
Mal Tech Services	150	21	$30,000,000
Rnet	200	15	n/a
Tier Resource Rentals	5	30	n/a
Services: Retail			
Sheetz Inc.	7,500	50	$1,700,000,000

Note: n/a = data not available due to private status of organization.

CompGraphics

A provider of advanced image character recognition technology and solutions, CompGraphics' systems process millions of check deposits daily, helping banks meet transit deadlines and reduce operational costs. Comp-Graphics is a subsidiary of a company providing machine vision solutions. Its main office is in Israel, with another branch office in the U.S. We interviewed its CEO, who suggests that managing high tech employees requires a lot of emphasis on recruitment, but also on providing clear values and exemplification. According to this CEO, "No one listens to you if you don't make sense."[10]

I Trust Bank

Founded in 1935, I Trust Bank is one of Israel's three largest banks with over 260 branches, subsidiaries and representative offices in Israel and abroad, providing domestic and international banking and financial services. With 170 branches in Israel, the bank also operates an international operational network encompassing the U.S., Latin America and Europe. We interviewed both the Chairman of the Board and the CEO of the bank. The Chairman emphasized inspirational and transformational leadership. The CEO highlighted transactional leadership as a first step to forming transformational leadership relationships with his employees.[11]

Magnum Credit Card

This large financial services/credit card company based in the eastern U.S. has operations throughout the U.S., Canada, Ireland and the United Kingdom. With managed loans of $95.4 billion, Magnum also provides retail deposit, consumer loans, and insurance products. In 2001, Magnum generated revenues of $3.2 billion dollars. To support their operations, Magnum has successfully integrated technology, such as Voice Response Units for their call centers, into their infrastructure in order to better serve its customers. As a result, Magnum has garnered excellent ratings for the strategic use of technology from *CIO Magazine* and *Business Week*. We interviewed Magnum's Chief Technology Officer for Human Resource area. With a strong background in social sciences, he was actively involved in academia and lectured at a large university in western Pennsylvania.[12]

Morton Finance

This major financial service company was founded in 1933 in New York City. This company was a pioneer both nationally and internationally in the use of technology and in the development of new financial tools and techniques that have redefined the meaning of financial services for individual, institutional and investment banking clients. In 2001, Morton's securities income after taxes was $2.36 billion, their investment management income after taxes was $545 million, and credit service income after taxes was $702 million. Morton's assets under management in August 2002 amounted to $424 billion. Employing more than 57,700 people, the company has over 700 offices all over the world, and most of them are in U.S. and Europe. We interviewed one of the key executives of the company. A young success-ful executive who is responsible for a budget of over $1 billion, he is recog-nized by associates as a highly enthusiastic leader who excels in making his employees identify with the company goals and utilize their budget to con-stantly improve the services that Morton provides to its customers.[13]

Union Bank of California

As the third largest commercial bank in California, Union Bank of Cali-fornia (UBC) has its headquarters in San Francisco, California. The com-pany was created when Union Bank and The Bank of California merged in 1996. UBC has about 260 branches in the U.S. and 18 international offices. It employs 9,297 people and has total assets over $36.1 billion. UBC is a full-service commercial bank providing a broad mix of financial services including consumer and small business banking, middle market banking, real estate finance, corporate banking, correspondent banking and trade finance (with a Pacific Rim orientation), investment and financial manage-ment, personal and business trust services, and private banking and global custody. We interviewed an Assistant President who was in charge of institu-tional investment.[14]

Vanguard Group

Jack Bogle founded the Vanguard Group in 1975 as a novel and more cost effective way to provide mutual fund investment products for inves-tors. He created an organization where each mutual fund was considered to be as a separate entity, owed by the fund holders, who contracted with Vanguard to provide administrative services at cost. With its 10,500 employ-ees and $540 billion in U.S. fund assets in 2001, Vanguard is the world's largest pure no-load mutual fund company. It also offers brokerage ser-vices, variable and fixed annuities, and life insurance, as well as financial planning, asset management, and trust services. Vanguard's organizational culture is built upon its core values of trusteeship of client assets (their cli-ents come first), ethical business practices, commitment to quality, and respect for the organization, its clients, and its fellow "crewmembers" (as Vanguard's employees are called). We interviewed Robert Snowden, senior principal at Vanguard. A 14-year crewmember, Snowden is responsible for managing Vanguard's Institutional Participant Service Business, which responds to incoming phone calls and e-mails from participants in com-pany sponsored retirement plans. Prior to his current post, Snowden man-aged a corporate accounting group where he gained experience in contributing to the strategic direction of the organization.[15]

Finance: Insurance

American Institute for CPCU/Insurance Institute of America

This 60-year old nonprofit organization offers education, certification, publications, and research reports to businesses and individuals in risk management and property-casualty insurance. The AICPCU/IIA harnesses the power of advanced information technologies to develop and offer distance education curriculums, educational materials, testing, and research materials to its clients. In 2001, this 200-employee organization generated revenues of $24 million. We interviewed Terrie E. Troxel, Ph.D., CPCU, CLU, ARP, who serves as President and CEO of the AICPCU/IIA. Dr. Troxel was recently honored by being named to the 100 Most Powerful People in the Insurance Industry-North America list.[16]

General Electric

This international conglomerate manufactures everything from jet engines to power generation, from financial services to plastics, from television to medical imaging, and provides services including news and information, financing, real estate, and auto insurance. In existence for 124 years, GE generated revenues of $126 billion in 2001 with the help of its 300,000 employees. The development, adoption, and harnessing of technology is a driving force that has propelled GE to produce consistent increases in product quality, customer satisfaction, employee development and profitability over its history. We interviewed Brian Duffy, President of GE's Auto Insurance division, who had previously worked for 25 years at Colonial Penn Insurance and Providian Insurance. Duffy's Wharton School MBA education has been further refined by several of the GE training programs, including Six Sigma and e-business training.[17]

Info Tech: Computers

Comptech

This company provides advanced technology solutions for electronics manufacturers to facilitate the production of printed circuit boards, flat panel displays, integrated circuit packaging and electronics assemblies. Comptech produces advanced hi-tech equipment for inspecting and imaging circuit boards and display panels. It employs approximately 1,600 employees of which more than a quarter are scientists and engineers. The company is based in Israel and has more than 50 offices worldwide. We interviewed Comptech's Director for New Technologies. In his position, this executive has to focus on strategy and technology. He manages mostly people who do not directly report to him. He highlights teamwork and agreement as means to spur excellent project management and to foster creativity.[18]

ILR Global

A well-known computing powerhouse, ILR Global manufactures and sells a wide variety of computer services, hardware and software. ILR Global operates in over 160 countries worldwide and more than half of the company's revenues are derived from sales outside the U.S. ILR Global can be classified as a leader within the computer services and hardware industry. We interviewed ILR's Director of Media Relations, and a Senior Manager for the ILR Global Accounts Payable, Fixed Assets and Property Control.[19]

International Chips

This company was started in 1974 with 5 employees. In 1974, International Chip's first design and development center outside the U.S., was set up in Haifa. Today International Chips employs 8,000 employees and is a leading branch of its parent corporation. We interviewed the organization's Vice President of the Technology and Manufacturing Group. This executive displays a very rational approach to leadership. His engineering background helps him understand employees' expectations and direct them towards the tough challenges that he faces.[20]

JNI Engineering

This 10-year old company located in San Diego, California is a leading designer and supplier of Fibre Channel hardware and software products that comment servers and data storage devices. Because of JNI's early and continuous focus on developing technology and products based on the Fibre Channel standard, the company has successfully developed a broad line of computer-related products that provide increased bandwidth for data communications, increased distance for high speed data transmission, guaranteed data delivery and scalability to large numbers of network connections. The company had a very successful IPO in 1999 and continued to be a market and technology leader. It generated $75 million in revenues in 2001 and has currently about 220 employees. We interviewed its VP of operations who previously had a successful career of managing several rapidly growing high tech companies.[21]

Info Tech: Consumer Electronics

Oswold Services

Oswold Services is a division of its parent organization, a solely-owned subsidiary of an international conglomerate. Its business is divided into seven groups: Electronics, Automotive Lighting, Photo Optics, General Lighting, Light Emitting Diodel and Materials. We interviewed the President and CEO of Oswold Services, and its Vice President and General Manager of its Chemical and Metallurgical Division. The President/CEO received his undergraduate degree in Engineering, Science and Math from Georgia Tech, and an MBA from Boston University. The VP/General Manager has been employed by Oswold Services since 1973, beginning as a sales trainee, and has previously served as the Director for Marketing in two different divisions: Electronic Components and Materials, and Chemical and Metallurgical Products.[22]

SNY Register Controls

Started as a partnership in 1966, SNY is a provider of "Retail Control Systems" through their cash register business. In 1987 SNY linked with IBM and eventually became a "premier" business partner, enabling SNY to provide superior customer service to such organizations as Hershey Park and the White House. We interviewed the CEO of SNY, who is a graduated from SUNY Canton where he majored in Business Management. In 1989, he became CEO of SNY, guiding the growth of this small start up from a regional, local organization in 1966 to the present organization which enjoys national clientele and exposure.[23]

Info Tech: Software

Adocuments

Provider of information solutions to the communications and Internet protocol industry, Adocuments offers customer relations management, billing and order management systems and business support systems for directory publishing companies. Adocuments has a global customer base of more than 200 communications providers around the world. The company spends $100 million a year on research and development, and is one of the largest high tech organizations in Israel, employing more than 10,000 employees worldwide. We interviewed the Chief Operations Officer of the company. The interview took place just before the company went through downsizing. The COO's leadership highlights intellectual stimulation and individualized consideration as a means to focus and motivate employees to achieve strategic goals.[24]

ADS Business Solutions

Established in 1993, ADS is a NASDAQ-listed developer of advanced digital technology for security purposes, such as early alert, miniaturized power sources and security monitoring systems, and data management services to support this technology. The company focuses on wireless data delivery for government, commercial, and private consumers. We interviewed an executive who was its CEO and President during 2001. Before joining ADS, she was a senior executive with AT&T. She earned her Master's degree from Harvard.[25]

CB Technologies

Successfully helping clients with innovative technologies since 1993, CB Technologies is a 200-employee privately-held provider of technology tools and services to the life science industries. The organization's targeted solutions help pharmaceutical, biotechnology, medical device and contract research organizations adopt more efficient processes throughout the life science product lifecycle from post discovery through commercialization. With its corporate headquarters in suburban Philadelphia, CB Technologies also has offices in Boston, New York, Charleston, San Francisco, San Diego and London. The organization recently completed a second round of financing, raising $12.5 million of venture capital. We interviewed Karen Borda, CB Technologies co-founder and former COO, a prominent and well-respected entrepreneur who is currently establishing another life sciences and technology company.[26]

ITV, Inc.

This organization, a division of a multinational electronics manufacturer, was acquired by four of its managing employees in 1988 to continue development of major product lines including imaging systems, sensing systems and analytic instrumentation. ITV, which employs over 400 people, has manufacturing plants located in the U.S., Canada, U.K., and Puerto Rico. We interviewed the organization's acting Chairman. Under this executive's leadership, ITV seeks to be a worldwide leader in design, manufacture, and marketing of specialty display, electronic systems, components and equipment.[27]

Kane Tech

Headquartered in a large city in the northeast U.S., Kane Tech partners with companies and government agencies to plan, build, and manage application software to enable their business strategies. Kane provides broad range of services and has multi-year outsourcing contracts. Kane delivers its services via an integrated network of branch offices in North America and the United Kingdom, as well other centers in Canada, and India. We interviewed a key director in the company. His leadership style is very instrumental given the nature of his job and the company's focus on providing outsourcing services. However, he also uses inspirational leadership to move the company forward and motivate employees.[28]

KES Software

KES is an emerging information technology leader located in San Diego, California. KES manufactures innovative systems solutions that provide customers with advanced systems engineering, systems integration and testing, and rapid prototype. As a privately-held company, KES was rated as the fastest growing company in San Diego region in 1998. We interviewed KES' founder and CEO John Yi, a University of California San Diego trained engineer who retooled into a successful entrepreneur. Yi is highly dedicated to the company's success and welfare of his employees. His enthusiasm toward embracing new technology and its commercialization has led to several business enterprises in the past 5 years.[29]

Mega Software Israel

Founded in 1999, Mega Software Israel is a partnership of a multinational software conglomerate and an Israeli Internet service provider. Mega Software Israel is a web portal that has similar structure as its parent's sites in other countries but its content is tailored to Israeli customers. It has its own Quick Messenger service and Hotmail as well as other web community services. Mega Software Israel has more than 800,000 unique users who view more than 60 million pages. We interviewed the former CEO of Mega Software Israel. In his early 30's, this executive is already seen as a highly charismatic leader. He makes the vision of the company will be apparent everywhere to all employees and customers. His enthusiasm and his dedication to the business are among the reasons for the success of this content-based portal during this challenging period for Internet companies.[30]

RDN Cognition

RDN Cognition's business covers E-commerce, E-marketing and E-tools. At the time of our interview, the company was focusing on developing "e-gambling" software that allows gambling games over the web. It had to deal with both the legal environment and the competitive and complicated Internet environment. We interviewed a senior Vice President of the company who has both a legal and business background. Working for a small company, he emphasizes consideration as means of getting employees to work together in such an unstable "dot com" environment.[31]

SCT

A 1,700-employee 35-year old suburban Philadelphia-based company, SCT provides advanced solutions and software for its clients in the higher education industry. According to its website, SCT "supports more than 1,300 client institutions worldwide with administrative and academic solutions; portal, community, and collaboration solutions; content management and workflow solutions; information access and integration solutions; and professional services." In 2001, SCT generated revenues of $345 million. We interviewed SCT's Corporate Vice President for Client Services, Amy Turner-LaDow, who exemplifies today's successful women leaders who recognize that being on the leading edge of technology offerings to customers/clients is difficult given the short life spans of technology today and the time required by product development life cycles to bring the products to market.[32]

Info Tech: Telecommunications

Aye Tech.com

As a privately held company based in Amsterdam, London, Madrid, Paris and Stockholm, and with an R&D center in Israel, Aye Tech.com provides a flexible pricing and promotion tools for telecom operators. The technology enables Aye Tech.com to increase revenues from existing subscribers and immediately match promotions launched by their competitors. We interviewed Aye Tech.com's former President and CEO. As a CEO of this startup company, this executive has to satisfy both venture capitalists and employees' expectations. He emphasizes individual responsibility, professionalism, teamwork, and cooperation.[33]

BB Net.com

This organization provides broadband multimedia networking solutions. It is a startup company, employing 90 people based in Israel and in the Silicon Valley. BB Net.com is founded and managed by leaders from communications and media companies such as Motorola and 3Com. The company is financially backed by venture capital funding, led by prominent high technology investment firms. We interviewed the organization's founder and CTO, an entrepreneur who successfully sold a company that he founded before BB Net.com. He emphasizes the personal and professional development of his employees and management's responsibility for it. He believes that leaders need to present the challenges that the company faces to employees as their own personal challenges.[34]

C Communications

The largest cellular phone company in Israel, C Communications is famous for expanding the cell phone market to all people. C Communications is jointly owned by several telecommunications firms, and by other smaller investors. C Communications employs about 3,500 people, who help to service its 2.4 million customers. We interviewed its CEO. As a former head of the security services of Israel, he is a well-known leader in Israeli industry. His reputation as a charismatic leader was supported by followers' evaluations and in his interview with us. He believes a top executive has to buffer employees from market or political forces. He leads by example and intervenes when he thinks he can signal to employees what are the critical strategic goals.[35]

Concord, Inc.

Concord, Inc. is based on technology and innovation. Over the past 150 years Concord, Inc. has developed the glass for Edison's light bulb and created the first commercially viable, low-loss fiber for use in telecommunications. We interviewed the organization's Chairman and CEO, and its Senior Vice President and Chief Technology Officer. The CEO received his MBA from Harvard in 1962 and began his career at Concord, the company his family founded in 1851. His decisiveness, sense of urgency, and belief in teamwork quickly became legendary. He set the stage for the company's transformation to a high technology firm, changing the company's name in 1989 to reflect the progressive, diversified nature of the organization. The Senior VP/CTO holds a doctorate in chemistry from Pennsylvania State University and is responsible for leading and setting the strategic direction for Concord's research and development efforts. He was appointed by former President Clinton to serve on the National Science Board, which oversees the National Science Foundation. We also interviewed Concord's Director of Optical and Digital operations.[36]

Dian Technologies

This company offers production-ready designs in the domain of embedded networking systems. Dian Technologies partners with large corporations such as Cisco, 3Com, and Lucent. It has 17 years of experience in designing complex switches and implementing various networking protocols. Dian Technologies is a member of a multi-billion dollar organization specializing in the development of LAN and WAN access solutions. We interviewed the company's CEO, who believes that innovation can be a result of effective leadership that highlights persuasion and consensus. He is highly informal and accessible to his coworkers and direct reports.[37]

Eastern Com

Formed by the merger of two large telecommunications companies, Eastern Com is one of the world's leading providers of high-growth communications services. Eastern Com's companies are the largest providers of wire line and wireless communications in the U.S., with nearly 135 million access line equivalents and over 30 million wireless customers. Eastern Com is also the world's largest provider of print and online directory information. A Fortune 10 company with more than 241,000 employees and $67 billion in 2001 revenues, Eastern Com's global presence extends to 45 countries in the Americas, Europe, Asia and the Pacific. We interviewed five key executives, responsible for the series of mergers the company experienced over its history. The executives we interviewed had technology-oriented rational influence styles, but also highlighted the importance of rewarding employees and sharing with them in company decisions.[38]

Mighty Tech

This organization designs and manufactures high-performance components and subsystems for the microwave electronics market. Located on Long Island, New York, the company employs over 600 people and has existed for more than thirty years. Mighty Tech's products include low-noise and medium power amplifiers, mixers and mixer-preamplifiers, multipliers, and switches among other products. We interviewed the president of Mighty Tech, whose leadership exemplifies the values of the company, which focus on precision and creating a high performance-oriented culture.[39]

NAGMEA Tech

NAGMEA Tech deals with enterprise storage and delivery of data and content. It is designed to enable enterprises to create global data management strategies. NAGMEA Tech had $1 billion revenue for fiscal year 2001. It is a member of both the S&P 500 and NASDAQ 100 index. Its systems are installed in over 70 countries around the world. The company has operations in Israel since 1992 and its branch there is mainly responsible for marketing in Israel, the Middle East, and Africa. We interviewed the CEO of the Israeli branch, who is also the area manager for this region. He directly oversees 15 employees and uses leadership as a marketing tool. He believes that his leadership style can provide an example that will help sales agents be more successful with clients.[40]

PCC Ltd.

The first global satellite messaging (GSM) mobile telephone network operator in Israel, PCC Ltd. commenced full commercial operations in January 1999 and by July 2002 had 1.7 million subscribers, representing an estimated 28% of the cellular market in Israel. The company uses its competitive GSM advantage to provide its customers seamless roaming in 103 countries worldwide, using over 246 networks. With about 3,000 employees, PCC is now considered the second largest cell phone provider in Israel. We interviewed the CEO of the company. This executive is considered one of the best CEOs in Israel and is often mentioned in the Israeli media. He is known for founding a company in a very competitive market and for generating a record increase in market share due to effective customer management and marketing of a new technology. Our interview reveals how he uses his SFL to highlight innovation at all costs to grow the company.[41]

Qualcomm

Qualcomm is best known as the company that pioneered Code Division Multiple Access (CDMA) technology, which is now used in wireless networks and handsets all over the world. The company was founded in 1985 by Dr. Irwin Jacobs, a former engineering professor at the University of

California San Diego. This 17-year old company has over 600 patents, is a member of the prestigious S & P 500 Index, and has been rated as one of the 100 best managed companies by *Industry Week* and as one of the America's Most Admired Companies in 2002 by *Fortune*. Qualcomm has about 6,500 employees and generated $2.7 billion in revenues in 2001. We interviewed a director of business development who received an MBA from San Diego State University and has spent several years working for Qualcomm.[42]

Tele Spondence Inc.

This organization was established in 1984, and provides engineering, administrative, and other services to the regional Bell Operating Companies. Tele Spondence Inc. supplies eighty percent of the software for the U.S. In 1997 the company was acquired by a Fortune 500 company that is the largest employee-owned research and engineering firm in the nation. Tele Spondence Inc.'s parent and its subsidiaries have more than 41,000 employees with offices in over 150 cities worldwide. We interviewed Tele Spondence Inc.'s CEO. This CEO has more than 22 years of experience in the communications industry. He had worked in a range of senior management positions at Nortel Networks, AT&T Bell Labs and Lucent Technologies. He holds an MBA from the University of Chicago. He strongly emphasizes building an organizational culture that boosts employee morale and enables communication of organizational strategy.[43]

Vee Jay Communcations

Founded in 1994, Vee Jay Communcations develops, manufactures and markets high-performance, multi-function personal and group videoconferencing systems designed for a variety of communication networks. The systems that the company produces are primarily targeted at business, distance learning, government and telemedicine, the delivery of medical services from a physically remote location. The company is based in Israel and holds subsidiaries in the U.S., Germany, Spain, France, United Kingdom and China. It has 150 employees world wide and generated $36.2 million of sales in 2001. We interviewed the President and CEO of the company. Having previously managed several large high tech companies, such as Citex, and with a background in the Israel Air Force, he brings an interesting SFL approach to Vee Jay during turbulent economic conditions.[44]

Life Sciences: Healthcare

Lancaster Radiology Associates, LTD.

This 30-year old incorporated radiology practice is committed to being recognized as a leader in imaging, consultative, and education services in diagnostic, interventional and therapeutic radiology. Lancaster Radiology Associates consists of an association of 29 physicians who market themselves under the name MRI Group and utilize the latest imaging and information technology to provide outpatient radiology, women's imaging, position emission tomography scanning, radiation oncology, and Gamma Knife operation services to the Lancaster County in southeastern Pennsylvania. In 2001, Lancaster Radiology Associates generated $20 million in revenues. We interviewed its Practice Manager/ COO, Robert T. (Bob) Still, who brings an interesting spectrum of leadership experience to his organization. Prior to joining the practice, Still served as a state senator in Delaware and earned his MBA from Penn State University. His experiences in state government and higher education have allowed Still to bring a solid understanding of legislative trends and SFL to Lancaster Radiology Associates.[45]

Mercy Community Hospital

Located in Havertown, Pennsylvania (near Philadelphia) and in existence for about 100 years, Mercy Community Hospital is a 64-bed hospital providing state-of-the-art outpatient programs in advanced radiology, outpatient surgery services in a broad range of specialties, a pain treatment program, and primary and specialty physician care. In 2001, the hospital generated $8 million in revenue. Mercy Community is part of the Mercy Health System, a diverse, integrated Catholic health-care system providing comprehensive services to people in all stages of life through seven acute-care hospitals, several ambulatory care centers, physician practices, two skilled nursing facilities, an independent living facility, a home health-care company, and managed care plans. The system employs about 8,000 health care professionals who serve over 500,000 patients and 600,000 HMO enrollees each year. We interviewed Mercy Community Hospital's CEO Martin McElroy, who is famous for the inspirational talks he gives to his employees, his dedication and devotion to his people, and the success he has had in elevating the morale of the organization and improving its financial stability through reorganizations.[46]

Scripps Health

Scripps is a non-profit health care network in San Diego, California, that includes five hospitals with 2,600 plus affiliated physicians, an extensive ambulatory care network, home health care and associated support services. Scripps has approximately 10,000 employees. The company was founded by Ellen Scripps in 1924 and is one of the oldest health care providers in Southern California. We interviewed Dr. David Shaw, who is Chief of Staff at Scripps Mercy Hospital, which is the biggest hospital in the Scripps system with over 900 affiliated physicians.[47]

Unified Hospital of New York

The mission of Unified Hospital of New York is to improve the health of the regional community through education, biomedical research and healthcare. One of only 125 of the country's medical training facilities, its educational offerings include the Colleges of Medicine, Graduate Studies, Health Professions and Nursing. We interviewed Unified's Chief Operating Officer, and it's Vice President for Public and Governmental Affairs. As COO, this female executive is responsible for managing several administrators who oversee University Hospital's day-to-day operations along various service lines. The Vice President is the principle officer responsible for public affairs, governmental relations, campus events and communications, including marketing, media relations, and publications.[48]

Unitary Medicine Associates

Unitary Medicine Associates was created in 1991 when a large health system acquired an independent group of 35 physicians practicing at two locations in upstate New York. Unitary Medicine Associates has become a not-for-profit, multi-specialty physician group affiliated with the large health system, records 425,000 patient visits per year, and generates gross revenue in excess of $100 million. We interviewed the CEO of Unitary Medicine Associates, who has held this executive position since the inception of the organization. He holds and undergraduate degree in Economics from Allegheny College and a Master's degree in Health Service Administration from George Washington University.[49]

Life Sciences: Pharmaceuticals/Biotech

UCB Pharma

In 1928 UCB Pharma was created as a result of the merger of several chemical laboratories. With global headquarters in Brussels, UCB has operations and subsidiaries in Europe, North and South America, and Asia and employs 8,800 employees worldwide. A truly multinational organization, UCB leverages international expertise and competencies through a global network of projects, its subsidiaries, and through licensees in countries where it has no permanent operations. The expansion of its operations has resulted in the discovery of a variety of drugs for treating allergic diseases and disorders of the central nervous system. Advanced technologies are used to promote innovation and collaboration among its business units by accessing modern technologies such as genomics, molecular biology, and combinational chemistry, acquired from specialized laboratories. In 2001, UCB generated $1.2 billion in sales. We interviewed UCB Pharma President Anthony Tebbutt, whose thoughtful style of SFL illustrates the need for executives to pay close attention to technology and industry trends, filtering out irrelevant information, and focusing on what is important for the success of the organization.[50]

Solid State Plasma

Solid State Plasma develops innovative encapsulated active ingredients for applications in the pharmaceutical, cosmetic, oral care and food additive global markets. It has licensed its proprietary platform technology invented at The Hebrew University of Jerusalem. The novelty of its technology is its production of transparent glass matrices capable of entrapping almost every possible existing molecule. Founded in 1997, the company is currently bringing its first of many projects into production. We interviewed its CEO and cofounder. He is a very informal executive who believes in "straight forward" leadership – employees must have fair wages but also have fun and interest in their work. His leadership has created the conditions that promote safety and regulation, but still allow the creativity that is necessary for an up and coming high tech company.[51]

Manufacturing: Construction

Architectural Concepts LLP.

Creativity and innovation are valued in this 28-year old privately-held full-service design firm located in suburban Philadelphia. Architectural Concepts offers architectural, engineering and interior design services with a staff of 25. The organization employs state-of-the-art computer-aided design, WebCam visualization, modeling, rendering and translation technologies to manage all stages of its projects from design creation, through drawing production, project management and construction administration. We interviewed Bruce D. Weinsteiger, AIA, who is one of three partners of Architectural Concepts. Over his 22-year career, he has successfully led the implementation of numerous commercial and residential architectural projects in the Pennsylvania, Delaware and West Virginia areas.[52]

Pulte Homes

With about 9,400 employees, Pulte Homes is the largest homebuilder in the U.S., with operations spanning more than 40 markets throughout the U.S., Argentina, Mexico and Puerto Rico. For over 50 years, Pulte has been providing homebuilding and financial services to its customers. In 2001, Pulte generated revenues of $5.3 billion. One of its newest business units is the Delaware Valley Division of Pulte Homes, which serves the southeastern Pennsylvania, New Jersey and Delaware markets. This division is led by its president, Bill Rieser, who we interviewed. Rieser entered the construction field working for a local builder in Atlanta.[53]

Manufacturing: Defense & Aerospace

Ebor Tech Systems

Ebor Tech Systems is one of Israel's largest and most successful high tech defense firms. It produces and upgrades aircraft/helicopter systems, unmanned airborne vehicle, combat vehicles, and space and aerial reconnaissance systems, among other defense systems. With 5,000 employees, it has markets in the U.S., Israel, Europe and Brazil and its stock is traded on the NYSE. In 2001 Ebor Tech generated revenues of $765 million compared to $372 million in 1997. We interviewed Ebor Tech's VP for Strategy and Business Planning, who is a former General in the Israeli Air Force—a fact that influences his leadership style. As an executive responsible for strategic planning in a very successful company, he highlights change initiatives and employee development as processes that promote SFL at all levels of the organization.[54]

Manufacturing: Energy

Dial-Rhodes

Dial-Rhodes is a wholly-owned business unit of a large U.S.-based infrastructure manufacturer and a leader in energy conversion technology, expanders, power generation packages and control systems. Dial-Rhodes' equipment is used for services such as gas lift/injection, gathering, storage, transmission, hydrocarbon processing and petrochemical production. We interviewed the organization's Vice President and General Manager, Painted Post Operations. He holds a BS in Mechanical Engineering from Virginia Tech and an MBA from the University of Rochester-Simmons School of Business.[55]

IS R&D Inc.

This San Diego California-based company is a major supplier, developer, and service provider of electric, hybrid-electric and fuel cell vehicle components. In business since 1994, IS R&D Inc. is leading the world in building environmentally clean transportation systems using sound designs and manufacturing processes. Its customers include the U.S. Air Force, Navy, and Army/Tacom, and United Airlines among many others. We interviewed the founder and head of IS R&D Inc. A Stanford graduate, this executive provides the spirit and the vision for his organization's success. Under his guidance the company has become a success story and his employees view him as a visionary leader.[56]

NC Utility

NC Utility is a subsidiary of a super-regional energy services and delivery company in the Northeast. NC Utility serves 830,000 electric customers and 250,000 natural gas customers across more than 40% of the state which it serves. We interviewed the President and Chief operating officer of NC Utility. He joined NC Utility in 1978 in the electric generation department. He was named President and Chief Operating Officer in 2000. He received his BS in Atmospheric Science and an MS in Atmospheric Physics from the State University of New York at Albany.[57]

Manufacturing: Furniture

Everfast, Inc

This privately-held 1,700-employee manufacturer and distributor of home fabrics and furniture manages its own retail store chain: Calico Corners, with its 111 unit chains operating at locations across the U.S. For 66 years, Everfast has made its mark by working hand in hand with customers who require solutions that are tailored to their personal needs. To support their plans for future expansion, Everfast is implementing new point-of-sale software, formalizing their IT policies and procedures, and adopting a team-based approach for IT solutions. We interviewed Everfast's CIO, Richard King who gained leadership experience over his 33 years of working for DuPont and then consulting prior to joining Everfast. King is well-known for his ability to communicate a positive outlook for Everfast, while providing clear descriptions of the goals and strategies of his organization.[58]

Manufacturing: Metals & Machinery

BA Reading

This organization had its beginning in 1922 when its founder purchased control of a small foundry and machine shop located in upstate New York. Under the founder's visionary leadership, the company invented the first successful hydraulic hand lift truck and the first hand pallet truck for double-faced pallets. The original company was acquired by a Swedish organization in 1997 and was renamed BA Reading. Some of the company's products include brand electric forklift trucks. We interviewed the President and CEO of BA Reading. This executive joined the company as Vice President of an upstate New York branch operational unit in 1993 and was elected President and COO by the board of directors in 1995. He holds an MBA from the University of Rochester and a Bachelor's degree from Lemoyne College.[59]

Unicorn Incorporated

This organization, a subsidiary of a Fortune 500 technology manufacturing company, produces capital equipment for the electronics industry. Its mission is to be a global supplier of automated electronic assembly technology, equipment, and support through product innovation and enhancement of customer productivity. We interviewed an executive who has been President of Unicorn Incorporated since July 2001. He earned a Civil Engineering degree from the Royal Military College. After serving in the British army for 10 years, he started his career in manufacturing as a Quality Engineer.[60]

Services: Media

Harcourt

Harcourt is a global education company serving students and teachers in Pre-K through grade 12, adult learners, and readers of all ages. Harcourt's companies provide a variety of books, print, and electronic learning materials, assessments, and professional development programs. We interviewed the CFO of Harcourt Trade Publishers (HTP) headquartered in San Diego, California. Founded in 1919, HTP has been producing high quality, award-winning books and related products for readers of all ages for more than eighty years. HTP books and related products are available through booksellers, libraries, gift and specialty stores, catalogs, and educational outlets. Since the company was acquired by Reed Elsevier several years ago, the company has been trying to utilize information technology to facilitate its global operations.[61]

Roote Information

Founded in the United Kingdom in 1851, Roote Information is the leading global provider of news, financial information and technology solutions to the world media, financial institutions, businesses and individuals. Roote Information's strength is its unique ability to offer customers around the world a combination of content, technology and connectivity. Its premier position is founded on a reputation for speed, accuracy, integrity and impartiality as well as continuous technological innovation. Roote

Information supplies the global financial markets and news media with the widest range of global solutions and technologies. The organization employs 18,140 employees in 220 cities in 97 countries, and in 2001 it achieved $5.6 billion in revenue. We interviewed one of the top leaders of Roote Information who valued inspirational leadership as an important motivational force.[62]

Scoope Tech Services

Scoope Tech Services supplies digital compression technology to the broadcasting industry. Based on over 20 years of research and expertise in digital compression algorithm development, Scoope's solutions provide superior flexibility at the highest quality and cost-performance. Scoope's clients are leading satellite broadcasters, cable and telecommunications operators and private networks. Scoope's has offices in San Diego, Miami, Beijing, San Paulo, Ahmadabad, India, Mexico City, and headquarters in Tel Aviv, employing about 140 people. The company's mission is to provide complete end-to-end system solutions for the delivery of digital TV and data over broadband networks. We interviewed the company's Vice President for Professional Services. This executive, an electrical engineer, is responsible for R&D at Scoope. He believes in paying close attention to employee needs and in integrity as critical for creating excellent relationships with both employees and customers.[63]

Services: Professional

Bloom Institute, Inc.

The managing of professional impressions is the mantra for this 10-year old privately-held organization, based in Bloomsburg, a historic and quaint town in central Pennsylvania. Here one finds the Bloom Institute, a center for behavioral change, professional and executive development, leadership training, executive coaching, and professional presence or impression management programs. While the Bloom Institute employs only 3 full time individuals, it is truly a "virtual organization" in the sense that it relies on numerous temporary contractual relationships with human resource development professionals to attain its organizational goals. We interviewed its CEO and founder, Beth Bloom Gardner whose expertise has been featured in *Inc.* and *Glamour* magazines and several books on impression management and career development. Gardner has been listed among America's most successful women entrepreneurs along with being a recipient of the prestigious Blue Chip Enterprise Initiative Award.[64]

DGM Information Systems

DGM Information Systems is a developer, producer and supplier of training and educational systems. The company operates in the general education and professional training markets. It offers a variety of products in the areas of science and technology, IT products and community centers. Among its customers are schools, universities, graduate research institutes, and industrial training facilities around the world. We interviewed the company's CEO, who believes e-learning will be more critical in the future and highlights future orientation as his main leadership approach. He is also a great believer in empowerment.[65]

Diversified Data Services

Time-honored traditions of the staid financial industry blend with innovative approaches to technology adoption at Diversified Data Services. This 250-employee privately-held organization has been in operation since 1992 providing professional systems integration and development services to public and private sector organizations across central and eastern Pennsylvania. Diversified Data Services takes pride in its advanced information technologies that support its network administration and integration services, knowledge management services, application development and programming on a wide range of platforms and languages, and computer telephony (call center) operations. In 2001, Diversified Data Services generated revenues of $15 million. We interviewed Craig Robinson, CPA, MBA, who is the organization's CFO. In addition to his SFL role at Diversified Data Services, Robinson is prominent in community and business development projects in the Lancaster, Pennsylvania region.[66]

Greencastle Associates Consulting, LLC.

Employing 14 associates who each possess military experience, Greencastle Associates Consulting is a six year old IT program and project management organization. Greencastle offers planning services at the tactical business level, business process mapping, management consulting, change management and project management as it relates to executing strategic business initiatives. In 2001, it generated revenues of $1.8 million. Greencastle's associates work with advanced technologies on a daily basis since most of their clients are in service businesses such as telecommunications, utilities, finance, health care, and pharmaceuticals. We interviewed one of Greencastle's founding partners, Celwyn Evans, who serves as its president. Evans served as a member of the U.S. Army Special Forces and is currently a Major in the Pennsylvania Army National Guard where he holds the position of Executive Officer in a military intelligence battalion. His military experience has helped him shape Greencastle into a mission-driven organization based on core values of service, adaptability, loyalty, teamwork, integrity, and enthusiasm.[67]

Greymatter, Inc.

The brainchild of four former DuPont employees, Greymatter Inc. is an emerging six-year old IT consulting organization based in Wilmington, Delaware. Employing 14 people, Greymatter delivers high-end IT consulting services to Fortune 1000 companies that have a need for innovative business solutions. Greymatter's business model involves synergizing the knowledge, skills and abilities of a team of highly-talented IT professional consultants with advanced information technology to provide quality IT solutions to help meet their clients business goals. As noted on their website, GreyMatter's industry-certified consultants possess a wide-range of experiences gained through working with small-mid-and-Fortune 500 companies and staying abreast of the latest industry technologies and trends. In 2001, it generated revenues of $2 million. We interviewed Shannon K. Watson, CEO/President of GreyMatter, Inc, who has served as a role model to his employees through his active involvement with innumerable IT outsourcing engagements in large and mid-sized corporations and in a variety of community service activities in the Pennsylvania, New Jersey and Delaware region.[68]

ITG Pathfinders

The traditions of the U.S. Marine Corps are evident at ITG Pathfinders, an emerging 4-year old 35-employee e-business and management consulting company based in Wilmington, Delaware. ITG advises clients in formulating business and technology strategies with respect to using the Internet. ITG's culture stresses loyalty, respect, and trustworthiness in all client and employee interactions while providing a variety of practice areas including, e-Manufacturing (supply chain management), strategy services, infrastructure and network engineering, solutions software development, systems integration and enterprise applications integration and technology lifecycle support. In 2001, ITG generated revenues of $3.1 million. We interviewed ITG's co-founder and COO, Russel Laraway, whose strategic leadership has been influenced by his experiences in the Naval ROTC program at the University of South Carolina and his service in the U.S. Marine Corps. In the military, Laraway's talents for leadership were recognized with rapid promotions to the level of Company Commander. Laraway's SFL involving goal setting and performance measurement using the balanced scorecard has helped ITG to gain recognition in 2002 as one of Delaware's "Companies to Watch."[69]

Mal Tech Services

Mal Tech Services, a public company traded on the Tel Aviv Stock Exchange, is one of Israel's leading system integration shops. Mal Tech Services has a staff of 150 employees and provides overall IT solutions to over 1,000 customers mostly in the public sectors in Israel and abroad, on all common hardware, software, database and communication platforms. We interviewed the CEO of Mal Tech Services. He emphasizes human resource management as a key to achieving the strategic goals of the company. He also uses surveys to monitor employees' expectations and tries to link these expectations with the goals of the organization.[70]

Rnet

Founded in 1988, Rnet is a New York City-based company in the computer network business. It employs about 200 people who are mostly engineers. We interviewed one of the cofounders of the company. The executive we interviewed is a strong believer in leadership that lets employees be involved in strategic planning. Such involvement not only is a strong motivator but also contributes to more effective planning.[71]

Tier Resource Rentals

A franchise division of a $4.5 billion, member-owned cooperative, Tier Resource Rentals and its sister-company carry 30 years of experience in the rental business and the buying power of its parent company, one of the largest hardware co-ops in the U.S. We interviewed an independent owner, operator and President of a Tier Resource Rentals operation in upstate New York. This executive's business combines profit centers that include party rentals, contractor rentals and homeowner rentals. His innovative marketing has enabled growth in his company despite local population declines and a shrinking economy.[72]

Services: Retail

Sheetz Inc.

From their famous hot dogs and hamburgers, fresh brewed coffee, and gasoline to their line of Made to Order (MTO) sandwiches and salads, Sheetz, Inc. represents the pinnacle of success in the convenience store industry. For 50 years, Sheetz has been a chain that has achieved remarkable growth in both profit and size. Based in Altoona, Pennsylvania, the organization currently has 7,500 employees and operates 275 stores in Pennsylvania, West Virginia, Maryland, Virginia and Ohio, with plans to open 14 additional stores. In 2001, Sheetz generated revenues of $1.7 billion and surpasses $2 billion in sales in 2002. With a recent investment of nearly $18 million in advanced technology systems, Sheetz has supported its success by implementing touch screen food ordering systems, upgraded back office computer software, ATMs at every store, Internet kiosks, and Z-Cards (smart cards) for purchases. We interviewed Joseph S. Sheetz, CFO of the privately-owned and operated family business. On his way to becoming CFO, Sheetz worked for the family business in various accounting and operations functions, completed his college education at the University of Pennsylvania's Wharton School, and then spent over six years working as an employee benefits consultant in Philadelphia before coming back into the family business.[73]

NOTES

CHAPTER 1

1. DiStefano, J. N. (2003, April 3). New course served for a losing firm. *The Philadelphia Inquirer*, E1-E2; Gilbert, A. (2000, October 30). VerticalNet unable to silence critics. *Informationweek*, 193; and Karpinski, R. (2002). VerticalNet exits e-marketplaces, buys tech firms, *BtoB, 87*(3), 28.

2. For more information on the high pace characteristics of technology intensive environment, see Brown, S. L., & Eisenhardt, K. M. (1998). *Competing on the edge*. Boston, MA: Harvard Business Press.

3. For examples of the destructive force of poor strategy-focused leadership, see Collins, J. C. (2001). *Good to great: Why some companies make the leap—and others don't*. New York: Harper Business; and Rowe, W. G. (2001). Creating wealth in organizations: The role of strategic leadership. *Academy of Management Executive, 15*, 81-94.

4. Models grounding this project's research include the work of Avolio, B. J., & Bass, B. M. (2002). *Developing potential across a full range of leadership: Cases on transactional and transformational leadership*. Mahwah, NJ: Lawrence Erlbaum Associates; Conger, J. A., & Kanungo, R. N. (1998). *Charismatic leadership in organizations*. Thousand Oaks, CA: Sage; and Shamir, B., & Howell, J. M. (1999). Organizational and contextual influences on the emergence and effectiveness of charismatic leadership. *The Leadership Quarterly, 10*, 257-283.

The Dream Weavers: Strategy-Focused Leadership in Technology-Driven
Organizations, pages 277–306
Copyright © 2004 by Information Age Publishing, Inc.
All rights of reproduction in any form reserved.
ISBN: 1-59311-110-X (paper), 1-59311-111-8 (cloth)

5.   Shackleton, E. (1914). *The heart of the Antarctic: Being the story of the British Antarctic Expedition, 1907-1909*. London: William Heinemann.

6.   For more critical examinations of Shackleton's expedition, see Gore-Langton, R. (2002). The importance of being Ernest. *The Spectator, 228,* 22-23; and Simons, T. (2002). What are the true lessons of Shackleton's survival saga? *Presentations, 16*(5), 6.

7.   Finkelstein, S. (2001). The myth of managerial superiority in Internet startups: An autopsy. *Organizational Dynamics, 30*(2), 172-185.

8.   For a detailed discussion of how executives gain discretion see Finkelstein, S. & Hambrick, D. (1996). *Strategic leadership: Top executives and their effects on organizations.* Minneapolis/St. Paul: West.

9.   Kaplan, R. S., & Norton, D. P. (1996). Strategic learning and the balanced scorecard. *Strategy & Leadership, 24,* 18-24.

10.   Ireland, R. D., & Hitt, M. A. (1999). Achieving and maintaining strategic competitiveness in the 21st century: The role of strategic leadership. *Academy of Management Executive, 13,* 43-57.

11.   Finkelstein & Hambrick (1996) as cited in Note 8.

12.   For a detailed critical review of strategic leadership see Boal, K. B., & Hooijberg, R. (2001). Strategic leadership research: Moving on. *The Leadership Quarterly, 11,* 515-549; and Priem, R. L., Lyon, D. W., & Dess, G. G. (1999). Inherent limitations of demographic proxies in top management team heterogeneity research. *Journal of Management, 25,* 935-953.

13.   See a review of the leadership literature by House, R. J., & Aditya, R. N. (1997). The social scientific study of leadership: Quo Vadis? *Journal of Management, 23,* 409-473.

14.   Hambrick, D. C. & Mason, P. A. (1984). Upper echelons: The organization as a reflection of its top managers. *Academy of Management Review, 9,* 193-206.

15.   Priem et al. (1999) as cited in Note 12.

16.   Rowe, W. G. (2001). Creating wealth in organizations: The role of strategic leadership. *Academy of Management Executive, 15,* 81-94.

17.   Sellers, P. (1999, June 21). CEOs in denial. *Fortune, 139,* 80-82.

18.   Yukl, G. (2002). *Leadership in organizations* (5th Ed.) Upper Saddle River, NJ: Prentice-Hall.

19.   Kelly, B. (Executive Producer). (2001, July 3). *State of Pennsylvania #1008: WARMland remembered—The mighty 590* [Television broadcast]. Pittston, PA: WVIA Public Broadcasting Service.

20.   http://www.businessweek.com/2000/00_39/b3700122.htm.   (accessed August 18, 2002).

21.   Excellent discussions of inspirational leadership and its effects on followers are provided in Bass, B.M. (1998). *Transformational leadership: Industry, military, and educational impact.* Mahwah, NJ: Lawrence Erlbaum Associates; Burns, J. M. (1978). *Leadership.* New York: Harper & Row; Shamir, B. (1991). The charismatic relationship: Alternative explanations and predictions. *The Leadership Quarterly, 2,* 81-104; and Shamir, B., Zakay, E., Breinin, E., & Popper, M. (1998). Correlates of charismatic leader behavior in military units: Subordinates' attitudes, unit characteristics, and superiors' appraisals of leader. *Academy of Management Journal, 41,* 387-409.

22.   Kelleher, H. (1997). A culture of commitment. *Leader to Leader, 4,* 1-6.

23. Mondy, R. W., Noe, R. M., & Premeaux, S. R. (2002). *Human resource management* (8th Ed.). Upper Saddle River, NJ: Prentice-Hall.

24. Anonymous. (2000). Study looks at how exemplary-practice companies use training and development efforts to attract and retain employees. *Training & Development, 54*, 78-79.

25. Anonymous. (2003, January 13). The best (& worst) managers of the year. *Business Week*, 67.

26. Devine, D. J., Clayton, L. D., Philips, J. L., Dunford, B. B., & Melner, S. B. (1997). Teams in organizations: Prevalence, characteristics, and effectiveness. *Small Group Research, 30*, 678-711.

27. http://www.commonwealth.com/Comm_Ink/CEO.htm. (accessed August 15, 2002).

28. Oz, E., & Sosik, J. J. (2000). Why information system projects are abandoned: A leadership and communication theory and exploratory study. *Journal of Computer Information Systems, 41*(1), 66-78.

29. Melymuke, K. (1997, April 28). Virtual realities. *Computerworld*, 70-72.

30. Expectations of how leaders and followers will interact through technology are discussed in Avolio, B. J., Kahai, S. S., & Dodge, G. (2001). E-leading in organizations and its implications for theory, research and practice. *The Leadership Quarterly, 11*, 615-668; and Oz, E. (2000). *Management information systems*. Cambridge, MA: Course Technology.

31. For a comprehensive discussion of the role of impression management in leadership, see Gardner, W. L., & Avolio, B. J. (1998). The charismatic relationship: A dramaturgical perspective. *Academy of Management Review, 23*, 32-58; and Sosik, J. J., Avolio, B. J., & Jung, D. I. (2002). Beneath the mask: Examining the relationship of self-presentation attributes and impression management to charismatic leadership. *The Leadership Quarterly, 13*, 217-242.

32. Interview with Lee Kranefuss conducted by Steve Dunn, June, 2002.

33. Anonymous (2001, October). Leaders develop leaders. *Association Management*, 16-17.

34. Shinseki, E. K., & White, T. E. (2001). *Army knowledge management strategic plan: A strategic plan for an agile force.* Washington, DC: Department of the Army.

35. Interview with Richard King conducted by Lisa D. K. Coutant, May 2001.

36. Excellent discussions of balanced scorecard approaches to strategy-focused leadership can be found in Kaplan, R. S., & Norton, D. P. (1996). *The balanced scorecard: Translating strategy into action.* Boston: Harvard Business School Press; Mahoney, A. I. (1999). For the customer: How webs of inclusion can create an organization with agility to face imperatives head-on. *Association Management, 51*, 101-108; Olve, N. G., Roy, J., & Wetter, M. (1999). *Performance drivers.* New York: Wiley.; and Puisis, J. (2001). BioTech's new business model. *Pharmaceutical Executive, 21*, 58-64.

37. Harvard Business School. (2000). *GE's two-decade transformation: Jack Welch's leadership.* Multimedia case 9-301-040. Boston: Harvard Business School Publishing.

38. Finkelstein & Hambrick (1996) as cited in Note 8.

39. The central role of vision is discussed by several authors including Ireland & Hitt (1999) as cited in Note 10, Kaplan & Norton (1996) as cited in Note 36, and Rowe (2001) as cited in Note 16.

CHAPTER 2

1. Interview with Amy Turner-LaDow conducted by Grant Galef, June 2002. Additional information on SCT obtained from http://www.sct.com/ (accessed November 10, 2002).

2. Interesting discussions of the integral role of information technology in future organizations can be found in Toffler, A., & Toffler, H. (1995). *Creating a new civilization : The politics of the Third Wave*. Atlanta, GA: Turner Publishing; Toffler, A. (1990). *Powershift: Knowledge, wealth, and violence at the edge of the 21st century.* New York: Bantam Books; and Toffler, A. (1989) *The Third Wave*. New York: Bantam Books.

3. Anonymous (2003, September 23). The good CEOs. *Business Week*, 80-88.

4. Leadership of organizations leveraging technology has been described in works by Annunzio, S., & Liesse, J. (2001). *eLeadership : Proven techniques for creating an environment of speed and flexibility in the digital economy*. New York: Free Press; Avolio, B. J., Kahai, S. S., & Dodge, G. (2001). E-leading in organizations and its implications for theory, research and practice. *The Leadership Quarterly, 11*, 615-668; Kostner, J. (1994). *Virtual leadership: Secrets from the round table for the multi-site manager.* New York: Warner Books; and Mills, D. Q. (2001). *E-leadership: Guiding your business to success in the new economy.* Paramus, NJ: Prentice Hall.

5. The topic of shared leadership is discussed by Avolio, B. J. (1999). *Full leadership development: Building the vital forces in organizations*. Thousand Oaks, CA: Sage; Gronn, P. (2002). Distributed leadership as a unit of analysis. *The Leadership Quarterly, 13*, 423-451; and Manz, C. C. & Sims, H. P. (1993). *Business without bosses: How self-managing teams are building high-performing companies*. New York: Wiley.

6. Anonymous (2003) as cited in Note 3.

7. Lawless, M. & Gomez-Mejia, L. R. (1990) *Strategic management in high technology firms*. Greenwich, CT: JAI Press.

8. Detailed descriptions and examples of technology-based organizations are provided in Anonymous. (2003, January 13). Industry Outlook 2003. *Business Week*, 95-134; Khandwalla, P. K. (1992). *Innovative corporate turnovers*. Newbury Park: Sage Publications; and Ricadela, A. (2002, July 29). Microsoft plans big R&D and hiring push. *InformationWeek, 899*, 22.

9. Hottenstein, M. (1990). Managing the design/manufacturing interface in selected high technology firms. In Lawless, M. & Gomez-Mejia, L. R. (Eds.). *Strategic management in high technology firms*. Greenwich, CT: JAI Press.

10. http://global-reach.biz/globstats/index.php3 (accessed June 9, 2003).

11. DiStefano, J. N. (2003, April 3). His troubles aside, Musser is still sailing. *The Philadelphia Inquirer,* E1,E3; and Rebon, M. A. (1999). *Safeguard Scientifics and its innovative approach to building shareholder value.* Unpublished masters thesis, Penn State University—Harrisburg; and http://www.safeguard.com/home.asp (accessed August 22, 2002).

12. http://www.dialog.com/products/casestudies/kpmg.shtml (accessed September, 24, 2002).

13. Kirkpatrick, D. (2003, May 12). Tech: Where the action is. *Fortune, 147*(9), 78-84.

14. Fascinating views of the future of the Internet and how we will interact with each other in the future are described in Bullinga, M. (2002). The Internet of the

future: To control or be controlled. *The Futurist, 36*(3), 27-33; and at the following web addresses www.motorola.com; oxygen.lcs.mit.edu; and www.ai.mit.edu/projects/iroom.

15.   *Business Week.* (2003, March 25). The tech outlook. *Spring 2003 special annual issue, 3826A,* 153-172.

16.   Details on the Enron and WorldCom scandals can be found in Geewax, M. (2002, July 25). Reform legislation clears hurdle Final version reflects wishes of Democrats. *The Atlanta Journal-Constitution,* H1; Iwata, E. (2002, August 21). Ex-Enron exec may plead guilty; Possible deal would lighten sentence for cooperation. *USA Today,* B.01; Mills. D. I. (2002). *Buy, lie, and sell high: How investors lost out on Enron and the Internet bubble.* New York: Prentice Hall; and Young, H. (2002, July 25). Comment & Analysis: The Interbrew wrangle gives succor to the crooks: In an age of corporate scandal, whistleblowers should be protected. *The Guardian,* 18.

17.   http://www.responsibleshopper.org/ (accessed August 22, 2002).

18.   For an overview of books on social betterment thinking see Marien, M. (2002). Utopia revisited: New thinking on social betterment. *The Futurist, 36*(2), 37-43.

19.   Senge, P. M. (1990). *The fifth discipline: The art and practice of the learning organization.* New York: Doubleday.

20.   Tomlinson, A. (2002). T&D spending up in U.S. as Canada lags behind. *Canadian HR Reporter, 15*(6), 1.

21.   Fulmer, R. M., & Goldsmith, M. (2001). *The leadership investment: How the world's best organizations gain strategic advantage through leadership development.* New York: American Management Association; and http://www.unisys.com/about__unisys/careers/growth__and__development/learn__more__about__uu.htm   (accessed August 26, 2002).

22.   Crawford, C. B., Brungardt, C. L., Scott, R. F., & Gould, L. V. (2002). Graduate programs in organizational leadership: A review of programs, faculty, costs, and delivery methods. *The Journal of Leadership Studies, 8*(4), 64-74.

23.   Cultural assessment techniques are described by O'Connell, C. (1999). A culture of change or a change of culture? *Nursing Administration Quarterly, 23*(2), 65-68; Reigle, R. F. (2001). Measuring organic and mechanistic cultures. *Engineering Management Journal, 13*(4), 3-8; Schein, E. H. (1992). *Organizational culture and leadership* (2nd Ed.). San Francisco: Jossey-Bass; and Svensson, M. & Klefsjo, B. (2000). Experiences from creating a quality culture for continuous improvements in the Swedish school sector by using self-assessments. *Total Quality Management, 11,* 800-807.

24.   Avolio, B. J., Sosik, J. J., Jung, D. I., & Berson, Y. (2003). Leadership models, methods and applications: Small steps and giant leaps. In W. C. Borman, R. J. Klimoski, D. J. Ilgen, & I. B. Weiner (Eds.) *Comprehensive handbook of psychology, Volume 12: Industrial and organizational psychology,* (pp. 277-307). New York: John Wiley & Sons.

25.   Postmes, T. Spears, R., & Lea, M. (2000). The formation of group norms in computer-mediated communication. *Human Communication Research, 26,* 341-371; and Sheehy, N., & Gallagher, T. (1996). Can virtual organizations be made real? *Psychologist, 9,* 159-162.

26.   Figura, S. Z. (2000). Human capital: The missing link. *Government Executive, 32*(3), 22-26.

27.   Warner, F. (2002, July). How Google searches itself. *Fast Company, 60,* 50-52.

28. Messmer, M. (2001). Encouraging employee creativity. *Strategic Finance, 83*(6), 16-18.

29. Anonymous. (2002, June 3). CEOs talk. *Canadian HR Reporter, 15*(11), 15-17.

30. Anonymous (2002) as cited in Note 29.

31. Details on how to promote creativity and innovation in organizations are provided by Bernacki, E. (2001). Building an idea factory. *New Zealand Management, 48*(5), 11; and DeSalvo, T. (1999). Unleash the creativity in your organization. *HRMagazine, 44*(6), 154-164.

32. Wrzesniewski, A., & Dutton. J. E. (2001). Crafting a job: Revisioning employees as active crafters of their work. *Academy of Management Review, 26,* 179-201.

33. The advantages and disadvantages of globalization are discussed by Anonymous. (2001, December 8). Finance and economics: Going global, globalization and prosperity. *The Economist, 361,* 67; Apter, D. E. (2002). Globalization and its discontents. *Dissent, 49,* 13-18; Hawkens, P. (2002). Globalization equals conformity and loss of diversity. *Whole Earth, 107,* 68; Potter, E. L. (2001). Settling the global frontier. *Association Management, 53*(2), 16; and Taylor, T. (2002). The truth about globalization. *Public Interest, 147,* 24-44.

34. Globalization's effects of spreading knowledge and raising average living standards at the expense of harming the world's poorest are eloquently described by Amartya Sen, the 1998 Nobel Laureate in Economic Science in Sen, A. (2002). How to judge globalism. *The American Prospect,* (Winter), A2-A6.

35. http://www.vodafone.co.uk/cgi-bin/COUK/arrival.jsp (accessed September 25, 2002).

36. Abate, T. (2002, June 10). Biotrends: Two major reports highlight the globalization of biotechnology and the battle within the U.S. for regional supremacy. *San Francisco Chronicle,* E1.

CHAPTER 3

1. Cranmer, M. (2002). *Strategic leadership analysis of Shannon Watson, CEO, Grey-Matter, Inc.* Malvern, PA: Penn State Great Valley School of Graduate Professional Studies; and http://greymatterinc.com/ (accessed September 5, 2002).

2. Discussions on the social and cognitive requirements of executive leadership can be found in Hunt, J. G. (1991). *Leadership: A new synthesis.* Newburry Park, CA: Sage; Jaques, E. (1986). The development of intellectual capacity: A discussion of stratified systems theory. *Journal of Applied Behavioral Science, 22,* 361-383; and Yukl, G. A. (2002). *Leadership in organizations* (5th Ed.). Upper Saddle River, NJ: Prentice-Hall.

3. Taylor, A. (2003, March 17). Just another sexy sports car. *Fortune, 147*(5) 76-80.

4. http://www.greencastleconsulting.com/ (accessed September 5, 2002); and interview with Celwyn Evans conducted by John J. Sosik and Maria Peterson, November 28, 2001.

5. Garr, D. (1999). *IBM redux: Lou Gerstner and the business turnaround of the decade.* New York: HarperBusiness.

6. Thomas, P. (2003, February, 18). Case study: Owner's contacts make new business a success. *The Wall Street Journal,* B.9.

7. Swartz, N. D. (2003, March 17). The Pentagon's private army. *Fortune, 147*(5), 100-108.

8. http://www.ucbpharma.com/INT/pages/corp4.php?ID=26 (accessed February 27, 2003).

9. http://www.techcouncil.org/aboutetc.cfm (accessed February 27, 2003).

10. Interview with executive conducted by Christine Alaimo, Frank Iacono, Tony Ng, and Jennifer Rounavaara, December 2001.

11. Hodara, S. (2002, April 14). Not a party or business meeting. *The New York Times,* 3.

12. Fombrun, C. J. (1996). *Reputation: Realizing value from the corporate image.* Boston: Harvard Business School Press.

13. Coffee, J. C. (2002). Understanding Enron: "It's about the gatekeepers, stupid." *The Business Lawyer, 57,* 1403-1420.

14. Interview with Anthony Tebbutt conducted by Andrew F. Hartnett, November 2001.

15. Scott, S. G., & Lane, V. R. (2000). A stakeholder approach to organizational identity. *Academy of Management Review, 25,* 43-62.

16. Gordon, R. A. (1996). Impact of ingratiation on judgments and evaluations: A meta-analytic investigation. *Journal of Personality and Social Psychology, 71,* 54-70; and Peale, N. V. (1987). *The power of positive thinking.* New York: Prentice Hall.

17. For a fuller, more theoretical consideration of the concept of individualized consideration, see Bass, B. M., & Avolio, B. J. (1994). *Improving organizational effectiveness through transformational leadership.* Thousand Oaks, CA: Sage.

18. Ante, S. E. (2003, March 17). The new blue. *Business Week, 3824,* 80-88.

19. Washer, P. (2002). Professional networking using computer-mediated communication. *British Journal of Nursing, 11,* 18-20.

20. http://www.corning.com/ (accessed March 3, 2003).

21. http://www.uic.com/wcms/WCMS.nsf/index/About_Universa l_0.html (accessed March 3, 2003).

22. Abels, E. (2002). Hot topics: Environmental scanning. *Bulletin of the American Society for Information Science, 28,* 16-17; and Kourtelli, L. (2000). Scanning the business environment: Some conceptual issues. *Benchmarking, 7,* 406-413.

23. http://flagship.vanguard.com/web/corpcontent/Corporat ePortal.html (accessed March 3, 2003).

24. Porter, M. E. (1985). *Competitive advantage: Creating and sustaining superior performance.* New York: Free Press.

25. Port, O., Arndt, M., & Carey, J. (2003, March 25). Smart tools. *Business Week, 3826A,* 154-155; and Schlosser, J. (2003, March 17). Looking for intelligence in ice cream. *Fortune, 147*(5), 114-120.

26. Details for implementing this intriguing tactic are described in Halliman, C. (2001). *Business intelligence using smart techniques: Environmental scanning using data mining and competitor analysis using scenarios and manual simulation.* Houston, TX: Information Uncover. A review of this tactic is provided by Subramanian, B. (2002). Software reviews. *Competitiveness Review, 12,* 115.

27.   Orndoff, K. (2002). Strategic tools for RIM professionals. *Information Management Journal, 36*, 65-71; and Yukl (2002) as cited in Note 2.

28.   Orndoff (2002) as cited in Note 27.

29.   Jennings, L. (2002). Scenario planning in a multicultural world. *The Futurist, 36*, 61-62; and Ogilvy, J. A. (2002). *Creating better futures: Scenario planning as a tool for a better tomorrow.* Oxford, UK: Oxford University Press.

30.   Wylie, I. (2002). There is no alternative . . . *Fast Company, 60*, 106-110.

31.   Schwartz, P. (1991). *The art of the long view: Planning for the future in an uncertain world.* New York: Currency Doubleday.

32.   Ante (2003) as cited in Note 18.

CHAPTER 4

1.   Interview with a key executive at Morton Finance conducted by Jon Goldberg, Michael Tumino, Ted Witryk, and Tom D'Antonio, December 2001.

2.   Frankl, V. E. (1959). *Man's search for meaning.* Boston: Beacon Press.

3.   Conger, J. A., & Kanungo, R. N. (1998). *Charismatic leadership in organizations.* Thousand Oaks, CA: Sage.

4.   N. Brinker (Personal communication, October 10, 1998).

5.   For detailed explanations of inspirational leadership, see Avolio, B. J., & Bass, B. M. (2002). *Developing potential across a full range of leadership: Cases on transactional and transformational leadership.* Mahwah, NJ: Erlbaum; and Bass, B. M. (1985). *Leadership and performance beyond expectations.* Mahwah, NJ: Erlbaum.

6.   Comparison sample is derived from Bass, B. M., & Avolio, B. J. (1997). *Full range leadership development: Manual for the Multifactor Leadership Questionnaire.* Palo Alto, CA: Mind Garden. Means (standard deviations) for inspirational leadership (IL) for executives in our sample were 3.2 (.60), and 2.69 (.91) for leaders in the Bass and Avolio (1997) sample ($t(1684) = 7.58$).

7.   Executives of manufacturing organizations ($M = 3.54$, $SD = .35$) were rated by their direct reports as displaying significantly ($p < .05$) higher levels of IL than executives of information technology ($M = 3.03$, $SD = .70$), finance ($M = 2.96$, $SD = .40$), and services ($M = 2.93$, $SD = .56$) organizations.

8.   Interview with a key executive at Roote Information conducted by Asanka Gunarrtane, Georgios Zois, Bill Manikakis, and Kenneth Mui, December 2001.

9.   Csikszentmihalyi, M. (1990). *Flow: The psychology of optimal experience.* New York: Harper Collins.

10.   Amabile, T.M. (1998). How to kill creativity. *Harvard Business Review, 76*(5), 77-87

11.   Interview with John Yi conducted by Don I. Jung and Sean Hutchens, June 2002.

12.   Eden, D. (1990). *Pygmalion in management.* Lexington, MA: D.C. Heath; and Manz, C. C., & Neck, C. P. (1999). *Mastering self-leadership: Empowering yourself for personal excellence.* Upper Saddle River, NJ: Prentice-Hall.

13.   Interview with Mighty Tech's president conducted by Dennie Beach, Shawn Belfast, Gordon Marshall, Edison Paul, Johnasttan Regalado, and Kamran Shaikh, December 2001.

14. Shamir, B., Arthur, M. B., & House, R. J. (1994). The rhetoric of charismatic leadership: A theoretical extension, a case study, and implications for research. *The Leadership Quarterly, 5*(1), 25-42.

15. Interview as cited in Note 8.

16. Sosik, J. J., & Dworakivsky, A. C. (1998). Self-concept based aspects of the charismatic leader: More than meets the eye. *The Leadership Quarterly, 9*(4), 503-526.

17. For more details on core message content, see Berson, Y., Shamir, B., Avolio, B. J., & Popper, M. (2001). The relationships between vision strength, leadership style, and context. *The Leadership Quarterly, 12,* 1-21; Conger, J. A. (1991). Inspiring others: The language of leadership. *Academy of Management Executive, 5*(1), 31-45; Conger, & Kanungo (1998) as cited in Note 3, and Shamir et al. (1994) as cited in Note 14.

18. http://www.connectlive.com/events/verizon/verizon-tra   nscript.html (accessed March 12, 2003).

19. Berson et al. (2001) as cited in Note 17.

20. For more details on core message composition or structure, see Emrich, C. G., Brower, H. H., Feldman, J. M., & Garland, H. (2001). Images in words: Presidential rhetoric, charisma, and greatness. *Administrative Science Quarterly, 46,* 527-557; Den Hartog, D. N., & Verbug, R. M. (1997). Charisma and rhetoric: Communicative techniques of international business leaders. *The Leadership Quarterly, 8*(4), 355-391; and Shamir et al. (1994) as cited in Note 14.

21. http://web66.coled.umn.edu/new/MLK/MLK.html (accessed March 13, 2003).

22. Interview with Russell Laraway conducted by Mark Hellerman, June, 2002.

23. For more information on core message style and delivery, see Conger (1991) as cited in Note 17; and Holladay, S. J. & Coombs, W. T. (1994). Speaking of visions and visions being spoken: An exploration of the effects of content and delivery on perceptions of leader charisma. *Management Communication Quarterly, 8*(2), 165-189.

24. Riefenstahl, L. (1934). *Triumph of the will.* [Videocassette]. Novi, MI: Synapse Films.

25. Interesting discussions of the role of emotions in leadership can be found in Englis, B. G. (1993). The role of affect in political advertising: Voter emotional responses to the nonverbal behavior of politicians. In E. E. Clark, T. C. Brock & D. W. Stewart (Eds.) *Attention, attitude and affect in responding to advertising* (pp. 223-247). Hillsdale, NJ: Erlbaum; Gardner, W. L., & Avolio, B. A. (1998). The charismatic relationship: A dramaturgical perspective. *Academy of Management Review, 23,* 32-58; and McHugo, G. J., Lanzetta, J. T., Sullivan, D. G., Masters, R. D., & Englis, B. G. (1985). Emotional reactions to a political leader's expressive displays. *Journal of Personality and Social Psychology, 49,* 1513-1529.

26. Mumford, M. D., Scott, G. M., Gaddis, B., & Strange, J. M. (2002). Leading creative people: Orchestrating expertise and relationships. *The Leadership Quarterly, 13,* 705-750.

27. It is beyond the scope of this book to elaborate upon strategic planning processes. Interested readers should refer to Dess, G. G., & Lumpkin, G. T. (2003). *Strategic management: Creating competitive advantages.* Boston, MA: McGraw Hill/ Irwin; and Harrison, J. S. (2003). *Strategic management of resources and relationships: Concepts and cases.* New York: Wiley.

28. Nonaka, I., & Konno, N. (1998). The concept of 'Ba': Building a foundation for knowledge creation. *California Management Review, 40,* 40-54.

29. Kaplan, R. S., & Norton, D. P. (1996). Strategic learning and the balanced scorecard. *Strategy & Leadership, 24,* 18-24.

30. Schein, E. H. (1992). *Organizational culture and leadership.* San Francisco: Jossey-Bass.

31. Interview with Dr. David Shaw conducted by Don I. Jung in June, 2002.

CHAPTER 5

1. Hitt, J. M., Bierman, L., Shimizu, K., & Kochlar, R. (2001). Direct and moderating effects of human capital on strategy and performance in professional service firms: A resource-based perspective. *Academy of Management Journal, 44,* 13-28; and http://www.hrmguide.co.uk/hrm/chap6/ch6-links1.htm (accessed March 28, 2003).

2. Rousseau, D. M. (1996). Changing the deal while keeping the people. *Academy of Management Executive, 10*(1), 50-59; and Sohag, R. A. (1992). The impact of technology on work groups. *Work Study, 41*(3) 14-15.

3. Mumford, M. D., O'Connor, J., Clifton, T. C., Connelly, M. S., & Zaccaro, S. J. (1993). Background data constructs as predictors of leadership behavior. *Human Performance, 6,* 151-195.

4. Interview with Anthony Tebbutt conducted by Andrew F. Hartnett, November 2001.

5. Anonymous. (2001). HR faces the challenges of 2002. *HR Focus, 78*(12), 14-15.

6. Kaplan, R. S., & Norton, D. P. (1996). Strategic learning and the balanced scorecard. *Strategy & Leadership, 24,* 18-24.

7. Interview with executive conducted by Tal Mor, Arye Chernovorov, Iris Reis, Shachar Ronen, Dana Lubevsky, and Nir Aviram, August 2002.

8. Anonymous. (2002). Why hiring/retention is still a problem . . . & what to do about it. *HR Focus, 79*(11), 3-5.

9. Interview with Rich Sanders conducted by Don I. Jung in June, 2002.

10. For a detailed discussion on selection processes, see Gatewood, R. D., & Field, H. S. (2001). *Human resource selection* (5th Ed.). Fort Worth, TX: Hartcourt; and Schmitt, N., Cortina, J. M., Ingerick, M. J., & Wiechmann (2003). Personnel selection and employee performance. In W. C. Borman, R. J. Klimoski, D. J. Ilgen, & I. B. Weiner (Eds.) *Comprehensive Handbook of Psychology, Volume 12: Industrial and Organizational Psychology* (pp. 77-105). New York: John Wiley & Sons.

11. Anonymous. (2002) as cited in Note 8.

12. Anthony, W. P., Perrewe, P. L., & Kacmar, K. M. (1998). *Human resource management: A strategic approach.* Fort Worth, TX: Dryden.

13. Stewart, T. (1998, February 16). In search of elusive tech workers. *Fortune,* 171-172.

14. Schmidt, F. L., & Hunter, J. E. (1998). The validity and utility of selection methods in personnel psychology: Practical and theoretical implications of 85 years

of research findings. *Psychological Bulletin, 124,* 262-274; and www.siop.org (accessed March 28, 2003).

15. Jung, D. I., & Avolio, B. J. (2000). Opening the black box: An experimental investigation of the mediating effects of trust and value congruence on transformational and transactional leadership. *Journal of Organizational Behavior, 21,* 949-964.

16. Interview with John Yi conducted by Don I. Jung in June, 2002.

17. Avolio, B. J., Sivasubramaniam, N., Murry, W. D., Jung, D., & Garger, J. W. (2003). Assessing shared leadership. In C. L. Pearce & J. A. Conger (Eds.), *Shared leadership: Reframing the hows and whys of leadership* (pp. 143-172). Thousands Oaks, CA: Sage.

18. House, R. J., & Aditya, R. N. (1997). The social science study of leadership. Quo Vadis? *Journal of Management, 23,* 409-473.

19. Cascio, W. F. (2003). Changes in workers, work, and organizations. In W. C. Borman, R. J. Klimoski, D. J. Ilgen, & I. B. Weiner (Eds.) *Comprehensive Handbook of Psychology, Volume 12: Industrial and Organizational Psychology* (pp. 401-422). New York: John Wiley & Sons.

20. Interview with Sandra Sherman conducted by Don I. Jung in June, 2002.

21. Interview with Terrie Troxel conducted by John J. Sosik and Maria Peterson, March 7, 2002.

22. Interview as cited in Note 9.

23. Interview with a key executive at Morton Finance conducted by Jon Goldberg, Michael Tumino, Ted Witryk, and Tom D'Antonio, December 2001.

24. For more information on the private and public self-awareness of IT managers, see Cringely, R. X. (1992). *Accidental empires.* Reading, MA: Addison-Wesley; Sosik, J. J., & Dworakivsky, A. C. (1998). Self-concept based aspects of the charismatic leader: More than meets the eye. *The Leadership Quarterly, 9*(4), 503-526; and Sosik, J. J., & Jung, D. I. (2003). Impression management strategies and performance in information technology consulting: The role of self-other agreement on charismatic leadership. *Management Communications Quarterly, 17*(2), 233-268.

25. For more information on emotional intelligence see Goleman, D. (1995). *Emotional intelligence.* New York: Bantam Books; and Megerian, L. E., & Sosik, J. J. (1996). An affair of the heart: Emotional intelligence and transformational leadership. *Journal of Leadership Studies, 3*(3), 31-48.

26. Interview with Karen Borda conducted by John J. Sosik and Maria Peterson, February, 4, 2002.

27. Interview with the executive conducted by Suzanne Buckley, Joshua Hogue, Andru Prescod, and Jeanine Prime and submitted December 20, 2002.

28. Interview with Brian Duffy conducted by Brian Viscusi, July 2, 2002.

29. Avolio, B. J., & Bass, B. M. (2002). *Developing potential across a full range of leadership: Cases on transactional and transformational leadership.* Mahwah, NJ: Lawrence Erlbaum Associates.

30. Comparison sample is derived from Bass, B. M., & Avolio, B. J. (1997). *Full range leadership development: Manual for the Multifactor Leadership Questionnaire.* Palo Alto, CA: Mind Garden. Means (standard deviations) for individualized consideration (IC) for executives in our sample were 2.78 (.85), and 2.62 (.94) for leaders in the Bass and Avolio (1997) sample (t(1684) = 2.27).

31. Executives of life sciences organizations (M = 3.24, SD = .35) were rated by their direct reports as displaying significantly ($p < .03$) higher levels of IC than exec-

utives of information technology (M = 2.72, SD = .65) and services (M = 2.56, SD = .66) organizations.

32. Bass, B. M. (1985). *Leadership and performance beyond expectations.* New York: Free Press.

33. For more details, see Avolio, B. J., & Bass. B. M. (1995). Individual consideration viewed at multiple levels of analysis: A multi-level framework for examining the diffusion of transformational leadership. *The Leadership Quarterly, 6,* 199-218.

34. Fields, M., & Weaver, V. (2002). Navigating the hurdles of measurement and retention. *HR Focus, 79*(1), 3-5; and www.shrm.org/hrresources/surveys_published/CMS_002958.pdf (accessed April 3, 2003).

35. Interview with Amy Turner-LaDow conducted by Grant Galef, June 2002.

36. Interview with Robert Snowden conducted by Gary Generose, July 1, 2002.

37. Messmer, M. (1998). Mentoring: Building your company's intellectual capital, *HR Focus, 75,* 11-12.

38. For details on mentoring as a leadership development tool, see Day, D. V. (2001). Assessment of leadership outcomes. In J. S. Zaccaro, & R. J. Klimoski (Eds.), *The nature of organizational leadership: Understanding the imperatives confronting today's leaders* (pp. 384-412). San Francisco: Jossey-Bass; Zelinski, D. (2000.) Mentoring up. *Training, 37,* 136-140; and http://www.mentors.ca/mentor.html (accessed April 2, 2003).

39. Noe, R. A., Greenberger, D. B., & Wang, D. B., Wang, S. (2002). Mentoring: What we know and where we might go. In G. R. Ferris (Ed.), *Research in personnel and human resource management: Vol. 21* (pp. 129-174). Oxford, England: Elseiver Science LTD; and Ragins, B. R. (1997). Diversified mentoring relationships in organizations: A power perspective. *Academy of Management Review, 22,* 482-521.

40. Interview with executive conducted by Wai-Ling Lam, May 28, 2002.

41. Interview as cited in Note 28; and www.gecareers.com (accessed July 10, 2002).

42. Descriptions of career development and psychosocial mentoring functions are based on the seminal work of Kram, K. E. (1985). *Mentoring at work: Developmental relationships in organizational life.* Glenview, IL: Scott Foresman.

43. Interview with Shannon K. Watson conducted by Michael Cranmer, May 20, 2002.

44. Interview with Bill Rieser conducted by Dana Roos and Maria Peterson, June 5, 2002.

45. Interview with executive conducted by Christine Alaimo, Frank Iacono, Tony Ng, and Jennifer Rounavaara, December 2001.

46. Interview with executive conducted by Stacia Babb, Wendy McDonald-Barbee, Jane Pirone, and Cherry Fe D. Trinidad, December 2001.

CHAPTER 6

1. Von Krohg, G., Ichijo, K., & Nonako, I. (2000). *Enabling knowledge creation.* New York: Oxford University Press.

2. Bass, B. M., Avolio, B. J., Jung, D. I., & Berson, Y. (2003). Predicting unit performance by assessing transformational and transactional leadership. *Journal of Applied Psychology, 88*(2), 207-218.

3. Interview with Celwyn Evans conducted by John J. Sosik and Maria Peterson, November 28, 2001.

4. Anonymous. (2003, May 26). Apple takes a big bite. *Fortune, 147*(10), 44; and Phillip, C. (2003, April 11). Apple singing Vivendi tune. *Orlando Sentinel,* C1-C2.

5. Shinseki, E. K., & White, T. E. (2001). *Army knowledge management strategic plan: A strategic plan for an agile force.* Washington, DC: Department of the Army.

6. Interview with Rich Sanders conducted by Don I. Jung in June, 2002.

7. DeSanctis, G., & Poole, M. S. (1994). Capturing the complexity in advanced information technology use: Adaptive structuration theory. *Organization Science, 5*(2), 121-147.

8. Oz, E., & Sosik, J. J. (2000). Why information system projects are abandoned: A leadership and communication theory and exploratory study. *Journal of Computer Information Systems, 41*(1), 66-78.

9. Avolio, B. J. (2000). *E-leadership: Here, there and everywhere.* [Videocassette]. Melbourne, Australia: MLQ Pty. Ltd.

10. Avolio, B. J., Kahai, S., & Dodge, G. E. (2001). E-leadership: Implications for theory, research, and practice. *The Leadership Quarterly, 11*(4), 615-668.

11. For a comprehensive review of the literature on IT failure rates, see Oz and Sosik (2000) as cited in Note 8; and Kandiah, V., Mohd Zailani, S. H., Nasirin, S., Oz, E., & Sosik J. J. (2001). Information systems (IS) project failure: New Evidence from Malaysia. *Sasin Journal of Management, 7*(1), 27-38.

12. Oz and Sosik (2000) as cited in Note 8.

13. Mumford, M. D., Scott, G. M., Gaddis, B., & Strange, J. M. (2002). Leading creative people: Orchestrating expertise and relationships. *The Leadership Quarterly, 13,* 705-750.

14. Interview with executive conducted by Uri Madar, Noa Shapira, David Bar, Michael Gur-Arye, Liat Nechmadi, Margalit Bennett, Taly Granit, and Raz Birman, August 2002.

15. Berson, Y., & Linton, J. D. (2003, August) *Leadership style and quality climate perceptions: Contrasting project versus process environments.* Paper presented at the Academy of Management Annual Meeting, Seattle, WA.

16. Interview with executive by Nataly Linsky, Eyal Rachamim, Tomer Farkash, Alex Schwartz, Arthur Mellikin, Yitzchak Rot, and Nataly Idi, August 2002.

17. Avolio, B. J., Howell, J. M., & Sosik, J. J. (1999). A funny thing happened on the way to the bottom line: Humor as a moderator of leadership style effects. *Academy of Management Journal, 42*(2), 219-227; and Bass (1990). *Bass & Stodgill's handbook of leadership.* New York: Free Press.

18. Comparison sample is derived from Bass, B. M., & Avolio, B. J. (1997). *Full range leadership development: Manual for the Multifactor Leadership Questionnaire.* Palo Alto, CA: Mind Garden. Means (standard deviations) for laissez faire (LF) for executives in our sample were .74 (.78), and .99 (.88) for leaders in the Bass and Avolio (1997) sample ($t(1684) = -3.79$).

19. Female executives were rated by their direct reports as displaying significantly lower levels of LF ($M = .42$, $SD = .29$) and MBE-P ($M = .85$, $SD = 1.29$) than male executives (LF $M = .78$, $SD = .58$; MBE-P $M = 1.29$, $SD = .62$). (For LF, $t(64) = -2.51$; for MBE-P, $t(64) = -2.06$).

20. Executives of emerging growth organizations ($M = 1.03$, $SD = .70$) were rated by their direct reports as displaying significantly ($p < .10$ and $p < .05$) higher levels of LF than executives of start-up ($M = .70$, $SD = .57$) and mature ($M = .67$, $SD =$

.50) organizations. These executives ($M = 1.59$, $SD = .50$) were also rated by their direct reports as displaying significantly ($p < .03$) higher levels of MBE-P than executives of mature ($M = 1.14$, $SD = .61$) organizations.

21.   Interview as cited in Note 6.

22.   Interview with Richard King conducted by Lisa D. K. Coutant, July, 2002.

23.   Dionne, S. D., Yammarino, F. J., Awater, L. E., & James, L. E. (2002). Neutralizing substitutes for leadership theory: Leadership effects and common-source bias. *Journal of Applied Psychology, 87*(3), 454-464; and Kerr, S. & Jermier, J.M. (1978). Substitutes for leadership: The meaning and measurement. *Organizational Behavior and Human Performance*, 22, 375-403.

24.   Jung, D., Chow, C., & Wu, A. (2003). The role of transformational leadership in enhancing organizational innovation: Hypotheses and some preliminary findings. *The Leadership Quarterly, 14*, 525-544.

25.   Avolio et al. (2001) as cited in Note 10.

26.   Interview with executive conducted by Christine Alaimo, Frank Iacono, Tony Ng, and Jennifer Rounavaara, December 2001.

27.   Avolio et al. (2001) as cited in Note 10.

28.   Thormahlen, A. (2001). *Flexiplace pilot 2000 IRS information technology services: Managing Teleworker performance using results.* Washington, DC: Internal Revenue Service.

29.   For overviews of e-leadership research see Avolio et al. (2001) as cited in Note 10; Kostner, J. (1994). *Virtual leadership: Secrets from the round table for the multi-site manager.* New York: Warner Books; Sosik, J. J., Avolio, B. J., & Kahai, S. S. (1997). Effects of leadership style and anonymity on group potency and effectiveness in a group decision support system environment. *Journal of Applied Psychology, 82*(1), 89-103. and Thormahlen (2001) as cited in Note 28.

30.   John-Steiner, V. (2000). *Creative collaboration.* Oxford, UK: Oxford University Press.

31.   Lancer, E. G. (2000). The corporate alliance advantage. *Healthcare Executive, 15*(6), 40-41, and Trask, R. (2000). Developing e-partnerships. *Association Management, 52*(11), 46-52.

32.   Anonymous. (2003, April 28). HP's beachhead in high-tech services. *Business Week*, 40.

33.   Gonzalez, M. (2001). Strategic alliances. *Ivey Business Journal, 66*(1), 47-51.

34.   http://www.thecollaborators.com/index.html (accessed April 23, 2003).

35.   Interview with executive conducted by Wai-Ling Lam, May 28, 2002.

36.   Interview with the executive conducted by Ophir Abramovich, Alon Avi, Brauner Alon, Engel Galit, Bakel Revital, Geva Chana, and Steinberg Sharon, August 2001.

37.   Sosik, J. J., & Dionne, S. D. (1997). Leadership styles and Deming's behavior factors. *Journal of Business and Psychology, 11*(4), 447-462.

CHAPTER 7

1.   Interview with Vee Jay Communications' executive conducted by Ophir Abramovich, Alon Avi, Brauner Alon, Engel Galit, Bakel Revital, Geva Chana, and Steinberg Sharon, August 2001.

2. Foust, D., Barrett, A., Hindo, B., Jespersen, F. F., Katzenberg, F., McNamee, M., & Pascual, A. M. (2003, Spring). The best performers, *Business Week, 3776A,* 44-58; and interview with Bill Rieser conducted by Dana Roos and Maria Peterson, June 5, 2002.

3. Mayer, R. C., Davis, J. H., & Schoorman, F. D. (1995). An integrative model of organizational trust. *Academy of Management Review, 20,* 709-734.

4. Robbins, S. P. (2003). *Organizational behavior* (10th Ed.). Prentice Hall: Upper Saddle River, NJ.

5. Interview with the executive conducted by Asanka Gunarrtane, Georgios Zois, Bill Manikakis, and Kenneth Mui, December 2001.

6. Interesting discussions of the role of trust in leadership can be found in Covey, S. R. (1991). *Principle-centered leadership.* New York: Simon & Schuster; Fukuyama, F. (1995). *Trust: The social virtues and the creation of prosperity.* New York: The Free Press; Mishra, A. K. (1996). Organizational response to crisis: The centrality of trust. In R. M. Kramer & T. R. Tyler (Eds.), *Trust in organizations: Frontiers of theory and research* (pp. 261-287). Thousand Oaks, CA: Sage; and Sheppard, B. H., & Tuchinsky, M. (1996). Micro-OB and the network organization. In R. M. Kramer & T. R. Tyler (Eds.), *Trust in organizations: Frontiers of theory and research* (pp. 140-165). Thousand Oaks, CA: Sage.

7. House, R. J. (1971). A path-goal theory of leadership effectiveness. *Administrative Science Quarterly, 16,* 321-338.

8. Information on the effectiveness of goal setting can be found in Locke, E. A., & Latham, G. P. (1990). *A theory of goal setting and task performance.* Englewood Cliffs, NJ: Prentice Hall; and Locke, E. A., & Latham, G. P. (1984). *Goal setting: A motivational technique that works!* Englewood Cliffs, NJ: Prentice Hall.

9. Comparison sample is derived from Bass, B. M., & Avolio, B. J. (1997). *Full range leadership development: Manual for the Multifactor Leadership Questionnaire.* Palo Alto, CA: Mind Garden. Means (standard deviations) for contingent reward for executives in our sample were 2.81 (.77), and 2.04 (.94) for leaders in the Bass and Avolio (1997) sample (t(1684) = 11.0).

10. Interview with Brian Duffy conducted by Brian Viscusi, July 2, 2002.

11. Interview with Karen Borda conducted by John J. Sosik and Maria Peterson, February, 4, 2002.

12. Reviews of the literature on classical conditioning and the motivating force of rewards can be found in Kazdin, A. E. (1994). *Behavior modification in applied settings* (5th Ed.). Pacific Grove, CA: Brooks/Cole; Lee, D. L., & Belfiore, P. J. (1997). Enhancing classroom performance: A review of reinforcement schedules. *Journal of Behavioral Education, 7*(2), 205-217; and Skinner, B. F. (1953). *Science and human behavior.* New York: Macmillan.

13. Ante, S. E., & Sager, I. (2002, February 11). IBM's new boss. *Business Week, 3769,* 66-72.

14. Interview with the executive conducted by Nataly Linsky, Eyal Rachamim, Tomer Farkash, Alex Schwartz, Arthur Mellikin, Yitzchak Rot, and Nataly Idi, August 2002.

15. Interview with the executive conducted by Gideon Elkan, Amos Levy, Ariel Shmuely, and Alex Berman, January 7, 2002.

16. Interview(s) with the executive(s) conducted by Asanka Gunarrtane, Georgios Zois, Bill Manikakis, and Kenneth Mui, December 2001.

17. Interview as cited in Note 10.

18.   http://www.gmu.edu/depts/psychology/homepage/thorndike.html (accessed May 8, 2003).

19.   Interview with Norm Thomas conducted by Don I. Jung in June 2002.

20.   Interview with John Yi conducted by Don I. Jung in June, 2002.

21.   There is a debate in the creativity literature regarding the detrimental effects of rewards. Those scholars who support the view that rewards have detrimental effects on creativity include Amabile, T. M. (1996). *Creativity in context: Update to the social psychology of creativity.* Boulder, CO: Westview; Deci, E. L., & Ryan, R. M. (1985). *Intrinsic motivation and self-determination in human behavior.* New York: Plenum Press; Kohn, A. (1993). *Punished by rewards.* Boston: Houghton Mifflin; and Lepper, M. R. (1981). Intrinsic and extrinsic motivation in children: Detrimental effects of superfluous social controls. In W. A. Collins (Ed.), *Aspects of the development of competence: The Minnesota Symposium on Child Psychology* (Vol. 14, pp. 155-214). Hillsdale, NJ: Erlbaum. In contrast, there are those who argue that detrimental effects of rewards on creativity can be restricted and easily avoided. These scholars include Eisenberger, R., & Cameron, J. (1996). Detrimental effects of reward: Reality or myth? *American Psychologist, 51,* 1153-1166; and Gupta, N., & Shaw, J. D. (1998). Let the evidence speak: Financial incentives are effective!! *Compensation & Benefits Review, 30*(2), 26-32.

22.   Interview with Beth Bloom Gardner conducted by John J. Sosik, July 1, 2002.

23.   Interview with Rich Sanders conducted by Don I. Jung in June, 2002.

24.   Avolio, B. J. (1999). *Full leadership development: Building the vital forces in organizations.* Thousand Oaks, CA: Sage.

25.   Sheen, F. J. (1967). *Guide to contentment.* New York: Simon & Schuster. Additional information on Bishop Sheen's ideas about character development can be found in Sheen, F. J. (1956). *Life is worth living.* New York: McGraw-Hill; and Sheen, F. J. (1980). *Treasures in clay: The autobiography of Fulton J. Sheen.* Garden City, NY: Double Day.

26.   Sheen (1956) as cited in Note 25.

27.   Gardner, W. L., & Cleavenger, D. (1998). Impression management behaviors of transformational leaders at the world-class level: A psychohistorical assessment. *Management Communication Quarterly, 12,* 3-41.

28.   Bass, B. M., & Avolio, B. J. (1997). *Full range leadership development: Manual for the Multifactor Leadership Questionnaire.* Palo Alto, CA: Mind Garden.

29.   Interview with executive conducted by Christine Alaimo, Frank Iacono, Tony Ng, and Jennifer Rounavaara, December 2001.

30.   Lord, R. G., & Maher, K. J. (1992). Cognitive theory in industrial and organizational psychology. In M. D. Dunnette & L. M. Hough (Eds.) *Handbook of Industrial and Organizational Psychology,* (2nd Ed., pp. 1-62). Palo Alto, CA: Consulting Psychologists Press.

31.   Comparison sample is derived from Bass and Avolio (1997) as cited in Note 28. Means (standard deviations) for idealized influence behavior (II-B) and attributes (II-A) for executives in our sample were 2.95 (.77) and 3.10 (.77), and 2.71 (.89) and 2.69 (.90) for leaders in the Bass and Avolio (1997) sample (t(1684) = 3.6 and 6.1, respectively).

32.   Executives of manufacturing organizations (M = 3.18, SD = .64) were rated by their direct reports as displaying significantly (p < .07) higher levels of II-B than executives of service (M = 2.72, SD = .56) organizations. These executives (M = 3.40,

SD = .50) were also rated by their direct reports significantly higher (*p* < .10) on II-A than executives of information technology (*M* = 3.03, *SD* = .70) and services (*M* = 2.93, *SD* = .56) organizations.

33. Interview with executive conducted by Tal Mor, Arye Chernovorov, Iris Reis, Shachar Ronen, Dana Lubevsky, and Nir Aviram, August 2002.

34. Interview with executive conducted by Stacia Babb, Wendy McDonald-Barbee, Jane Pirone, and Cherry Fe D. Trinidad, December 2001.

35. House, R. J. (1996). Path-goal theory of leadership: Lessons, legacy, and a reformulated theory. *The Leadership Quarterly, 7*, 323-352; and Vogelstein, F. (2003, May 26). Mighty Amazon. *Fortune, 147*(10), 60-74.

36. Interview as cited in Note 34.

37. Ambler, T. E. (undated). The strategic value of values. The CEO Refresher: Brain food for business, http://www.refresher.com/!taevalues.html (Accessed May 18, 2003).

38. Collins, J. C., & Porras, J. I. (1997). *Built to last: Successful habits of visionary companies*. New York: Harper Business.

39. Interview with the executive conducted by Suzanne Buckley, Joshua Hogue, Andru Prescod, and Jeanine Prime and submitted December 20, 2002.

40. Interview with the executive conducted by Nataly Linsky, Eyal Rachamim, Tomer Farkash, Alex Schwartz, Arthur Mellikin, Yitzchak Rot, and Nataly Idi, August 2002.

41. Swartz, M., & Watkins, S. (2003). *Power failure: The inside story of the collapse of ENRON*. New York: Double Day.

42. Interview with Dr. David Shaw conducted by Don I. Jung in June, 2002.

43. Interview with Martin McElroy conducted by Jacob Kretzing, Jr., April, 2002.

44. Interview with the executive conducted by Pat Galarza in December 2002.

45. Interview with executive conducted by Wai-Ling Lam, May 28, 2002.

CHAPTER 8

1. Dundon, E., & Pattkos, A. N. (2001) Leading the innovation revolution: Will the real Spartacus stand up? *Journal for Quality & Participation, 24*(4), 48-52.

2. Tushman, M. L., & O'Reilly, C. A. (1997). *Winning through innovation*. Cambridge, MA: Harvard Business School Press.

3. Gallagher, J. (2003). Success depends on IT/business link. *Insurance & Technology, 28*(6), 34.

4. For a summary of research on innovation and leadership, see Mumford, M. D., Scott, G. M., Gadis, B., & Strange, J. M. (2002). Leading creative people: Orchestrating expertise and relationships. *The Leadership Quarterly, 13*, 705-750.

5. Dundon & Pattkos (2001) as cited in Note 1.

6. For more details see Brown, S. L., & Eisenhardt, K. M. (1998). *Competing on the edge: Strategy as structured chaos*. Boston, MA: Harvard Business Press.

7. Amabile, T. M. (2000). Stimulate creativity by fueling passion. In E. Locke (Ed.). *Handbook of principles of organizational behavior* (pp. 331-341). Malden, MA: Blackwell.

8.   Mumford, M. D. (2002). Leading creative people: Orchestrating expertise and relationships. *The Leadership Quarterly, 13*, 705-750.

9.   Jung, D.I. (2001). Transformational and transactional leadership and their effects on creativity in groups. *Creativity Research Journal, 13*, 185-195.

10.   Interview with the executive conducted by Uri Madar, Noa Shapira, David Bar, Michael Gur-Arye, Liat Nechmadi, Margalit Bennett, Taly Granit, and Raz Birman, August 2002.

11.   Interview with the executive conducted by Suzanne Buckley, Joshua Hogue, Andru Prescod, and Jeanine Prime and submitted December 20, 2002.

12.   Rostan, S. M. (1998). A study of young artists: The emergence of artistic and creative identity. *Journal of Creative Behavior, 32*, 278–301.

13.   For more information see Shamir, B., House, R., & Arthur, M. (1993). The motivational effects of charismatic leadership: A self-concept based theory. *Organization Science, 4*, 1-17.

14.   Inspiring innovation. *Harvard Business Review, 80*(8), August 2002.

15.   For a discussion of intellectual stimulation, see work on transformational leadership, such as Bass, B. M. (1985). *Leadership and performance beyond expectations.* New York: Free Press; or Bass, B. M., & Avolio, B. J. (1994). *Improving leadership effectiveness through transformational leadership.* Thousand Oaks, CA: Sage.

16.   Farson, R., & Keyes, R. (2002). The failure tolerant leader. *Harvard Business Review, 80*(8), 64-76.

17.   Mumford et al. (2002) as cited in Note 4.

18.   Bass, B. M. (1985). *Leadership and performance beyond expectations.* New York: Free Press.

19.   Comparison sample is derived from Bass, B. M., & Avolio, B. J. (1997). *Full range leadership development: Manual for the Multifactor Leadership Questionnaire.* Palo Alto, CA: Mind Garden. Means (standard deviations) for intellectual stimulation (IS) for executives in our sample were 2.79 (.70), and 2.50 (.86) for leaders in the Bass and Avolio (1997) sample (t(1684) = 4.53).

20.   Executives of life sciences organizations (M = 3.03, SD = .22) were rated by their direct reports as displaying significantly ($p <$ .03) higher levels of IS than executives of services (M = 2.54, SD = .62) organizations.

21.   Our discussion of stumbling blocks to intellectual stimulation (IS) and methods of IS that can be used by executives is derived from Avolio, B. J., & Bass, B. M. (1990). *Manual for advanced workshop: Full range leadership development.* Binghamton, NY: Center for Leadership Studies, State University of New York at Binghamton.

22.   See more details in Mumford et al. (2002) as cited in Note 4.

23.   Interview with the executive conducted by Ovadia Cohen and Yossi Chen, August 2002.

24.   Interview with Lee Kranefuss conducted by Steve Dunn, June, 2002.

25.   Interview with the executive conducted by Ovadia Cohen and Yossi Chen, August 2002.

26.   Sessa, V. I. (1998). E = GR2P: A model for managing research and development teams. In D. J. Sessa & J. L. Willett (Eds.), *Paradigm for the successful utilization of renewable resources* (pp. 17–29). Champagne, IL: AOCS Press.

27.   Farson & Keyes (2002) as cited in Note 16.

28. Kluger, A. N., & DeNisi, A. (1996). The effects of feedback interventions on performance: A historical review, a meta-analysis, and a preliminary feedback intervention theory. *Psychological Bulletin, 119*, 254-284.

29. Interview with Brian Duffy conducted by Brian Viscusi, July 2, 2002.

30. Interview with Russell Laraway conducted by Mark Hellerman, June, 2002.

31. Interview with the executive conducted by Asanka Gunarrtane, Georgios Zois, Bill Manikakis, and Kenneth Mui, December 2001.

32. Farson & Keyes (2002) as cited in Note 16.

33. Interview with Karen Borda conducted by John J. Sosik and Maria Peterson, February, 4, 2002.

34. Mumford et al. (2002) as cited in Note 4.

35. Interview with the executive conducted by Batia Admony, Edna Azulay, Omer Harpaz, Zcharia Inbal, and Naftaly Kaikov, January 2002.

36. Interview with executive conducted by Don I. Jung in June, 2002.

37. Interview with executive conducted by Don I. Jung in June, 2002

38. Interview with the executive conducted by Jon Goldberg, Michael Tumino, Ted Witryk, and Tom D'Antonio in December 2001.

39. Interview with the executive conducted by Uri Madar, Noa Shapira, David Bar, Michael Gur-Arye, Liat Nechmadi, Margalit Bennett, Taly Granit, and Raz Birman, August 2002.

40. Interview with the executive conducted by Suzanne Buckley, Joshua Hogue, Andru Prescod, and Jeanine Prime and submitted December 20, 2002.

41. O'Donnell, A. (2003). Leading a new approach to tech investment. *Insurance & Technology, 28*(6), 40-42.

42. O'Donnell (2003) as cited in Note 41.

43. Interview with Brian Duffy conducted by Brian Viscusi, July 2, 2002.

44. Interview with the executive conducted by Tova Halifin, Shmulik Regev, Ram Segal, Hilat Elrom, Niv Sever, and Emanuel Ilyonesky, August 2002. For more information on SIT, see http://www.sitsite.com.

45. Amabile (2000) as cited in Note 7.

46. Gallagher (2003) as cited in Note 3.

47. Interview with the executive conducted by Rosanne McDonald and Val Zimmerman and submitted December 20, 2002.

CHAPTER 9

1. Yukl, G. (2002). *Leadership in organization* (5th Ed.) Upper Saddle River, NJ: Prentice Hall

2. Robbins, S. (2003). *Organizational behavior* (10th Ed.). Upper Saddle River, NJ: Prentice Hall

3. Useem, J. (2002, August 12). Jim McNerney thinks he can turn 3M from a good company into a great one. *Fortune*, 127-131.

4. Robbins (2003) as cited in Note 2.

5. http://www.roughnotes.com/rnmagazine/2003/sept03/09p160.htm (accessed September 3, 2003).

6. http://www.microsoft.com (accessed August 23, 2003).

7. http://www.sas.com (accessed March 23, 2003).

8. http://www.roughnotes.com/rnmagazine/2003/sept03/09p160.htm (accessed September 3, 2003).

9. Kreitner, R., & Kinicki, A. (1997). *Organizational behavior.* Boston, MA: Irvin McGraw-Hill.

10. Interview with the executive conducted by Scott Beattie and Charles Tolbert and submitted December 20, 2002.

11. Slater, R. (1999). *Saving big blue: Leadership lessons and turn around tactics of IBM's Lou Gerstner.* New York: McGraw-Hill.

12. Denison, D. (1990). *Corporate culture and organizational effectiveness.* New York: John Willey & Sons.

13. Slater (1999) as cited in Note 11

14. Robbins (2003) as cited in Note 2.

15. Meredith, R. (2002, January 21). Car guy. *Forbes,* 50-51.

16. Interview with the executive conducted by Suzanne Buckley, Joshua Hogue, Andru Prescod, and Jeanine Prime and submitted December 20, 2002.

17. Interview with John Yi conducted by Don I. Jung and Sean Hutchens, June 2002.

18. Interview with Ronald Kendrick conducted by Don I. Jung, October 2002.

19. Berner, R. (2003, July 7). How A.G. Lafley is revolutionizing a bastion of corporate conservatism. *Business Week,* 52-63.

20. Interview with Rick Sanders conducted by Don I. Jung and Sean Hutchens, August 2002.

21. Schein, E. (1992). *Organizational culture and leadership.* San Francisco: Jossey-Bass.

22. Interview with John Yi conducted by Don I. Jung and Sean Hutchens, June 2002.

23. Bass, B. M., & Avolio, B. J. (1993). Transformational leadership and organizational culture. *International Journal of Public Administration, 17*(1), 112-121.

24. Bass, B. M. (1996). *A new paradigm of leadership: An inquiry into transformational leadership.* Alexandria, VA: U.S. Army Research Institute for the Behavioral and Social Sciences.

25. For the contrast of LF between Moderated 4Is and Coasting organizations, $F(1,64) = 7.56$, $p < .008$; for the contrast of LF between Moderated 4Is and Predominately Bureaucratic organizations, $F(1,64) = 3.71$, $p < .06$; and for the contrast of MBE-P between Moderated 4Is and Coasting organizations, $F(1,64) = 5.71$, $p < .02$.

26. For the contrast of CR between Predominately 4Is and Predominately Bureaucratic organizations, $F(1,64) = 4.43$, $p < .04$; for the contrast of CR between Moderated 4Is and Coasting organizations, $F(1,64) = 6.68$, $p < .01$; for the contrast of CR between Moderated 4Is and Predominately Bureaucratic organizations, $F(1,64) = 10.71$, $p < .002$; For the contrast of CR between Moderated 4Is and Pedestrian organizations, $F(1,64) = 4.00$, $p < .05.$; for the contrast of CR between Coasting and Predominately Bureaucratic organizations, $F(1,64) = 6.54$, $p < .02$; for the contrast of CR between Coasting and Moderated Bureaucratic organizations, $F(1,64) = 3.90$, $p < .05$; for the contrast of CR between Moderated Bureaucratic and Predominately Bureaucratic organizations, $F(1,64) = 8.77$, $p < .004$; and for the contrast of CR between Moderated Bureaucratic and Pedestrian organizations, $F(1,64) = 4.20$, $p < .05$.

27. For the contrast of IM between Predominately 4Is and Predominately Bureaucratic organizations, $F(1,64) = 7.66$, $p < .007$; for the contrast of IM between Moderated 4Is and Coasting organizations, $F(1,64) = 4.19$, $p < .05$; for the contrast of IM between Moderated 4Is and Predominately Bureaucratic organizations, $F(1,64) = 12.29$, $p < .001$; for the contrast of IM between Coasting and Predominately Bureaucratic organizations, $F(1,64) = 8.57$, $p < .005$; for the contrast of IM between Moderated Bureaucratic and Predominately Bureaucratic organizations, $F(1,64) = 6.69$, $p < .01$; and for the contrast of IM between Pedestrian and Predominately Bureaucratic organizations, $F(1,64) = 7.36$, $p < .009$.

28. Bass (1996) as cited in Note 24.

29. Conger, J., & Kanungo, R. (1998). *Charismatic leadership in organizations.* Thousand Oaks, CA: Sage.

30. Bass (1996) as cited in Note 24.

CHAPTER 10

1. Interview with Robert T. Still conducted by John J. Sosik, Maria Peterson and John Gronski, December 19, 2001.

2. Mason, J. M., & Jablokow, K. W. (2003). *Organizational culture for change: Innovation and intellectual capital.* Malvern, PA: Penn State Great Valley Working Paper series. Detailed information on Metcalf's Law can be found in Shapiro, C., & Varian, H. R. (1999). *Information rules: A strategic guide to the network economy.* Boston, MA: Harvard Business School Press.

3. Avolio, B. J. (2000). *E-leadership: Here, there and everywhere.* [Videocassette]. Melbourne, Australia: MLQ Pty. Ltd.; and Rosenbush, S., Crockett, R. O., & Haddad, C. (2003, January 13). Telecom: At last, the depression is lifting. *Business Week, 3815,* 120.

4. Lord, R. G., Binning, J. F., Rush, M. C., & Thomas, J. C. (1978). Effect of performance and leader behavior on questionnaire ratings of leader behavior. *Organizational Behavior and Human Performance, 21,* 27-39.

5. Interview with Lee Kranefuss conducted by Steve Dunn, June, 2002.

6. Garrison, T. W. (1999). The true value of customer service. In R. Crandell (Ed.) *Celebrate customer service: Insider secrets* (pp. 3-24). Corte Madera, CA: Select Press; and The Garrison Report #2003-7 http://www.TedGarrison.com/specialinfo.cfm (accessed July 7, 2003).

7. Interview with the executive conducted by Rosanne McDonald and Val Zimmerman and submitted December 20, 2002.

8. Interview with the executive conducted by Christine Alaimo, Frank Iacono, Tony Ng, and Jennifer Rounavaara, December 2001.

9. Interview with Russell Laraway conducted by Mark Hellerman, June, 2002.

10. Interview with the executive conducted by Suzanne Buckley, Joshua Hogue, Andru Prescod, and Jeanine Prime and submitted December 20, 2002.

11. Interview with Bruce Weinsteiger conducted by Chen Cheng, May 19, 2002.

12. Meisenheimer, C. (1992). *Improving quality: A guide to effective programs.* Aspen, CO: Aspen Publishing, Inc.; and Sosik, J. J., & Dionne, S. D. (1997). Leader-

ship styles and Deming's behavior factors. *Journal of Business and Psychology, 11*(4), 447-462.

13.   Interview with Bill Rieser conducted by Dana Roos and Maria Peterson, June 5, 2002.

14.   Jung, D., Avolio, B., & Berson, Y. (2003). *Effect of individual and team transformational leadership on unit performance: A moderating role of individual perceptual agreement.* Manuscript under review.

15.   Detailed discussions of shared leadership can be found in Avolio, B. J. (1999). *Full leadership development: Building the vital forces in organizations.* Thousand Oaks, CA: Sage; Gronn, P. (2002). Distributed leadership as a unit of analysis. *The Leadership Quarterly, 13,* 423-451; Manz, C. C. & Sims, H. P. (1993). *Business without bosses: How self-managing teams are building high-performing companies.* New York: Wiley; and Perry, M. L., Pearce, C. L., & Sims, H. P. (1999). Empowered selling teams: How shared leadership can contribute to selling team outcomes. *The Journal of Personal Selling & Sales Management, 19*(3), 35-51.

16.   Pearce, C., & Conger, J. (2003). *Shared leadership: Reframing the hows and whys of leadership.* Thousand Oaks: Sage.

17.   Interview with Celwyn Evans conducted by John J. Sosik and Maria Peterson, November 28, 2001.

18.   We found that the age of organizations in our sample was negatively related to direct reports' perceptions of executives' display of LF ($r = -.21$, $p < .09$), MBE-P ($r = -.29$, $p < .02$), MBE-A ($r = -.23$, $p < .06$) and positively related to II-A ($r = .25$, $p < .05$), and direct reports' ratings of unit effectiveness ($r = .25$, $p < .04$), satisfaction with the executive ($r = .23$, $p < .06$), and extra effort exerted ($r = .36$, $p < .01$).

19.   For details on the life-cycle classification scheme we used, please refer to Jawahar, I. M., & McLaughlin, G. L. (2001). Toward a descriptive stakeholder theory: An organizational life cycle approach. *Academy of Management Review, 26*(3), 397-414. Alternative perspectives on organizational life cycle classifications and characteristics can be found in Quinn, R. E., & Cameron, K. (1983). Organizational life cycles and shifting criteria of effectiveness: Some preliminary evidence. *Management Science, 29,* 33-51; and Vicere, A. A. (1992). The strategic leadership imperative for executive development. *Human Resources Planning, 15*(1), 15-31.

20.   Interview with Karen Borda conducted by John J. Sosik and Maria Peterson, February, 4, 2002.

21.   Interview with Norm Thomas conducted by Don I. Jung in June 2002.

22.   Executives of emerging growth organizations ($M = 1.03$, $SD = .70$) were rated by their direct reports as displaying significantly ($p < .05$) higher levels of laissez-faire (LF) than executives of mature ($M = .67$, $SD = .50$) organizations. These executives were also rated by their direct reports significantly higher ($p < .10$) on LF than executives of start-up ($M = .70$, $SD = .57$) organizations, and significantly higher ($p < .03$) on passive management-by-exception ($M = 1.59$, $SD = .50$) than executives of mature organizations ($M = 1.14$, $SD = .60$).

23.   Hrebeniak, L., & Joyce, W. (1985). Organizational adaptation: Strategic choice and environmental determination. *Administrative Science Quarterly, 30,* 336-349.

24.   Interview with Steve Torres conducted by Don I. Jung in June, 2002.

25.   Executives of mature organizations ($M = 1.39$, $SD = .62$) were rated by their direct reports as displaying significantly ($p < .05$) *lower* levels of MBE-A leadership

than executives of start-up ($M = 1.68$, $SD = .41$) and emerging growth ($M = 1.75$, $SD = .46$) organizations.

26. Interview with Martin McElroy conducted by Jacob Kretzing, Jr., April, 2002.

27. Grove, A. S. (1999). *Only the paranoid survive: How to exploit the crisis points that challenge very company.* New York: Currency-Doubleday.

28. For details on why some CEOs derail their own careers, see Charan, R., & Colvin, G. (1999, June 21). Why CEOs fail. *Fortune, 139*(12), 69-78; and Sellers, P. (1999, June 21). CEOs in denial. *Fortune, 139* (12), 80-82.

29. Interview with the executive conducted by Greg Jensen and Rajneesh Moudgil and submitted December 20, 2002.

30. We examined self-other rating agreement using a simple qualitative assessment using three categories of agreement as originally proposed by Atwater, L. E., & Yammarino, F. J. (1992). Does self-other agreement on leadership perceptions moderate the validity of leadership and performance expectations? *Personnel Psychology, 45,* 141-164. However, these authors, in various articles (e.g., Atwater, L. E., Ostroff, C., Yammarino, F. J., & Fleenor, J. W. (1998). Self-other agreement: Does it really matter? *Personnel Psychology, 51,* 577-598; and Atwater, L. E., & Yammarino, F. J. (1997). Self-other rating agreement: A review and model. *Research in Personnel and Human Resource Management, 15,* 121-174.) proposed four categories of agreement by distinguishing between "in-agreement/good" and "in-agreement/poor" performers. The former have other ratings above the grand mean and the latter have other ratings below the grand mean. Atwater and Yammarino proposed that in-agreement/good managers have the highest outcomes, while in-agreement/ poor managers have low outcomes. The self-aware managers and executives we refer to here are "in-agreement/good."

31. For a comprehensive review of the literature on self-other rating agreement on transformational leadership, see Sosik, J. J., & Godshalk, V. M. (In press). Self-other rating agreement in mentoring: Meeting protégé expectations for development and career advancement. *Group & Organization Management;* Sosik, J. J., & Jung, D. I. (2003). Impression management strategies and performance in information technology consulting: The role of self-other rating agreement on charismatic leadership. *Management Communications Quarterly, 17*(2), 233-268; and Yammarino, F. J., & Atwater, L. E. (1997). Do managers see themselves as others see them? Implications of self-other rating agreement for human resources management. *Organizational Dynamics, 25,* 35-44.

32. We thank Edward M. Drost, a long-time advocate of healthy eating and living, for pointing out research on the benefits of probiotic nutrients, and recommending to us Sarnat, R., Schulick, P., & Newmark, T. M. (2002). *The life bridge: The way to longevity with probiotic nutrients.* Brattleboro, VT: Herbal Free Press.

33. Charan and Colvin (1999) as cited in Note 28.

34. Collins, J. (2003, July 21). The 10 greatest CEOs of all time. *Fortune, 148*(2), 54-68.

35. Interested readers may find the following books by Mother Teresa to be inspiring and spiritually enriching: Mother Teresa, Benenate, B., & Durepos, J. (1997). *No greater love.* Novato, CA: New World Library; and Mother Teresa, Gonzalaz-Balado, J. L., & Playfoot, J. N. (1985). *My life for the poor.* San Francisco, CA: Harper & Row.

APPENDIX

1. Albers-Mohrman, S., Gibson, C. B., & Mohrman Jr., A. M. (2001). Doing research that is useful to practice: A model and empirical exploration. *Academy of Management Journal, 44*(2), 357-375.

2. Berson, Y., & Avolio, B. J. (2000, May). *An exploration of critical links between transformational and strategic leadership.* Paper presented at the annual meeting of the Society of Industrial and Organizational Psychology, New Orleans, LA.

3. Comprehensive discussion of the Full Range Leadership model is provided in Avolio, B. J., & Bass, B. M. (2002). *Developing potential across a full range of leadership: Cases on transactional and transformational leadership.* Mahwah, NJ: Lawrence Erlbaum Associates; Bass, B. M. (1985). *Leadership and performance beyond expectations.* New York: Free Press; and Bass, B. M., & Avolio, B. J. (1994). *Improving organizational effectiveness through transformational leadership.* Thousand Oaks, CA: Sage.

4. Meta-analyses demonstrating the effectiveness of transformational leadership include Fuller, J. B., Patterson, C., Coleman, E. P., Hester, K., & Stringer, D. Y. (1996). A quantitative review of research on charismatic leadership. *Psychological Reports, 78*(1), 271-287; Gaspar, S. (1992). *Transformational leadership: An integrative review of the literature.* Unpublished doctoral dissertation, Western Michigan University, Kalamazoo; and Lowe, K. B., Kroeck, K. G., & Sivasubramaniam, N. (1996). Effectiveness correlates of transformational and transactional leadership: A meta-analytic review. *The Leadership Quarterly, 7,* 385-425.

5. For detailed information on the MLQ's specific measures and their validity and reliability, please refer to Avolio, B. J., Bass, B. M., & Jung, D. I. (1999). Reexamining the components of transformational and transactional leadership using the Multifactor Leadership Questionnaire. *Journal of Organization and Occupational Psychology, 72,* 441-462; Bass, B. M., & Avolio, B. J. (1997). *Full range leadership development: Manual for the Multifactor Leadership Questionnaire.* Palo Alto, CA: Mind Garden; and Carless, S. A. (1998). Assessing the discriminant validity of transformational leader behavior as measured by the MLQ. *Journal of Occupational and Organizational Psychology, 71,* 353-358.

6. For detailed information on the ODQ's specific measures and their validity and reliability, please refer to Bass, B. M., & Avolio, B. J. (1993). Transformational leadership and organizational culture. *International Journal of Public Administration, 17*(1), 112-121.

7. Excellent overviews of qualitative research methodology are provided by Giles, D. C. (2002). *Advanced research methods in psychology.* New York: Routledge; and Patton, M. Q. (2002). *Qualitative research and evaluation methods.* Thousand Oaks, CA: Sage.

8. For more details about using multiple sources of data to validate leadership research see Jick, T. D. (1979). Mixing qualitative and quantitative methods: Triangulation in action. *Administrative Science Quarterly, 24,* 602-611.

9. Hershey, R. D. (1999, April 25). The indexing giant nobody knows. *The New York Times,* Section 3; and http://www.barclaysglobal.com/ (accessed September 4, 2002); and interview with Lee Kranefuss conducted by Steve Dunn, June, 2002.

10. Information accessed and obtained from the organization's web site on October 18, 2002. Interview(s) with the executive(s) conducted by Raphael Elkayam, Gilad Zarfati, Zadok Osherovich, Ronny Zikeshvilli, and Shachar Levy,

August 2002. Due to their request to be anonymous, however, the names of the company and executive(s) we interviewed are not provided here.

11. Information accessed and obtained from the organization's web site on October 18, 2002. Interview(s) with the executive(s) conducted by Omer Unger, Yael Gal, Orly Salomon, Oded Shany, David Pauker, and Michal Naor and Shirly Cohen, Jenny Karkshon, Dotan Nave, Sagi Asraf, Omer Vidan, Arik Amichay, and Daniel Klinger in August 2001. Due to their request to be anonymous, however, the names of the company and executive(s) we interviewed are not provided here.

12. Interview with executive conducted by Wai-Ling Lam, May 28, 2002; and Lam, W. L. (2002). *Strategic high tech leadership.* Malvern, PA: Penn State Great Valley School of Graduate Professional Studies.

13. Information accessed and obtained from the organization's web site on October 18, 2002. Interview(s) with the executive(s) conducted by Jon Goldberg, Michael Tumino, Ted Witryk, and Tom D'Antonio in December 2001. Due to their request to be anonymous, however, the names of the company and executive(s) we interviewed are not provided here.

14. http://unionbank.com/UBoCHTML/L3A?OpenDocument&A2 (accessed September 18, 2002); and interview with executive conducted by Don I. Jung in June, 2002.

15. http://flagship.vanguard.com/web/corpcontent/CorporatePortal.html (accessed September 5, 2002); and interview with Robert Snowden conducted by Gary Generose, July 1, 2002.

16. AICPCU-IIA. (2001). *We help people succeed: 2001 report American Institute for CPCU Insurance Institute of America.* Malvern, PA; http://www.aicpcu.org/default.htm (accessed September 4, 2002); and interview with Terrie Troxel conducted by John J. Sosik and Maria Peterson, March 7, 2002.

17. http://www.ge.com/company/index.htm (accessed September 4, 2002); and interview with Brian Duffy conducted by Brian Viscusi, July 2, 2002.

18. Information accessed and obtained from the organization's web site on October 18, 2002. Interview(s) with the executive(s) conducted by Tova Halifin, Shmulik Regev, Ram Segal, Hilat Elrom, Niv Sever, and Emanuel Ilyonesky, August 2002. Due to their request to be anonymous, however, the names of the company and executive(s) we interviewed are not provided here.

19. Information accessed and obtained from the organization's web site on March 20, 2003. Interview(s) with the executive(s) conducted by Rosanne McDonald and Val Zimmerman and submitted December 20, 2002. Due to their request to be anonymous, however, the names of the company and executive(s) we interviewed are not provided here.

20. Information accessed and obtained from the organization's web site on October 18, 2002. Interview(s) with the executive(s) conducted by Nataly Linsky, Eyal Rachamim, Tomer Farkash, Alex Schwartz, Arthur Mellikin, Yitzchak Rot, and Nataly Idi, August 2002. Due to their request to be anonymous, however, the names of the company and executive(s) we interviewed are not provided here.

21. http://www.jni.com/aboutus (accessed September 18, 2002); and interview with executive conducted by Don I. Jung in June, 2002.

22. Information accessed and obtained from the organization's web site on March 20, 2003. Interview(s) with the executive(s) conducted by Vito Latini, Daniel Patton, Leslie Trudeau, and Damon Walker and submitted December 20, 2002.

Due to their request to be anonymous, however, the names of the company and executive(s) we interviewed are not provided here.

23. Information accessed and obtained from the organization's web site on March 20, 2003. Interview(s) with the executive(s) conducted by Scott Beattie and Charles Tolbert and submitted December 20, 2002. Due to their request to be anonymous, however, the names of the company and executive(s) we interviewed are not provided here.

24. Information accessed and obtained from the organization's web site on October 18, 2002. Interview(s) with the executive(s) conducted by Ronen Liroz, Gady Leichter, Avital Grossman, Yariv Grossman, and Halit Chernovrov, January 2002. Due to their request to be anonymous, however, the names of the company and executive(s) we interviewed are not provided here.

25. Information accessed and obtained from the organization's web site on February 14, 2003. Interview(s) with the executive(s) conducted by Stacia Babb, Wendy McDonald-Barbee, Jane Pirone, and Cherry Fe D. Trinidad, December 2001. Due to their request to be anonymous, however, the names of the company and executive(s) we interviewed are not provided here.

26. http://www.cbtech.com/ (accessed September 4, 2002); http://www.pabiotech.org/Members/CBTechnologiesPage.htm (accessed September 4, 2002); and interview with Karen Borda conducted by John J. Sosik and Maria Peterson, February, 4, 2002.

27. Information accessed and obtained from the organization's web site on March 20, 2003. Interview(s) with the executive(s) conducted by Kathy Healy and Richard Quinn and submitted December 20, 2002. Due to their request to be anonymous, however, the names of the company and executive(s) we interviewed are not provided here.

28. Information accessed and obtained from the organization's web site on October 18, 2002. Interview(s) with the executive(s) conducted by Darryl Inge, December 2001. Due to their request to be anonymous, however, the names of the company and executive(s) we interviewed are not provided here.

29. http://www.kes.com/profile.htlm (accessed September 18, 2002); and interview with executive conducted by Don I. Jung in June, 2002.

30. Information accessed and obtained from the organization's web site on October 18, 2002. Interview(s) with the executive(s) conducted by Batia Admony, Edna Azulay, Omer Harpaz, Zcharia Inbal, and Naftaly Kaikov, January 2002. Due to their request to be anonymous, however, the names of the company and executive(s) we interviewed are not provided here.

31. Information accessed and obtained from the organization's web site on October 18, 2002. Interview(s) with the executive(s) conducted by Liat Klein-Bareket, Yifat Baron, Shlomo Hochman, and Tammy Bril, August 2001. Due to their request to be anonymous, however, the names of the company and executive(s) we interviewed are not provided here.

32. http://www.sct.com/ (accessed September 5, 2002); and interview with Amy Turner-LaDow conducted by Grant Galef, June 2002.

33. Information accessed and obtained from the organization's web site on October 18, 2002. Interview(s) with the executive(s) conducted by Ilana Stupel, Tal Eisman, Alon Zipory, Erez Ginati, Lior Carmel, and Oren Golan, January 2002. Due to their request to be anonymous, however, the names of the company and executive(s) we interviewed are not provided here.

34. Information accessed and obtained from the organization's web site on October 18, 2002. Interview(s) with the executive(s) conducted by Barak Lavi, Moshe Aharon, Sharon Geva, Noa Rom, Sarit Olami, Guy Olami, and Shai Peretz, August 8, 2002. Due to their request to be anonymous, however, the names of the company and executive(s) we interviewed are not provided here.

35. Information accessed and obtained from the organization's web site on October 18, 2002. Interview(s) with the executive(s) conducted by Uri Madar, Noa Shapira, David Bar, Michael Gur-Arye, Liat Nechmadi, Margalit Bennett, Taly Granit, and Raz Birman, August 2002. Due to their request to be anonymous, however, the names of the company and executive(s) we interviewed are not provided here.

36.   Information accessed and obtained from the organization's web site on March 20, 2003. Interview(s) with the executive(s) conducted by Suzanne Buckley, Joshua Hogue, Andru Prescod, and Jeanine Prime and submitted December 20, 2002. Due to their request to be anonymous, however, the names of the company and executive(s) we interviewed are not provided here.

37. Information accessed and obtained from the organization's web site on October 18, 2002. Interview(s) with the executive(s) conducted by Michael Wacsman, Genady Soroche, and Benny Anor, August 2001. Due to their request to be anonymous, however, the names of the company and executive(s) we interviewed are not provided here.

38. Information accessed and obtained from the organization's web site on October 18, 2002. Interview(s) with the executive(s) conducted by Christine Alaimo, Frank Iacono, Tony Ng, and Jennifer Rounavaara, December 2001. Due to their request to be anonymous, however, the names of the company and executive(s) we interviewed are not provided here.

39. Information accessed and obtained from the organization's web site on October 18, 2002. Interview(s) with the executive(s) conducted by Dennie Beach, Shawn Belfast, Gordon Marshall, Edison Paul, Johnasttan Regalado, and Kamran Shaikh, December 2001. Due to their request to be anonymous, however, the names of the company and executive(s) we interviewed are not provided here.

40. Information accessed and obtained from the organization's web site on October 18, 2002. Interview(s) with the executive(s) conducted by Meir Katz, Gil Tene, Zvika Meidan, Ephraim Ben-Natan, and Dafna Aduram, January 2002. Due to their request to be anonymous, however, the names of the company and executive(s) we interviewed are not provided here.

41. Information accessed and obtained from the organization's web site on October 18, 2002. Interview(s) with the executive(s) conducted by Gideon Elkan, Amos Levy, Ariel Shmuely, and Alex Berman, January 7, 2002. Due to their request to be anonymous, however, the names of the company and executive(s) we interviewed are not provided here.

42.   http://www.qualcomm.com/about/index.html (accessed September 18, 2002); and interview with executive conducted by Don I. Jung in June 2002.

43. Information accessed and obtained from the organization's web site on December 22, 2002. Interview(s) with the executive(s) conducted by Pat Galarza in December 2002. Due to their request to be anonymous, however, the names of the company and executive(s) we interviewed are not provided here.

44. Information accessed and obtained from the organization's web site on October 18, 2002. Interview(s) with the executive(s) conducted by Ophir Abramov-

ich, Alon Avi, Brauner Alon, Engel Galit, Bakel Revital, Geva Chana, and Steinberg Sharon, August 2001. Due to their request to be anonymous, however, the names of the company and executive(s) we interviewed are not provided here.

45. http://www.mrigroup.com/index.html (accessed September 5, 2002); and interview with Robert T. Still conducted by John J. Sosik, Maria Peterson and John Gronski, December 19, 2001.

46. http://www.mercyhealth.org/community/ (accessed September 5, 2002); interview with Martin McElroy conducted by Jacob Kretzing, Jr., April, 2002; and Kretzing, J. E. (2002). *Leadership interview of Martin Mc Elroy.* Malvern, PA: Penn State Great Valley School of Graduate Professional Studies.

47. http://www.scrippshealth.org/aboutus.asp (accessed September 18, 2002); and interview with Dr. David Shaw conducted by Don I. Jung in June, 2002.

48. Information accessed and obtained from the organization's web site on March 20, 2003. Interview(s) with the executive(s) conducted by Ann Curran, Barbara McLean, Tanya Miller, and Debra Prudhon and submitted December 20, 2002. Due to their request to be anonymous, however, the names of the company and executive(s) we interviewed are not provided here.

49. Information accessed and obtained from the organization's web site on March 20, 2003. Interview(s) with the executive(s) conducted by Angela Iocavelli and Jinu Thomas and submitted December 20, 2002. Due to their request to be anonymous, however, the names of the company and executive(s) we interviewed are not provided here.

50.   http://www.central-nervous-system.com/profiles/cns/cns0800.cp/ucb pharma_inc.htm   (accessed   September   5,   2002);   http://www.pharma.ucb-group.com/ (accessed September 5, 2002); and interview with Anthony Tebbutt conducted by Andrew F. Hartnett, November 2001.

51. Information accessed and obtained from the organization's web site on October 18, 2002. Interview(s) with the executive(s) conducted by Arye Kestenbaum, Adi Kaplan, Amos Alter, Sima Yacobovich, Sharon Seivery, August 2002. Due to their request to be anonymous, however, the names of the company and executive(s) we interviewed are not provided here.

52. Architectual Concepts. (2001). *Firm profile and company literature.* Exton, PA; http://www.arconcepts.com/ (accessed September 4, 2002); and interview with Bruce Weinsteiger conducted by Chen Cheng, May 19, 2002.

53. http://www.pulte.com/Default.asp (accessed September 5, 2002); and interview with Bill Rieser conducted by Dana Roos and Maria Peterson, June 5, 2002.

54. Information accessed and obtained from the organization's web site on October 18, 2002. Interview(s) with the executive(s) conducted by Tal Mor, Arye Chernovorov, Iris Reis, Shachar Ronen, Dana Lubevsky, and Nir Aviram, August 2002. Due to their request to be anonymous, however, the names of the company and executive(s) we interviewed are not provided here.

55. Information accessed and obtained from the organization's web site on March 20, 2003. Interview(s) with the executive(s) conducted by Greg Jensen and Rajneesh Moudgil and submitted December 20, 2002. Due to their request to be anonymous, however, the names of the company and executive(s) we interviewed are not provided here.

56. Information accessed and obtained from the organization's web site on October 18, 2002. Interview(s) with the executive(s) conducted by Louise D'Angelo and Andrew Simon, December 2001. Due to their request to be anony-

mous, however, the names of the company and executive(s) we interviewed are not provided here.

57. Information accessed and obtained from the organization's web site on March 20, 2003. Interview(s) with the executive(s) conducted by Anne Reichert and Timothy Windert and submitted December 20, 2002. Due to their request to be anonymous, however, the names of the company and executive(s) we interviewed are not provided here.

58. http://www.calicocorners.com/ (accessed September 4, 2002); Milford, M. (1994, January 2). Rags to riches tale comes true. *Sunday News Journal,* Business Section, Wilmington, DE; and interview with Richard King conducted by Lisa D.K. Coutant, July, 2002.

59. Information accessed and obtained from the organization's web site on April 26, 2003. Interview(s) with the executive(s) conducted by Kevin Trenga and Kyung Woo Kang and submitted December 20, 2002. Due to their request to be anonymous, however, the names of the company and executive(s) we interviewed are not provided here.

60. Information accessed and obtained from the organization's web site on March 20, 2003. Interview(s) with the executive(s) conducted by Andrew Gates and Raghu Nippani and submitted December 20, 2002. Due to their request to be anonymous, however, the names of the company and executive(s) we interviewed are not provided here.

61. http://www.harcourt.com/bu_info/harcourt_trade.html (accessed September 18, 2002); and interview with executive conducted by Don I. Jung in June, 2002.

62. Information accessed and obtained from the organization's web site on October 18, 2002. Interview(s) with the executive(s) conducted by Asanka Gunarrtane, Georgios Zois, Bill Manikakis, and Kenneth Mui, December 2001. Due to their request to be anonymous, however, the names of the company and executive(s) we interviewed are not provided here.

63. Information accessed and obtained from the organization's web site on October 18, 2002. Interview(s) with the executive(s) conducted by Yochi Memech, Dima Mabzus, Koby Blank, Yacov Vigoshin, Zafrir Feiman, and Uri Simchon, August 2001. Due to their request to be anonymous, however, the names of the company and executive(s) we interviewed are not provided here.

64. http://www.bloominstitute.com/ (accessed September 4, 2002); and interview with Beth Bloom Gardner conducted by John J. Sosik, July 1, 2002.

65. Information accessed and obtained from the organization's web site on October 18, 2002. Interview(s) with the executive(s) conducted by Ovadia Cohen and Yossi Chen, August 2002. Due to their request to be anonymous, however, the names of the company and executive(s) we interviewed are not provided here.

66. http://www.divdata.com/ (accessed September 4, 2002); and interview with Craig Robinson conducted by John J. Sosik and Maria Peterson, January 23, 2002.

67. Gronski, J. L. (2002). *Research summary: For partial fulfillment of the requirements for Independent Study on Strategic High Tech Leadership.* Malvern, PA: Penn State Great Valley School of Graduate Professional Studies; http://www.greencastleconsulting.com/ (accessed September 5, 2002); and interview with Celwyn Evans conducted by John J. Sosik and Maria Peterson, November 28, 2001.

68. Cranmer, M. (2002). *Strategic leadership analysis of Shannon Watson, CEO, GreyMatter, Inc.* Malvern, PA: Penn State Great Valley School of Graduate Professional

Studies; http://greymatterinc.com/ (accessed September 5, 2002); and interview with Shannon K. Watson conducted by Michael Cranmer, May 20, 2002.

69. Anonymous. (2002, March 17). Companies to watch. *Wilmington News Journal*; http://www.delawareonline.com/newsjournal/business/2002/03/17best inbiz30.html (accessed September 5, 2002); http://www.itgpathfinders.com/ (accessed September 5, 2002); and interview with Russell Laraway conducted by Mark Hellerman, June, 2002.

70. Information accessed and obtained from the organization's web site on October 18, 2002. Interview(s) with the executive(s) conducted by Meir Baron and Meir Nakar, August 14, 2002. Due to their request to be anonymous, however, the names of the company and executive(s) we interviewed are not provided here.

71. Information accessed and obtained from the organization's web site on October 18, 2002. Interview(s) with the executive(s) conducted by S. Andre' Neblett, Antonette Reid, Gary Trotter, and Jeffery Tseng, December 2000. Due to their request to be anonymous, however, the names of the company and executive(s) we interviewed are not provided here.

72. Information accessed and obtained from the organization's web site on March 20, 2003. Interview(s) with the executive(s) conducted by Jason Miller and Tom Steinke and submitted December 20, 2002. Due to their request to be anonymous, however, the names of the company and executive(s) we interviewed are not provided here.

73. http://www.sheetz.com/sheetzweb/flashy.jsp (accessed September 5, 2002); interview with Joseph S. Sheetz conducted by William Young, April 10, 2002; and Pas, R., & Grabarek, B. (2002). The secrets of Sheetz's success. *Convenience Store/Petroleum, 13*(2), 42-46.

ABOUT THE AUTHORS

John J. Sosik (Ph.D., State University of New York at Binghamton) is an associate professor of management and organization at The Pennsylvania State University, Great Valley School of Graduate Professional Studies in suburban Philadelphia, where he has received awards for excellence in research, faculty innovation and teaching. Dr. Sosik teaches organizational behavior, leadership, strategic high-tech leadership, and managerial accounting classes. He is an expert on transformational/charismatic leadership, group dynamics and mentoring, having published over 50 scholarly articles and book chapters and delivered about 45 academic conferences presentations since 1995, conducted training and organizational development programs, and serves on the editorial boards of *The Leadership Quarterly* and *Group & Organizational Management*. He is also a Certified Public Accountant in Pennsylvania and Certified Management Accountant.

Don (Dongil) Jung (Ph.D. from the State University of New York at Binghamton) is a Professor of Management at San Diego State University. He teaches Organizational Behavior, Leadership and Group Processes, and International management. His research interests include transformational/charismatic leadership, cross-cultural leadership, team dynamics and international management. Some of his publications have appeared in many top-tier scholarly journals such as the *Academy of Management Jour-*

The Dream Weavers: Strategy-Focused Leadership in Technology-Driven
Organizations, pages 307–308
Copyright © 2004 by Information Age Publishing, Inc.
All rights of reproduction in any form reserved.
ISBN: 1-59311-110-X (paper), 1-59311-111-8 (cloth)

nal, Journal of Applied Psychology, Leadership Quarterly, Group and Organization Management, Group Dynamic, Journal of Applied Behavioral Science, Journal of Organizational Behavior, and Journal of Occupational and *Organizational Psychology* among others. Professor Jung has provided a number of workshops and executive training programs to many for-profit and not-for-profit organizations. He was selected for inclusion in the Marquis *Who's Who in Business Higher Education* and the recipient of the Ascendant Scholar Award from the Western Academy of Management in 2004.

Yair Berson (Ph.D., State University of New York at Binghamton) is an assistant professor of management in the Institute for Technology and Enterprise at Polytechnic University, located in New York City. His research includes a multi-method approach to the measurement of leadership constructs, examining linkages between transformational and strategic leadership, leadership, innovation, and job crafting, high technology leadership, visionary leadership and cross-cultural leadership. Since 2000 he has published in *Journal of Applied Psychology, The Leadership Quarterly,* and *Attachment and Human Development Journal.* Dr. Berson is also a certified industrial/organizational psychologist in Israel, where he worked as a career counselor, and conducted leadership training with organizations from the high tech industry, as well as military and educational institutions.

Shelley D. Dionne (Ph.D., State University of New York at Binghamton) is an assistant professor of Organizational Behavior and Leadership in the School of Management at Binghamton University and a fellow in the Center for Leadership Studies. Her research interests focus on the effects of leaders on creativity and group process, learning, training and development, as well as levels of analysis in leadership. Her research has been published in scholarly journals such as *Journal of Applied Psychology, The Leadership Quarterly,* and *Human Relations.* She is also a registered dietitian and has served as a board member for the Southern Tier of New York Dietetic Association.

Kimberly S. Jaussi (Ph.D., University of Southern California) is an assistant professor of Organizational Behavior and Leadership in the School of Management at Binghamton University and a fellow in the Center for Leadership Studies. She received the School of Management's Teaching Award. Her research interests include unconventional leader behavior, creativity and leadership, strategic leadership, organizational commitment, and identity issues in diverse groups. Dr. Jaussi's research has been published in the *Academy of Management Journal* and the *Academy of Management Learning and Education Journal.*

SUBJECT INDEX

The Dream Weavers: Strategy-Focused Leadership in Technology-Driven Organizations, pages 309–317
Copyright © 2004 by Information Age Publishing, Inc.
All rights of reproduction in any form reserved.
ISBN: 1-59311-110-X (paper), 1-59311-111-8 (cloth)

Printed in the United States
52078LVS00001B/69

9 781593 111106